I0419215

100
GREAT
EASTERN
WORKS
OF ART

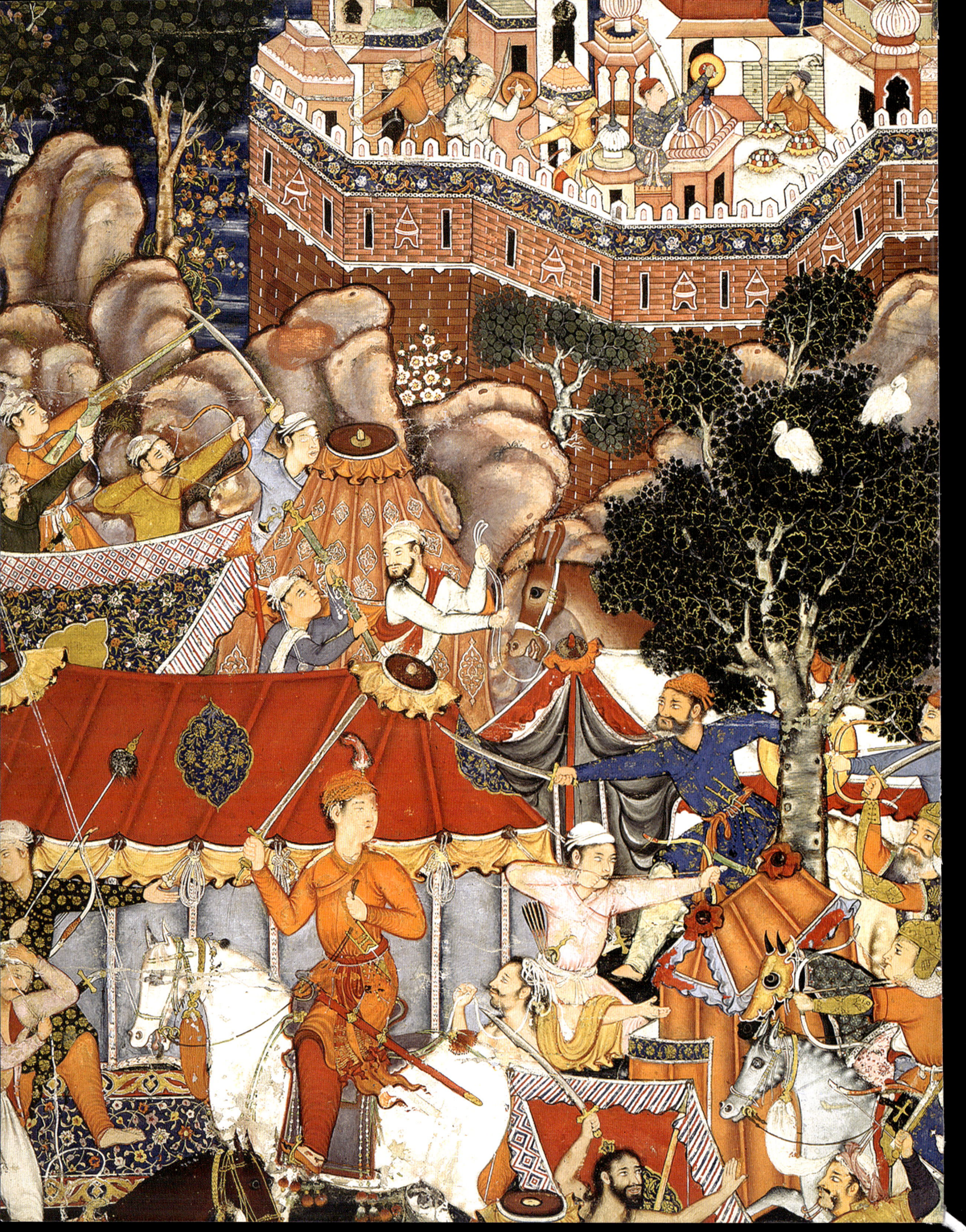

100
GREAT EASTERN WORKS OF ART

JOHN FINLAY

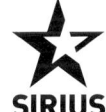

SIRIUS

Acknowledgements

Exceptional thanks go to the splendid Deidre (Dee) Sullivan (Lecturer on the Creative Technologies, WelTec, Wellington, New Zealand) for her advice and expertise on art and photographic history. Many thanks to Andrew Drummond and Christian Hidaka, for their ideas and permission to reproduce images of their work. I also want to thank everyone for their encouragement in numerous ways, particularly Emily and Elizabeth Finlay-Bliss, Judith Edwards and Judy Leicht.

Picture Credits

Alamy: 21; 28; 35; 42; 52–3; 104 & 105; 116; 148; 152; 171; 180 (Photo: Nick Ut), 202; 205. **Ans Westra:** 177 (Courtesy of Suite Tirohanga and by permission of the estate of Ans Westra [Ans Westra, Ruatoria, 1963]. **Auckland War Memorial Museum Tāmaki Paenga Hira:** 60–1 (Tangonge, Kuwaha. Auckland War Memorial Museum Tāmaki Paenga Hira. 6341, 71, and by permission of Te Rarawa Marae Committee); 121; 167. **Courtesy of Todd Barlin Oceanic Arts Australia:** 129. BPK/Museum für Asiatische Kunst, SMB: 64–5; 151. **Bridgeman Images:** 30–31; 92 (British Library Archive); 118 (© NPL – DeA Picture Library/G. Sioen); 137 (© NPL – DeA Picture Library/G. Nimatallah); 175 (Photo © Agnew's, London); 183 (Photo © Art Gallery of South Australia / South Australian Government Grant and by permission of Aboriginal Artists Agency Ltd); 195 (© Laila Shawa. All Rights Reserved 2024). **The British Museum:** 100; 110; 131; 138–9; 140; 165; 188. **The Bruschettini Foundation for Islamic and Asian Art:** 75. Cai Studio: 199 (Photo by Elio Montanari). **Diomedia:** 47. **Andrew Drummond:** 201. **Christian Hidaka:** 207. **The Ebara Hatakeyama Memorial Foundation/Hatakeyama Memorial Museum of Fine Art:** 44, 80–1. **Los Angeles County Museum of Art:** 112 (Gift of Jane Greenough Green in memory of Edward Pelton Green (AC1999.127.45)); 124 (Purchased with funds provided by the Eli and Edythe Broad Foundation with additional funding by Jane and Terry Semel, the David Bohnett Foundation, Camilla Chandler Frost, Gayle and Edward P. Roski, and The Ahmanson Foundation (M.2008.66.13)). **Library of Congress:** 163. **The Metropolitan Museum of Art:** 27 (Rogers Fund, 1918); 78 & 79 (Rogers Fund, 1920); 95 (Gift of Stephen and Sharon Davies Collection, 2015). **Yasumasa Morimura:** 190 (© Yasumasa Morimura; Courtesy of the artist and Luhring Augustine, New York). **Museum of Archaeology and Anthropology, Cambridge:** 133. **Museum der Kulturen, Basel:** 134 (© Museum der Kulturen Basel, Vb 30227; collection Volker Schneider 1982; photograph by Markus Gruber, 2007); 169 (© Museum der Kulturen Basel, Vb 7525; collection Eugen Paravicini 1929; photograph by Derek Li Wan Po, 2011). **Museum of New Zealand Te Papa Tongarewa:** 145 (Tā Moko panel, 1896–1899, Rotoiti, Lake, by Tene Waitere. Commissioned 1899. Te Papa (ME004211) with thanks to the Ngāti Tarawhai Iwi Trust;172 (Ngatu (tapa cloth), circa 1940s, Tonga, maker unknown. Gift of Valerie Morris, 1989. © The copyright holder. Te Papa (FE008723). **National Gallery of Victoria, Melbourne:** 107. **Nelson Atkins Museum of Art:** 17 (Ritual Disc with Dragon Motifs (bi), China, Eastern Zhou Dynasty (771–256 B.C.E.). Jade (nephrite), 6 1/2 inches (16.5 cm). **The Nelson-Atkins Museum of Art, Kansas City, Missouri. Purchase:** William Rockhill Nelson Trust, 33-81. Photo courtesy Nelson-Atkins Media Services, Joshua Ferdinand). **Philadelphia Museum of Art:** 126 (Purchased with funds contributed by Ann McPhail and Marion Boulton Stroud, 1991). **John Pule (with thanks to Auckland Art Gallery Toi o Tāmaki):** 197. **Public Domain:** 2, 9 (both); 10; 11; 12; 19; 20; 24; 37; 38; 39; 40; 50t; 58; 62; 70–1; 72; 77; 82; 95; 97; 103; 109; 114–15; 123; 142; 146–7; 155; 157; 159; 160–1; 184; 186–7. **RMN-Grand Palais/Bèatrice Hatala/Konstantinos/Dist. Foto SCALA, Florence:** 192. **Rijksmuseum:** 86; 87; 89. **Te Pātaka Toi Adam Art Gallery, Victoria University of Wellington:** 178. **The Board of Trustees of the Royal Botanic Gardens, Kew:** 99. **Shutterstock:** 15; 22; 32; 48; 50b; 54–5; 55; 56; 57; 66; 83; 84; 85; 90. **Wellcome Collection:** 68–9.

This edition published in 2025 by Sirius Publishing, a division of Arcturus Publishing Limited,
26/27 Bickels Yard, 151–153 Bermondsey Street,
London SE1 3HA

Copyright © Arcturus Holdings Limited

All rights reserved. No part of this publication may be reproduced, stored in a retrieval system, or transmitted, in any form or by any means, electronic, mechanical, photocopying, recording or otherwise, without prior written permission in accordance with the provisions of the Copyright Act 1956 (as amended). Any person or persons who do any unauthorised act in relation to this publication may be liable to criminal prosecution and civil claims for damages.

ISBN: 978-1-3988-4446-9
AD011631UK

Printed in Malaysia

Contents

Introduction

The subject of the arts of the East is undeniably a vast enterprise to characterize within the scope of a solitary text. Therefore, a survey of 'Great Eastern Art' will always have its limitations. This book's scope is restricted in terms of geography. It incorporates works from the Middle East, Central Asia, East Asia, Southeast Asia and the Pacific. Naturally, the choice is guided by an interest in the works themselves, so it does not always match the vicinity of a country's terrain to the 180th Meridian, which formed one of the geographical boundaries. And while the selection reflects the most eastern point in the course of travel, it has, for the sake of succinctness, left out the easternmost territories of the United States, Russia and Antarctica. Nor does it cover art of the Near East and the interconnected cultural worlds of the medieval East and West.

In the main, the objective of this selection has been to capture the power of Eastern art, including buildings and objects rightly deemed a tour de force of religious symbolism. No less remarkable, however, is a genre of extraordinary artefacts that have at times been overlooked: carved stone boulders, rock paintings, sand paintings, bags and other textiles, painted fans and scrolls, feasting bowls, and more besides. As well as great workmanship and visual brilliance, the selection highlights the uncommonly creative ways in which knowledge is frequently conveyed by symbolic or religious methods – 'meaning' perhaps relayed via complex artistic or ritual performance, often accompanied by dance, music and song. As exceptional occurrences and works of artistic creativity, they fascinate and appeal to the imagination and hence demand our due consideration and praise.

Scholars have persistently debated that the word 'art' does not have accurate equivalents outside the Western sphere, and that this type of aesthetic categorization is often inapt or 'alien'. Thinking along these lines seems like pigeon-holing when it comes to defining art, since every culture has arguably some type of associated classification. To help with this difficult issue, I have adopted the aesthetic adage that looking is always prejudiced by our learned 'assumptions' and the constructs of interpretation that have been put in place to try and make sense of them. Notably, 'seeing' through Western eyes not only concerns looking but interpreting the patois of images, something that has habitually led to distortion, obfuscation and relegation in terms of the appreciation of artworks. Thus, it is possible to view Eastern artworks as dynamic instruments of mediation with interactive histories of arbitration, caricature, humour, engagement and confrontation that reveal them to be brilliantly alive. In doing so, one can acknowledge that the ideas laid down in this book will always belong to others – the work of countless anthropologists, linguists, art historians, artists, writers and thinkers. In attempting to bring all this material and information under one banner, however, I hope the reader will find the selection engaging and entertaining as well as challenging and fulfilling.

1 Bhimbetka Rock Paintings
(10,000 BCE)

Artist(s): Unknown

Country of origin: India

Dimensions: 1,893 hectares (7⅓ square miles)

Material(s): Rock, vegetable-based paints containing charcoal, magnesium oxides and red haematite

Although the site of these rock paintings dates back 500,000 years, the earliest paintings are from approximately 10,000 BCE and are the oldest known example of rock art in India, while the latest were added during medieval times. The rock shelters in which they were found are sited on the southern edge of the Vindhya range within the Ratapani Wildlife Sanctuary in the Raisen district in the state of Madhya Pradesh, about 45 km (28 miles) southeast of Bhopal.

The earliest exploration of the Bhimbetka rock shelters took place in the late 1950s, led by the Indian archaeologist Vishnu Shridar Wakanar (1919–88), but the true extent of the region's caves was not revealed until the 1970s; the Bhimbetka site alone contains some 243. Wakanar divided the rock paintings into seven different periods, covering the Upper Palaeolithic, Mesolithic, Chalcolithic, two Early Historic and two Medieval eras. They form a fascinating study of the progression of early human development, with the earliest dated images showing linear figures dancing or hunting; this continues in the Mesolithic artworks but with additional decorations on the bodies as well as various types of recognizable weapons that include spears, sticks and bows and arrows. Later images show increasing interaction with agrarian communities, most likely those of the Malwa plains to the north, and the appearance of religious symbols, such as spirits representing fertility and nature (known as *yakshas*), indicating the formation of more sophisticated communities and belief systems.

A survey conducted by Yashodar Mathpal, an archaeologist, conservationist and expert on the rock paintings of Bhimbetka, identified a huge variety of animals portrayed in the shelters, including elephants, horses, antelopes, bears, monkeys, rats, fish and turtles among many others. Some are shown as being hunted or caught, while others appear to be part of battles.

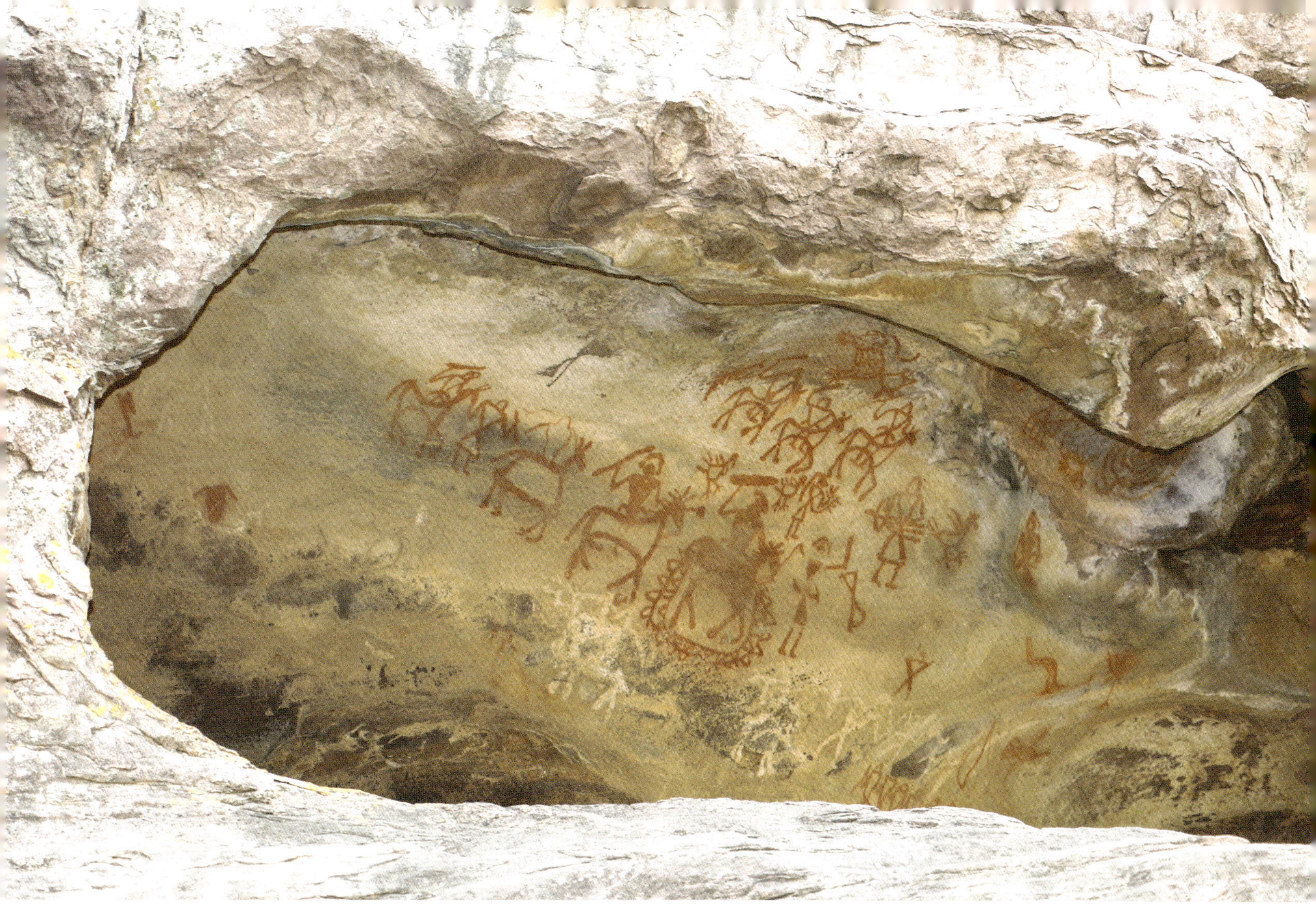
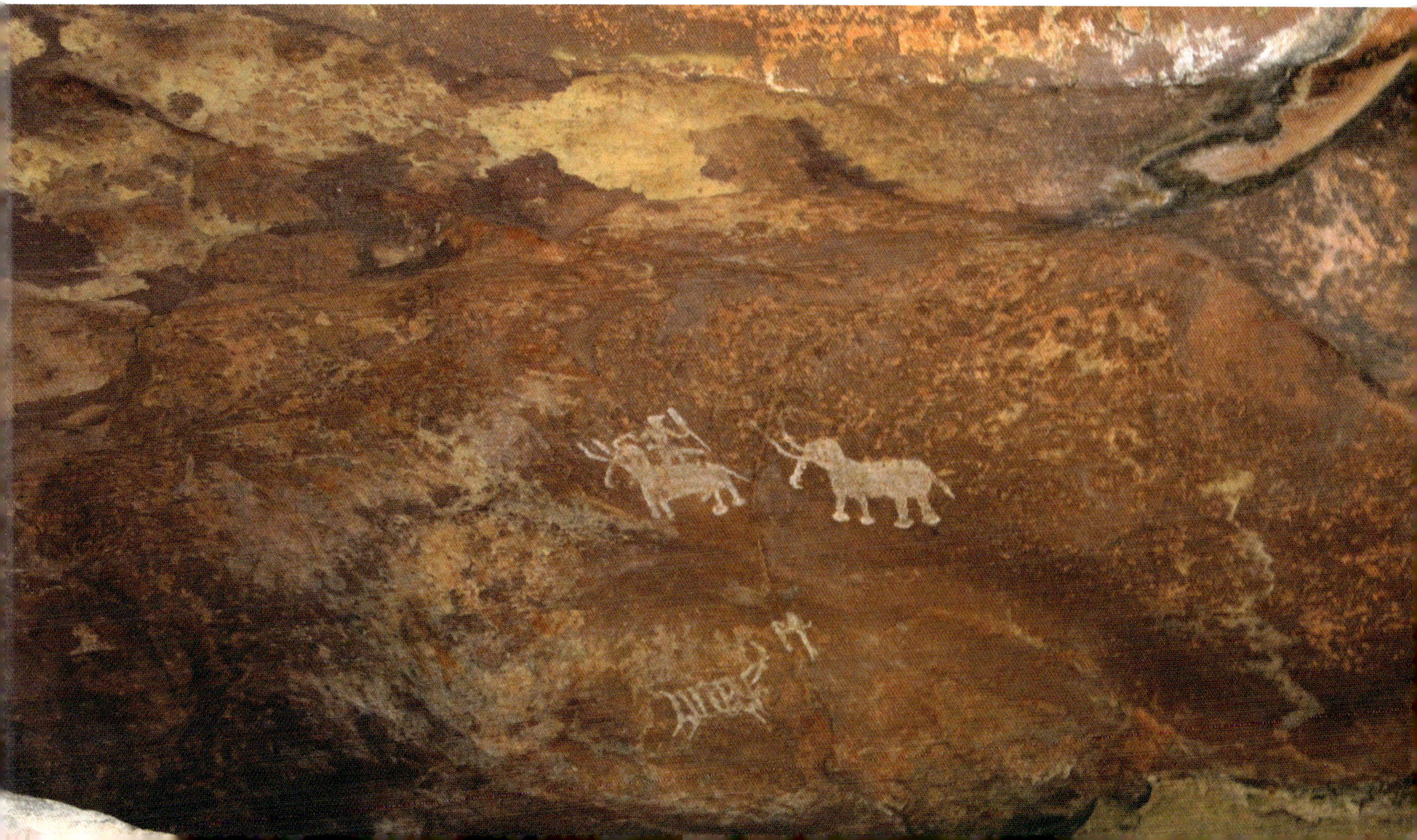

2 'Ain Ghazal Statues
(7200–6250 BCE)

Artist(s): Unknown

Country of origin: Jordan

Dimensions: 30 cm–1 m (1–3¼ ft)

Material(s): Lime plaster and reeds

Consisting of 32 statues, busts and heads, these anthropomorphic figures date from the Pre-Pottery Neolithic C period. They were found in 1974 at an archaeological site at 'Ain Ghazal in Amman in Jordan and then excavated during the course of two digs in 1984–5 and 1993–6. Although other similar figures have been found – in Jericho – they had broken into fragments, while the 'Ain Ghazal statues were exceptionally well preserved and stand as testament to the likely home-grown development of pottery techniques in a settlement that is mainly considered to have flourished before such skills became commonplace.

Remarkable for being some of the earliest known models of the human form, the statues and busts include representations of men, women and children; though detailed anatomical features are missing, the female forms include breasts and curved bellies. There are signs that they were painted and would have sported wigs, and in all cases it is still possible to see the outlines of the eyes and the irises that were made using bitumen. In addition, there are differences between the two sets of figures

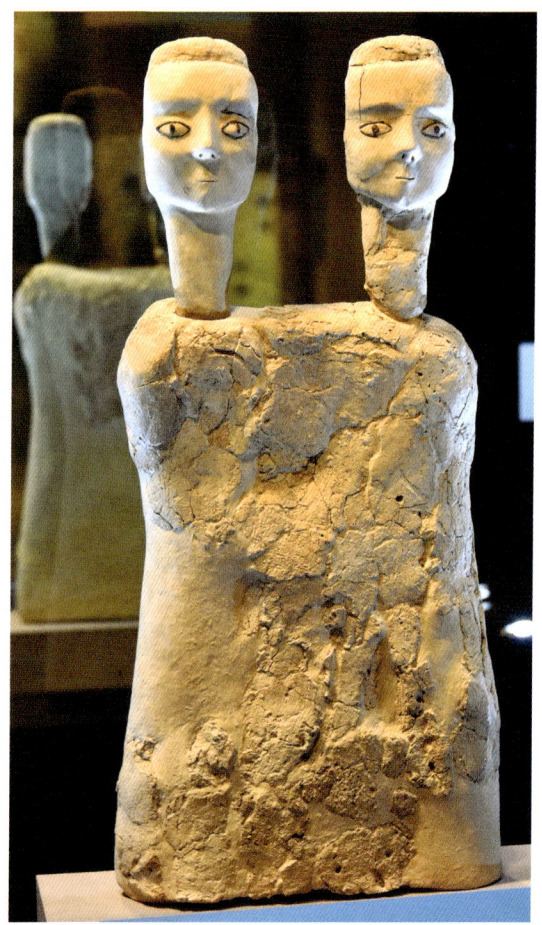

discovered during the digs: those from the earlier dig have small arms, while the eyes of the second set are more almond-shaped and their arms appear not to have been delineated from the torsos.

Made using separate bundles of reeds for the torsos, heads and legs, which were then covered in a lime-based plaster mix, the statues are approximately 1 m (3¼ ft) high, while the smallest bust is approximately 30 cm (1 ft). Viewed from the side, they are somewhat flat compared to classical statues, and a number of the statues and busts are two-headed. What purpose they served remains unclear. It is thought that the figures may well have been part of a religious ritual, given the way they were created and buried, possibly because during that period the dead were often dug up, once a period of time had passed and it was assumed that the flesh had decayed, so that their skulls could also be covered in the same kind of plaster. Although the statues are very fragile, having lost their reed cores to deterioration, conservation work using protective acrylic coatings is helping to preserve them.

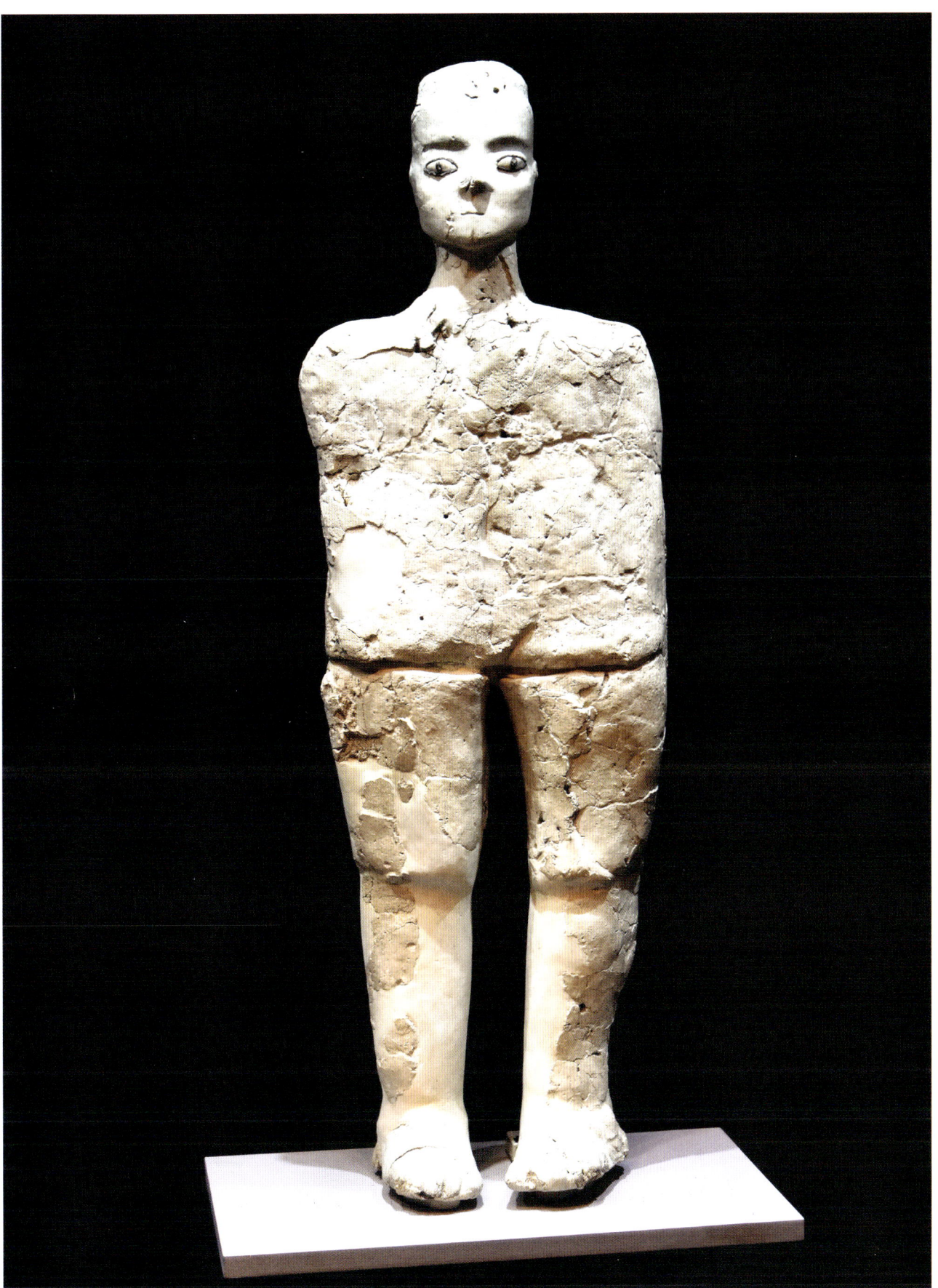

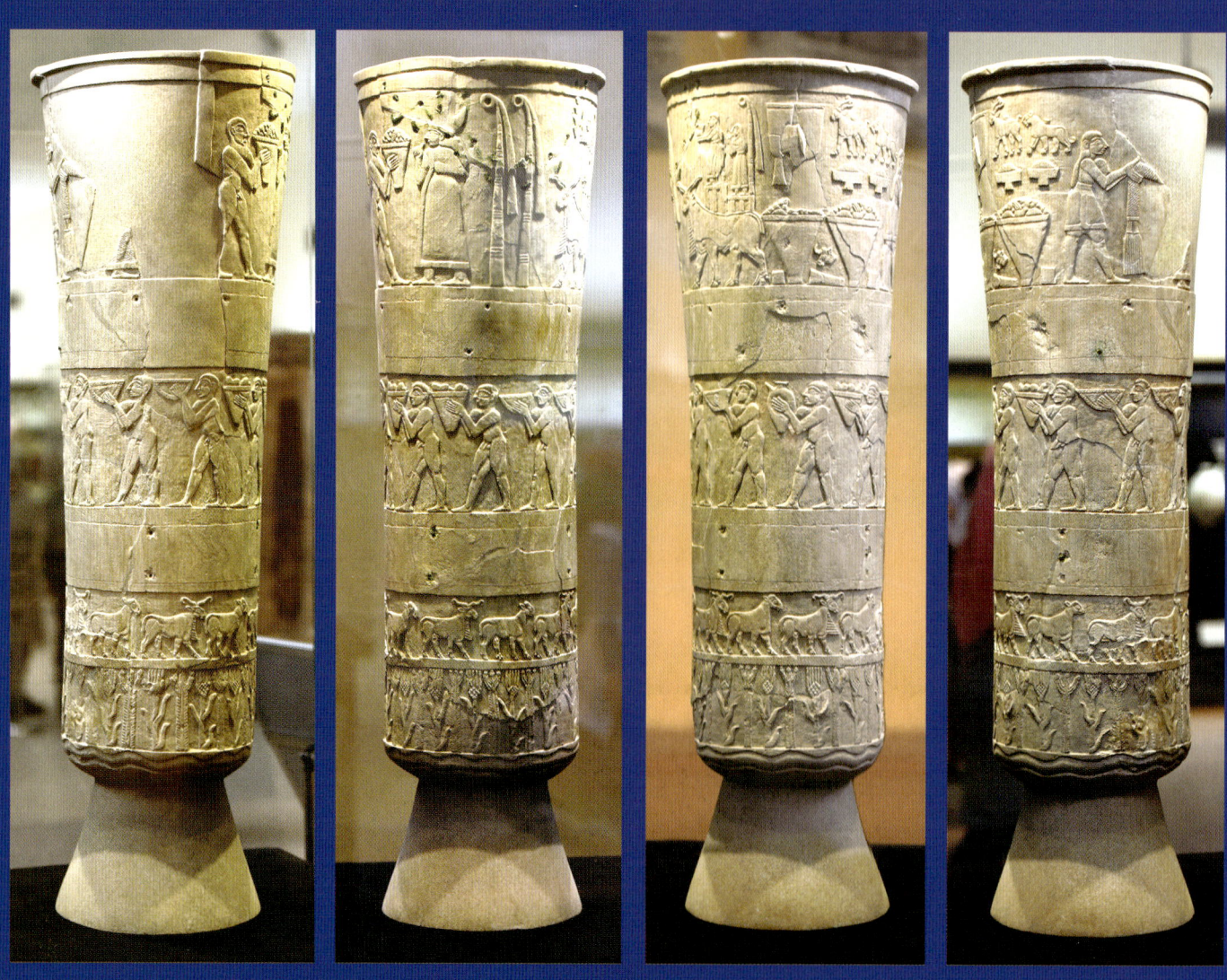

Warka Vase
(*c.* 3200–3000 BCE)

Artist(s): Unknown

Country of origin: Assyria (now Iraq)

Dimensions: 1.05 m (3½ ft)

Material(s): Alabaster

On 12 June 2003, a red Toyota car drove up to the National Museum of Iraq in Baghdad and three young men got out and unloaded an object wrapped in a blanket. The American guards at the museum entrance braced themselves, unsure as to what was happening. Then the blanket was peeled back to reveal one of the museum's most important treasures, which had been looted two months earlier during the invasion of Iraq to overthrow Saddam Hussein's regime.

It was the Warka Vase, an alabaster vessel that had been discovered by German archaeologists studying the Assyrian civilization during a 1933–4 excavation of the temple complex of the Sumerian goddess Inanna in the ruins of the city of Uruk (now known as Warka). According to legend, Uruk was the capital city of Gilgamesh, a hero of ancient Mesopotamian mythology.

Inanna, who is depicted on the vase, was the ancient Mesopotamian goddess of love, war and fertility. To some cultures, such as the Babylonians and the Assyrians, she was known as Ishtar, although it has been suggested that Inanna and Ishtar were originally separate deities.

Decorated with three rows (also known as registers) of bas-relief sculpture, with the bottom register divided into lower and upper sections, the vase would have been considered a sacred object at the time it was produced. The reliefs in the lowest register celebrate the fertility of the land, with depictions of crops such as barley and reeds that, together with the sheep in the upper layer, signified productivity, while the male figures in the middle register carry the riches garnered from the land – baskets of fruits and flagons of wine. These were gifts to offer in sacrifice during ceremonies. The topmost register portrays one fluid scene that shows the procession arriving at the temple, led by the *en* (ruler) of Uruk. He is seen facing the goddess Inanna (who can be identified by the fact that there are two stacks of reeds behind her), for whom the sacrifice is intended. Although unconfirmed, it is speculated that the plainer bands between the registers may have been covered in painted decorations that have worn away over time.

The vase is now on display in the National Museum, restored once more.

Temple of Shiva
(Commenced *c.* 835 BCE)

Artist(s): Unknown

Country of origin: Indonesia

Dimensions: Main tower height: 47 m (154 ft)

Material(s): Stone

The impact of Indian religious beliefs helped scatter its artistic styles throughout southeast Asia and Indonesia, with Buddhist and Hindu art later spreading to Sri Lanka and Java. One of the great buildings influenced by Indian religion is a group of temples dedicated to Shiva, Vishnu and Brahma – a magnificent, picture-perfect Hindu-Javanese complex near the village of Prambanan in central Java. The tallest of these temples is dedicated to Shiva, with those on either side devoted to Brahma and Vishnu, and this trio of holy 'mountains' is of paramount importance to religious belief and ancient cosmogony in southeast Asia.

On Java, mountains were thought of as places of contemplation, the home of the gods and a holy site for the ancestors. The shrines would originally have housed three statues to their gods, but only one, that of Nandi, the sacred bull of the Hindu god Shiva, is still intact. Two reduced temples within reach of the north and south gates and eight small peripheral *candi* (a shrine to a deity) are held within the enclosing wall. This wall divides the central temple area from the neighbouring space, which was originally peppered with 224 smaller shrines, proportionally organized in four descending rows and corresponding to the four enclosing walls. Outside is a courtyard, where activities pertaining to the temples' upkeep and those of its worshippers took place.

Of the three temples at Prambanan, the Shiva temple is the tallest and most graceful-looking. The effect is engineered by groups of tiny towers fusing almost indiscernibly into one single structure. Encompassing the lower section of the temple wall are 24 bas-relief panels representing *lokapāla*, custodians of the compass points, accompanied by various followers. Carved scenes from the Indian epic *Ramayana* appear alongside sculpted images of celestial beings. At interludes, there are large clusters of dancers and musicians whose postures relay the refinement and delight of heavenly dances. Helpers and other lesser characters primarily act as observers, while birds, animals and other creatures watch on from a landscape or forested environment. The influence is naturally Javanese; numerous relief sculptures echo carvings at Borobudur (see pages 40–1), and several may even have been sculpted by the same carvers. In the Shiva temple, one of the reliefs depicting the deity might be misconstrued as a bodhisattva (one who seeks enlightenment) were it not for the inclusion of a trident and lotus flower topped by a skull: symbols that clearly distinguish him as Shiva. This and other figures appear to have been correspondingly switched from Buddhism to Hinduism. The manner of art diverges from Indian aesthetics, with more soothing shapes and less voluptuous female characters. Whatever the aesthetic influence, the relief scenes at Prambanan essentially outline everyday life with wit and vitality.

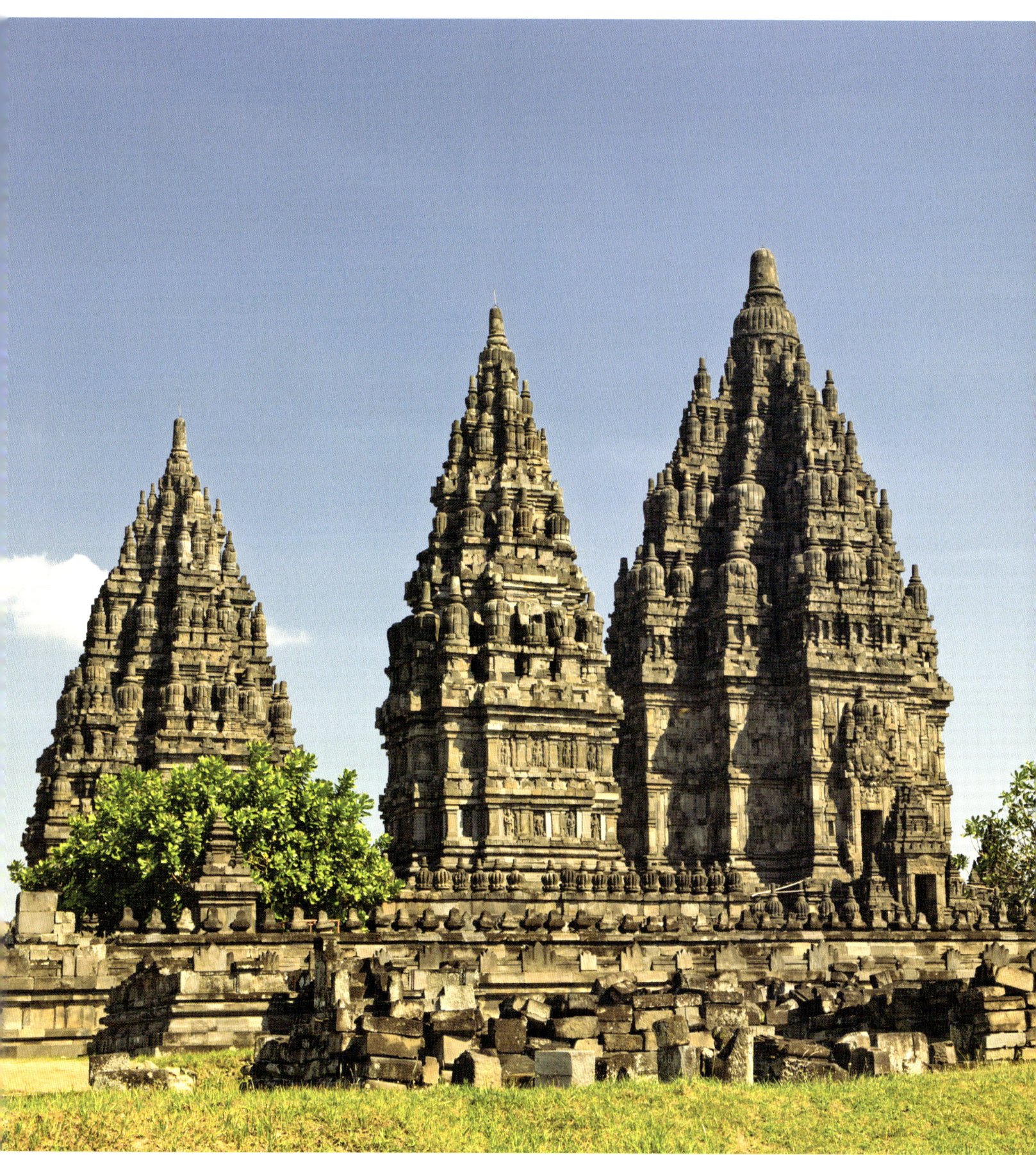

5 *Bi*
(771–256 BCE)

Artist(s): Unknown
Country of origin: China
Dimensions: 16.5 cm (6½ inches)
Material(s): Jade (nephrite)

Early archaeological discoveries from Liangzhu city in the Yangtze River Delta area of eastern China have revealed élite burials sites from the late Neolithic period. These sites contained large quantities of worked jade, which was placed around the interred body. Chinese archaeologists and scholars have been somewhat confounded about the purpose of such objects, and thorough research of the relevant cultures is multifaceted and ongoing. However, Liangzhu people must have believed jade artefacts protected the deceased body in some manner, and these objects certainly signified an individual's lofty status.

Bi, in Chinese art, are jade objects carved in the shape of a flat disc with an inner symmetrical hole whose proportional size varies from one to another. Early examples from Liangzhu may either be a symbol of the circle of heaven, emblematic of the sun, or possibly an astrological sign.

Jade comes in a well-renowned green as well as other colours, and it is resilient, solid and has intricate surface decoration. To make the *bi*, skilled artisans used unrefined jades as opposed to more glassy stone jadeites, which were chosen for small adornments of the type favoured in later periods. Neolithic objects were obviously manufactured before the invention of metal tools, with marks left by stone implements helping to date this particular *bi* to the late Zhou dynasty.

The making of jade jewels and ceremonial objects for entombment reached its height during the Zhou era (*c.* 1050–256 BCE). Zhou artists used jade and lacquer to honour the extravagant demands of grandiose feudal courts that competed in unrestrained demonstrations of aesthetic ostentation. The jade *bi* shown has formalized dragon motifs along the exterior edge and the disc's centre. Nephrite buffs to a radiant, slightly milky appearance, while jadeite, favoured in earlier times, is lustrous in finish. In China, jade's aesthetic merits became ciphers for the strength and ethical faultlessness of an admirable individual, with Han dynasty rulers entombed entirely in jade attire. Jade involves the laborious processes of sawing, boring, scraping and furbishing the stone. Fashioning jade required great technical skill and tenacity on the part of Zhou artisans, who worked with elementary hand tools, so the sophisticated carving of the dragons on the *bi* demonstrates their technical mastery.

As for its symbolism, Chinese dragons were once believed to journey between the heavenly and earthly realms to convey rain, and these magical creatures have always been a sign of fortuity in eastern Asia. Dragons also stood for a ruler's power to intercede between the celestial and human realms. In China, jade *bi* indicate a culture 'in which civilization could grow, and for the fortunate few, the leisure time to ponder on the mysteries of fertility and harvest, the cycle of the seasons, life and death, and the nature of the gods'.[1]

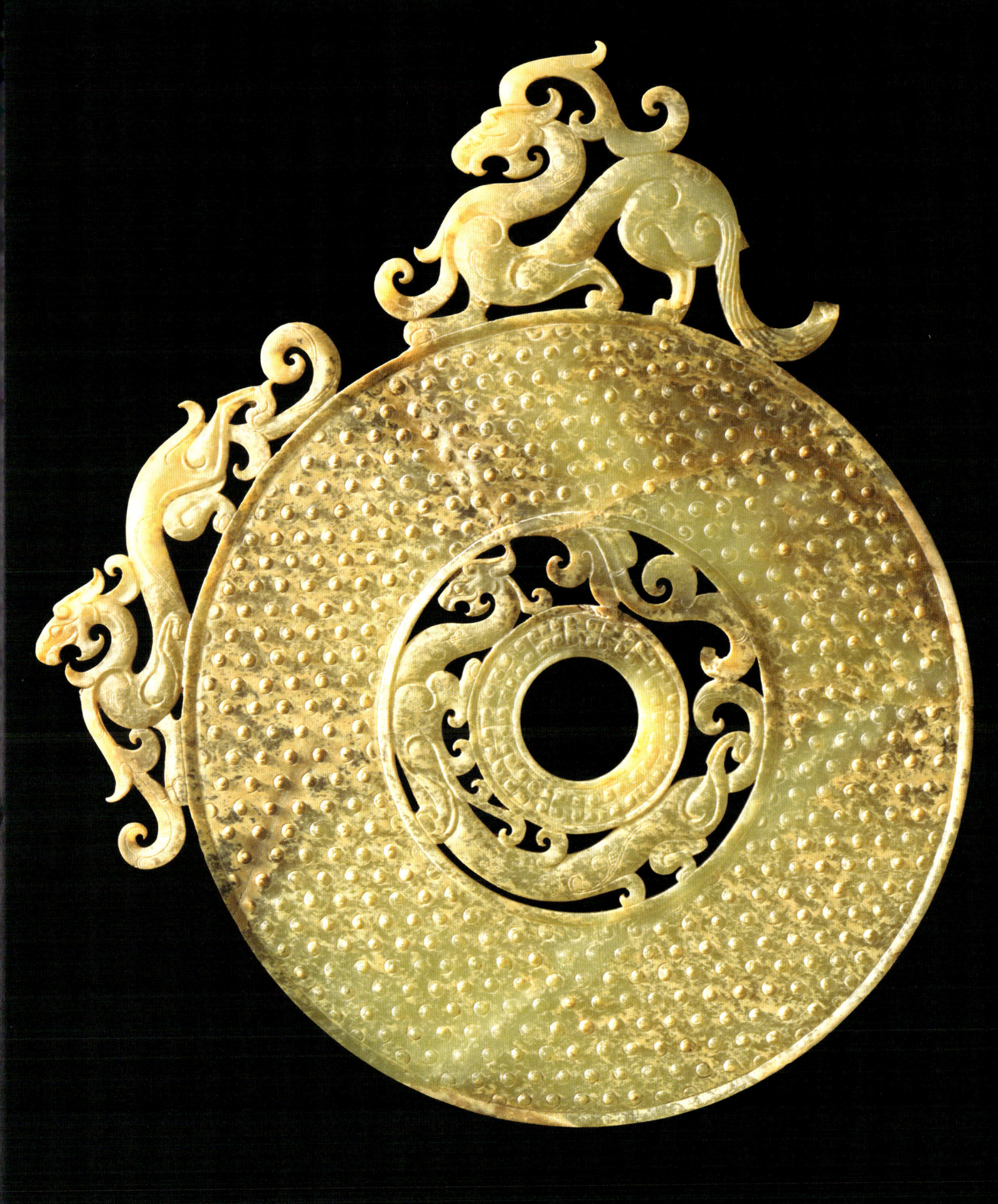

6 The Lion Hunt of Ashurbanipal
(645–635 BCE)

Artist(s): Unknown

Country of origin: Assyria (now Iraq)

Dimensions: 97 x 183 cm (38 x 72 inches)

Material(s): Alabaster haematite

This series of bas-relief slabs (or orthostats), excavated by Hormuzd Rassam and William Loftus between 1852 and 1854, once decorated the North Palace of the Assyrian city of Nineveh, which is in present-day northern Iraq. They depict a hunt by King Ashurbanipal (reigned 669–631 BCE), whose rule prefaced the decline of the Assyrian Empire. By any standards, these hunts were cruel, using lions that had been captured and then released solely in order for the king to track and kill them. At the time, only royalty was allowed to kill a lion, and it is believed that this may have had some connection with religious ritual. Although these extraordinary reliefs tell the story of a typical hunt, the main intention would have been political, to convey the power and bravery of the Assyrian king – the action man of his age – defeating a foe (represented by the lion) with ease.

Considered to be a masterpiece of Assyrian art, these reliefs were probably painted originally, making the palace appear very bright and colourful. The paint would have helped to preserve the gypsum from which the reliefs were carved using either iron or copper chisels, gouges or knives.

As with other Assyrian reliefs, there is a narrative depicted through this series of low-reliefs that runs from left to right. In some areas, individual scenes stretch the whole height of the slabs from top to bottom, but other panels present the progress of the hunt in three levels (or registers). In one section, in the topmost register, a lion is shown being released, while the middle register shows a lion being distracted by a horseman and the lower register portrays Ashurbanipal celebrating his kill.

Although the reliefs portray figures from a typical two-dimensional perspective – usually in profile – the quality of the details is extremely high. For example, the realistic poses and naturalistic representation of the lions, as well as the attention to the ornamentation of the clothes worn by the king and huntsmen make the scenes feel very dynamic.

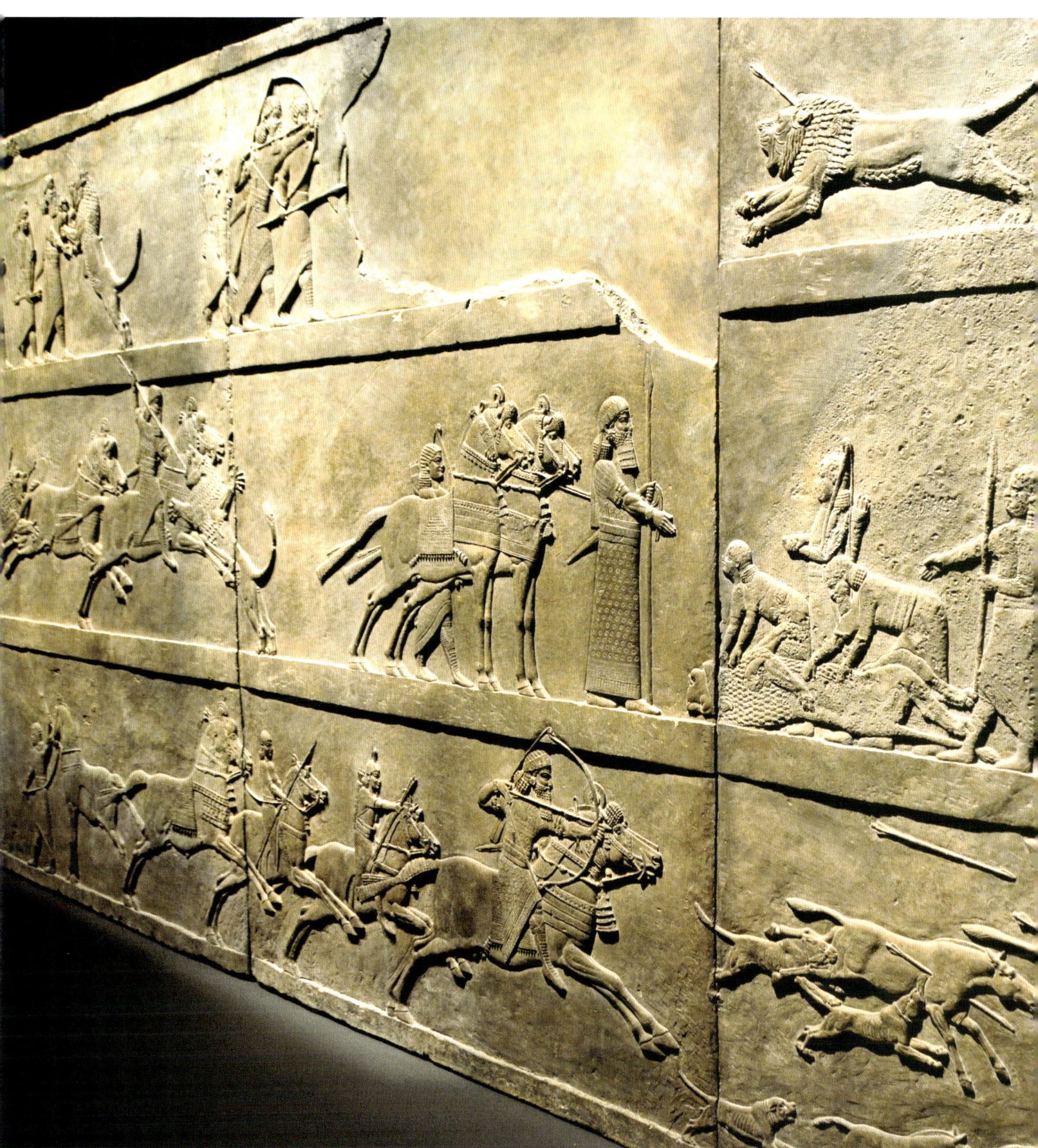

The Oxus Chariot
(5th–4th Centuries BCE)

Artist(s): Unknown

Country of origin: Tajikistan

Dimensions: 7.5 x 19.5 cm (3 x 7¾ inches)

Material(s): Gold

This delightful example of Achaemenid metalwork is considered to be one of the most outstanding pieces that were found as part of what is known as the Oxus Treasure (named after the nearby River Oxus – also known as the Amu Darya). The actual site of the discovery is unknown. Some believe it was found near Kobadiyan (now in Tajikistan). There are approximately 180 pieces of gold and silver work but, given that the treasure was looted by local people when it was found around 1877–80, it is estimated that the original number of items was in excess of 1,500.

Drawn by four horses, some of whose legs are now missing but whose physical features and harnesses are shown in intricate detail, the chariot is box shaped with an open back and finely worked decorations at the front and on the sides. Inside the chariot is a seat made from a strip of gold. While the charioteer holds the reins of the horses, the second figure is dressed in a long robe and wears a cap and a torc around his neck, suggesting that he was a man of relative wealth or prominence. Both figures are fixed to the seat by wires. Originally, the chariot's studded wheels would have rotated but they were soldered to the axle at some point.

The Oxus Treasure also contained other statuettes as well as jewellery, coins, votive plaques, scabbards, bowls and jugs. The treasure passed through numerous hands – from robbers to merchants

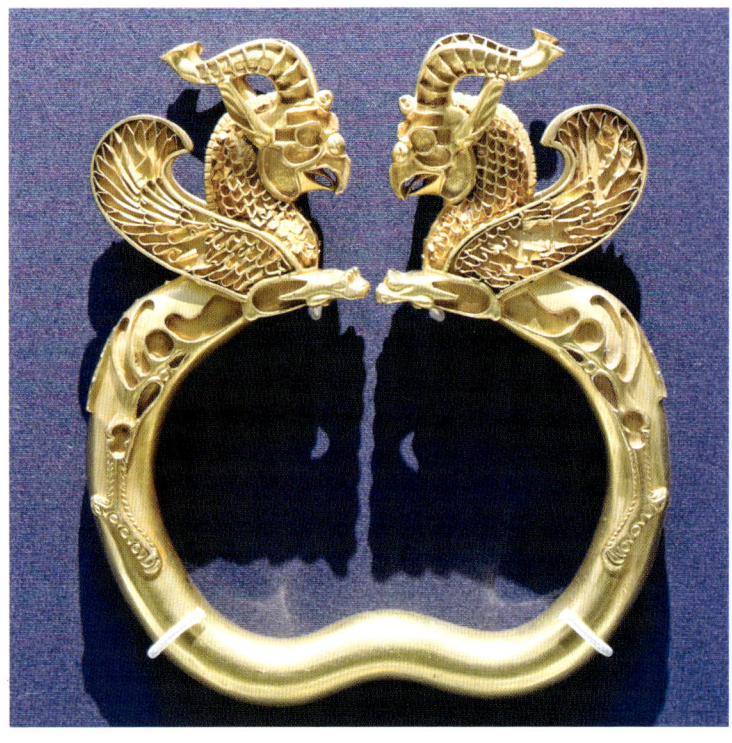

to other robbers – but it was rescued in the main by a British Army officer, Captain Francis Charles Burton, who was serving in Afghanistan in the early 1880s and who retrieved much of the treasure from thieves. Other items were bought from merchants and tribesmen by Sir Alexander Cunningham, the first Director of the Archaeological Survey of India. There is no evidence as to the origin of the items or in what situation they were found; some speculate that they may have been located in a temple. Now, the vast majority of the items that comprise the treasure are housed in the British Museum in London.

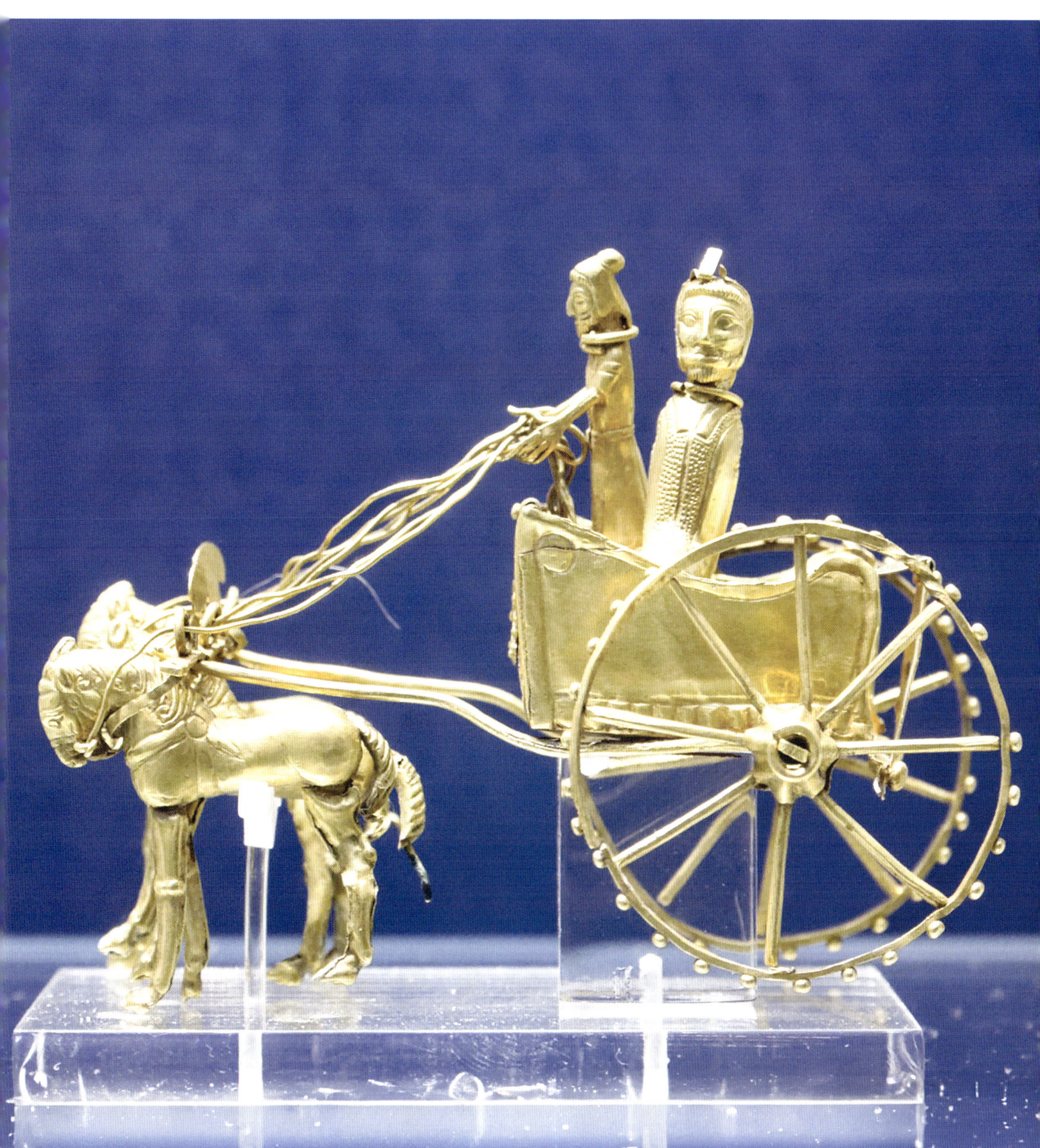

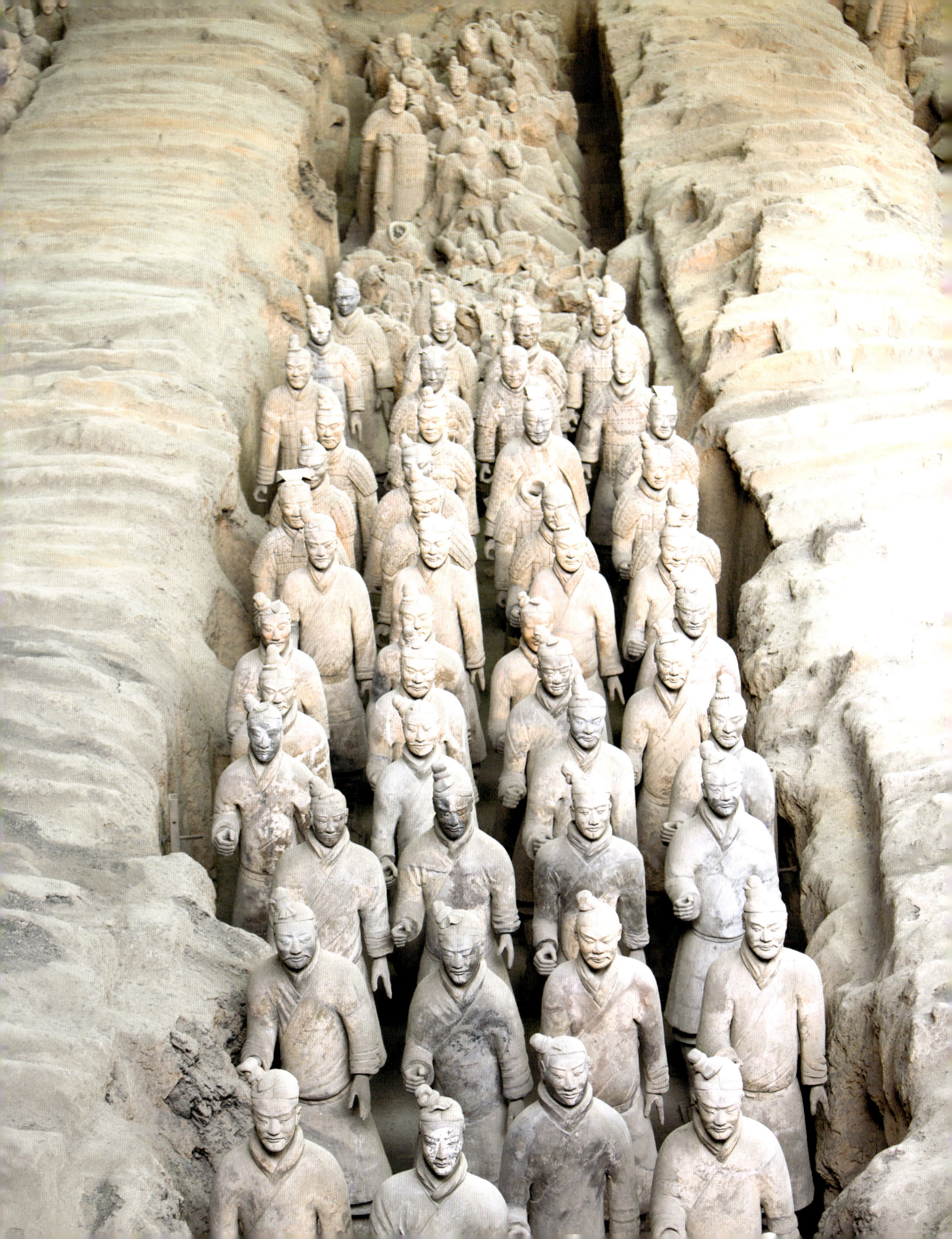

Terracotta Warriors, Mausoleum of Qin Shi Huang
(*c.* 221–209 BCE)

Artist(s): Unknown

Country of origin: China

Dimensions: Height range: 1.75–2 m (5¾–6½ ft)

Material(s): Terracotta clay and paint

We have the Han-dynasty chronicler Sima Qian (145 BCE–*c.* 86 BCE) to acknowledge for his description of the extravagant imperial tomb complex constructed for the first Qin Emperor of China, Qin Shi Huangdi (also known as King Zheng), who ruled from 221 to 210 BCE. Albeit a short-lived reign lasting just 11 years, his was a ruthless 'autocratic approach without which the road to unification could never have been followed'.[2] Nonetheless, 'He is popularly associated with the construction of the Great Wall, the burning of books, the burying alive of 460 scholars, the ostentatious expenditure on the Epang Palace, the building of the artificial Mount Li and his own sumptuous mausoleum nearby, and the deaths of hundreds of thousands of his subjects as they toiled in his service or infringed details of the state law code.'[3]

Qin Shi Huangdi's dynasty and various policies had a lasting effect on Chinese culture and society, crucially setting a path for the Han dynasty (206 BCE–220 CE), and his legacy was the systematizing of language, weights and measures as well as modifying the country's infrastructure. Nowadays, he is memorialized by his terracotta warriors, an accidental find made in 1974 by farmers roughly 1.5 km (1 mile) from the site of the emperor's tomb near the city of Xi'an, when they uncovered the first clay warrior. Local archaeologists later unearthed an enormous pit containing a larger-than-life-size clay model army, accompanied by chariots and cavalry horses, archers, lancers and hand-to-hand fighters. Despite various captivating theories, what the 'army' was for remains a mystery. However, new theories and a broader understanding of the mausoleum suggests a chiefly ritual purpose to do with the afterlife, Chinese intellectuals generally 'assuming that if an image… had the correct features, then the features gave the figures the powers of the thing or person depicted'.[4] While some believe that the significance of the find lies in the creative abilities of the ceramicists.

The warriors weighed approximately 150–200 kg (330–440 lb), and often comprised seven major modules made separately and later assembled, with the hands, heads, facial features, hairstyles and eyebrows finished with sharp realism to give the illusion of individuality. In the final stage, 'the pink and white-faced warriors… adorned by variegated and always brightly coloured clothes were intended to reflect contemporary taste and fashion'[5] as well as adding individual 'personality'. Hence the makers could fulfil Qin Shi Huangdi's demand for 'a magic army that would protect his tomb for eternity'.[6]

But while the emperor's guard stand ready for battle, the wider inclusion of acrobats, seated musicians, wrestlers, weightlifters, animals and birds (live birds were traditionally trained to 'dance' to orchestral sounds) indicates the tomb was built for longevity, including entertainment in the afterlife. As part of a long tradition of human and animal tomb art, however, the terracotta warriors form one of the most mysterious mausoleums of the ancient world.

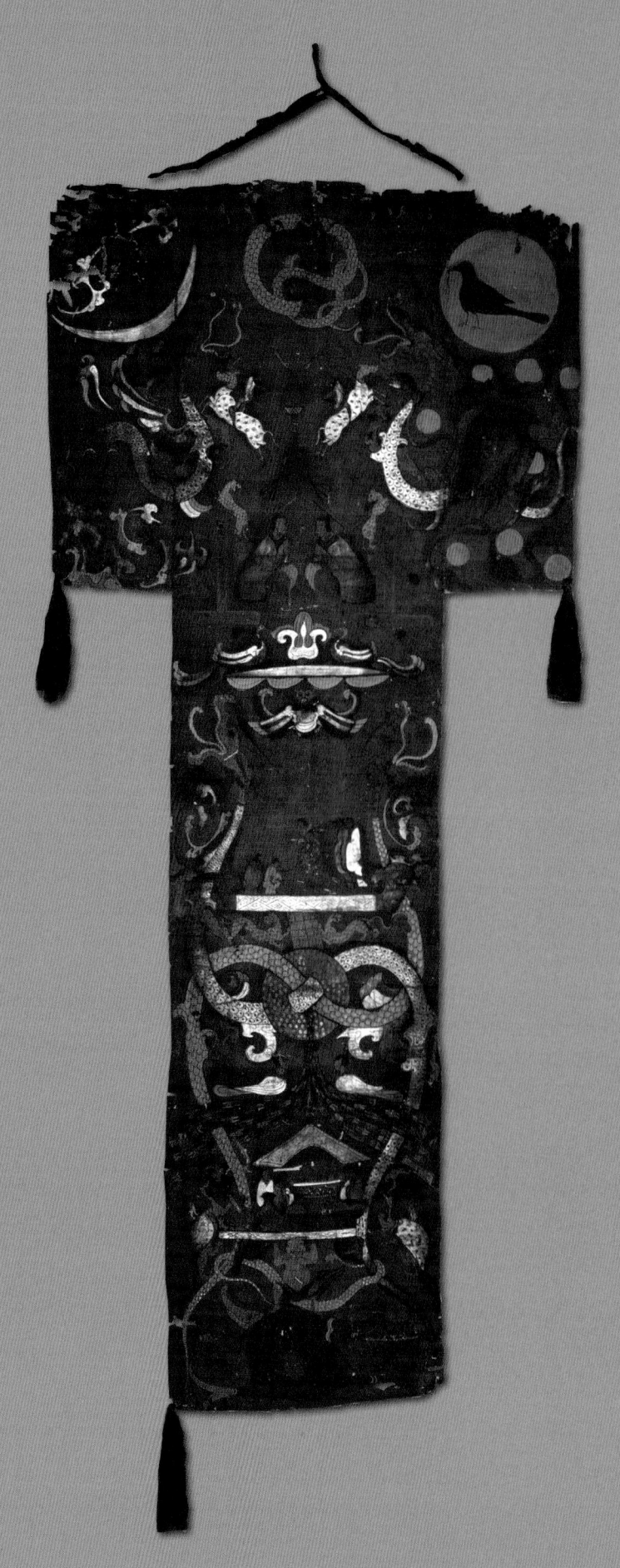

Funerary Banner of Marchioness Dai
(*c.* 168 BCE)

Artist(s): Unknown

Country of origin: China

Dimensions: 205 x 92 cm (80¼ x 36¼ inches)

Material(s): Silk

Writings from China's Han dynasty (206 BCE–220 CE) as well as approximately 10,000 archaeological artefacts from the excavations at Mawangdui, near the city of Changsha in Hunan province, have revealed that the living were in essence interested in preserving life after death. The notion that the dead would require sustenance and fostering in the afterlife was made plain from the royal mausoleums of the second-millennium-BCE Shang period, something that has endured after a fashion all through Chinese society. Sacrificial rituals of military leaders, convict-workers, slaves and animals had been carried out, but this was less common by the Spring and Autumn Era (popularly ascribed to 722–481 BCE), when Confucius condemned the practice. Nonetheless, the custom of burying wooden figures alongside the deceased persisted, something evidenced by the tomb of Marquis Yi of Zeng at Leigudun, who, in 433 BCE, was buried with more than 10 tonnes (11 tons) of bronze objects.

By the Han period, the mausoleums of aristocrats were elaborately equipped with specially selected artefacts, including human figures cast in the bronze *cire perdue* or 'lost wax' process. The welfare of the human body and its two souls – the *hun* (the spiritual soul) and the *po* (the physical soul) – had to be preserved in order to survive the journey to the otherworldly realm. The philosophy of comforts in the next life was also essential to the new post-Zhou élite. So, *mingqi* (burial figurines) have much to tell of peoples' lives, lifestyles, social structures, fashions, entertainments and belief systems, thus providing a 'portrait' of the tomb owners.

In the tomb of Marchioness Dai, a painted silk T-shaped funerary banner was draped over the coffin, described as a *fei yi* ('flying garment'). From top to bottom, the banner is roughly divided into three zones: a heavenly sphere, the earthly domain and the underworld, its iconography adhering to the philosophical concerns of the period. More precisely, the 'ornamental motifs clearly present a programmatic theme, wishing for the protection and survival of the dead.'[7] The ritual reasoning behind the banner is nonetheless hotly debated. While some Sinologists believe it was held aloft ahead of the funeral march, others, persuaded by a report of it in a funeral ledger as a 'flying garment', consider it a ceremonial robe. Another novel interpretation views the garment as a 'name banner', a high-born funerary 'passport' to aid Lady Dai's entry into heaven. On the banner, halfway, the earthly realm materializes as a female figure with her serving maids, possibly confirming the 'name garment' hypothesis. However, the banner may be notable for another reason. Is it the first-known 'portrait' in 'naturalistic' Chinese painting?

Dōtaku (Ritual Bell)
(1st–2nd Century CE)

Artist(s): Unknown

Country of origin: Japan

Dimensions: 110.5 cm (43½ inches)

Material(s): Bronze

This clapperless Japanese ritual bell (*dōtaku*) was cast in the mid to late Yayoi period (*c.* 300 BCE–250 CE), when Jomon culture had slowly given way to Yayoi. It is known that *dōtaku* were produced during a period of close connections between Japanese and Korean societies, which brought about huge social, technological and material changes.

More than 400 *dōtaku* cast-bronze bells have been uncovered in western Japan, created using metals imported from Korea and China, which together were a major production centre for high quality bronze two and half thousand years ago. Stone or clay moulds have also been unearthed at the sites of Yayoi foundries and 'the thinness of their walls and the high quality of their finish attest to the high degree of skill involved in their manufacture'.[8] But the process of casting means that *dōtaku* could not resonate, their function was principally ritualistic. However, historical reseach does suggest that they are based on earlier Chinese bell formations, which were similarly designed, decorated and not meant to be rung. *Dōtaku* are thought to have derived from smaller Korean bells that garlanded domestic animals and horses. They are found buried, individually, in braces and in large clusters, intermittently with bronze mirrors and weapons, frequently in remote sites or atop a mound, possibly to guarantee agronomic fruitfulness.

Bells were cast in clay moulds and commonly feature incised figural motifs including tooth, spiral and herringbone decorative bands carved into the surface. Three-quarters of this *dōtaku* is partitioned at the rear and front into six sections framed within wide and ornate lattice strips and a surplice design, which is somewhat evocative of a Buddhist monk's vestment. Within each section there would have been an image, most likely a simple line drawing, which in this instance has eroded. Where visible, however, they offer an insight into life throughout the Yayoi era, and some of the first instances of pictographic art in Japan. The precise meaning of the designs on *dōtaku* are nonetheless still debated. Various theories have likewise been offered regarding the actual purpose of *dōtaku* and the motivation for their burial, which could have been related to religious belief structures of the time.

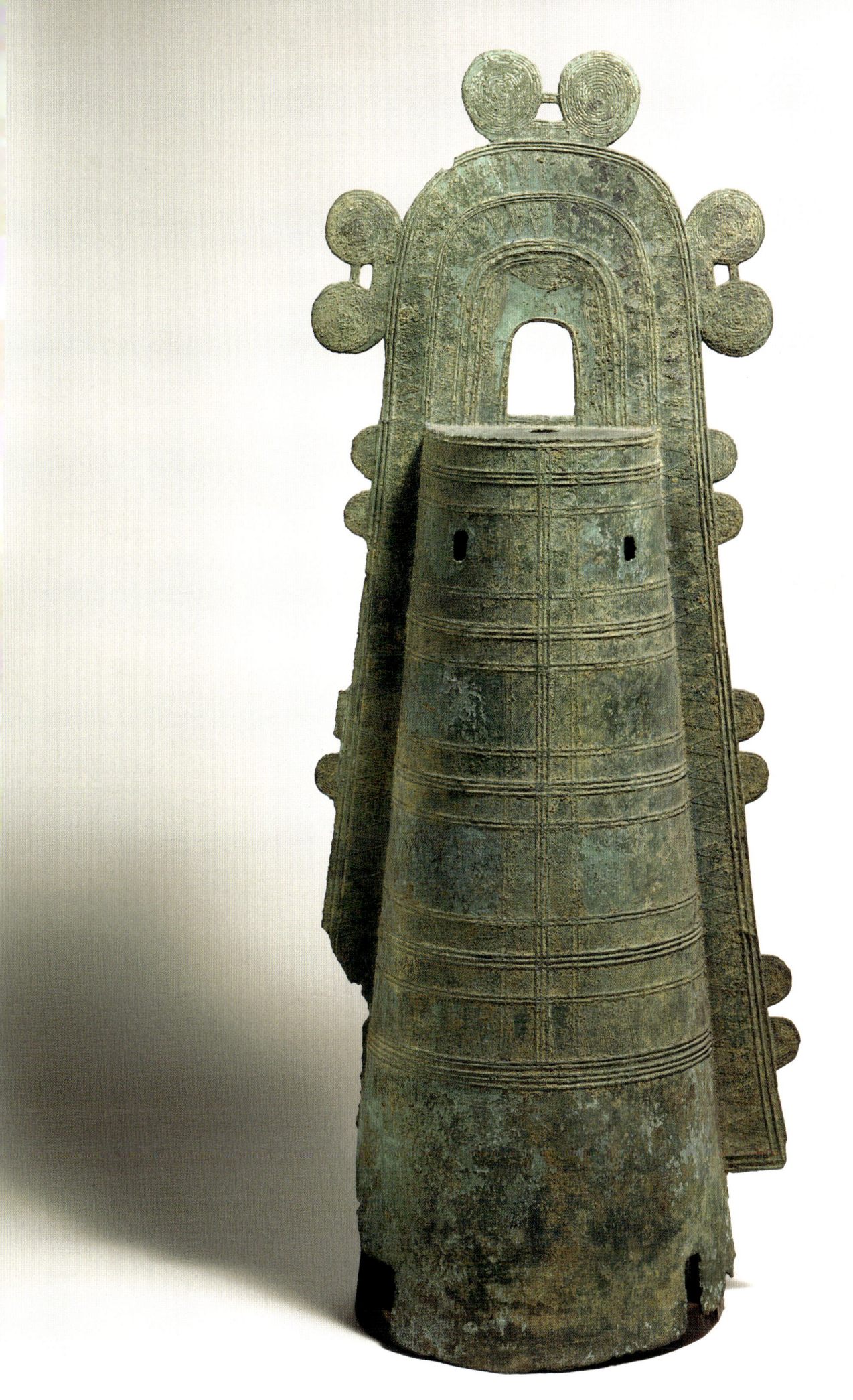

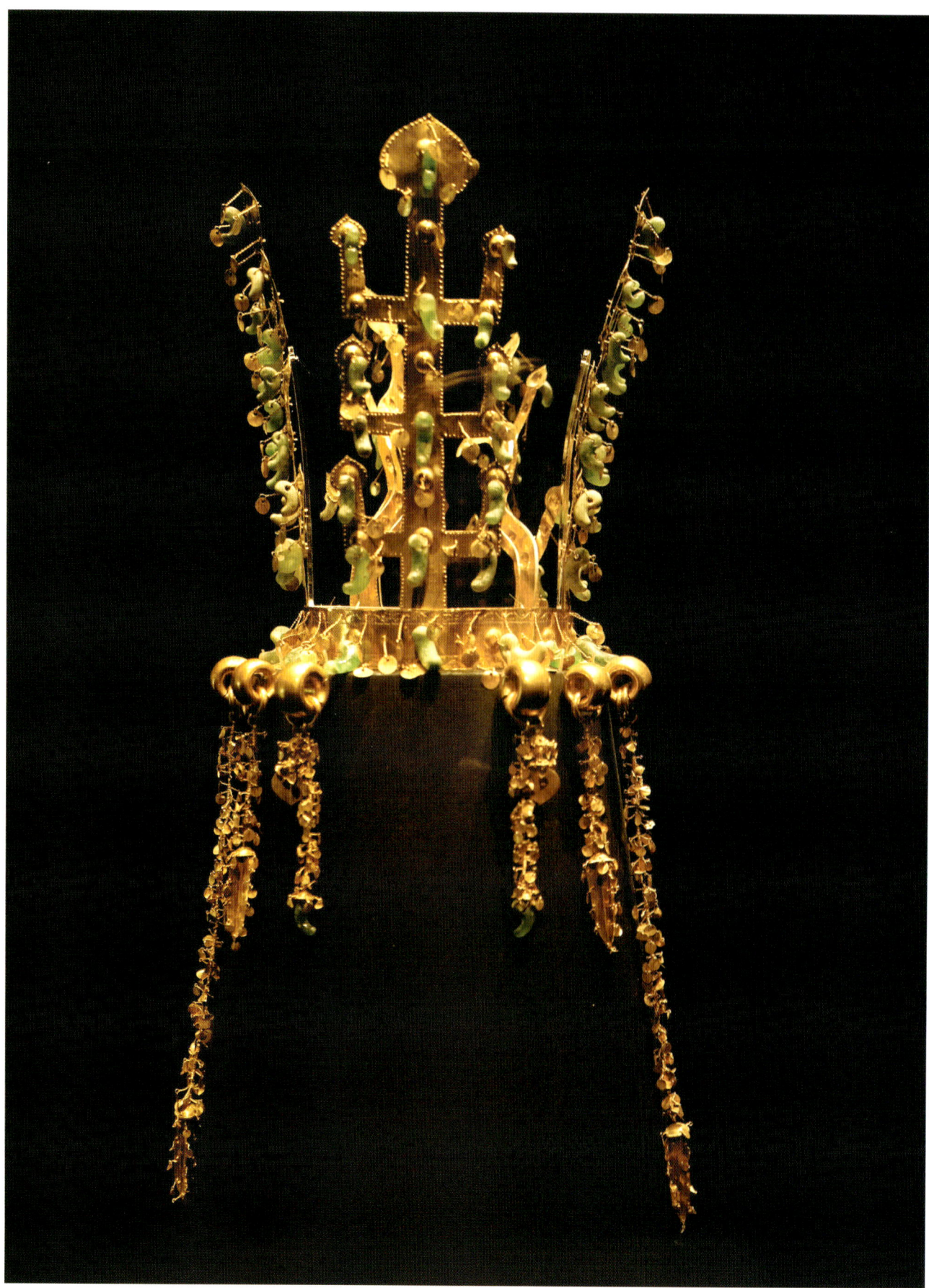

Gold Cap and Crown
(5th–6th Century)

11

Artist(s): Unknown

Country of origin: Korea

Dimensions: Gold, inner cap height 19 cm (7½ inches); Outer crown height 27.5 cm (11 inches)

Material(s): Gold and jadeite

The finest examples of Korean metalwork date from the Three Kingdoms era (c. 57 BCE–668 CE). In recent decades, archaeology has brought to light spectacular finds in gold and silver. The discoveries suggest that these precious materials were used not only for Buddhist imagery but also for individual embellishment. Gold is an 'inactive' chemical element, so exposure to air, low-grade heat, humidity and most diluents does not affect its composition. Hence the most spectacular artefacts found are made from gold.

With the exception of Japan, this crown is unlike anything unearthed so far in neighbouring countries – places traditionally under the cultural sway of Korea. Found in the north mound of Tomb 98 or the Hwangnamdaechong Tomb at Gyeongju (formerly romanized as Kyongju), it is a testament to the artistry of its metalworkers. It makes use of subtle filigree work in which gold grains are affixed to the surface to manufacture a mesmerizing dance of light, a method that recalls the artistry of Central Asia and the Middle East rather than countries bordering Korea. In fact, the peaked gold cap and crown (*daegwan*) are from the old Silla Kingdom (pre unification in 668).

Although the conical cap (*mogwan*) is traditionally the inner constituent of a circlet crown, contemporary mural paintings from China demonstrate that it could be worn separately to indicate individual rank or social status. Together, the crown is a construction of sorts, comprising of an internal *mogwan* made of thinly punched gold and encompassed by a crown made from delicate gold sheets with upright and horizontal offshoots. It was worn by royalty, so the design has applications in terms of decoration and practicality. While the inner cap has two rearward facing 'wings', the outer crown is festooned with gold sequins and cedilla-shaped beads made from jadeite, suspended from coils of gold thread. It is surmised that the uprights of the crown signify a tree and deer antlers and its design is very similar to headwear unearthed from tumuli in southern Russia. This points to ancient connections with roaming tribes that were strewn across the great Eurasian steppe from Hungary to China. There are no equivalents in Chinese art, so it likely relates to Siberian artistic forms.

Bracelets, earrings, rings and necklaces studded with valuable stones and jewels would probably have complemented it. Gold is eternally the colour of veneration and worship; it inspired great admiration and was used to intimidate or instil wonderment, its magnetism found in the mineral's rarity and unequal division. When viewed from the front, the shimmering radiance of the uprights and horizontal bars of the crown may have been intended to double as a golden throne.

12 Aboriginal 'Rainbow Serpent' Rock Art
(*c.* 6th Century)

Artist(s): Unknown

Country of origin: Australia

Dimensions: 6.1 m (20 ft)

Material(s): Natural pigment paints on sandstone

In the Arnhem Land escarpment in the Northern Territory of Australia, data suggests that painting on rock happened some 50,000 years ago, pre-dating the oldest European Palaeolithic parietal art (wall art) *c.* 45,000–30,000 years ago by *Homo sapiens*. Early New Guinea and Australian peoples also made rock paintings dated to the last Glacial Maximum, around 20,000 years ago. Rock art paintings not only indicate that the earliest inhabitants of Australia were long-practised artists, but also demonstrate that they created objects and images 'that they found powerful and meaningful'.[9] In the later rock art, *c.* 3,000–6,000 years ago, images of supernatural beings and creator ancestors such as the 'Rainbow Serpents' first appear. The term is pervasive in Aboriginal Australia and is illustrative of a number of preternatural entities in their appearances as snakes, particularly Wititj, the great python.

This image represents a huge rainbow serpent, painted on the sandstone overhang: a long-bodied imaginary creature that amalgamates the characteristics of various animals along the form of a massive snake. Rainbow serpent images often combine the features of a crocodile, emu or kangaroo and are frequently found around waterholes or in caverns where they are believed to hide. The presence of a rainbow is hence an indication of the great rainbow serpent rising from the waterhole where it dwells.

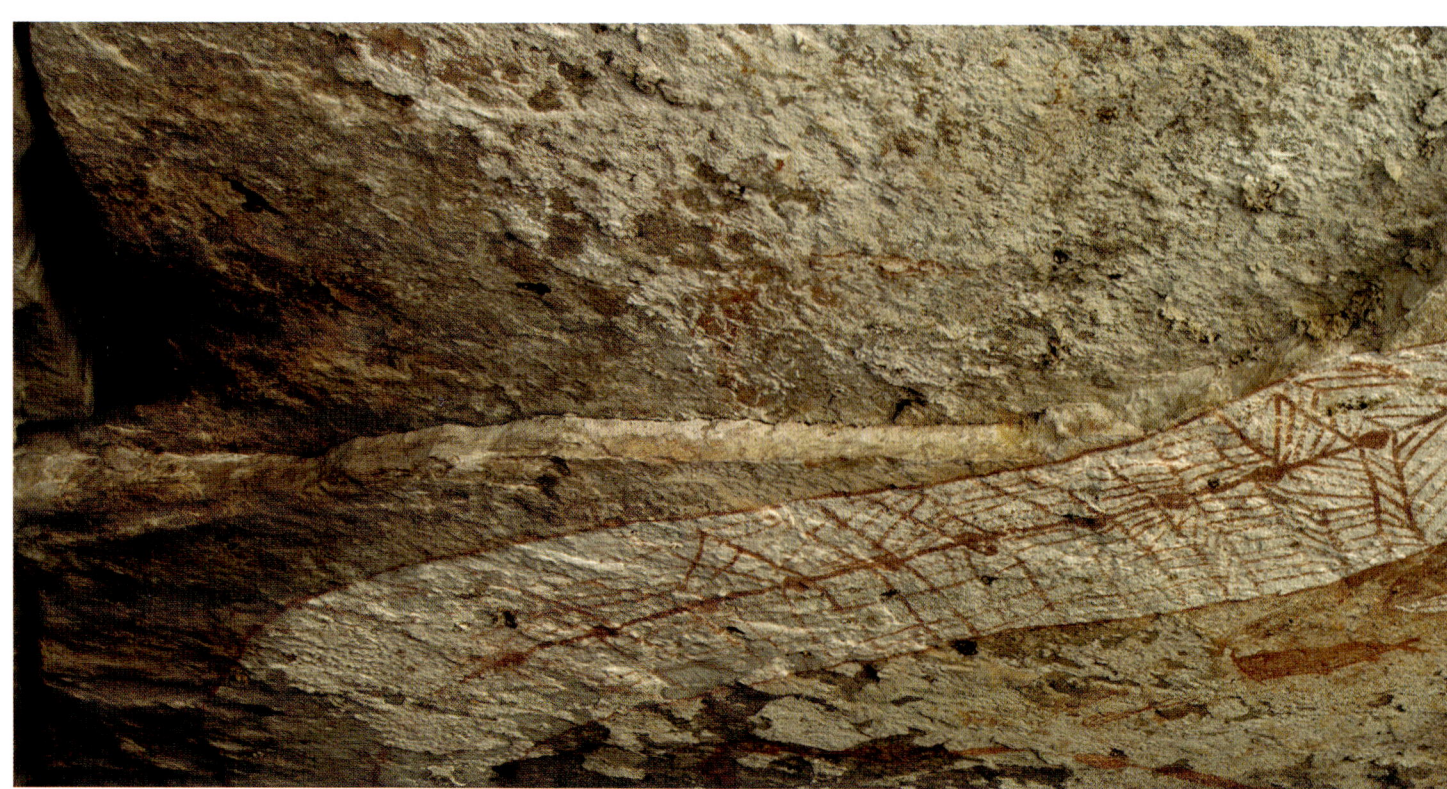

Nowadays, the image is connected with provincial ceremonies that draw in the wider community and highlight matters of fecundity and acquaint Aboriginal peoples with their land and country. As the master of all ancestral beings (*djang*), therefore, the rainbow serpent signifies the imaginative possibility of every individual, its image correlated with virtually every ancestral place. There is one caveat regarding Western Arnhem Land rock art – that these interpretations are provisional and probably part of a far more multifaceted history that will never be wholly retrieved.

For Aboriginal artists, painting is also a way to achieve dominion over the scheme of things, a way of grasping their world and cosmology. For instance, red-coloured rocks may represent the blood of ancestors, and in many parts of Australia petroglyphs and rock paintings are seen as a verification of spirits (*mimis*) soaked into the rock itself. As Howard Morphy further suggests: 'There are many Aboriginal equivalents to the image of Christ on the Turin Shroud: signs that mark an infinite presence on the surface of the earth.'[10] This state of mind, where there are no definitive boundaries between, say, the visible and invisible world, is clearly outlined by a mode of representation known as 'x-ray art' on Ubirr rock, where the interior organs and structure of humans and animals are akin to photographic x-rays. So, rock art is not only a record of the past but also for Aboriginal peoples a way of looking beyond the superficial and making sense of the quintessential aspects of nature, the world and universe. Art is fundamental to Aboriginal life and its making intimately tied to the spiritual life, which focuses on the concept of 'the Dreaming' (see pages 182).

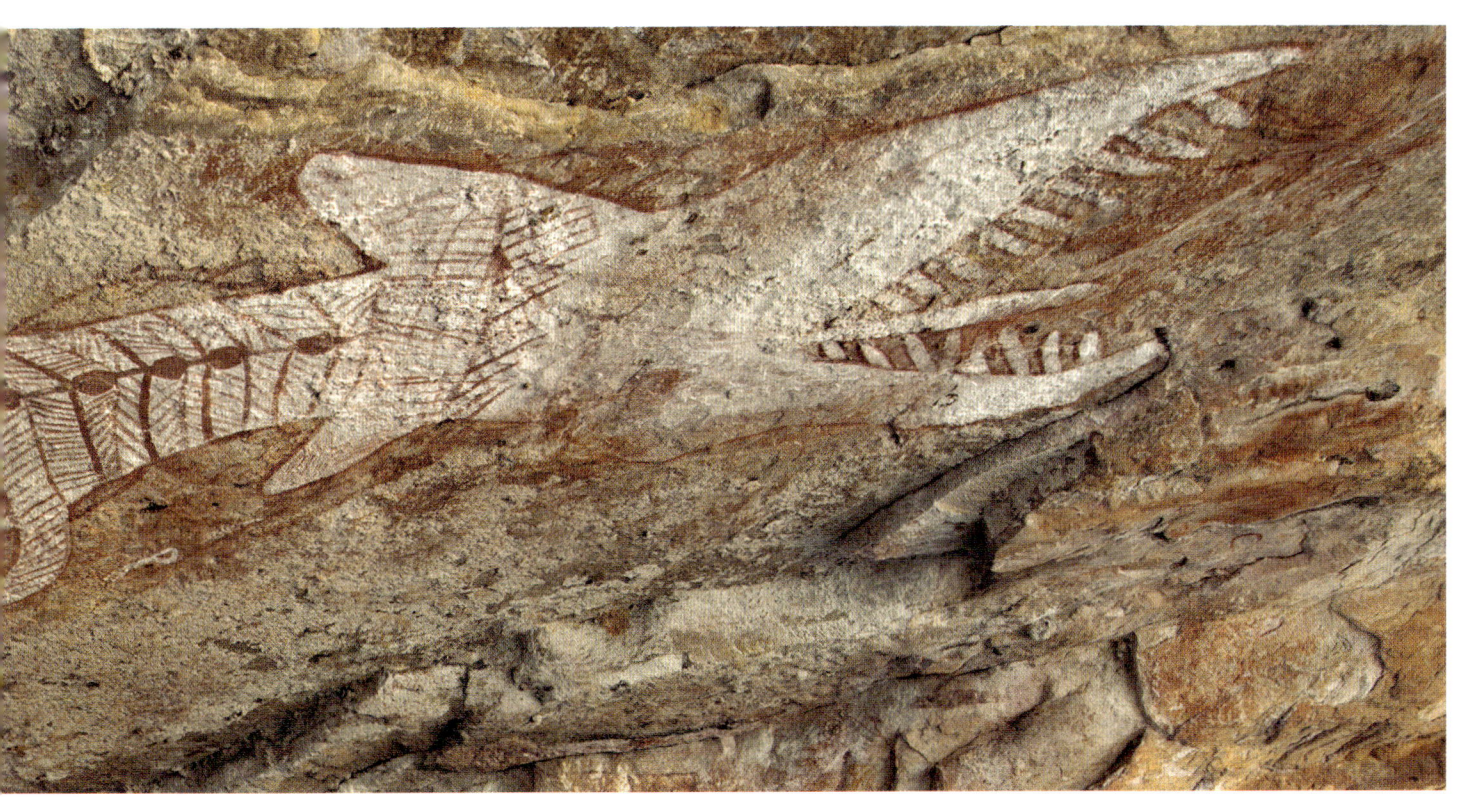

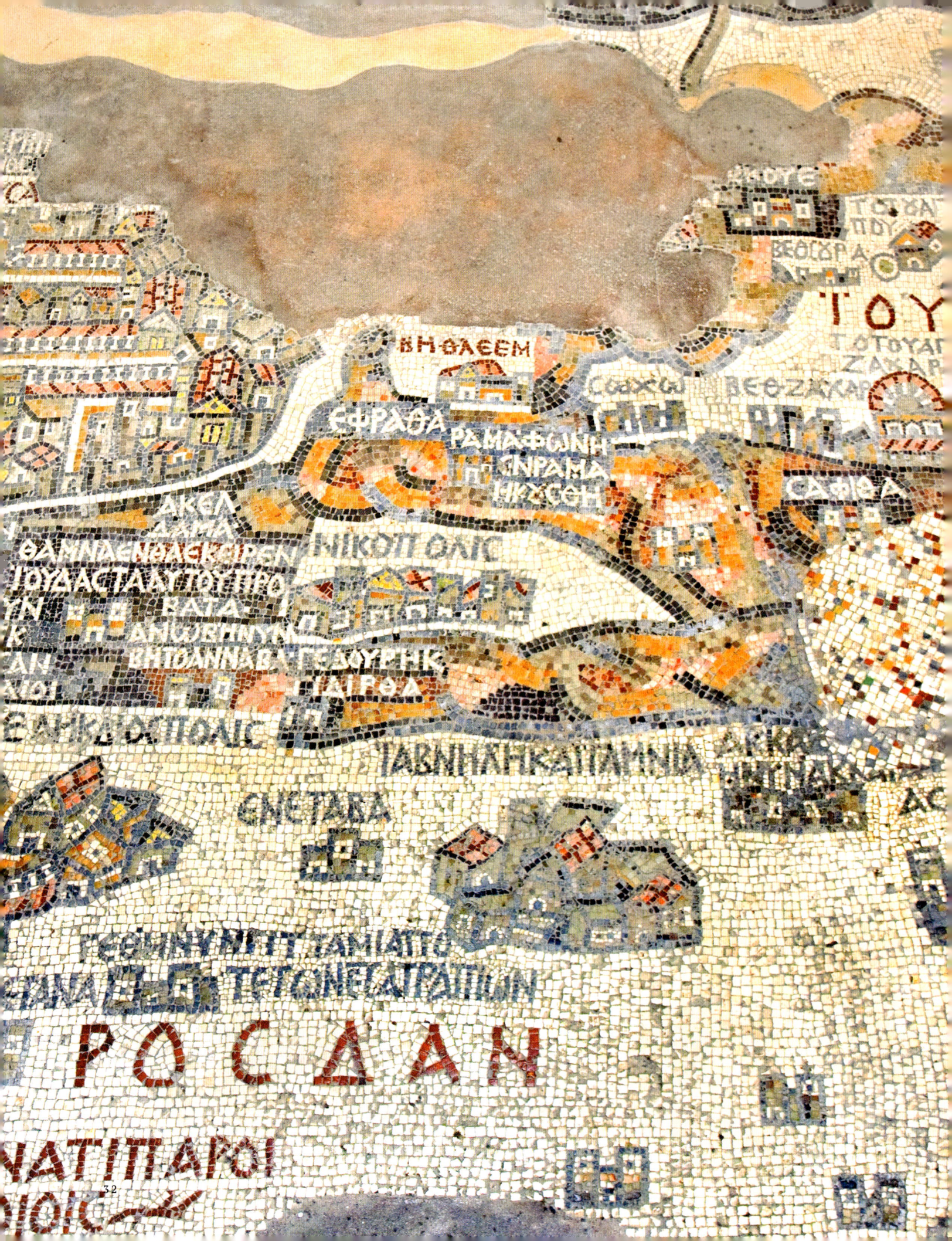

13 Madaba Map
(*c.* 542–570 CE)

Artist(s): Unknown

Country of origin: Jordan

Dimensions: 15.7 x 5.6 m (51½ x 18¼ ft)

Material(s): Stone tesserae (c. 2 million)

Located in the apse of the Byzantine Church of St George in Madaba in Jordan, this beautiful mosaic is the oldest known map of the Holy Land. It shows an area stretching from Lebanon in the north to the Nile delta in the south and from the Mediterranean in the west to the part of the Sahara Desert lying east of the Nile.

Madaba is located in central Jordan about 30 km (18½ miles) from the capital Amman, and is well known for its mosaics from the Byzantine Empire and Umayyad Caliphate era. There has been a settlement there since the Bronze Age, but it was almost destroyed by an earthquake in 746 CE and consequently abandoned. In the mid-1880s, small parts of the mosaic were noted during the foundation work for a new Greek Orthodox church on the site, but little was done to investigate it. Then, ten years later, after the new church had been built and preparations for a new cement floor were underway, the mosaic was rediscovered, and the floor was laid around it. Subsequently, the mosaic suffered some damage due to fire but was renovated thanks to a grant from the Volkswagen Foundation in the mid-1960s.

The mosaic contains some wonderful pictorial elements, such as palm trees, bridges and lions hunting gazelle or fishing boats floating in the Dead Sea, but it also provides a vital understanding of the topography of Jerusalem, which sits at the centre of the map, in the early centuries of the first millennium CE. Visible are notable sites, such as the Church of the Holy Sepulchre and the Tower of David as well as the Damascus Gate, the Lions' Gate and others.

Inscriptions are in Greek and include references to the 12 tribes of Israel as well as biblical quotations, all leading to the belief that the creators of the mosaic would have relied on a gazeteer or directory of place names called the *Onomasticon* that was compiled by Eusebius of Caesarea in the 4th century. Its accuracy has been proven by archaeological excavations in Jerusalem which have revealed that sites such as the Cardo Maximus (the Roman street that would have run north to south) were exactly where the map said they were.

14 Harihara Statue
(Late 7th Century)

Artist(s): Unknown
Country of origin: Cambodia
Dimensions: 1.97 m (6½ ft)
Material(s): Sandstone

There is no unassailable proof for the age of this extraordinary Harihara sandstone statue, found at the small temple of Prasat Andet, Kampong Thom. However, it probably dates from the final quarter of the 7th century, during the reign of Jayavarman I (ruled approximately 655/657–680/681 CE), or possibly Jayadevi, his daughter, who subsequently reigned, *c.* 681–*c.* 713. This pre-Angkor (802–1431) image is remarkable for its manifestation as half Vishnu or Hari (right side) and half Shiva or Hara (left side), hence the name Harihara.

Important signs for Harihara would have been the attributes held in the now missing four hands, but otherwise the differentiation between the two sides of the sculpture is minimal. The separation is registered only in the head, as evidenced by just half of his third eye showing and in the rather ascetic treatment of Shiva's headdress of snaked and curling ringlets. These shapes are typical of the *Shaivite jatamukuta* coiffure, which contrast with the smooth portion of Vishnu's cylindrical and regal-looking mitre. The base of the headdress and the band of overlapping verdant shapes below possibly denote the authority of a crown, heralding the diadems that typify subsequent representations of Vishnu. To a degree, the coiled locks of the Prasat Andet Harihara evoke the braided and extravagantly decorated *jatamukuta* hairstyle, which signifies an aesthetic or deity in difficult to classify female divinities. This style of hair is depicted in other Cambodian statues of the period (or slightly later).

The long end of Harihara's *sampot* (traditional Cambodian garment), incised in delicate relief with a knot swathed to suggest an airy pocket of loose fabric, anticipates what was to become the prevailing dress style for future representations of Harihara. More crucially, this type of modelling gave prominence in the later Angkor era to sacerdotal imagery that exemplified *ashana*, the imperviousness to physical and worldly tasks. The frontal stance is slightly flexed in the left hip and knee joint, suggesting a state of neutrality, but the benevolent composure in the face aligns neatly with this sophistication of form, supposing a formal linkage with earlier pre-Angkorian sculptures. The Harihara from Prasat Andet is possibly the most divine and unquestionably the most sophisticated of all Khmer divinities. Unlike nearly all stone sculpture in Indonesia, depicted in relief on slabs and steles, it is produced in the round and with the weight placed on the ankles and arms reaching into space. The Khmer sculptors intended viewers to see their sculpture from all viewpoints and, in this instance, experience it in three dimensions at the centre of the *garbhagriha* brick-and-sandstone temple, the most holy of places, where the Harihara sculpture was found. The temple was also orientated slightly north of due east, a custom that 'may imply a veneration of the northeast as the sacred of cardinal or sub-cardinal points [and] an estimation that prevails in Indonesia'.[11]

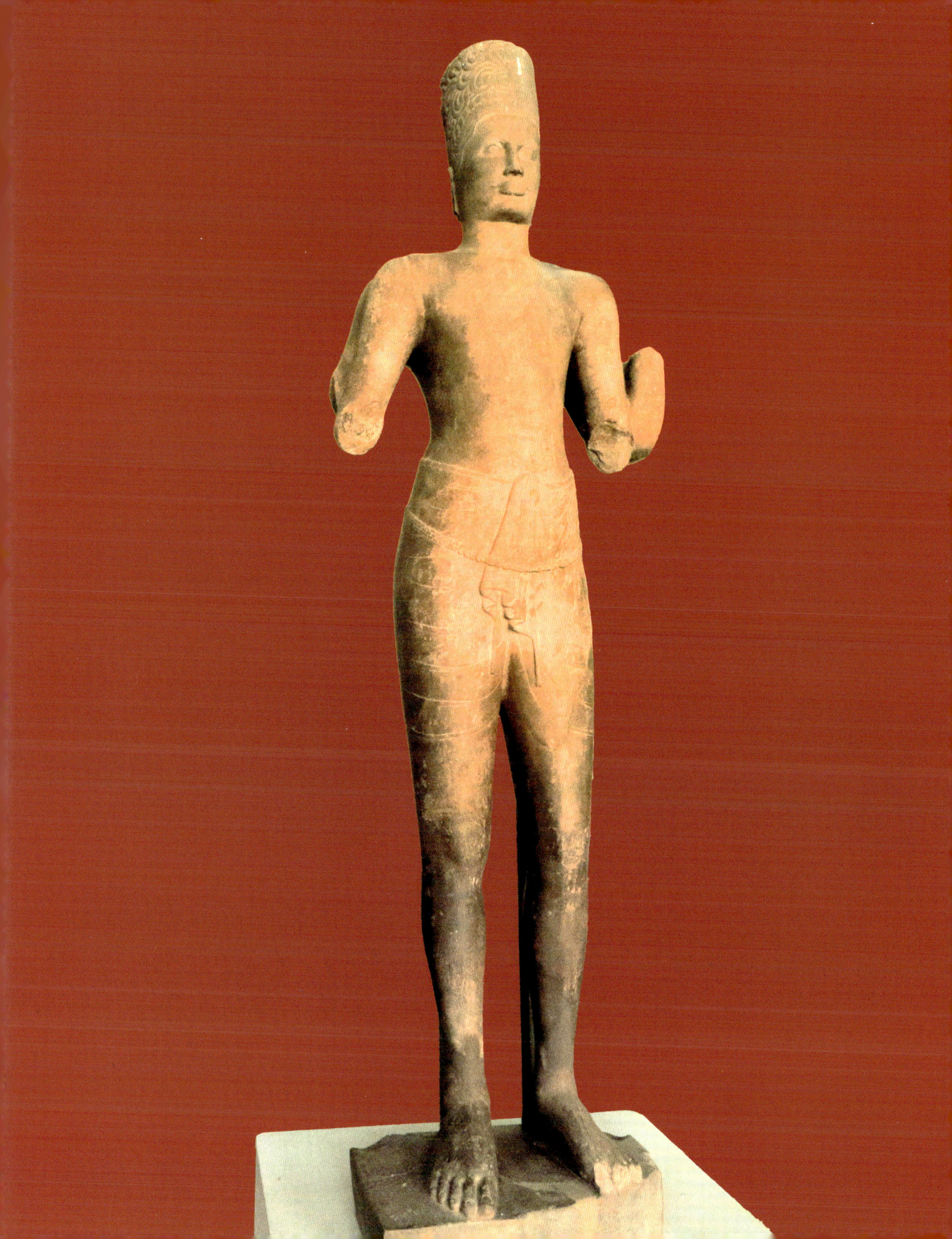

15 Afrāsiāb Murals
(Mid 7th Century)

Artist(s): Unknown

Country of origin: Uzbekistan

Dimensions: 3.4 x 11.5 m (11 x 37¾ ft) each

Material(s): Vegetable-based paints on limestone plaster

These murals, also called *The Paintings of the Ambassadors*, are some of the finest examples of Sogdian art. The Sogdians lived predominantly in a group of city states known as Sogdiana (*c.* 700 BCE–1000 CE) that covered an area between the Amu Darya and Sri Darya (rivers in Central Asia) through which passed the Silk Road and which straddles the present-day countries of Uzbekistan, Turkmenistan, Tajikistan, Kazakhstan and Kyrgyzstan. Although Sogdians were also to be found in China, where they were renowned for their roles in the military and government under the Tang dynasty (619–906 CE), they were in fact an ancient Iranian civilization that followed various religions, including Zoroastrianism and Buddhism, before converting to Islam in the 9th–10th centuries.

Sogdiana had no official capital, but Samarkand was the main focal city. In 1965, local authorities began work on a new road in the Afrāsiāb mound, the original site of pre-Mongol Samarkand (pre 1220), and excavations revealed a house in which the murals were found covering the four walls of one of the rooms. Sogdian art is renowned for its 'narrative' focus, with the emphasis on figurative elements rather than backgrounds and settings which are suggested using colour and line.

The Afrāsiāb murals were painted during the reign of King Varkhuman, *c.* 650–670 CE. There were originally two registers of murals on each wall, but the upper registers were destroyed by bulldozers working on the road that led to their discovery. Thus each wall now only shows its lower register. Samarkand and the veneration of King Shishpir (Varkhuman's predecessor) are the theme of the south wall, while the other murals depict various cultures with whom the Sogdians would have had trading and cultural relationships. The west wall contains ambassadors and their entourages from China, escorted by Turks, and other delegations from neighbouring territories, such as Chaghaniyan, Chach, Tibet and the Korean kingdom of Goguryeo. The north wall is known as the 'Chinese panel' and shows the Emperor Taizong out hunting and the empress on a boat. Of the four walls, the east wall is the most deteriorated with very little of the original artwork remaining, but it is speculated that it would probably have shown travellers from India. Considered together, the murals are testament to the numerous cultural exchanges that were stimulated by trade along the Silk Road.

From top to bottom: North, South, East and West walls.

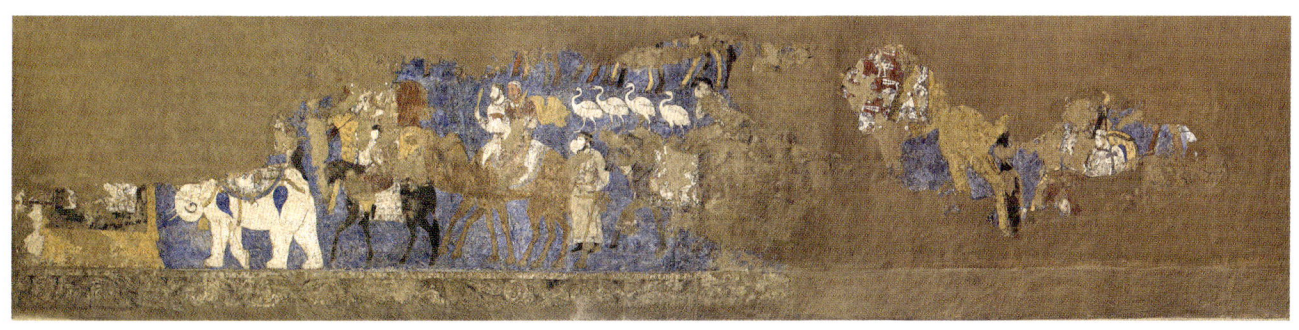

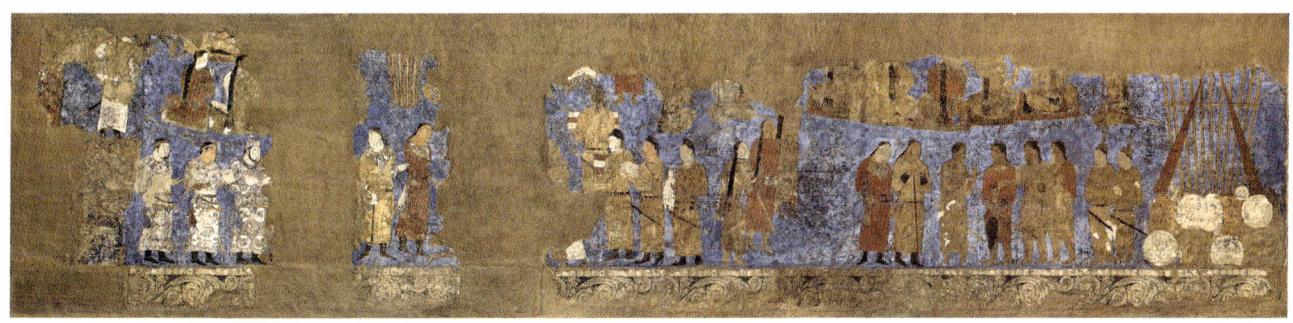

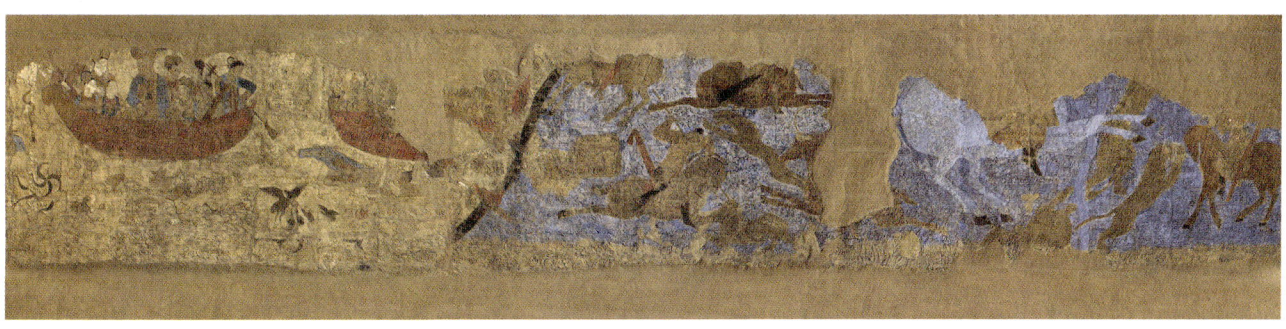

16 Buddha Statue, Temple of Seokguram
(774 CE)

Artist(s): Unknown
Country of origin: South Korea
Dimensions: Height 3.5 m (11½ ft)
Material(s): Granite

Until recently, Korean art was virtually unknown in the West. Despite the cultural shadow of China, incursions by the Mongols and Japanese and internal hostilities, Korea has managed to conserve its own national identity, language and artistic style. In addition, a destructive civil war left little physical evidence of Korea's former cultural glory. Yet what has survived after such a turbulent history provides a cultural chronicle of extraordinary variety and richness.

The Korean peninsula synthesized cultural influences from China and Europe, archaeological evidence revealing 'prehistoric stone cairns and dolmans that would normally be more associated with the ancient Celtic world'.[12] Another import was Buddhism, which arrived from China *c*. 372–384 CE, during the Three Kingdoms period, and was adopted as a state philosophy in 535 CE. Countless small bronze statues, stylistically similar to those manufactured in China, evidence Buddhism's appeal. With China's help, Silla was the first united dynasty to rule over the entire Korean peninsula. Korea's golden age lies in this epoch (668–935 CE).

Silla's leaders viewed Buddhism as a defensive entity rather than a religion, subsidizing the construction of temples in and around the city of Gyeongju (formerly romanized as Kyongju) as a preternatural protection against outside forces. None of these buildings survived Korea's stormy history, but the superb Buddhist cave-temple of Seokguram (formerly romanized as Sokkuram), just east of the capital, begun in 742 CE and completed in 774, 'stands as a sentinel of an architectural tradition from India'.[13] The primary, circular area sits under a high domed room (rotunda), which, despite only being 6 m (20 ft) in diameter, is filled with a sense of light and space. The chapel is constructed from hundreds of pieces of cut-granite blocks held in place with stone rivets rather than traditional mortar.

The 'Ten Disciples of the Buddha' line the lower wall while small statues of seated bodhisattvas and worshippers fill eight niches above. All the sculptures face inwards towards a granite statue of the Shaka

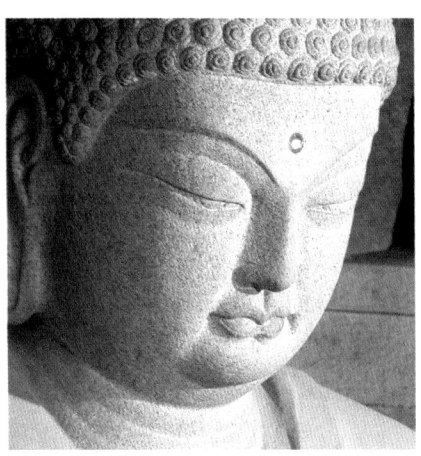

Buddha, sitting on a lotus leaf, with his right arm lowered in a gesture identified as 'calling the earth to witness' Buddha's enlightenment, the left arm in the lap denoting his meditative state. The facial expression is one of both self-possession and all-embracing mindfulness. Here, the Seokguram Buddha echoes its iconographic roots in Indian sculpture, especially the 5th-century *Seated Buddha Preaching his first Sermon* from Sarnath, yet it also encompasses figurative elements found in Tang China (619–906 CE), particularly in the face and drapery, and even 'has a distinctively broad-shouldered dignity combined with harmonious proportions that are without close precedents'.[14]

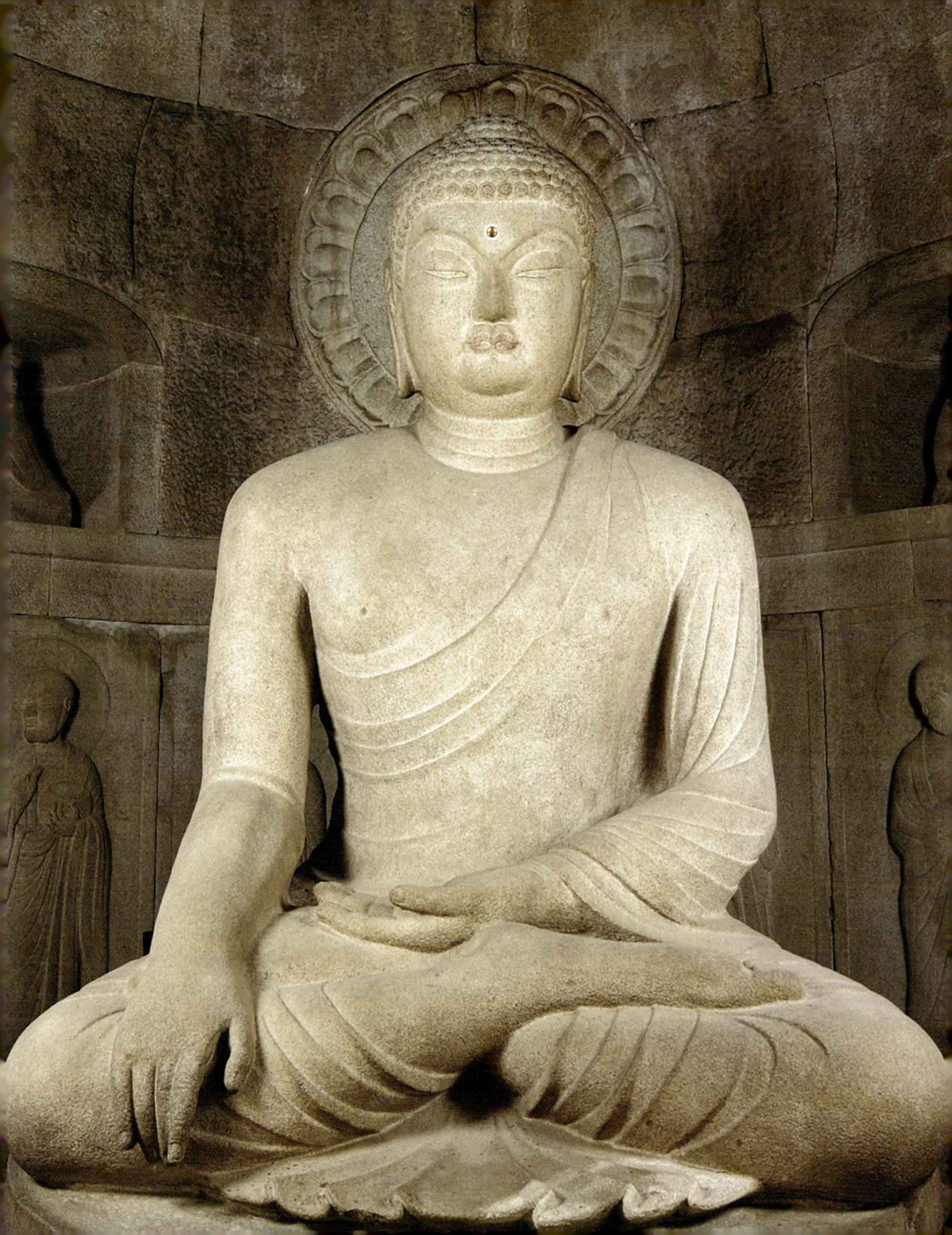

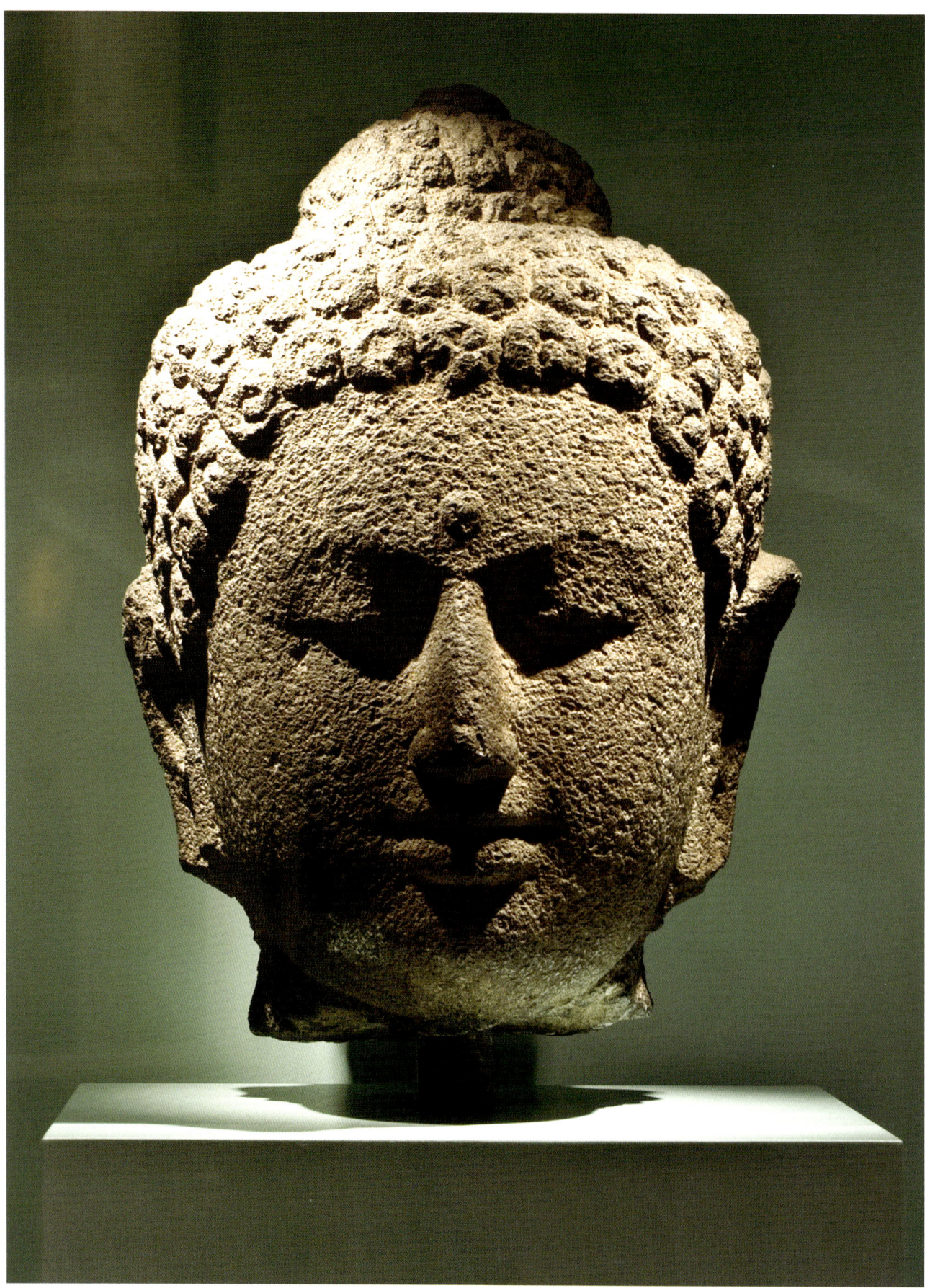

Borobudur Buddha Head
(780–840 CE)

Artist(s): Unknown
Country of origin: Indonesia
Dimensions: Height 33 cm (13 inches)
Material(s): Stone

This stone head hails from Borobudur ('world mountain') on the Indonesian island of Java, a few degrees south of the equator. It's the site of a supreme architectural and cultural triumph: a vast, concentric, square-stepped monument, covered with more than 4.8 km (3 miles) of relief carvings and peopled with 504 statues of Buddha. Although its symbolism is not entirely clear, Borobudur represents the Buddhist concept of the universe in stone. Ascending the structure's terraces is symbolic of the material path from ordinary life, sin, war and suffering to eventual spiritual awakening.

The Indonesian temple was for some reason abandoned soon after its completion. It's worth noting that Buddha was originally represented via a set of simple signs, not the archetypal image we see today. He was an actual historical figure, not a deity. According to historic sources, Siddhartha Gautama (*c.* 560–480 BCE) was born in Nepal, and renounced his wealth, privilege and power to search for spiritual enlightenment. (One famous relief panel at Borobudur depicts the Prince cutting off his hair as a symbol of his rejection of the physical world.) The story of his life, past incarnations and experiences influenced much of the art based on his teachings. After countless happenings and acts of meditation, he finally became the Buddha, the 'Enlightened' or the 'Awakened One'.

This Buddha has his eyes downcast in a serene state of contemplation. He has very long earlobes that suggest years of wearing weighty gold earrings as a prince, signifying his life before spiritual awakening. His mouth has the timeless half-smile that we recognize in sculptures of Vishnu, the iconography of Hinduism retained within Buddhism. Some of the first human representations of the Buddha were made in northwestern India around 500 years earlier. Beyond these religious references, a relief carving of a ship from about 800 CE at Borobudur is evidence of seaborne contact taking place between the two great civilizations, which occurred well over a thousand years before Borobudur was constructed.

The sculptures at Borobudur, and undeniably much of Javanese culture, owe a great debt to prolonged and nonstop contact with India. As an extremely fertile, wealthy, populous and strategically vital island, Java is probably the best illustration of how maritime Southeast Asian trade allowed Buddhism to reach beyond the peripheries of its origins and develop as a worldwide faith. But this head reveals a strange contradiction about all great religious enterprises, from Borobudur to the great Gothic edifices in Europe: monuments that took hundreds of years to construct and involving immense material riches are fundamentally designed to encourage humanity to leave all earthly pursuits behind. So as the Buddhist writer Stephen Batchelor indicates, the Borobudur Buddha head '… embodies something that goes beyond just metaphysics or religious doctrine and stands for something vital about what the human spirit can achieve'.[15]

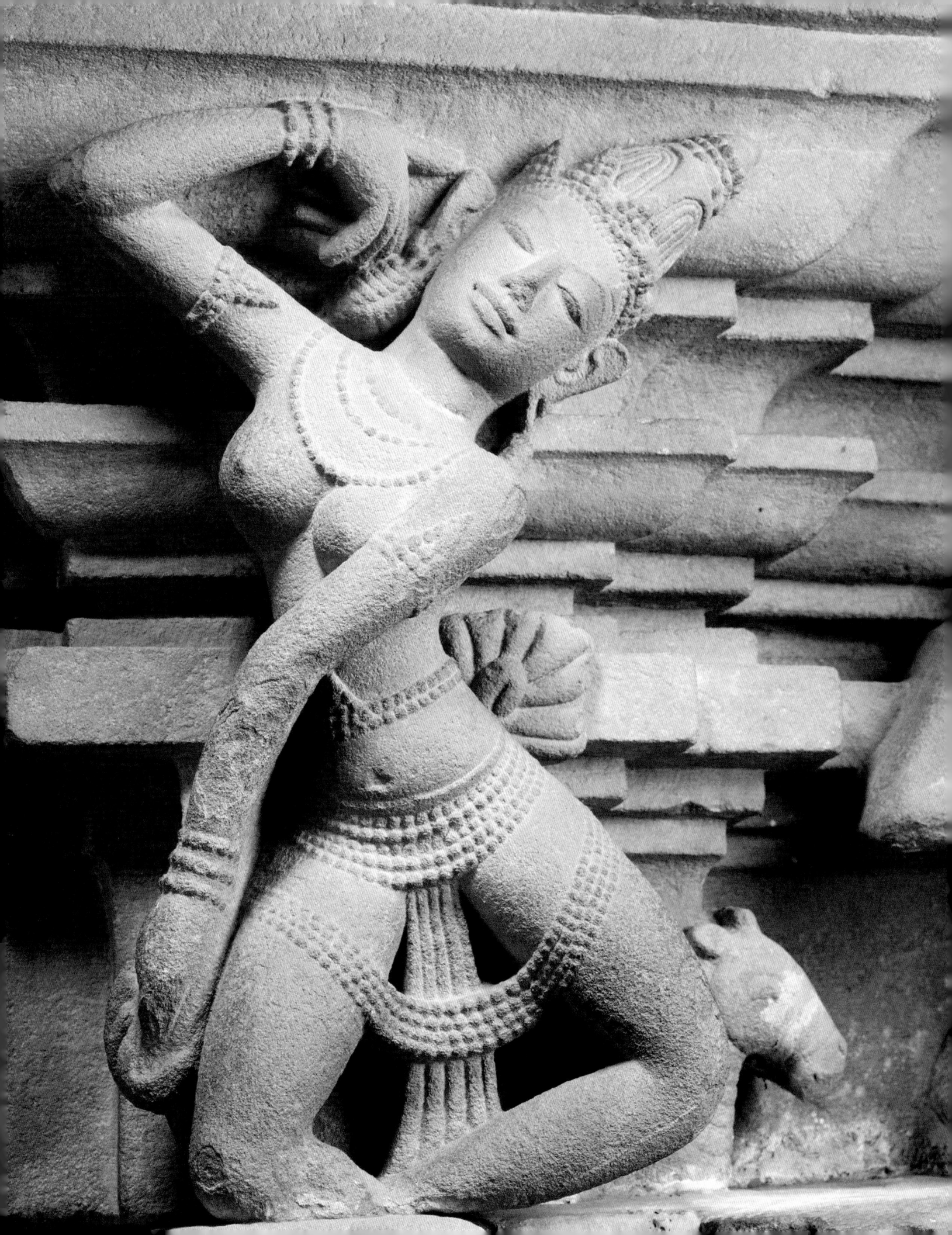

18 Dancer from the Mỹ Sơn 'pedestal'
(10th Century)

Artist(s): Unknown

Country of origin: Vietnam

Dimensions: Height: 6.3 m (20¾ ft)

Material(s): Fine buff sandstone

From the 4th to the 13th centuries, in the kingdom of Champa in modern-day Vietnam, Mỹ Sơn ('beautiful mountain') was a holy place that contained more than 70 Hindu temples. During the Vietnam War (1955–75), the archaeological site of Mỹ Sơn – the heart of Cham religious practice in the 10th century – became a war zone. In 1968, the US Air Force destroyed around 50 temples at Mỹ Sơn, with Vietnamese fighters believed to be hiding inside the structures.

Of all the Champa monuments, the kalan, a tower-like edifice, was of utmost significance. Traditionally, kalan were arranged in rows of three and haphazardly aligned on a north–south axis, the towers permanently calculated to look over the vicinity. However, the sites were chiefly selected and built upon to harness nature and practise religious observance. At Mỹ Sơn, imposing pedestals were a typical architectural feature, including the colossal Trà Kiệu platform-shrine. What lay on these structures is not yet wholly understood, and explanations for the carved imagery on these pedestal-shrines is still deliberated. Interpretations include the hypothesis that the platform was an altar and support for linga-yoni (male and female) worship, a place of interaction with Shiva, and that its iconography featuring archers and gambolling apsaras strengthened the military might and cultural life of the Champa, who had close ties to the courts of Cambodia, East Java and China. It was in sculpture and carving that its artists excelled, particularly highly technical, free-standing carved figures in high relief.

This celebrated dancer illustrates the supreme accomplishments of Hindu art. Her smiling countenance, fleshy lips and softly modelled body express serene beauty, something heightened by the many rows of bead-like jewellery on the arms, neck and waist, a prominent feature in later Cham art. It's a characteristic example of an apsara performing a technically intricate, semi-divine dance manoeuvre – a highly elegant three-bends posture or tribhanga. The deft carving not only illustrates gracefulness and control in the dance, but also 'the ability of Cham sculptors to create images of power and balance while representing the anatomically impossible poses necessitated by the technical demands of high relief'.[16] Of late, art historians such as Pierre Baptiste have argued that there is an important difference to be drawn between 'the pedestals for deity, offering altars, and the basement decoration of the Classical Cham Kalan'. In fact, as Baptiste argues, the Trà Kiệu dancers were '[m]ost probably... part of the outer decoration on the tower itself'.[17] The architectural and sculpted wonders of the long-lost Champa kingdoms have made Mỹ Sơn a UNESCO world heritage site.

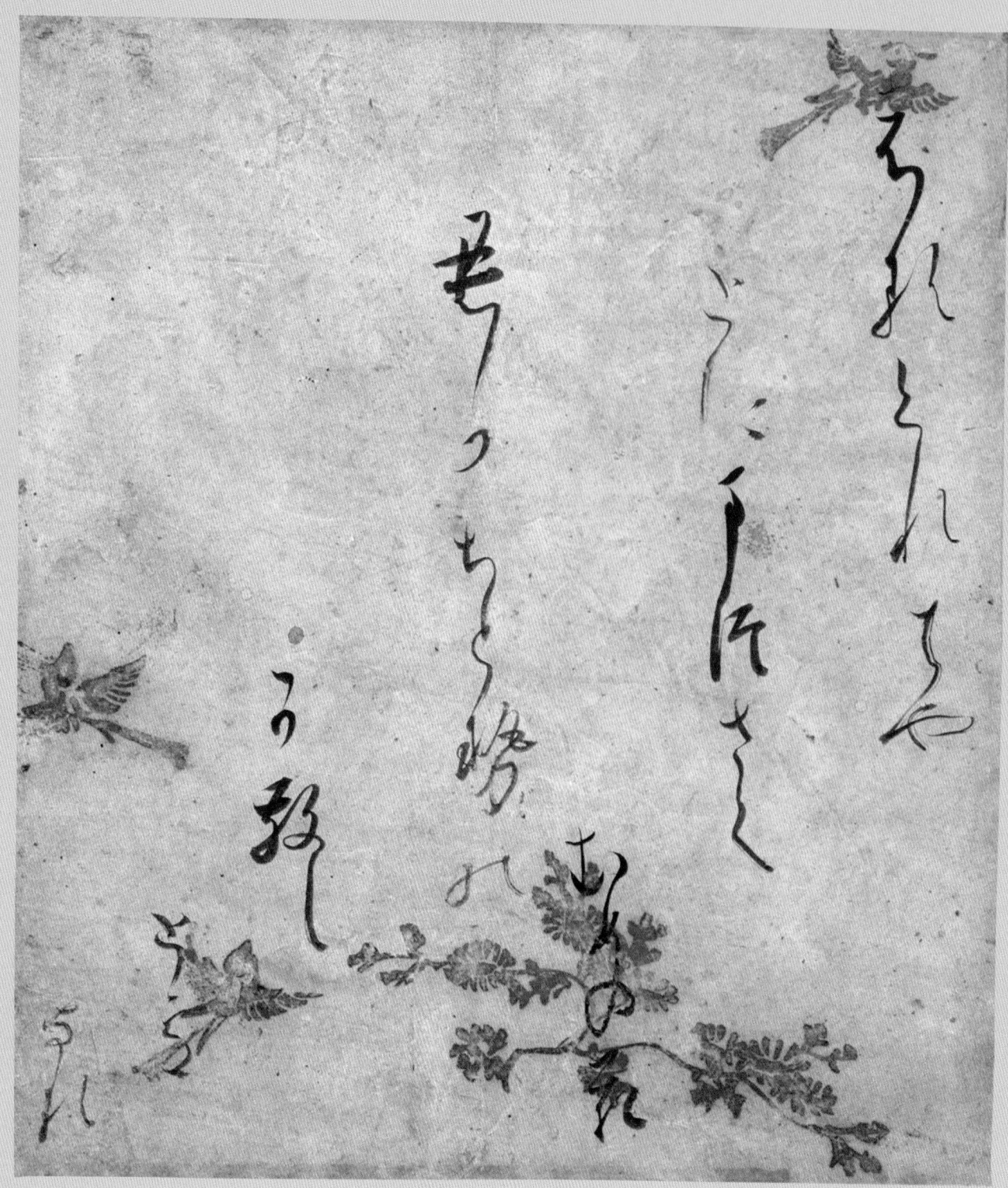

Segment of *Kokin Wakashū* (abbrev. as *Kokinshū*)
(Early–Mid 11th Century)

Artist(s): Calligraphy attributed to Fujiwara no Kintō

Country of origin: Japan

Dimensions: 21.9 x 18.5 cm (8½ x 7¼ inches)

Material(s): Paper and ink

Written Chinese symbols derive from pictograms that were created over 3,000 years ago. This early form of writing, known as 'characters', can be traced back to the Shang dynasty (*c.* 1600–1046 BCE), with some inscribed on the shoulder-bones of oxen and the plastrons (belly-shells) of turtles. These early symbols employ a flowing cursive form that illustrates physical things or ideas. This form of writing is still in use today. In succession, written Chinese was adopted by Korea, Japan and some areas of southern Vietnam, where it was adapted for regional or local dialects. Across the Far East, calligraphy is a proficiency that every individual is required to cultivate, at least to master basic literacy. In Japan, it was generally believed that there were no early forms of writing until contact with China in the 3rd century CE; that is, the beginning of the 'Tumulus' period, also termed the '"Great Burial Period" (*c.* 250–552) of tomb culture in Japan'.[18]

It was not until 1999 that the discovery of a piece of pottery, unearthed from a late Yayoi site in Mie Prefecture, between Nagoya and Osaka, revealed Chinese characters dated to the mid 2nd century. It is now thought that at that point well-established contact had transpired between Japan and China, but the precise origins of writing in Japan are still uncertain. From the 6th century onward, in any case, Japanese scribes took on the challenge of interpreting Chinese characters. The adaptation of Chinese ideograms was only the start since the dialect was very different to the Chinese tongue. As Michael Dunn has indicated, 'accommodation took some three centuries to accomplish... a system of writing... developed using Chinese ideographs together with two phonetic "alphabets" that have been simplified from Chinese characters, the pronunciation of which more-or-less approximated the sounds of spoken Japanese.'[19]

As a result, the Japanese have been enthusiastic masters of the artistic aspects of calligraphy, with calligraphy and painting intrinsically interlinked. An early example of this elegant and expressive form of writing includes a segment of writing known as *Sakai-jikishi*, part of the *Kokin Wakashū*, a celebrated scroll of poems penned in the flowing 'grass-style'. It is thought to be the work of Fujiwara no Kintō (966–1041). The paper is beautifully illustrated with chrysanthemums and mythological flying phoenixes represented in a faded silver, which has aged to a pleasing tone of grey.

More recently, calligraphy has transcended traditional boundaries to narrow the gap with painting, with Japanese calligraphers such as Saki Hasetsu (1912–) and Shiko Munakata (1913–75) leaning in the direction of abstraction or drawing as opposed to prose. Western artists such as Franz Kline (1910–62), Robert Motherwell (1915–91), Mark Toby (1890–1972) and many others have grasped the pictorial possibilities of Oriental calligraphy. Their use of more-or-less abstract forms indicates, consciously or not, whence calligraphy derived.

20 Maebyong Vase
(*c.* 918–1000)

Artist(s): Unknown

Country of origin: Korea

Dimensions: Height: 42 cm (16½ inches)

Material(s): Celadon porcelain with inlaid decoration

In the 13th century, the fame of Korean ceramics reached such a pitch that the Chinese author Taiping Laoren claimed, 'The celadons of Korea … all are first under Heaven.' That is to say, the ceramic works of China and Japan were outshone by Korean wares during the Goryeo or Koryŏ (918–1392) and Yi (1392–1910) dynasties. Archaeological finds from China confirm that Goryeo celadons were deemed of such excellence and status that they were imported into China in large numbers and even bartered for goods such as silk and tea. Japanese tea connoisseurs similarly admired the 'rustic' charms and beauty of *Buncheong* or *Punch'ŏng* pottery created by early Yi potters.

It was during the Three Kingdoms (*c.* 57 BCE–668 CE) and Unified Silla (668–935 CE) periods that immigrants from the Han dynasty established a Chinese colony in Korea and introduced the potter's wheel and the climbing chamber kiln, which was able to create the high temperatures needed to produce celadon stoneware. Koreans were blessed with plenty of good clay and timber for fuel. More crucially, the makers fostered a knowledge of how the unrefined materials fused 'in a magical way' in the heat of the furnace, resulting in a tranquil blue-green colour frequently typified as 'the blue of the sky after rain'.[20] Such was its beauty that a highly extravagant 12th-century monarch, King Uijong, had his entire palace roof furnished with splendid blue-green celadon tiles and covered with flower and leaf patterns.

This kind of broad-shouldered celadon vase is known as *maebyong* in Korea (*meiping* in China), its shape typical of the early Goryeo period and widely admired around the world today. To create its renowned pale green colour, the potters used translucent iron-pigmented glazes fired in an oxygen-starved kiln. This example also has colourful variations created by designs delicately carved or stamped into the clay. The artist incorporated images of cranes flying in different directions with some depicted inside circular roundels that were then filled with white and coloured clay slip. Here, the disparity in the positioning of motifs demonstrates the maker's unquestionable appreciation of 'the dynamic relationship between ornamentation and ceramic volume'.[21]

Ancient Korean art took shape within the wider circumstances of an East Asian – particularly Chinese-dictated – sphere, but its art is not merely imitative; it has a palpable indigenous identity. In fact, Japan's world-renowned ceramic art would not have attained such plentiful variation without consecutive upsurges of immigrant potters from Korea who brought new methods, shapes and its astonishing 'local style' to Japanese culture. Indeed, the Japanese arbiters of taste saw in these unpretentious celadon wares a type of ideal beauty.

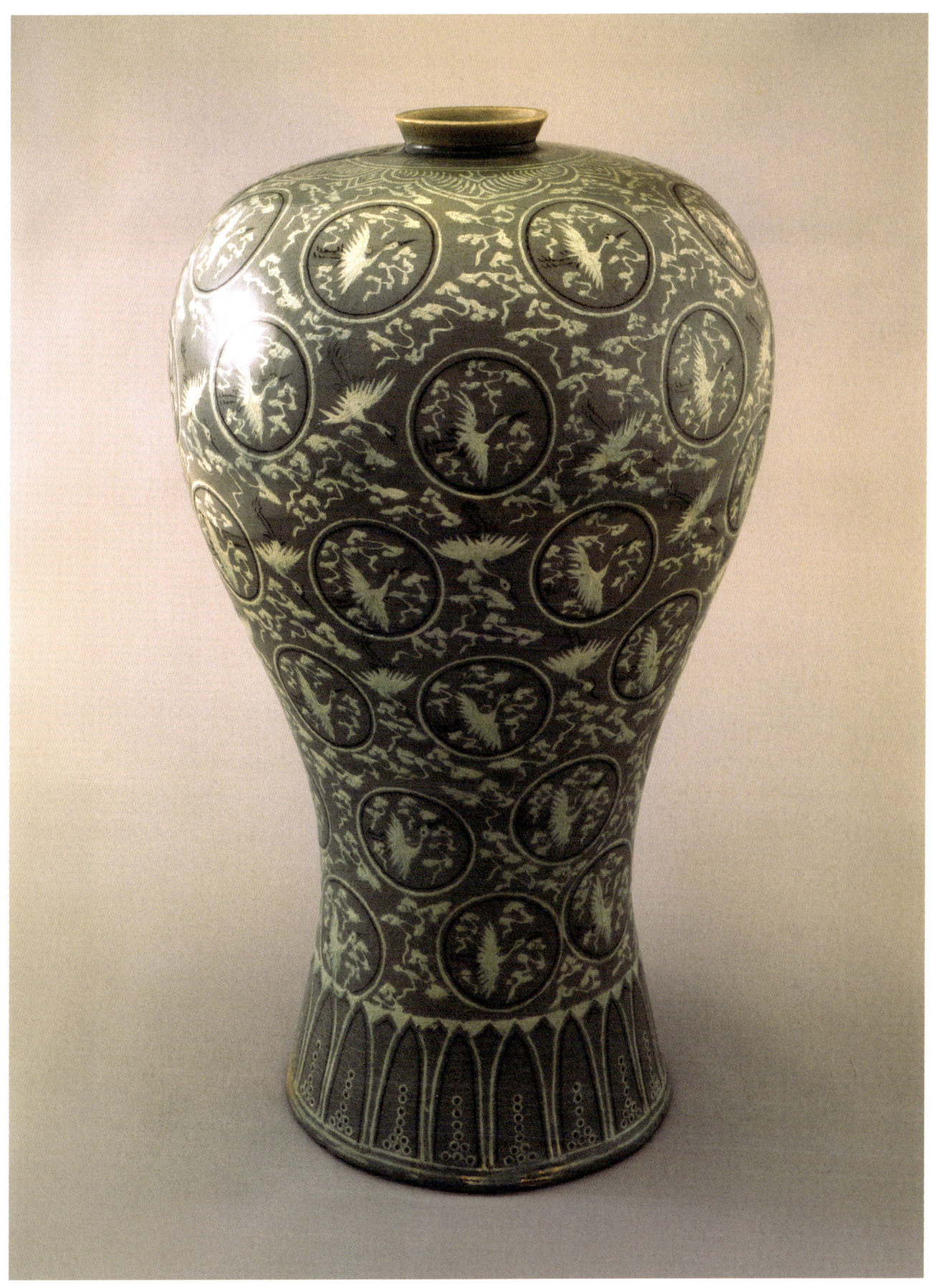

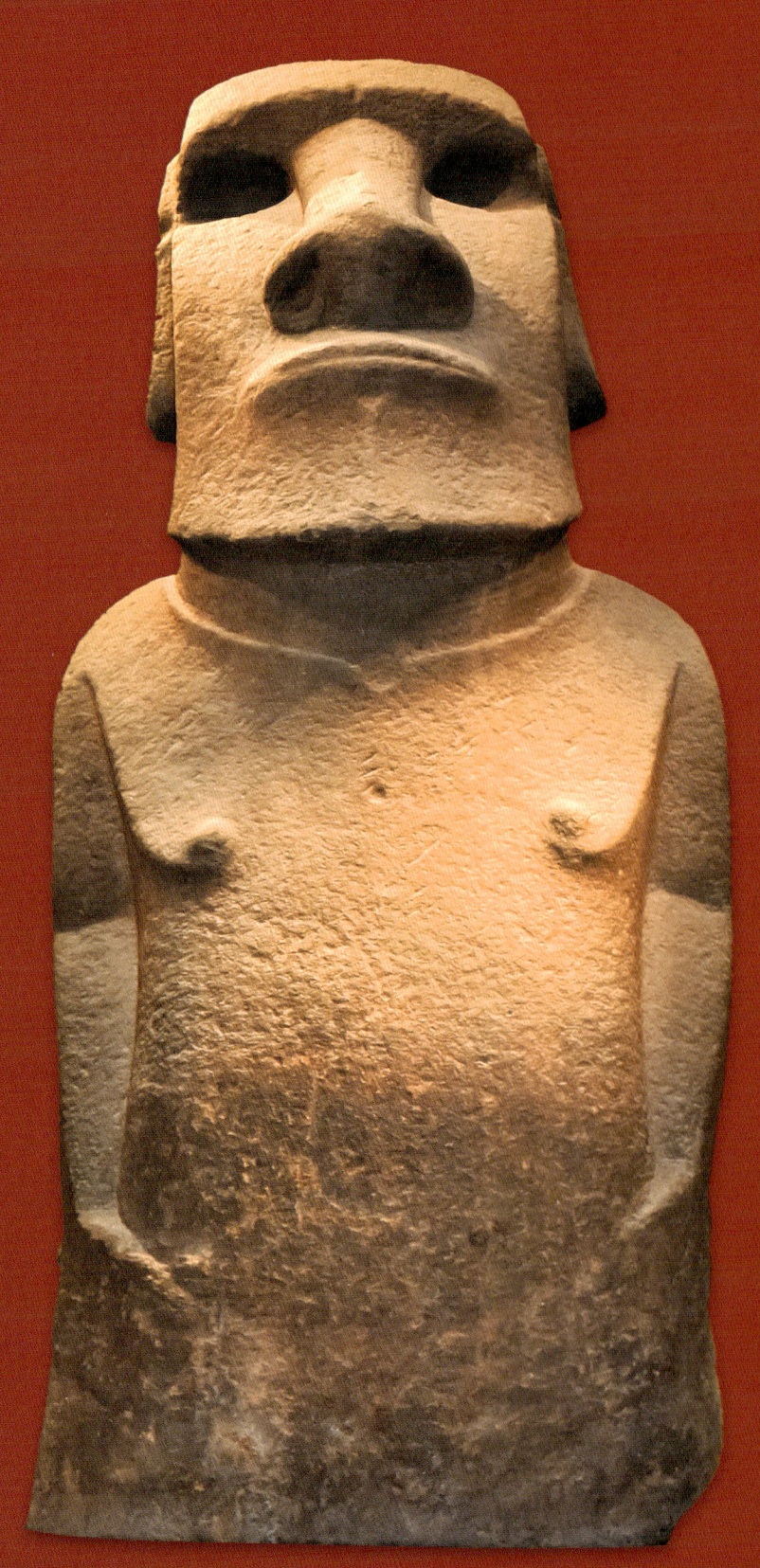

Hoa Hakananai'a of Rapa Nui
(1000–1200)

21

Artist(s): Unknown

Country of origin: Rapa Nui (Easter Island), Chile

Dimensions: Height 2.42 m (8 ft)

Material(s): Basalt

'**For some five hundred years** the *moai* statues of Rapa Nui embodied the continuity of a metaphysical order of deified ancestors that sustained the authority of clan chiefs, defined the nature of social roles and gave religious meaning to the world.'[22] The power of deified ancestors was hence bound up with the *ahu moai* (monolithic human figures) phase on Rapa Nui (the indigenous name for Easter Island, today a special territory of Chile).

In the 16th century, however, statue construction collapsed, the dire impact of ecological disaster, overpopulation and the subsequent rise of warring *matato'a* warrior chiefs. The inhabitants had pressed the island's fragile ecosystem to the point of collapse by cutting down virtually all its trees, and through the predation of land birds.

The *matato'a* of Rapa Nui usurped the old *ahu moai* and founded a new religion. By the 18th century, the *Tangata manu* (birdman) cult held sway under the auspices of the deity Makemake – the supreme god of Rapa Nui. The *tangata manu* not only legitimized the powerful militant clan but also engendered a new political sovereignty for a single year. Endowed with sacred *mana* (prestige), the reigning birdman took on a 'birdman' entity, which helped to bolster the accomplishments of his clan.

Hoa Hakananai'a must have been an important idol because a stone building was specifically constructed to protect it from competing clans. The statue was recorded by English sailors as 'Hoa Hāka Nāna Ia' ('stolen or hidden friend'). Its title is highly evocative, slightly mocking and probably made up. Carved on the back of the Hoa Hakananai'a sculpture – 'added several hundred years later ... [with] the carving style ... [very] different from the front' – are the principal features of the *tangata manu* religion: two birdmen with human limbs and the head of a frigate bird (*Fregata minor* or *makohe*). Above, a bird with an open beak suggests a fledgling sooty tern, while on either side of this creature stands an *ao* – a wooden ceremonial dance paddle – symbol of the birdman's *mana*, and seasonal omens of Makemake. Originally, these were painted in red and white 'so that this cluster of potent symbols could be easily recognized and understood'. In addition, the right ear of the statue has four shallow and abstracted relief representations of female genitalia, perhaps indicating females of the same lineage.

Initially, the Rapa Nui peoples appear to have tailored their lifestyle to the altering environmental conditions. The *Tangata manu* cult remained for nearly 100 years after first contact with Europeans (*c.* 1722), the final 'birdman' taking his 'crown' in 1867. In the 19th century, however, three principal potencies arrived from overseas to hasten the demise of the *Tangata manu*: Christianity, slavery and death. In 1868, Hoa Hakananai'a was presented to the sailors by the now baptized chiefs, and it was taken to England and later displayed at the British Museum. Here, and perhaps sadly, Hoa Hakananai'a 'faces south-east, looking towards Rapa Nui, 14,000 km (8,500 miles) away'[23] from his ancestral home at the end of the world.

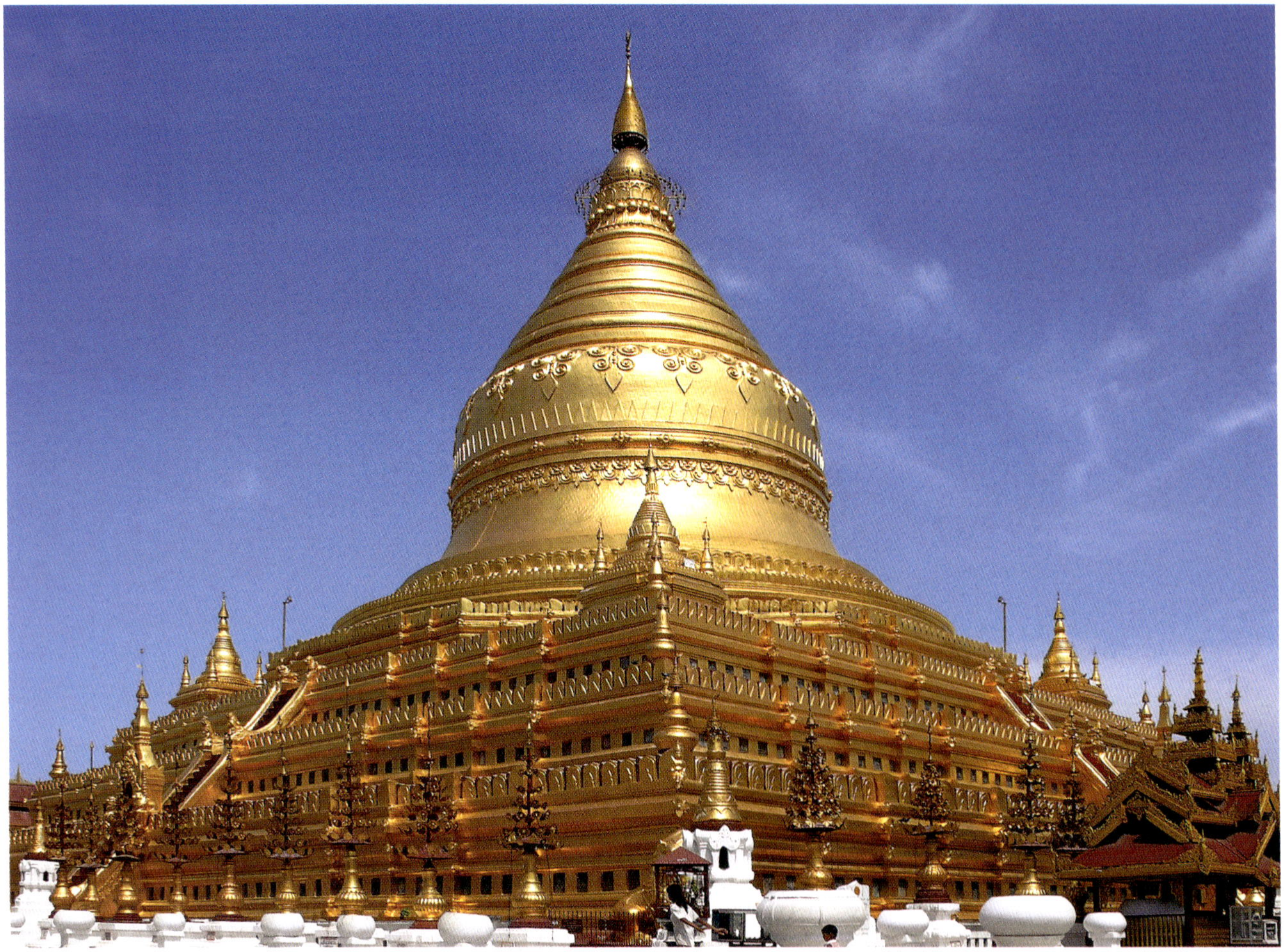

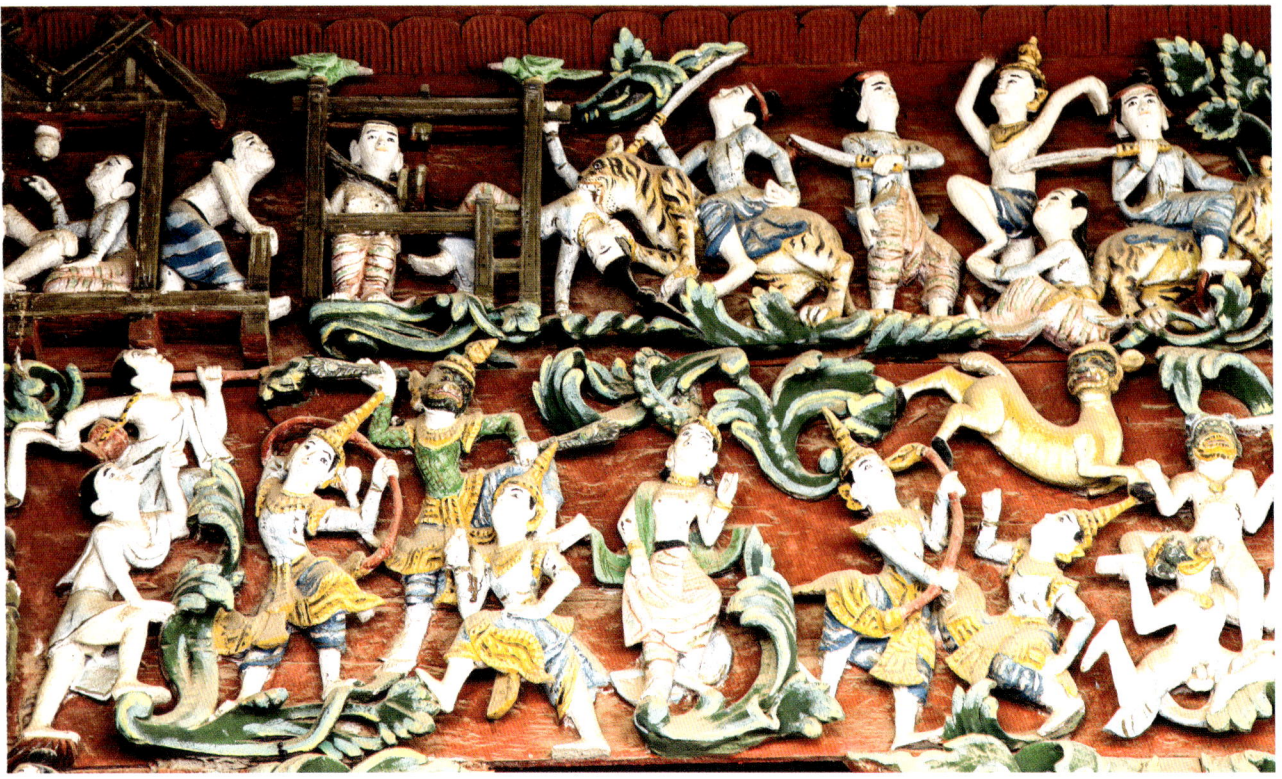

22 Shwezigon Pagoda
(Completed 1084)

Artist(s): Unknown

Country of origin: Myanmar

Dimensions: Height: 49 m (160 ft)

Material(s): Stone, terracotta tiles, bronze and gilding

The construction of the Shwezigon near Pagan (or Bagan) in Myanmar was begun during the reign of King Anawrahta (1044–77) and it is the largest temple of the period. Shwezigon was a central hub of the new Theravada ('The Way of the Elders') stem of Buddhism, a belief system set down in the earliest Pāli scriptures, probably in the 1st century BCE. On the orders of King Anawrahta, a holy vestige of the Buddha was put on the back of a white elephant and the animal was left to roam freely; where it stopped, a temple was to be built. Shwezigon means 'golden stupa on the sandbank', the pagoda said to have been constructed on the site where the elephant bent down by the river.

Myanmar (formerly known as Burma) is dubbed 'the land of pagodas' because they are so numerous, an archetypal religious signpost for Buddhists across the land. This pagoda's shrine is believed to house part of the Buddha's skull, collarbone and a tooth. As the first monument in a customary Burmese style, the Shwezigon Pagoda became an exemplar model for bell-shaped stupas. Though it was completed by King Kyansittha, later embellishments and refurbishment work is due to an array of successive patrons.

The gilded stupa ascends over five terraces, three on square, two on circular foundations, bordered by four rectangular sanctuaries and occupied by enormous bronze Buddha statues. Two huge mythological leogryph statues, *chinthes*, guard the main entrance gate at Shwezigon. A modest side chamber also houses 37 *nats* (god-like spirits) from the previous religious tradition, whose veneration Anawrahta allowed during transition to Theravada Buddhism, something still upheld today.

Although stupas, provincially called *dagabas*, were established from the 3rd century, they were built on ever grander scale by rulers seeking to surpass their antecedents. Theravada orthodoxy was partly responsible for disseminating artistic ideas and approaches drawn from Sri Lankan culture, which was fundamentally viewed as a wellspring of untainted Buddhist doctrine. Consequently, religious pilgrimage helped to generate close ties between the two Theravada Buddhists lands. Naturally, building religious structures was a vital means for world faiths to secure, sanction and ratify the power of their rulers. They built awe-inspiring monuments, temples, columns and other religious edifices, routinely embellished with edifying murals, relief sculptures and free-standing statues. At the Shwezigon Pagoda, sculptures of Buddha in *vitarka mudra*, the stance of revelation, would probably have been viewed as aiding a particular Burmese ruler in pursuit of rebirth in heaven.

Vishnu Lying on the Cosmic Ocean
(Later 11th Century)

Artist(s): Unknown

Country of origin: Cambodia

Dimensions: 122 x 222 x 72.5 cm (48½ x 87½ x 28½ inches)

Material(s): Bronze

The grace of 'Baphuon style', under King Udayadityavarman II (1050-66), is revealed in this magnificent bronze fragment of *Vishnu Lying on the Cosmic Ocean* – one of the largest bronze sculptures in antiquity. Vishnu is one of three principal deities in the Hindu pantheon, here in the attitude of cosmic slumber, epitomized by his characteristic half-smile. Despite missing body parts and other key embellishments, the sleeping Vishnu undoubtedly illustrates the Hindu myth of creation. Not only are a large section of the lower torso and two arms and legs missing, but also the exquisite metal and stone inlays that would have decorated the facial features, as well as a mitre, for which the fastening clips are still detectable. Vishnu, the prime mover who gives birth to the universe, is recumbent on the serpent Ananta, representing the boundless waters of time.

Besides building the enormous temple mountain Baphuon (at Angkor, near Siem Reap, *c.* 1060) in honour of the god Shiva, Udayadityavarman also completed the construction of the West Baray reservoir and erected the West Mebon temple, with an artificial island in its centre. Here, a raised platform of sandstone stood in the middle of a large pond with the platform penetrated by a sunken well. In 1936, among the ruins of the well, fragments were discovered of the *Vishnu Lying on the Cosmic Ocean*. The four-armed Hindu god's original

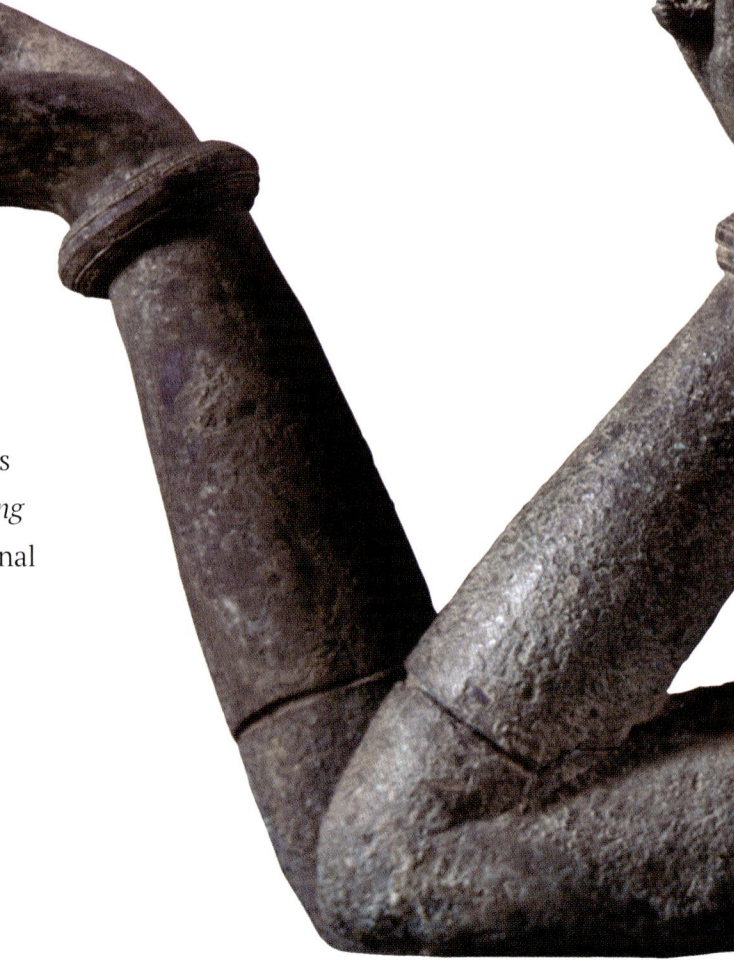

length would have been 6 m (20 ft). Surrounded by the waters at Angkor, the giant statue represents the ancient myth of Vishnu floating on the nascent ocean. Traditionally a lotus stem sprouts from Vishnu's bellybutton, the flower holding up Brahma, the creator god who instigates the next living cycle. The Vishnu Anantashayin also had a waterspout in his navel, which intimates not only the god's ability to protect the Earth and create Brahma and Shiva, but also fashion the waters of time.

Khmer bronze metallurgists were masters of the *cire perdue* or 'lost wax' process, in which molten metal is poured into a mould created from a wax model – an ancient casting technique used in China, India and Europe, and still in use today. Evidence suggests that this bronze Vishnu was cast at a vast workshop near the ancient Royal Palace of Angkor. Despite its fragmented state, the statue of Vishnu reminds one of the excellence of ancient metal-casting techniques by the 'artisans of Angkor'. More crucially, it reiterates the authority, legitimacy and royal might of Udayadityavarman, as well as the power of the gods in ancient Cambodia.

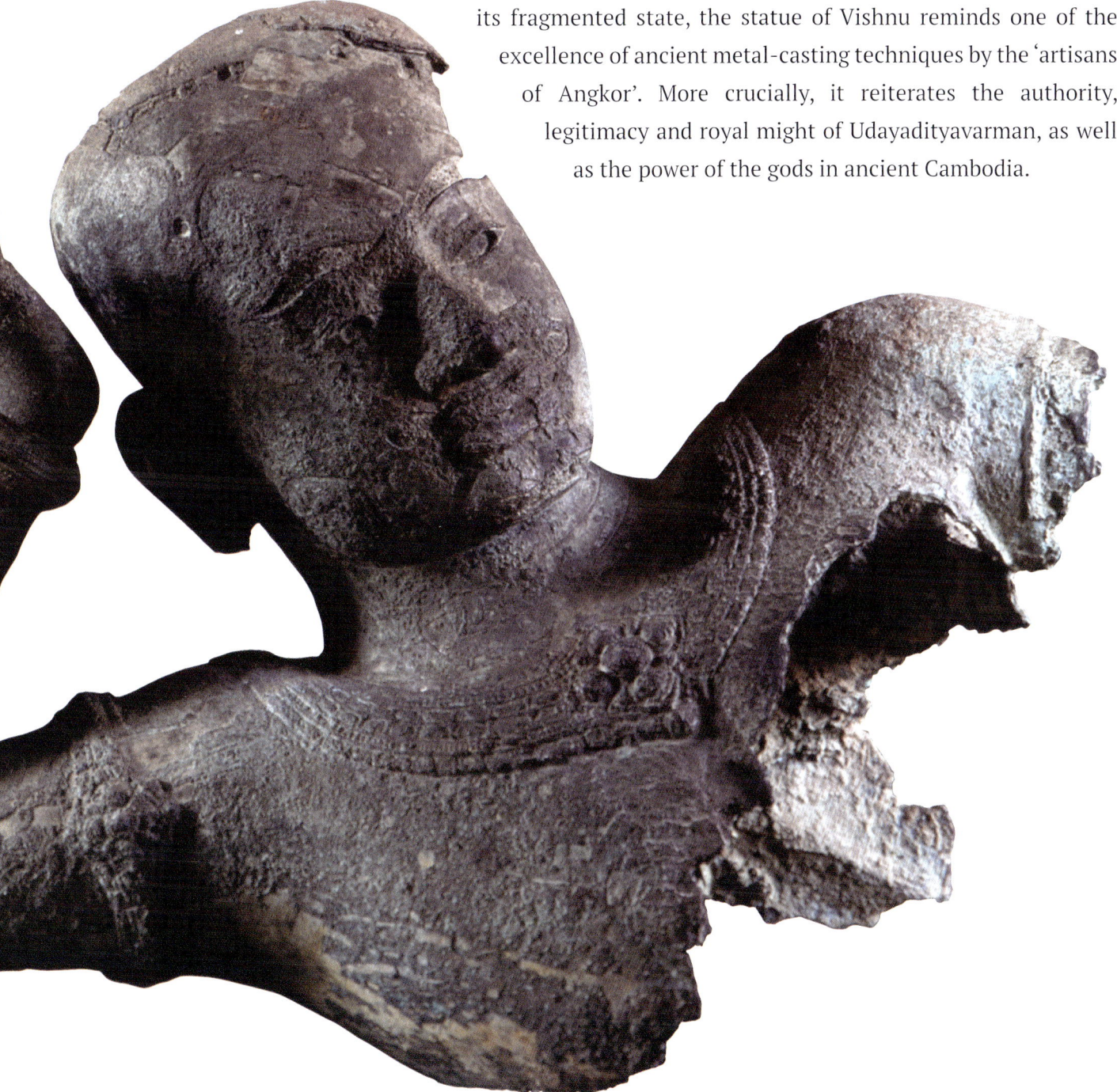

24 Angkor Wat
(12th Century)

Architect(s): Unknown

Country of origin: Cambodia

Dimensions: Complex 162.6 hectares (402 acres)

Material(s): Sandstone

The finest achievements of Cambodia's Khmer rulers were the stone temples built in the 9th–12th centuries. The grandest of all was Angkor Wat ('temple of the capital'), an architectural anthem to the gods. It was begun in the reign of Suryavarman II (died *c.* 1150), his tomb and temple dedicated to Vishnu, the foremost deity of Hinduism, and was continued by each Khmer ruler king into the 1400s, honouring a benefactor deity – Vishnu, Shiva or Buddha.

Under the auspices of King Jayavarman VII (*c.* 1120/25–*c.* 1220) – a Buddhist monk who twice rebuffed the throne – Angkor Wat came to an astounding pinnacle. During this period, Angkor Wat was possibly the largest city in the world and known for its astonishing riches. In the late 13th century, Chinese emissary Zhou Daguan described one royal procession as follows: 'Last came the king, standing on an elephant, the gold sword in his hand and the tusks of his elephant encased in gold.'[24] At the root of this transformation was the ruler's ability to gather considerable financial resources and human labour.

Great religious and political change had brushed through Southeast Asia during the early first millennium CE, and into the middle of the second. It was in the 9th century, however, under Jayavarman

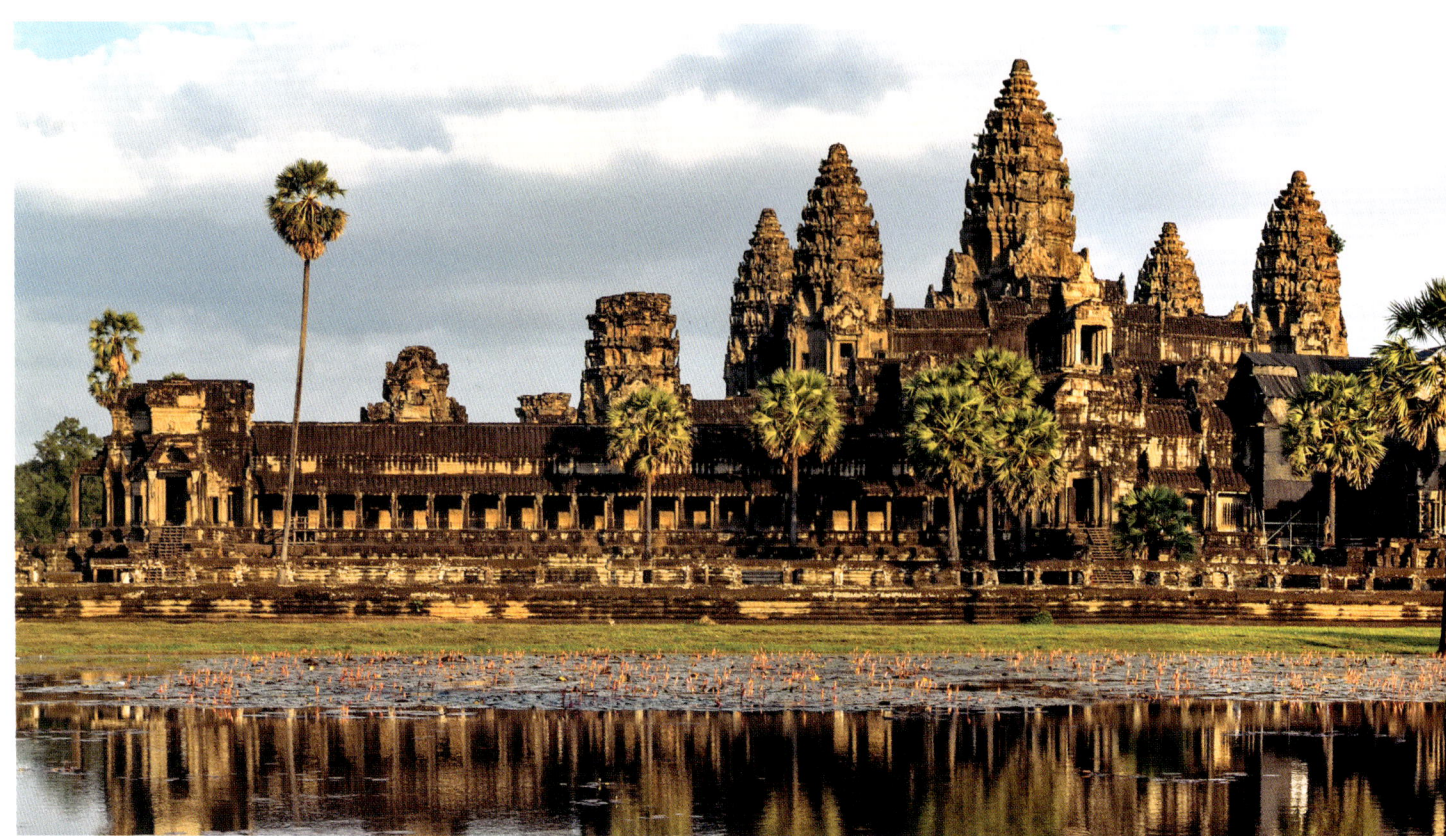

II, that the Khmer had extended control over Cambodia. Subsequently, the Empire became a leading power that left a wealthy heritage of architecture and sculpture.

Angkor Wat consists of limestone blocks bound together by iron clinches, its corbelled roofs rising to around 60 m (197 ft), encircled by sheltered passageways and a huge moat roughly 4 km (2½ miles) in circumference. A plan of the temple shows that it is turned – as in many world cultures – towards the west, following cosmological principals in relation to design and the regimented pictographical programme of its sculpture. The central shrine – initially housing a metal effigy of Vishnu – and four reduced shrines surmounted by spires and based on the Indian *sikhara* ('mountain peak') symbolize the five summits of Mount Meru according to Hindu and Buddhist tenets, while the wide moat represents the oceans that encircle it. The temple was situated to view the solar apex above the central spire, traditionally at the beginning of the cosmological year in Indian astronomy (nowadays 21 June).

Intrinsically, the structure was a highly appropriate edifice devoted to Suryavarman II, because his name means 'protected by the sun'. As the Chinese writer Han Suyin observed of Angkor in 1972: 'None of these temples or monuments was intended to serve human beings as dwelling-places... Angkor is not the Parthenon or Colosseum; it was built as an expression of the idea of the divine: it is the realization in stone of the divine power of the kings of Angkor...'. Angkor – 'city state' (from the Sanskrit *nagara*) – was, from the outset, 'the beginning of a new era in Khmer civilization'.[25] Unsurprisingly, Angkor Wat later captured the imagination of Europeans who drew and photographed the site comprehensively.

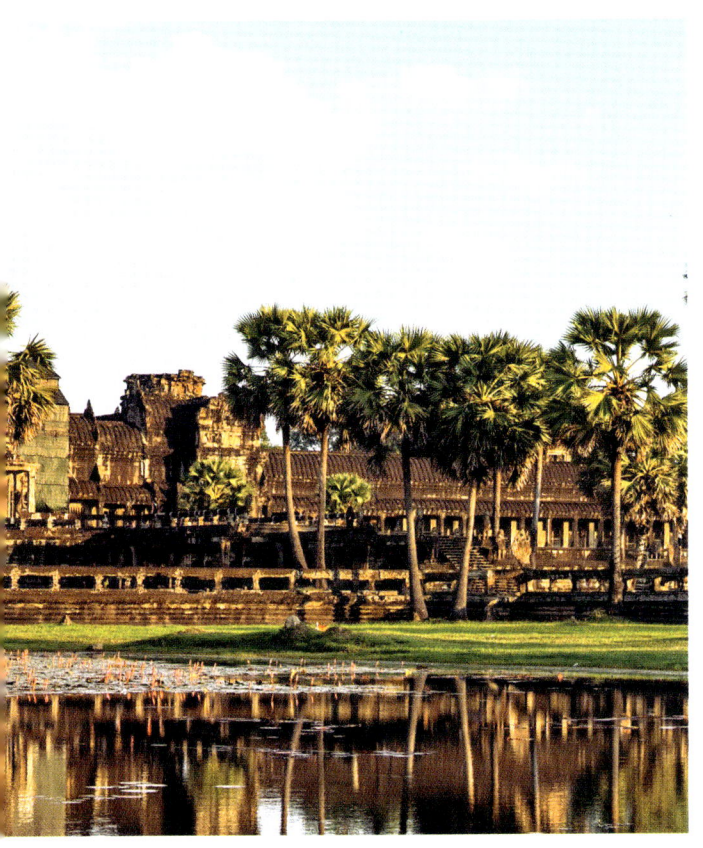
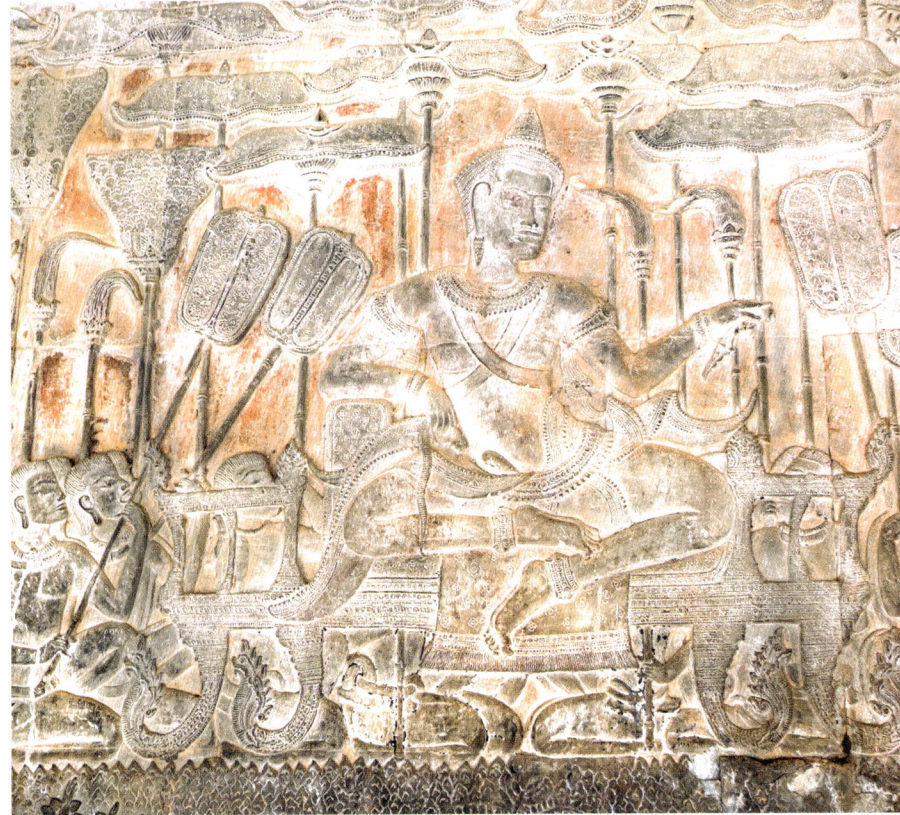

25 The Minaret of Jam
(*c*. 1190–4)

Artist(s): Unknown

Country of origin: Afghanistan

Dimensions: Height 65 m (213 ft); Diameter at base 9 m (29½ ft)

Materials: Brick

This beautifully decorated minaret is thought to be one of the few remnants of Firozkoh, the summer capital of the Ghurid dynasty that was situated in the Ghor district in what is now central Afghanistan from the 8th to the beginning of the 13th century. Now designated as a UNESCO World Heritage site (Afghanistan's first), it is under threat, due partly to neglect and partly as a result of damage caused by an earthquake that hit western Afghanistan in 2022.

Minarets are most often associated with mosques, being the place from which a muezzin calls the faithful to prayer, but the term 'minaret' is derived from the Arabic word *manar*, meaning place of light, and sometimes minarets were constructed to show that the area was Islamic. This minaret stands among ruins of several buildings, including

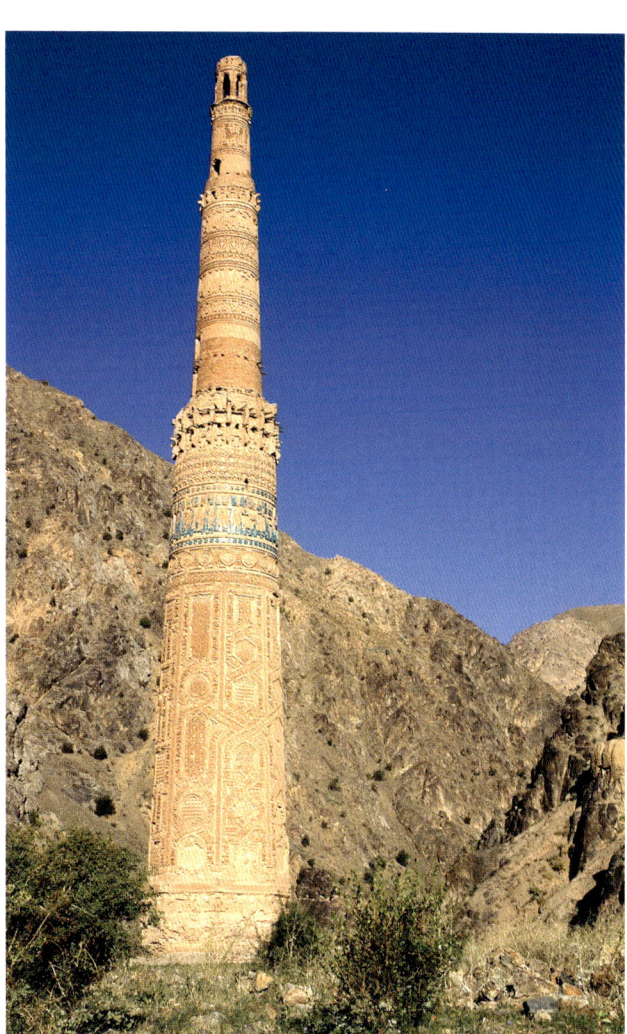

a fortification of some kind, a pottery kiln and a Jewish cemetery. It is 65 m (213 ft) high and sits on a 9-m- (29½-ft-) diameter octagonal base.

Built by order of the Ghurid Sultan Ghiyas-ud-Din (1153–1203) of baked clay bricks, the Minaret of Jam is renowned for its intricate decoration of bands of stucco work and glazed tiles that contain quotes from the Qur'an in two types of calligraphy – one Arabic (Kufic) and the other Islamic (Naskh). In both its architectural engineering features and its decoration, it blends elements from the surrounding region and in turn it influenced similar structures in India.

It is uncertain as to why the minaret was constructed. One theory is that it commemorates Sultan Ghiyas-ud-Din's victory over the Ghaznevids in 1186, but another theory is that it commemorates a different victory, that of Mu'izz ad-Din over Prithviraja III, a king of the Chauhan dynasty that ruled Sapadalaksha, a region which now forms part of Rajasthan in India.

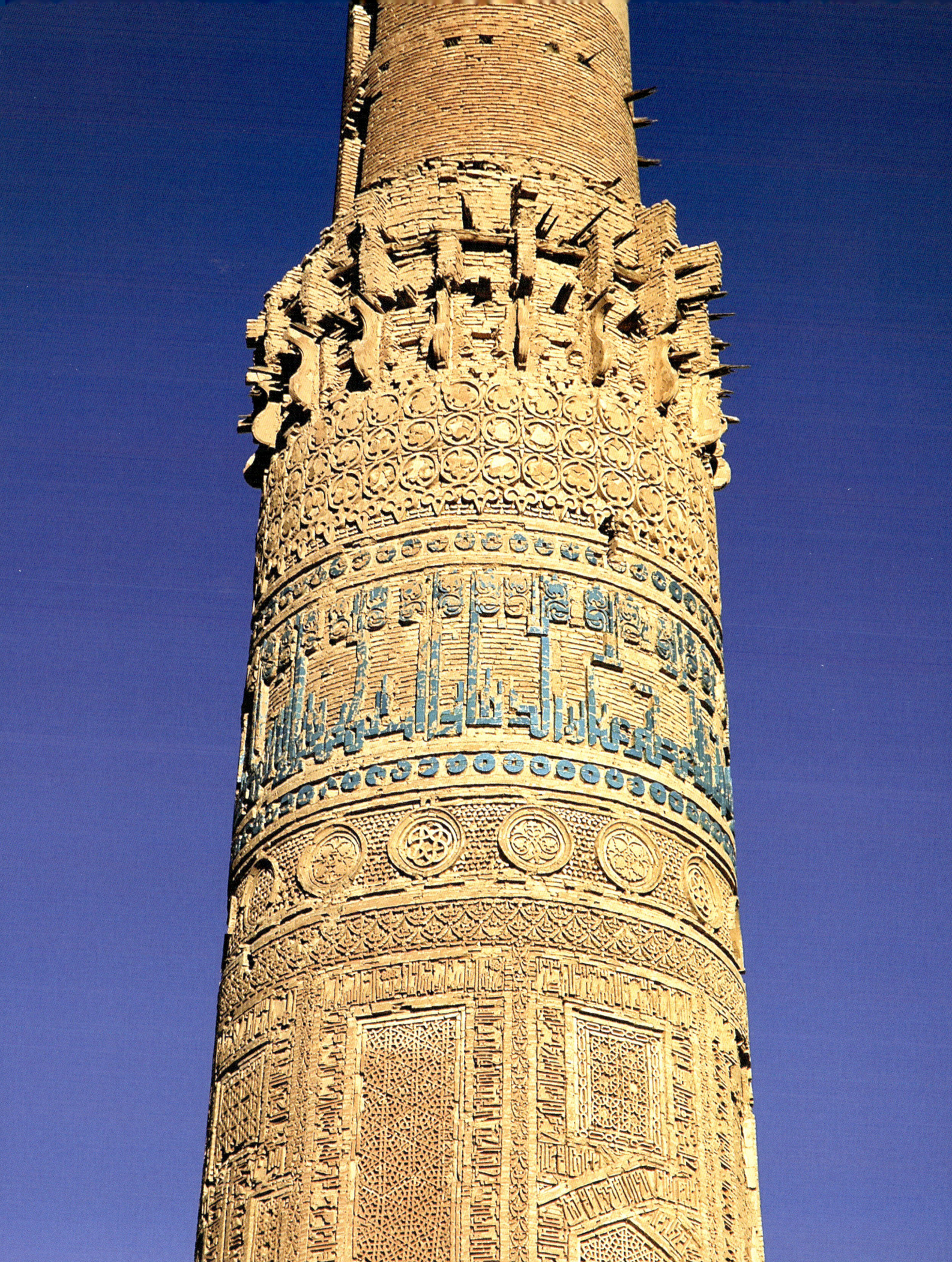

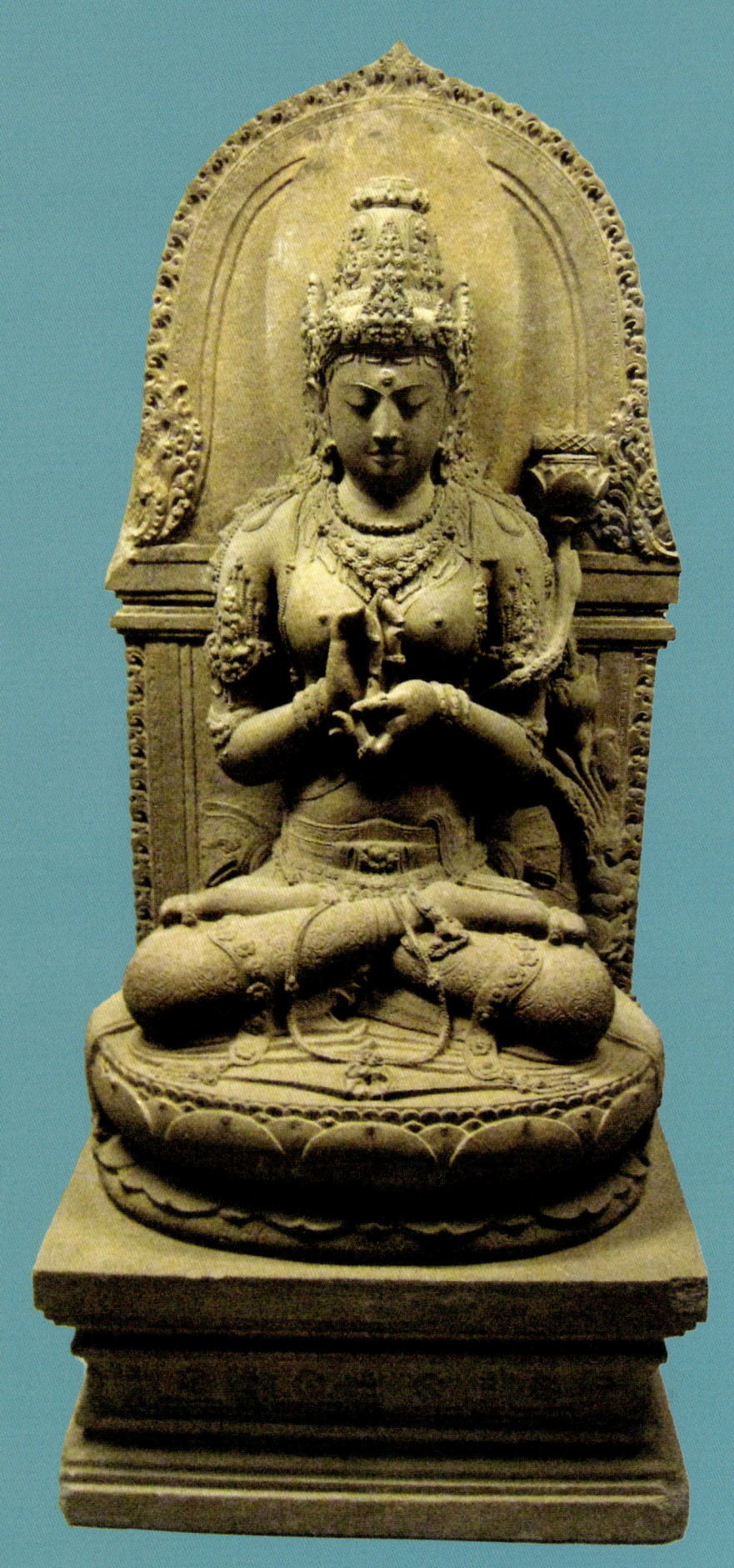

26 Statue of the Goddess Prajnaparamita
(*c.* 1300)

Artist(s): Unknown

Country of origin: Indonesia

Dimensions: Height 1.26 m (4 ft); Width 50 cm (19½ ft)

Material(s): Andesite stone

As Buddhist teaching reached Southeast Asia, there was a schism within the discipline. The first teachings had stressed the aim to achieve enlightenment, thereby attaining emancipation from the circle of rebirth. However, roughly 100 years after the death of its founder Siddhartha Gautama (the Buddha, *c.* 563–483 BCE), the school of Mahayana Buddhism deemed this unachievable.

Rather, it emphasized the bodhisattvas, those who helped others in the pursuit of enlightenment. Mahayanism held a belief in five great Buddhas, four of whom protected the cardinal points, with one deity, Vairocana, at the heart, and all individually linked with assorted deities and bodhisattvas. The most important was Avalokiteshvara, typically associated with Prajnaparamita ('Perfection of Wisdom') and, in Vajrayana (Tantric) Buddhism, described as the female consort of the Adi-Buddha (first Buddha) or Mother of All Buddhas.

Signs of Mahayana Buddhism are found throughout Southeast Asia. The statue of the Goddess Prajnaparamita is thought to be a portrait of Putri Dedes, wife of Kertanagara, the first king of Singhasari in Java, who died in 1292. Images of the incarnate Prajnaparamita were recorded as early 400 CE, but all existing examples date from 800 onwards.

Dated to the 13th century, this statue was carved at the time when imperial power had shifted to East Java, and Buddhism and Hinduism were both given royal patronage. Prajnaparamita is traditionally represented by yellow or white colours and is akin to the earlier Bodhisattva Samantabhadra (Candi Plaosan, Central Java, 8th–9th century), who redirects the light of the sun and moon emblematically and in reality. The figure has all the attributes of a deity. She is crowned with the piled tresses of the *jatamukuta* crown, with her hands in the teaching gesture of the *dharmachakra mudra* or 'wheel of law' and path to enlightenment. A lotus flower twisted around her left arm holds up a tiny version of the *Sutra*. Regularly associated with Prajnaparamita are prayer beads, a sword (to slice away ignorance), a thunderbolt (*vajra*, a symbol of the void) and a beggar's bowl (a rejection of the material and a precondition of wisdom). Although Prajnaparamita is adorned like a queen, her facial expression has the serenity of a god. Her eyelids are lowered, the visage and body posture suitably motionless and detached from this realm, with a large oval projecting slightly from the back of her 'throne' representing her halo. As Rose Gan and the museum volunteers at National Museum of Indonesia have pointed out, 'The effect of the whole has the power of a Madonna, and... stands equal to any medieval work in the Christian tradition.'[26]

27 Tāngonge *Waharoa* ('The Kaitaia Carving')
(May be *c.* 1300–1400, or more recent)

Artist(s): Unknown

Country of origin: Aotearoa New Zealand

Dimensions: 225 cm (7¹/₃ ft)

Material(s): Wood

In 1920, the drainage of the Tāngonge swamp near the northern North Island town of Kaitaia unearthed a carving embedded in the clay at the bottom of the swamp. Previously, swamps were often adopted as secure depositories for sacred (*tapu*) Māori objects during times of war or unrest. What came to light was originally named the 'Kaitaia Lintel', later 'Tāngonge *Waharoa*', and thought to be around 600 years old.

Not long after the carving's acquisition by the Auckland War Memorial Museum in 1921, the ethnologist H. D. Skinner penned a short article entitled 'Te Awanui Lintel', to which the editor of the journal added in brackets 'the Kaitaia carving'. As Skinner argued, 'It resembles other Māori lintels in essential characters, and there can be no doubt of its Māori origin. But the points of difference are important, and justify the general interest aroused by its discovery.' Those points of disagreement have meant that no early Māori carving has since garnered such conjecture as to its derivation. Today, the carving is widely thought to be a part of a *waharoa* – a gateway to a *pā* or main entranceway. As specialists have observed, moreover, 'The unpretentious anthropoid figure at its centre, animal figures at its end, chevron infilling, and notched edges distinguish it from most other pre-contact Māori carving, where *tiki* and zoomorphic figures are highly abstracted and adornment is often a complex system of surface patterns.'

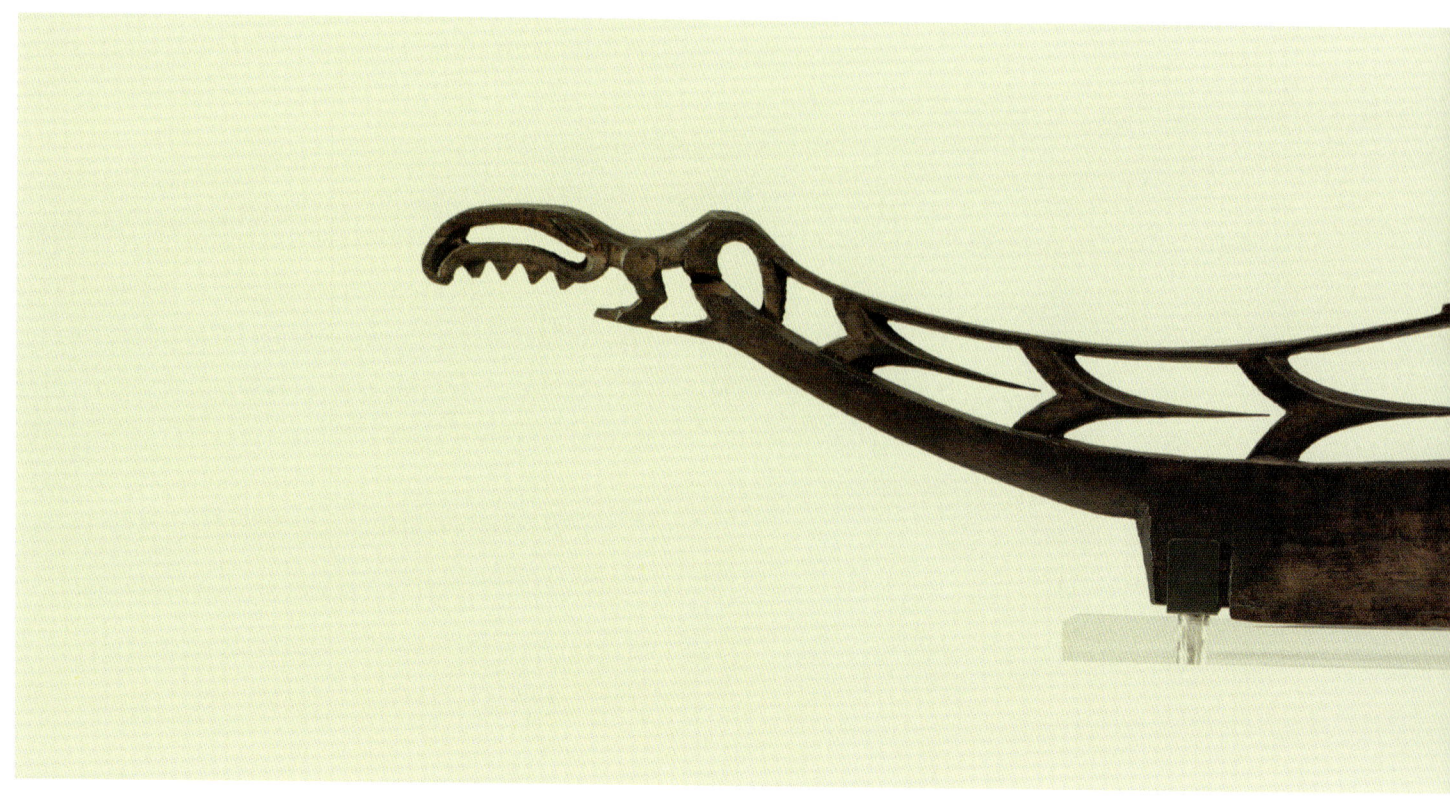

Similar stylistic features place the work within the broader context of Polynesian art. Scholars offer *Carving with Two Janus Figures and a Dog* (Museum of Archaeology and Anthropology, Cambridge), probably from the Austral islands, as evidence that the Kaitaia carving is an earlier carved 'prototype', and confirmation that Māori carving originated in the far north of Aotearoa New Zealand. Alternatively, one theory suggests that the Kaitaia carving travelled to New Zealand via early Polynesian mariners. However, the piece was whittled out of tōtara wood (*Podocarpus totara*), a tree native to New Zealand, making this notion very unlikely.

The carving is now a treasured possession (*taonga*), owing to its seemingly distant past, which affords the piece sacredness (*tapu*), prestige and authority (*mana*) in Māori artistic culture. As a result, the Kaitaia carving has enthused other Māori artists, including the painter Kura Te Waru Rewiri, who employs an image of the carving in her 1994 painting *Ia ra, Ia po* (*In Te Po there are many beginnings*) as a way to denote the roots of Māori culture and challenge traditions and ideas in Māori art, particularly *whakairo* (woodcarving) being the preserve of Māori men. Notably, the carving was also adopted as a logistic emblem by the *iwi* (tribal group) and tribal council Te Rūnanga o Te Rarawa. As the historian Deidre Brown suggests, 'its most enduring influence, it could be argued, is on a new generation of carvers who have copied its form for a *pare* (lintel) of at least three recent meeting houses built within the Te Rarawa tribal district.'[27]

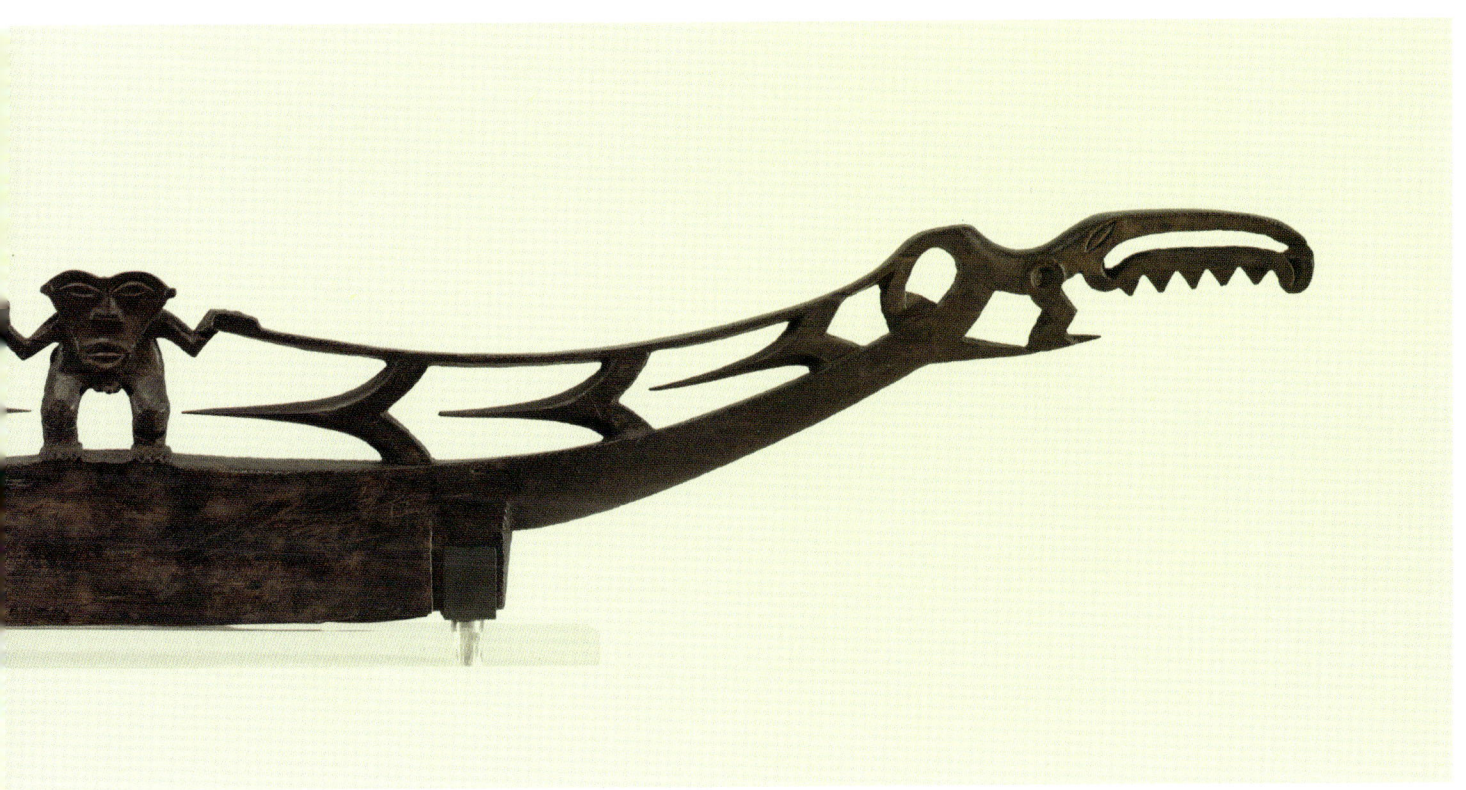

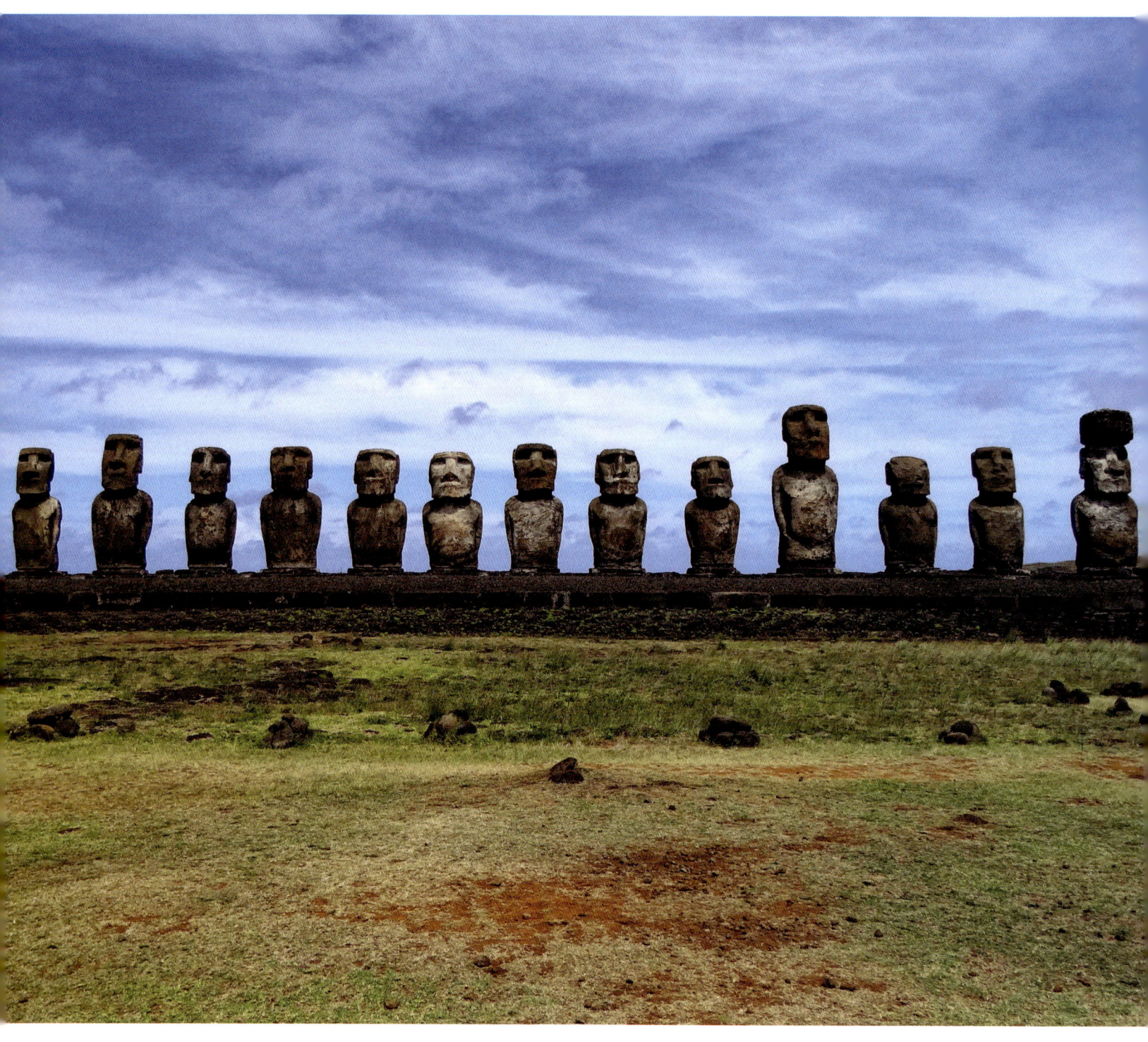

28 Ahu Tongariki
(1300–1500)

Artist(s): Unknown

Country of origin: Rapa Nui (Easter Island), Chile

Dimensions: 5.6–8.7 m (18⅓–28½ ft) (at Ahu Tongariki)

Material(s): Volcanic tuff, coral and scoria

A small eastern Polynesian island of 14,000 hectares (34,600 acres), Rapa Nui (or Easter Island), is home to the extraordinary Ahu Nau Nau ceremonial site at Anakena. Here stand an awe-inspiring group of 15 stone *moai* (human figures) carved out of soft volcanic tuff, the largest of which is Ahu Tongariki. A number have *pukao* (or *hau*) red cylinders balanced atop their heads like hats, and faces decorated with white coral and red scoria eyes. It is believed that the statues memorialized important ancestors or ancestor gods. Rapa Nui is roughly 1,930 km (1,200 miles) from the closest inhabited island and approximately 3,220 km (2,000 miles) from any nearby landmass, becoming inhabited at the time of Polynesian diaspora between 600 and 800 CE. It is one of humanity's greatest achievements, given it was perhaps the farthest-flung place on Earth to be permanently settled.

It was a thousand years before the European explorer Jacob Roggeveen and his crew saw 'a low flat island' and gave it the name of Paasch Eyland on Easter Sunday 1722. While there is no solid evidence from earlier periods, settlers of central Polynesia, including those who arrived in Hawai'i, Rapa Nui and Aotearoa (New Zealand), surely brought with them the concept of *marae*: a large communal and ceremonial space containing a stone platform or *ahu*, which functioned as an altar for religious worship or as a burial site. The precise nature of the ceremonies performed is unknown, but it is believed that they centred on birth, fertility, death and deification of *ariki* (chiefs). At Rapa Nui, the *moai* are surmounted on the *marae,* a walled platform up to 7 m (23 ft) high in places, placed along the coast and turned to face inland to oversee the lineage lands. Notably, the eye sockets were carved subsequent to erection and coral and red scoria eyeballs placed in the sockets at a ritual ceremony.

The colossal stone *moai* – one abandoned statue is 20.5 m (67½ ft) tall and weighs some 180 tonnes (200 tons) – were carved in a local quarry and pulled to a particular *ahu* by means of rolling logs. Manifold statue-raising with hundreds of *moai* still occupying the island and the widespread presence of *ahu* sites on Rapa Nui (there are 245) corroborate the significance of assiduously erecting statues and ancestral temples in *c.* 1000–1500. However, quite suddenly, from about 1500, the monolith-making ceased when population numbers reached 10–15,000 or more. A combination of food scarcity, soil damage and exploitation of a delicate ecosystem appear to have been the key stress factors. This resulted in the rise to power of the *matato'a* – a warrior class who resisted traditional tribal leadership, carrying out raids and toppling statues from countless *ahu*. The war leaders and the religious structure commonly known as the 'birdman cult' (*tangata manu*) came to dominate island life and superimposed their own key emblematic signature on the sacred sites and statues, including on the back of the famous Rapa Nui statue *Hoa Hakananai'a* (see p. 48).

29

Spring Clouds in the Linggu Mountains
(Early–Mid 15th Century)

Artist(s): Dai Jin (or Dai Wenjin)

Country of origin: China

Dimensions: 31.5 x 124 cm (12½ x 49 inches)

Material(s): Ink colour on silk

In the Ming dynasty (1368–1644), calligraphy and painting were considered élite art forms. The graphic arts took the format of folding fans and screens, hanging or hand scrolls and albums. It's an aesthetic form that occurred in China by way of Japan. Three artistic tendencies can be pinpointed: the painting of the court Academy, who followed the 'classic' Southern Song painters (960–1279), literati painters or leisure painters, and specialized non-court artists of the Zhe school. Essentially, professional painters harked back to the earlier painterly tradition that depicted lyrical scenes from the natural world, a practice established in the Han period (206 BCE–22 CE). Southern Song painters had revitalized previous lyrical tendencies by producing landscapes that combined poetry, calligraphy and painting.

Many of the Zhe artists also featured in the Academy. Here, landscape painting was heavily underpinned by aesthetic theory, an approach documented from the 1000s onwards and a tendency still extant today. Among Ming era painters, Dai Jin (or Dai Wenjin) was a highly prominent mid-15th-century artist (1388–1462), who is seen as the progenitor of the Zhe artistic coterie. As with earlier Song landscapes, Zhe artists sought to convey philosophies about the natural world, minuscule

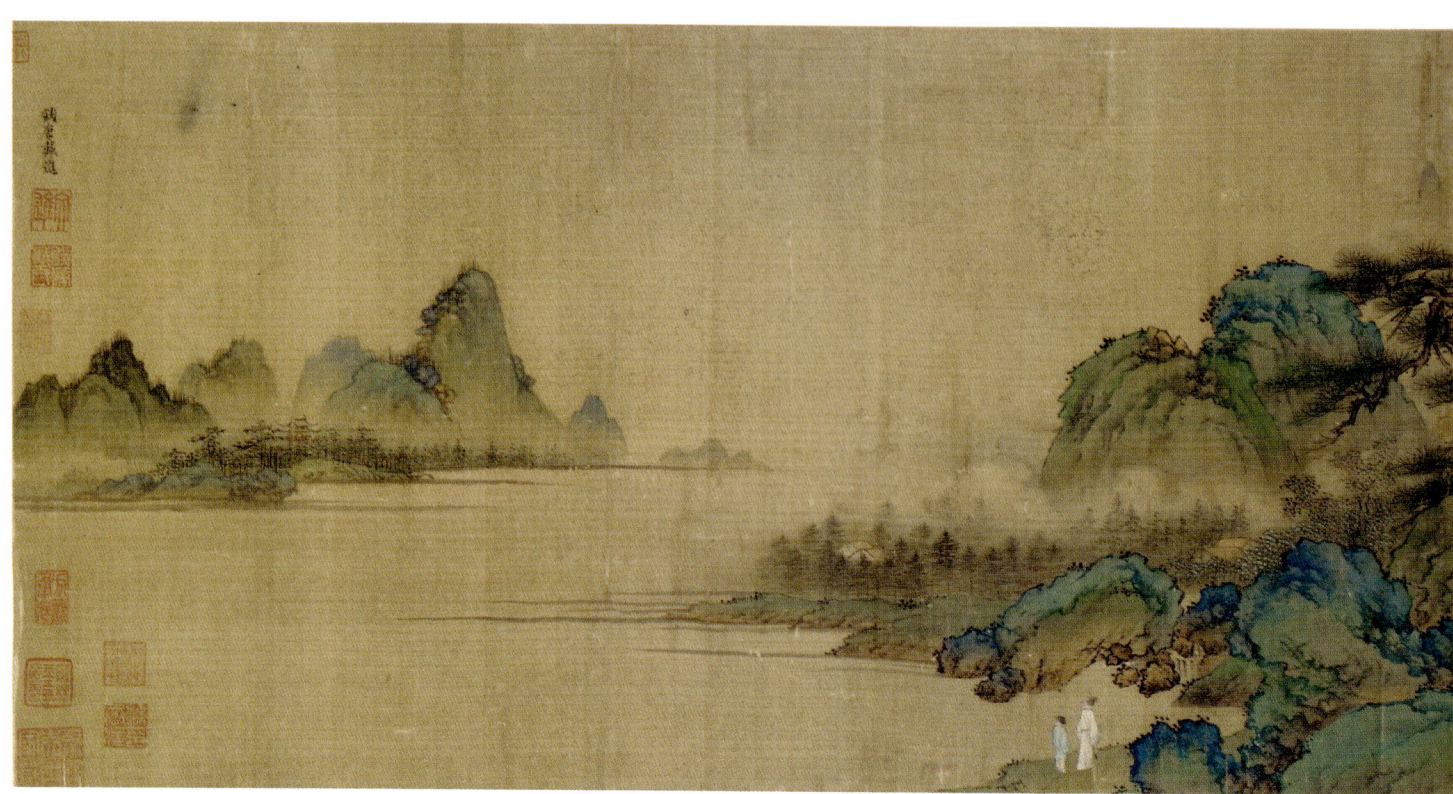

figures tending to express the majesty of nature, the human connection with the landscape and the ephemerality of life itself.

In Jin's *Spring Clouds in the Linggu Mountains*, trees, massifs, waterfalls and a large stretch of water dwarf virtually unseen figures. The painting is typical of Zhe artists, showing sharp contrasts of tone between light and dark areas, broad sweeps of colour, with tall trees, rocky cliffs and soaring mountains used as compositional framing devices. Pictorially, these paintings appear 'flat' with ink and colour washes manufacturing the internal space. Misty effects leave large areas 'blank', or, to use European Modernist language, 'give the eye a chance to add imaginatively to the variations already recorded'.[28] While elevations and towering trees climb out of the haze, the eye is led by a wide stretch of river toward peaks on the distant shoreline. It's a scene meant to characterize 'the scholars' ideal society… cut off from the world – if only for a little while.'[29]

Buyers of this type of art were the merchant classes, government officials of various rank and emperors. The Zhe artists' painterly repertoire typically included the events and lives of individuals 'from Confucianist, Daoist, and historical literature',[30] who sought out a highly idealized image of life. Paradoxically, it was a life many officials could not possibly have because their obligations prevented them doing so. The first colophon inscribed by the official Nie Danian (1402–56) on Dai Jin's painted silk handscroll is an invitation for his son to travel, accompanied by a favoured picturesque landscape that speaks of the official's yearnings.

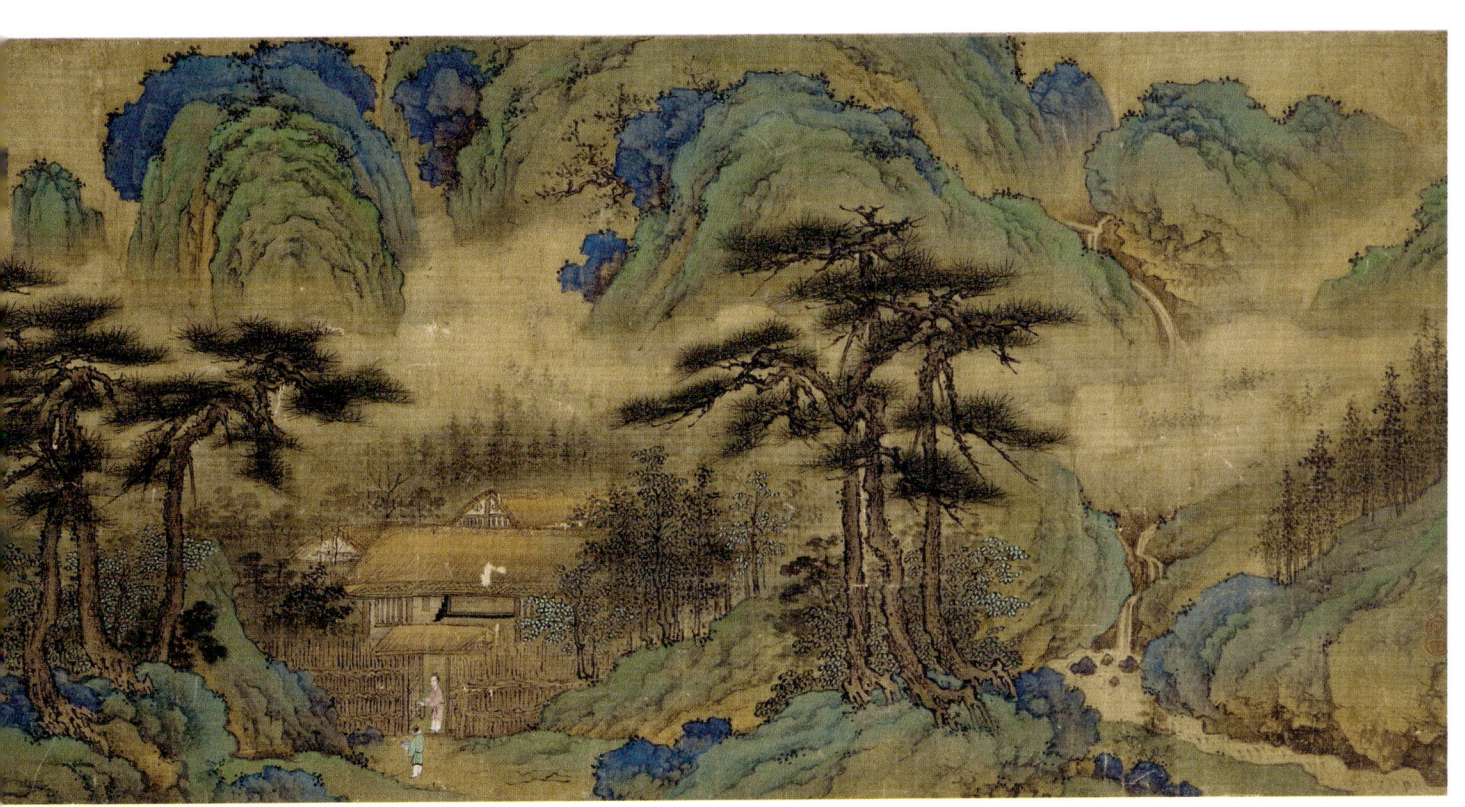

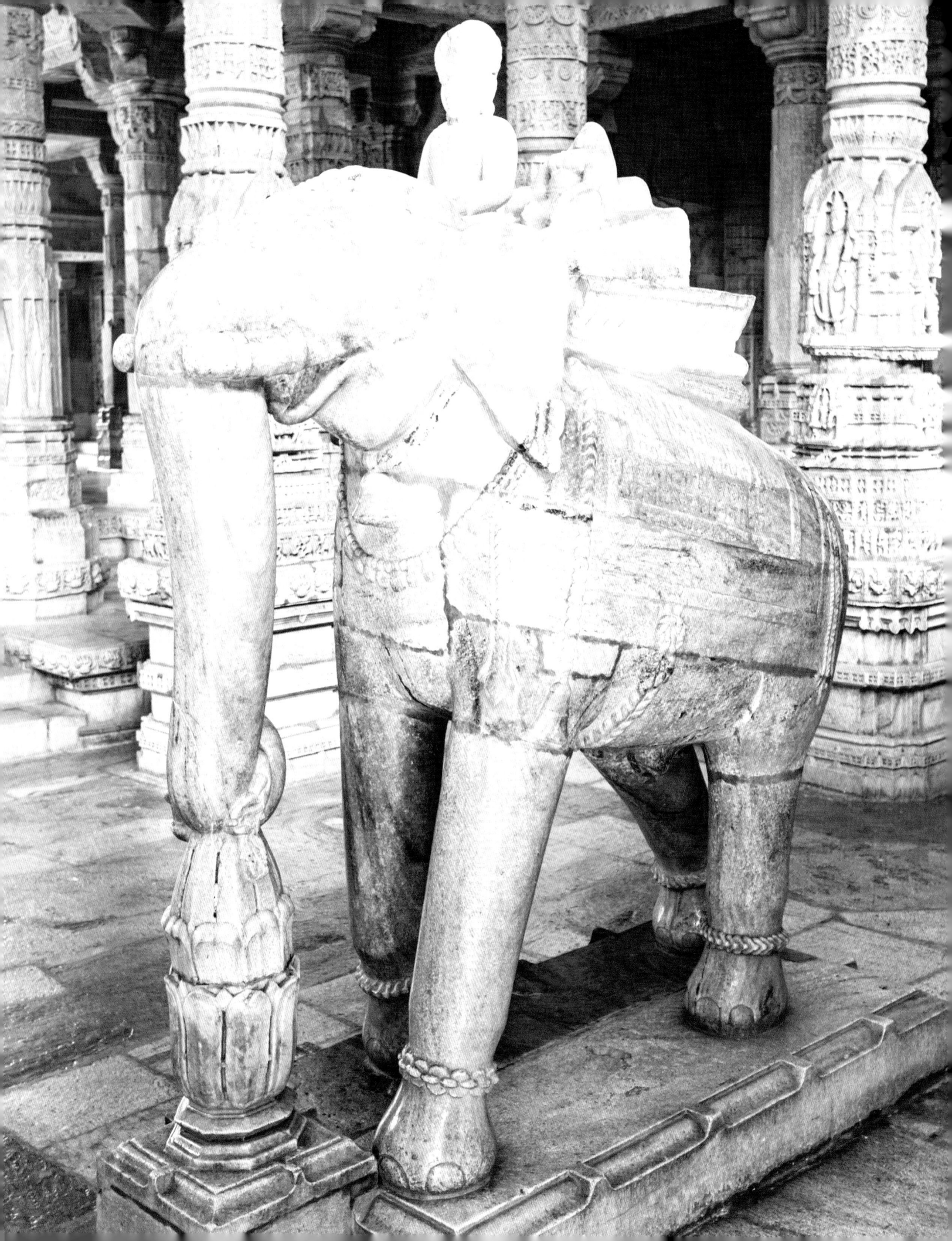

30

Chaturmukha Jain Temple of Rishabhanatha
(1389–*c.* 1439)

Artist(s): Depa and various unknown architects and artists

Country of origin: India

Dimensions: 4,460 sq m (48,000 sq ft)

Material(s): Marble

This beautiful complex of shrines (84 in total) is the result of a vision experienced by a businessman of the Porwal community, Dharana Shah, during a dream he had after an encounter with the spiritual leader Acharya Somasundarsuriji. Dharana Shah expressed a desire to build a temple dedicated to Rishabhanatha, who was the first *Tirthankara* (supreme preacher) of Jainism and who is also known as Adinatha (which literally means 'First Lord'). Supported by the local ruler Rana Kumbha, the Maharana of Mewar, Dharana Shah asked various architects to come up with designs. It was a sculptor named Depa (also Depaa) who produced a plan that most closely resembled Dharanashah's vision of what it should look like. Building work began in 1389 and would take more than 50 years to be completed. By 1439, with work still to be done, Dharana Shah was at an advanced age and so decided that the idol of the principal deity should be installed in the temple.

Hidden in a peaceful valley among the Aravalli Hills in Rajasthan, the temple sits on a huge plinth and is built in the Māru-Gurjarat (or Solanki) architectural style prevalent in West India in the 11th–13th centuries, but is unique in shape and in its interior decoration which consists of highly intricate carvings and sculptures. The form of the temple is said to resemble the Nalini-Gulma Vimana, a sort of flying palace of the gods. Executed in white marble, there are four entrances to the temple and approximately 1,444 pillars inside, each of which is individually carved. In the Gabhara, the innermost sanctuary of the temple, there is a 2-metre- (6-ft-) high idol of Rishabhanatha with four heads that face in the four cardinal directions. One of the most famous carved idols is that of Parshvanatha, which was made out of a single slab of marble and has 1,008 snake heads.

Although for many years the temple was deserted, with pilgrims dissuaded by the remoteness of its situation and the wild animals that roamed the surrounding area, it stands as a testament to the faith of Dharana Shah in his vision.

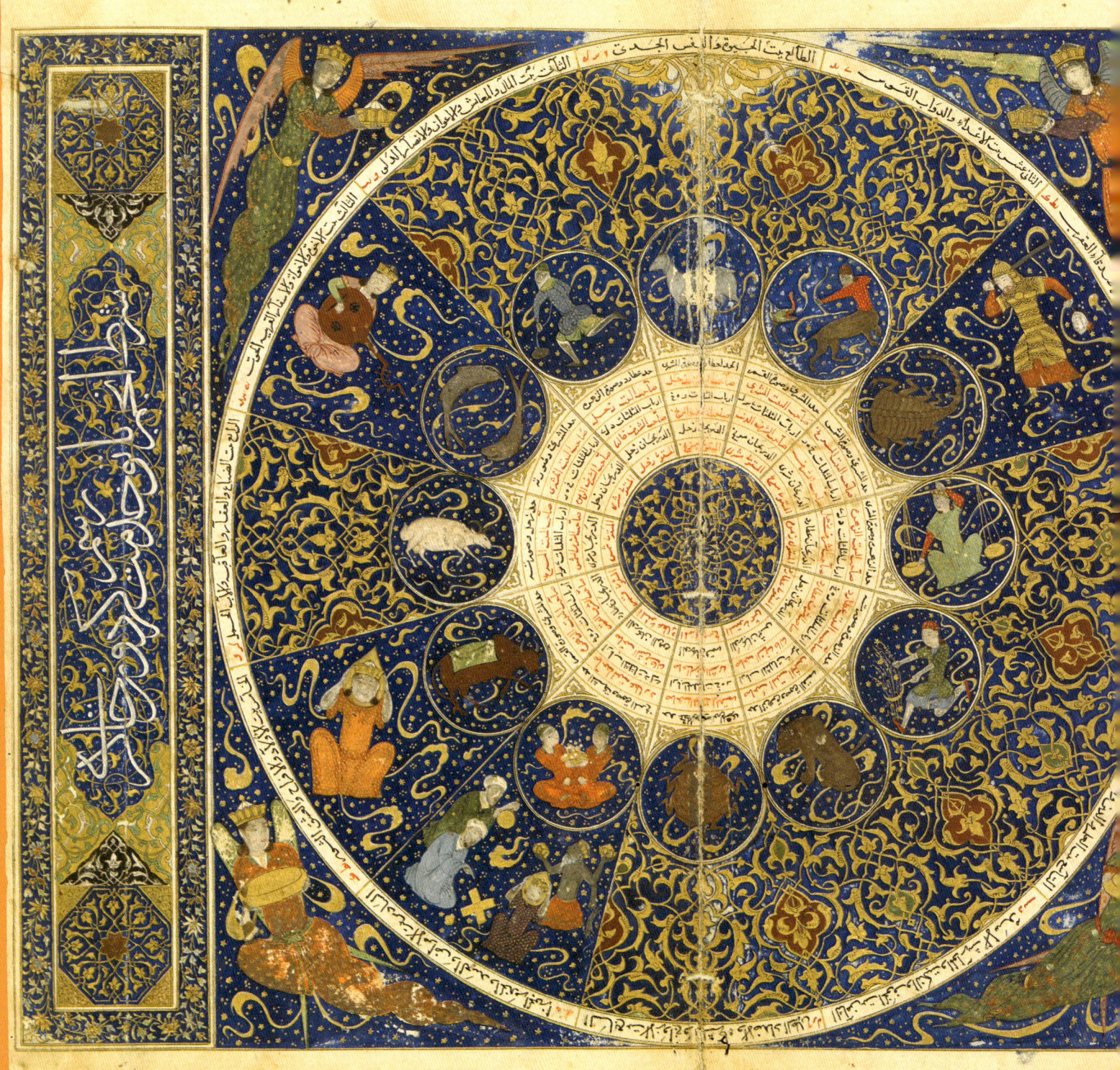

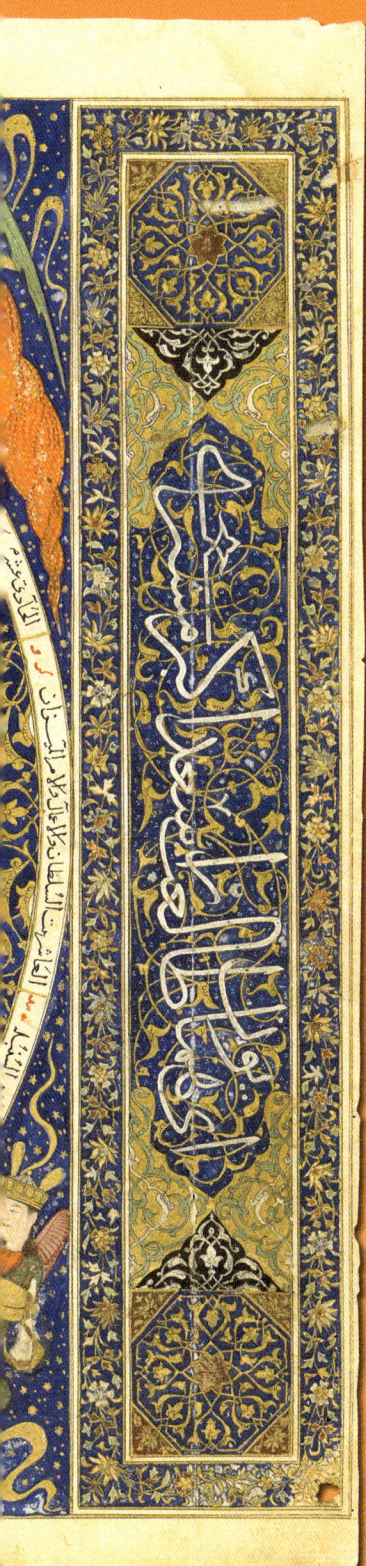

The Iskandar Horoscope
(1411)

Artist(s): Unknown

Country of origin: Timurid Empire (now Iran)

Dimensions: 26.5 x 34 cm (10½ x 13⅓ inches); Single folio 26.5 x 17 cm (10½ x 6¾ inches)

Material(s): Medium thick Oriental paper, ink, watercolour, gold

Also known as *Kitab-i viladat-i Iskandar* (*The Book of Birth of Iskandar*), this is a manuscript written by the court astrologer of Iskandar Sultan in 1411. Iskandar (1384–1415) was the grandson of Timur (1336–1405), who founded the Timurid Empire which encompassed an area that stretched across Iran, Afghanistan and Central Asia. Although Timur was succeeded by his brother, Shah Rukh, there was much infighting among Timur's grandsons for control of his empire, with Iskandar and his elder brother, Pir Mohammad, among them. Iskandar eventually established himself as ruler of Shiraz and set about conquering other cities, including Isfahan, which he made his capital. His ambitions brought him into conflict with Shah Rukh, who rallied his troops and defeated Iskandar. Despite capture and exile, Iskandar attempted another unsuccessful coup, which led to his execution in 1415.

In addition to his military ambitions, Iskandar took a great interest in the arts and sciences, promoting the production of books that included poetry and works on astronomy. This beautiful horoscope, part of a manuscript consisting of 86 folios, details the positions of the planets at the time of Iskandar's birth. It was prepared by Mahmud bin Yahya bin al-Hasan al-Kashi, whom Professor Fateme Keshavarz (who documented the manuscript on behalf of the Wellcome Collection) notes was most likely the grandfather of Ghiyath al-Din Jamshid bin Masud bin Mahmud al-Kashi, the well-known mathematician and astrologer of Ulugh Beg's court in Samarkand.

The manuscript is written in Naskh, a form of Islamic calligraphy much used by scribes in the preceding centuries. Together with circular depictions of the 12 astrological signs, there are four angels bearing gifts, one in each corner of the image. On the outside margins of each page are decorated rectangles bearing poetic verses that have not been identified. The planets are represented by figures, such as Venus playing a lute, while Mars is shown brandishing a sword. Around the horoscope and side panels there are exquisite patterns of flowers, trailing stems of leaves and stars, all of which have been outlined in black ink and then filled with red, blue, green or gold. The result is one of the greatest examples of the Shiraz School of Painting.

The Spirit Avenue at the Imperial Ming Tombs
(1435)

Artist(s): Unknown

Country of origin: China

Dimensions: Maximum height 4 m (13 ft)

Material(s): Stone

The process of constructing imperial tombs to bury rulers, abolished in the Song dynasty (960–1279), was re-established by the founder of the Ming dynasty (1368–1644), Emperor Hongwu (Zhu Yuanzhang). The majority of Ming tombs – 13 of them – lie just north of Beijing (in contrast to 18 Tang tombs near the former capital Xi'an). Only one tomb, the Dingling mausoleum of the Wanli ruler (*c.* 1573–1620), has been meticulously unearthed.

All these tombs were planned in advance and lend invaluable insight into the lives of past emperors and their subjects. Those of the élite contained elaborate interiors richly equipped with grave goods and decorated with *al secco* wall paintings. The walls of the tomb of Prince Zhanghuai (707 CE), for instance, are covered with colourful paintings showing riders playing polo, and a hunting scene with horses and camels. Emperor Qin Shi Huang's famous tomb of 'magic' terracotta warriors (see page 22) indicates that it, too, was constructed for pleasure in the hereafter.

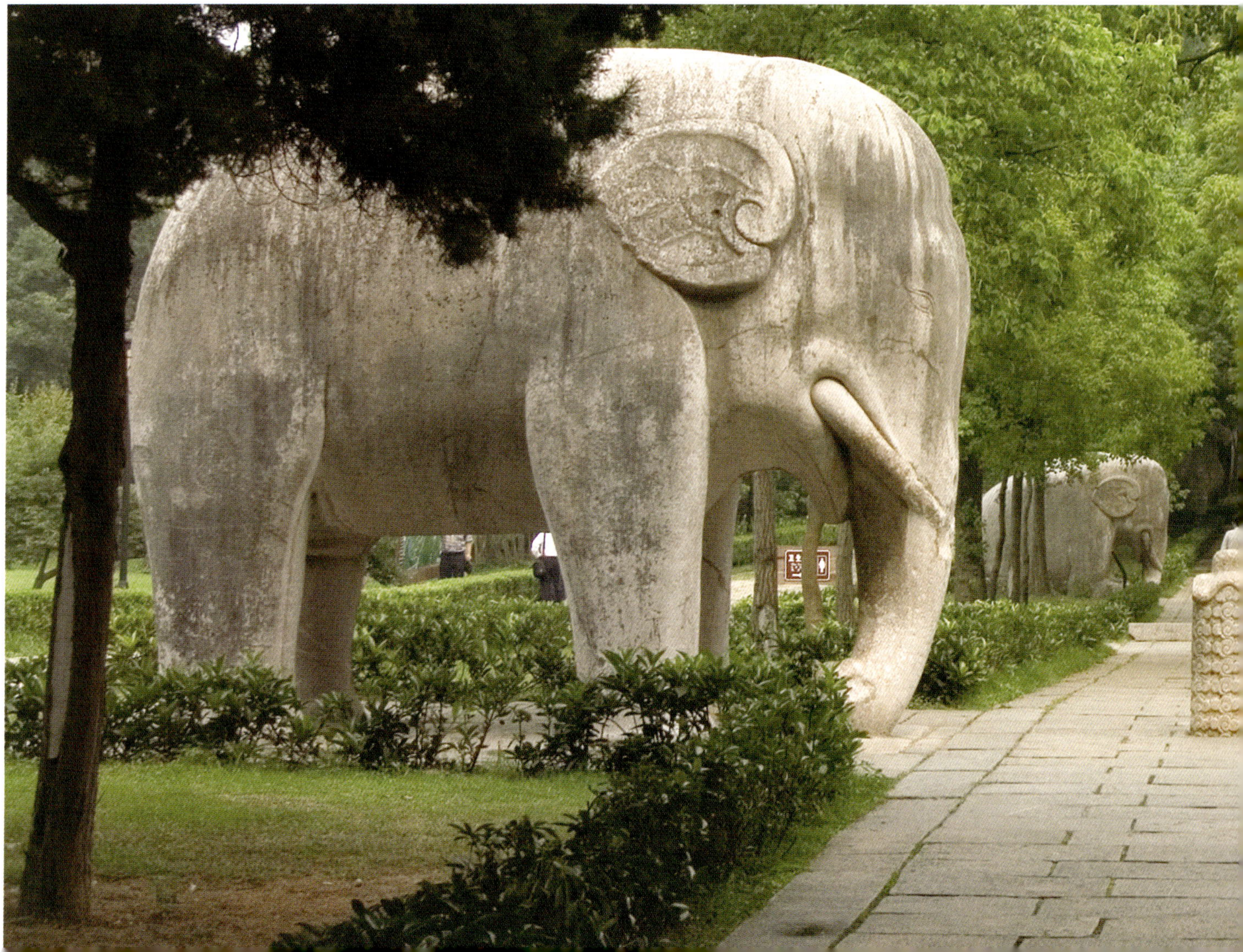

Tombs were constructed below and above ground and were approached by a solitary 'Spirit Way' (*Shéndào*), with sculptures placed on either side of the pathway. For instance, the Tang rulers' Way of Souls has monumental, free-standing and fully rounded stone figures standing in pairs lining the approach road to various tomb complexes.

Fundamentally, the layout for each imperial tomb is indistinguishable from others, but in details they differ in accordance with tradition, discernment, notoriety and the reputation of an individual emperor. Building-wise, the mausoleum of the Hongwu emperor at Nanjing, Xiaoling, is compatible with the 13 tombs near Beijing. However, the Beijing mausolea – known as the Ming or Thirteen Tombs – have a meandering Way of Souls that serves the complete valley of mausolea. The figures along the Spirit Avenue might encompass councillors, civil (*wen*) and military (*wu*) figures. That of the Ming Tombs is 'a combination of human beings, animals and mythological beasts. Their purpose was to guard and bless the departing spirit.'[31]

An ancient belief in geomancy probably governed the choice of site, which relinquished the traditional north–south axis. As one Sinologist observes: 'This group of imperial burials is one of the most impressive sets of mausolea in the world, covering a site of some 40 sq. km (15½ sq. miles).'[32]

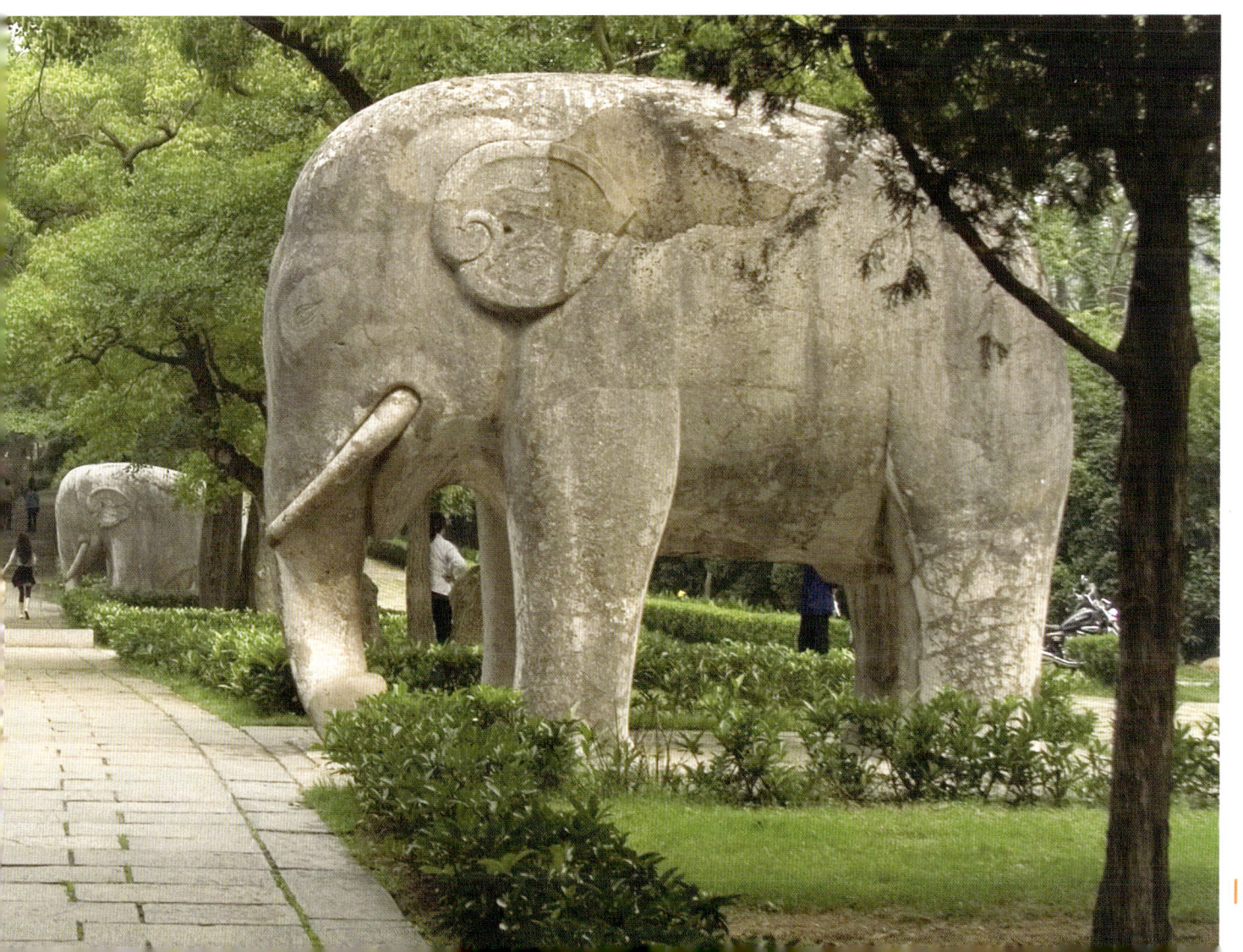

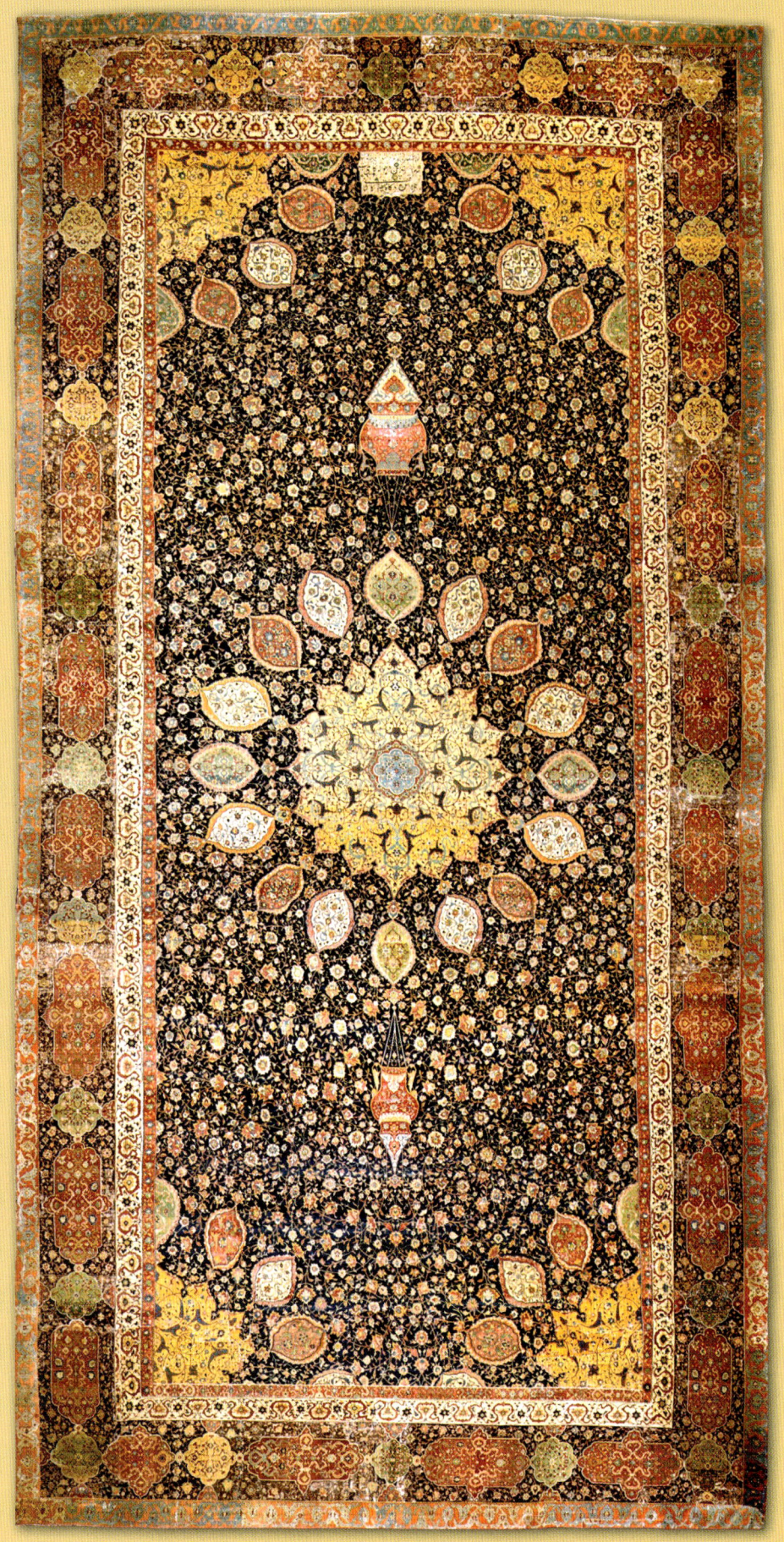

The Ardabil Carpet
(1539–40)

Artist(s): Unknown

Country of origin: Persia (now Iran)

Dimensions: 1.04 × 0.53 m (34 ft 3 inches × 17 ft 7 inches)

Material(s): Wool and vegetable dyes

For hundreds of years, Persian carpets have been renowned for their craftsmanship and artistry. The Ardabil Carpet is one of the oldest known examples still in existence. It was originally much larger, but the carpet's restoration in the 19th century resulted in a reconstruction that omitted some pieces which were then used to create a second Ardabil Carpet. The larger one is in the collection of the Victoria & Albert Museum in London in the UK, while the smaller is to be found in the Los Angeles County Museum of Art in California, USA.

Woven using the loop method, the Ardabil Carpet is a beautiful example of the rugs produced during the Safavid period (1501–1732) and took approximately four years to create. It was made in Kashan, a small city in the area of Isfahan in northern Iran that is now a UNESCO World Heritage site. The carpet was thought to have been made for the mausoleum of Sheikh Safi al-Din Khanegah, but this now seems unlikely. It made its way to London in the 19th century, where the artist and designer William Morris persuaded the Victoria & Albert Museum to purchase it.

The Ardabil Carpet was an original, though subsequently much copied, design that reflects the typical use of a central medallion but with two lamps (one smaller than the other that some experts believe provides varying perspectives depending from which end it is viewed) on either side, all of which is set against a background filled with flowers and surrounded by further intricate, repeated floral patterns and traditional shapes used in the design of Persian carpets. In the case of the Ardabil Carpet, it contains a woven inscription by the poet Hafiz Shirazi (1325–90) that reads:

I have no refuge in the world other than thy threshold.

There is no protection for my head other than this door.

The work of the servant of the threshold Maqsud of Kashan in the year 946.

Of huge historical importance, it has continued to influence carpet design for many years.

Greek and Chinese Painter Competition
(c. 1540–50)

Artist(s): Unknown

Country of origin: Iran

Dimensions: 22 x 14 cm (8½ x 14½ inches)

Material(s): Opaque watercolour, ink and gold on paper 22 x 14 cm

The debate between ancient Greek artists in painting is a legendary subject in the history of art. The tale of naturalism in Greek painting is recounted in Pliny the Elder's *Natural History* (77 CE). Zeuxis paints a bunch of grapes with such eye-fooling illusionism as to deceive the birds, while Parrhasius renders a curtain that hoodwinks Zeuxis. A similar tale emerges in early Islamic literature, from the Iranian poet Nizami (d. 1209) who describes a rivalry between a Greek and Chinese artist in which the Greek suffers defeat.

However, in this image from a manuscript of *Masnavi-I-Ma'navi* (*Spiritual Couplets*) by Jalal al-Din (Maulana) that stems from the Sufi writer Rumi (born 1207), whose epic tells of a Sultan's demand that two artistic groups compete to establish a superior form of painting, the story is upturned.[33]

The upper tier shows the two rivals, while below the spectators watch or debate the competition. Accordingly, while the Chinese artist renders relatively 'conventional' colourful Islamic flowers and streams, the astute Greek painter, whose work is free of colour, buffs the wall as if shining a mirror, echoing a belief in the heavenly quintessence of light described in Rumi's manuscript:

The mirror's purity is like the heart's,
receiving images beyond all number.
… the mirror of the heart is free of limits ….

In the right margin, a touch of 'realism' is brought to the debate, a mountainous landscape – with a (now discoloured) silver stream bordered by rocks, trees and plants – intimates 'real nature'. Alternatively, the compact *nasta'liq* calligraphy, together with the geometricized palace building, the compressed space, 'flat' shapes and dazzling colours, visualize complex, up-to-date, theoretical learning concerning representation in the arts. It has been suggested that earlier middle Eastern scientific and philosophical ideas to do with light, reflection and human optics inspired the poets and Sufis in their musings regarding representation and the practice of allegory to rationalize it.

Islamic visual culture has often been pigeonholed by European scholarship as principally decorative in nature. Thankfully, such stereotypes have now been dislodged, despite recurring periodically. In terms of literary and artistic exchange between all types of peoples, the painter envisages aesthetic contention as an important visual and intercultural occurrence.

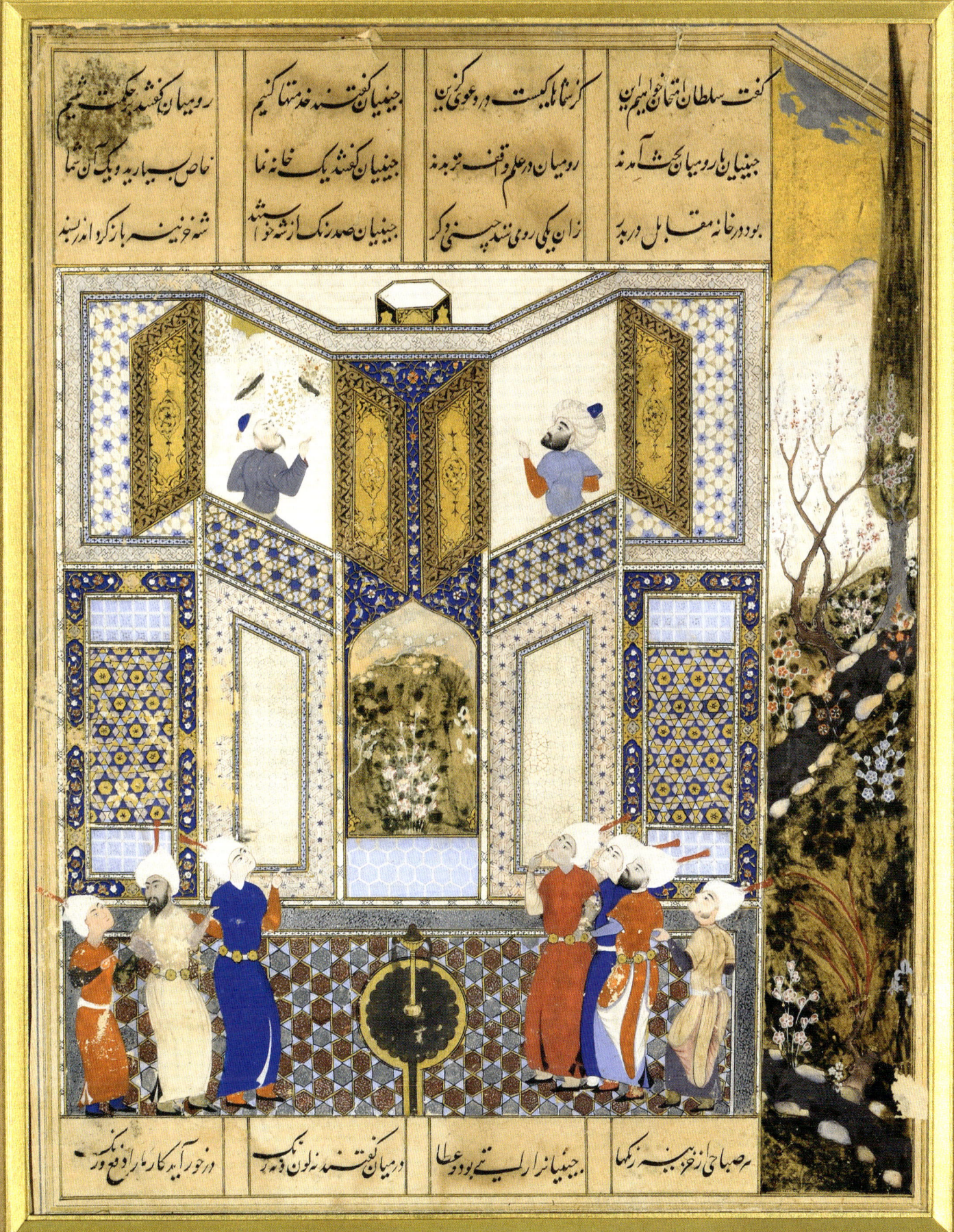

'Assad Ibn Kariba Launches a Night Attack on the Camp of Malik Iraj', Folio from *Hamzanama* (*The Adventures of Hamza*)

(1564–69)

Artist(s): Basawan

Country of origin: India

Dimensions: 69 x 54 cm (27 x 21¼ inches)

Material(s): Opaque watercolour, ink and gold on cloth, mounted on paper

A wonderful example of Mughal art, the *Hamzanama* is an extensive manuscript that contains 1,400 miniatures filled with exquisite detail which illustrate the adventures of an Arab warrior called Hamza. Originally passed down through generations in the oral tradition of storytelling, the *Hamzanama* is a typical example of Dastan (Central Asian oral history) storytelling that is similar to *One Thousand and One Nights*, filled with tales of heroic princes fighting dastardly enemies and encountering magicians, genies and beautiful princesses along the way. One line of thought is that the Hamza mentioned was the uncle of the Prophet, Hamza ibn Abdul-Muttalib, who was killed at the Battle of Uhud (625 CE), while another says that the character could be based on Hamzah ibn Abdullah, a member of the Kharijites, an Islamic sect dating from 656–661 that was eventually wiped out during the Abbasid period (750–1258).

The *Hamzanama* was commissioned by the Mughal Emperor Akbah, who loved the stories. Divided into 14 volumes, the images reflect a hybrid style exhibiting Persian and Mughal artistic traits. Certainly, the lively composition reflects the Mughal taste for dramatic imagery. Overseen by Mir Sayyid Ali and, subsequently, Abdus Samad, some 30 artists, most of whom are unknown, created the most beautiful scenes full of action and drama. The example selected here is attributed to the painter Basawan (or Basavana) who was working between 1580 and 1600. He is known to have been interested in the techniques of Western art, but here he follows those of traditional Mughal painting, using strong colours and creating a sense of depth to the scene in which the action in the background is as vital as that of the foreground.

Depicted here is a supporter of Hamza, Assad ibn Kariba, who can be seen clad in orange on a horse, leading an attack on a group of unbelievers (non-Muslims) who are thrown into chaos and disarray and begin attacking one another. Full of detail, from the decorations on the tent in the bottom left-hand corner to the brickwork of the fortified city in the background, Basawan conveys with great precision the furore of battle. This particular image is now in the collection of the Met Museum in New York. Further pages can be found in museums across the world, including the Museum of Applied Arts in Vienna, Austria, and the Victoria & Albert Museum in London in the UK.

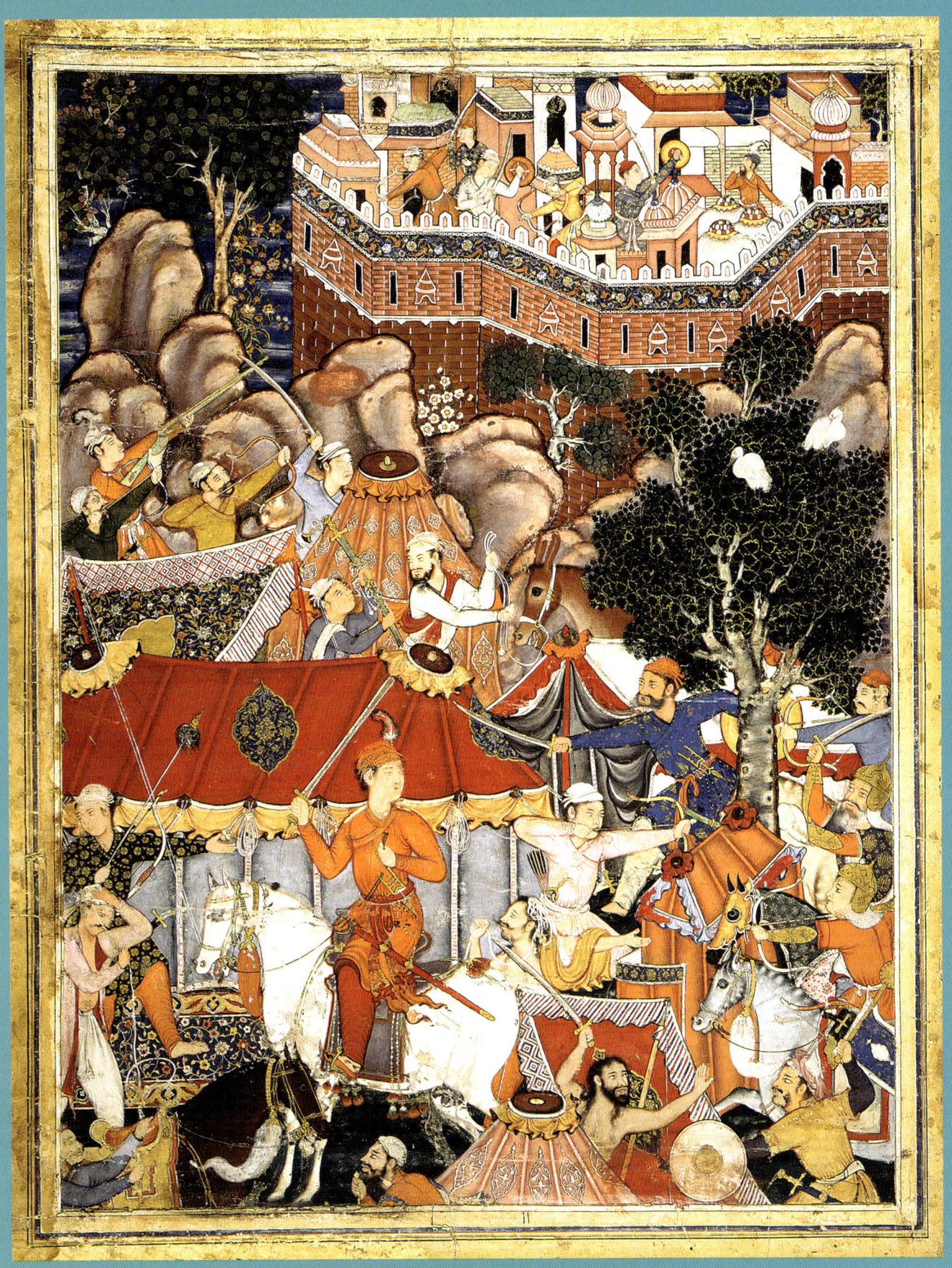

36 Ming Vase
(1587)

Artist(s): Unknown

Country of origin: China

Dimensions: Height 60 cm (23¼ inches); Base diameter 20 cm (8 inches)

Material(s): Porcelain and cobalt-blue paint

The blue-and-white porcelain of the Ming dynasty (1368–1644) is something many admirers of Chinese porcelain have come to recognize and the style has been copied the world over, particularly in Europe – for example, in the tin-glazed ware of Delft in the Netherlands. This vase portrays the Zhou-dynasty poet, cosmologist and philosopher Zhou Dunyi, and dates from the period of the Ming Emperor Wanli, who ruled from 1572 until 1620.

It was under the first Ming emperor, Hongwu, that the kilns in the southern Chinese city of Jingdezhen (from which this vase originates) were brought under imperial supervision. By the time of Wanli's reign, Chinese porcelain was regularly exported, with many items fashioned according to Western tastes, but the famous Jingdezhen blue-and-white style first appeared during the Yuan dynasty (1276–1368) that had been established by the Mongol leader Kublai Khan, although some evidence of blue-decorated pottery dating from the Tang and Song dynasties has also been found.

The blue patterns were made using a blue pigment made from cobalt oxide, originally by an artist using a brush (as techniques became more automated, brushwork was replaced by stencils and transfer prints). The cobalt was imported from Persia and, at the beginning of Hongwu's reign, it was in such short supply that the blue colour on most of the porcelain produced then is very faint. Later examples of Ming porcelain show much deeper blues against crisper white backgrounds. The blue could also show through the glazes placed on top, creating an almost black colour and adding to the substance of a pattern or figure.

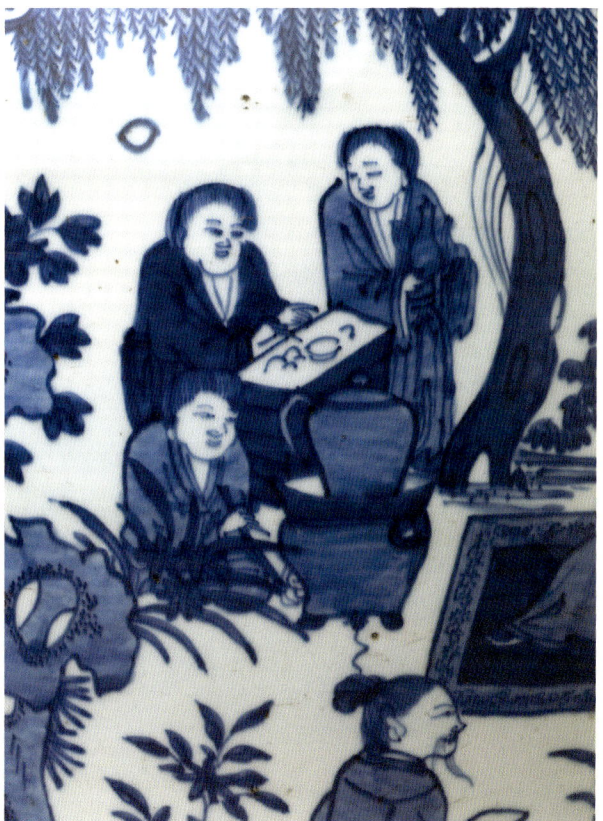

As can be seen in this example, patterns using flower, bird and dragon motifs took inspiration from traditional Chinese painting, and figurative scenes were often copied from woodblock illustrations. Around the vase are little vignettes and signs of everyday life: attendants making tea with Zhou Dunyi shown drinking a cup beneath a willow tree by a lotus pond, and various pots and baskets lying on the ground. The vase was produced for one of the outlying palaces in the southwest of the empire.

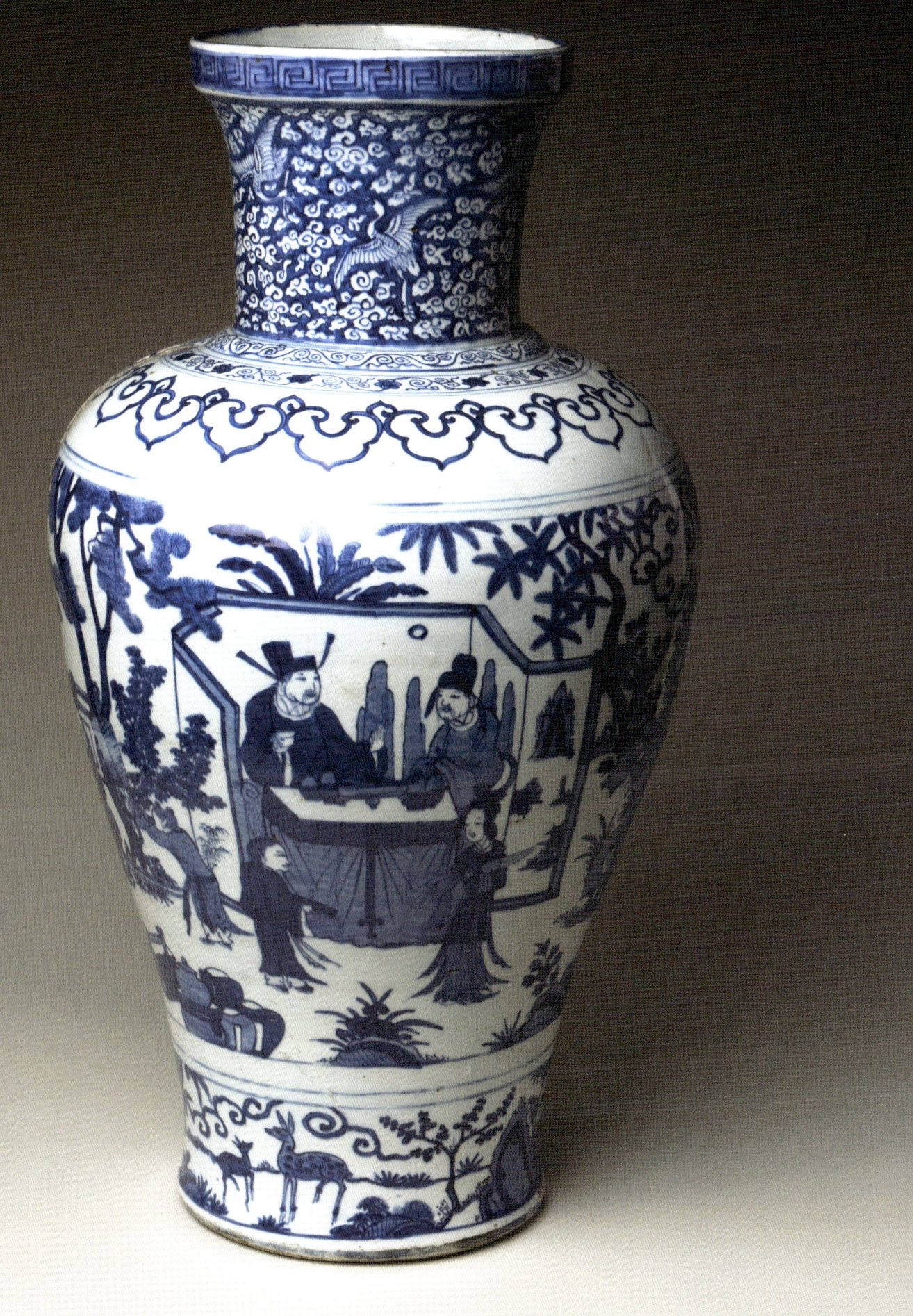

37 *Rabbit and Moon* **Fan Painting**
(Early 17th century)

Artist(s): Hon'ami Kōetsu

Country of origin: Japan

Dimensions: 18 x 54.4 cm (7 x 21¹/₂ inches)

Material(s): ink colours, and gold on paper.

In Japan, as in China, calligraphy and painting were never entirely separate entities. Indeed, artists frequently wrote on handmade paper with exquisitely painted images. The artist and craftsman Tawaraya Sōtatsu (approx. 1570–1643) is often associated with master calligrapher Hon'ami Kōetsu (1558–1637). Relatives by marriage, they collaborated on images that mingle poetry and painting, with a number of scrolls dating from the early 17th century combining the calligraphy of Kōetsu with designs by Sōtatsu.

Separately from his matchless calligraphy, Kōetsu also excelled at poetry, *raku*-style pottery, landscape gardening, lacquer work and painting and arts centered on the Japanese world of tearoom aesthetics. Kōetsu was born into a prosperous family in imperial Kyōto, and he and Sōtatsu entered his father's vocation as supplier of swords to the imperial court.

Together with Sōtatsu, he established the Rinpa school of painting, a 'movement' characterized by a brightly colourful and decorative manner in the traditional style of Yamato-*e* ('Japanese painting'). Kōetsu also explored painting, the only acknowledged instance being

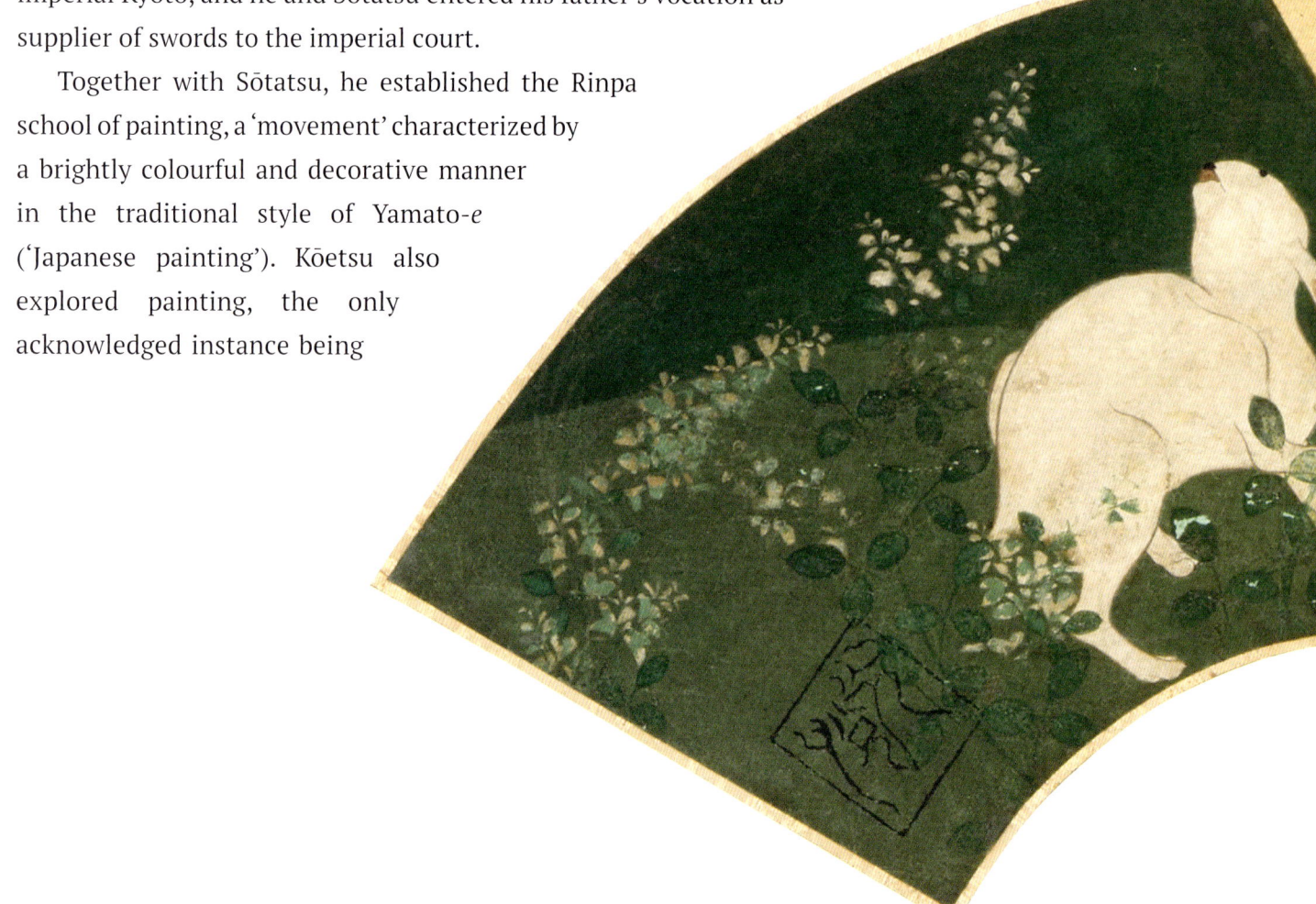

this delightful fan-painting of the moon and a rabbit in autumn, with attendant calligraphy written after Fujiwara no Hideyoshi (died 1240). Caught unawares among flowering bush clover (*hagi*), the rabbit's head is turned awkwardly with the ears curled backwards, the animal alert to the unseen. The flat gold area acts as the setting for Fujiwara's passionate poem, which Kōetsu has penned in highly graceful, coal-black lettering. The poem has reverberations of the painted backdrop and reveals 'how the tears shed by a lady for her loved one soak into the sleeves of her kimono and softly reflect the full moon of fall'.

In a mood matching the rabbit with the phase of a full moon, Kōetsu blends traditional myth with poetic and expressive potential. The moon rabbit legend is prevalent across Asian cultures, with the first reference to the fable recorded in the Western Han dynasty, in the *Chu Ci*, the Songs of Chu. In Chinese folklore, 'The rabbit in the moon pounds the medicine in vain,' writes Li Bai (701–762), the famous Tang poet, in his lauded song, translated into English as 'The Old Dust', and denoting 'life's vaporous glory', fleetingness and 'brief journey betwixt heaven and earth'. Kōetsu's famous painting typifies the sense of taste, philosophical bent and unexpectedness of the early Rinpa painters. As Michael Dunn observes of *Rabbit and Moon*: 'Most startling is the "telephoto lens" depiction of just the edge of the moon in gold leaf across the top right of the fan, in a composition that would have been unimaginable in any other country of the time.'[34]

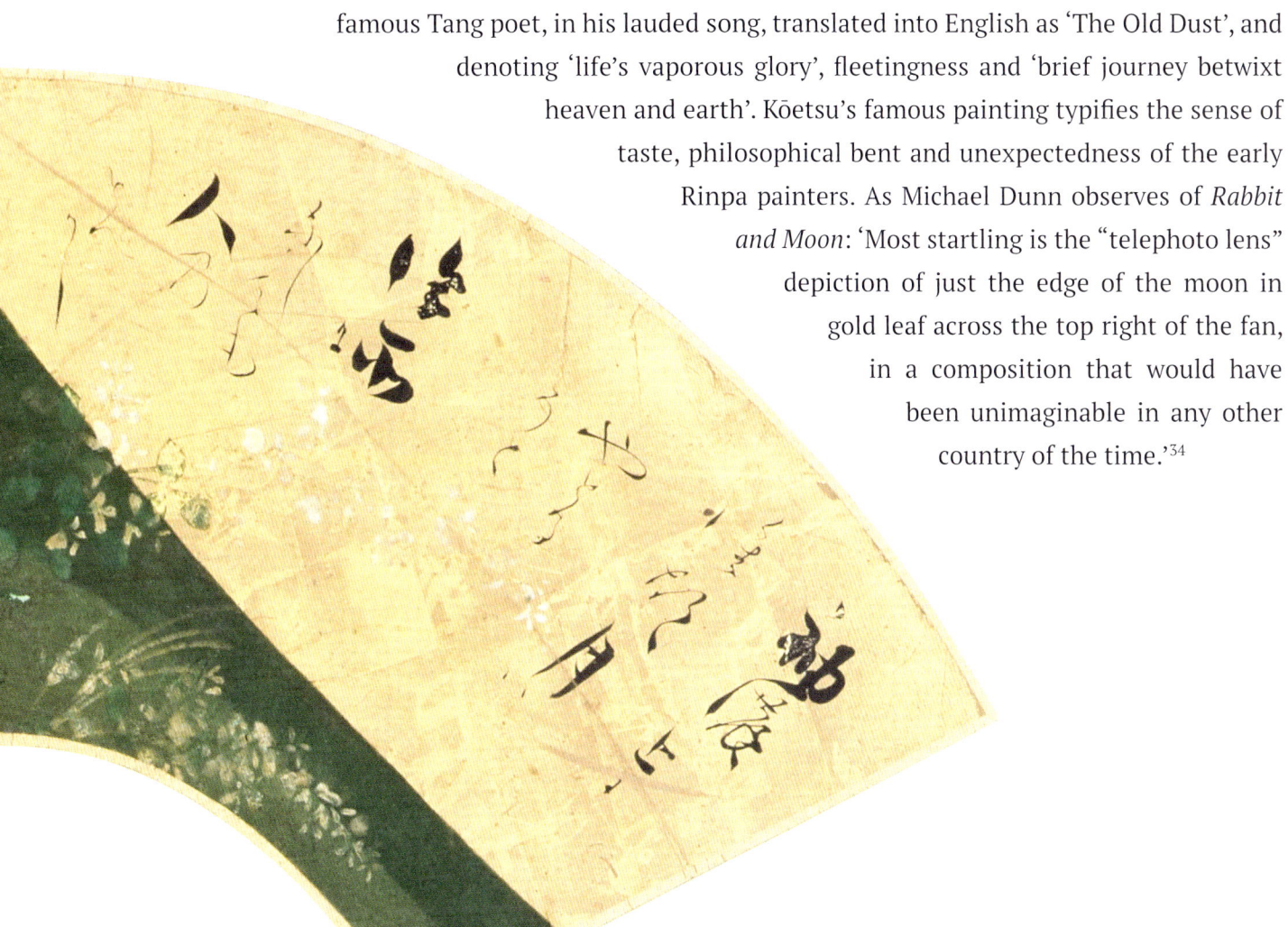

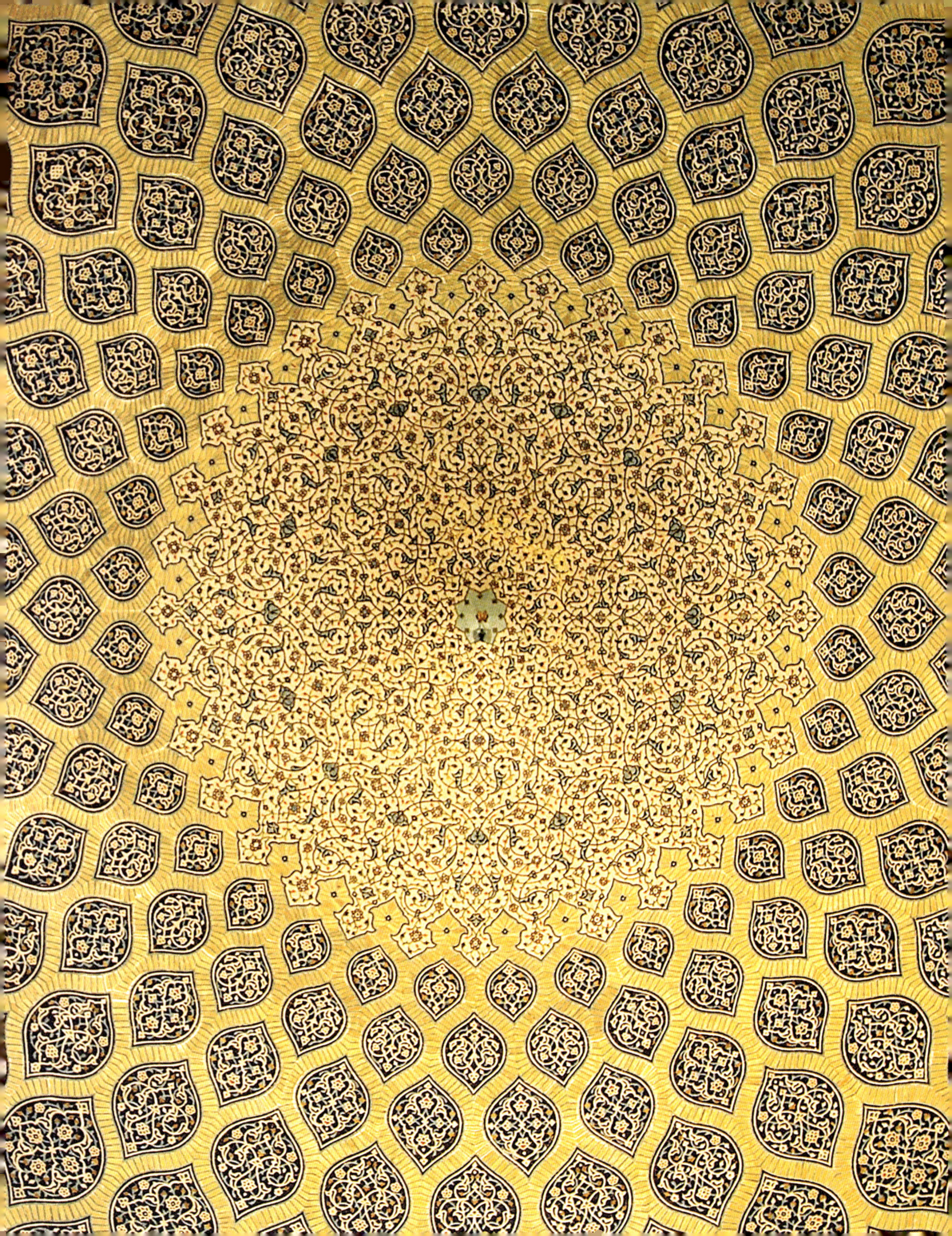

Sheikh Lotfollah Mosque
(1603–19)

Architect(s): Sheikh Baha'i and Ustad Mohammad Reza Isfahani

Country of origin: Iran

Dimensions: Height 32 m (105 ft); Dome diameter 22 m (72 ft)

Material: Stone, marble, ceramic tiles

Considered one of the masterpieces of Iranian architecture, the Sheikh Lotfollah mosque occupies the eastern side of Naqsh-I Jahan Square in Isfahan. It was built under the guidance of the architects Sheikh Baha'i and Ustad Mohammad Reza Isfahani by the orders of Shah Abbas I of Persia. Also known as Abbas the Great, the shah was the fifth ruler of the Safavid dynasty, which ruled much of western and central Asia between 1501 and 1736.

The mosque was intended for use by the royal household rather than for general worship, and Shah Abbas had a tunnel built so that he could move privately between the Ali Qapu Palace on the opposite side of the square and the mosque. Although the mosque has been known by several names, it is most often called the Sheikh Lotfollah Mosque after a famous imam who conducted prayers for the royal court when the mosque opened.

Smaller than many mosques, it has no minarets or courtyard but was described by the historian Iskandar Munshi as a mosque of 'great purity and beauty', while the travel writer Robert Byron considered it to be extremely fine, saying, 'Each part of the design, each plane, each repetition, each separate branch or blossom has its own sombre beauty.' It is renowned for its exquisite tile work laid out in arabesque patterns of blue, turquoise, yellow and white, depicting intricate, intertwining forms of flowers and leaves, and for the 'peacock'-tail effect that can be seen if one stands at the entrance to the inner hall and looks up towards the centre of the dome. Dark blue and white tiles contain verses from the Qu'ran in

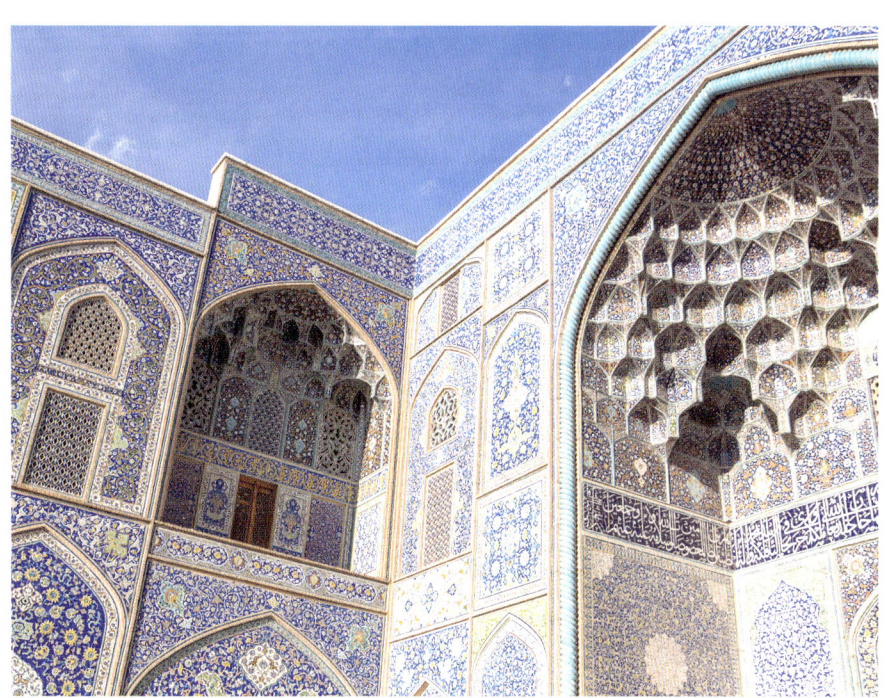

the Thuluth and Nasta'liq calligraphic styles, whose creation was overseen by Ali Reza Abbasi, the chief calligrapher of Shah Abbas's court. Viewed at different times of the day, it is clear that the architects took the time to consider the effect that light would have on the mosque's impact on visitors and, unsurprisingly, it has subsequently influenced numerous mosque designs around the world.

39 Taj Mahal
(1631–53)

Architects: Ustad Ahmad Lahauri (leader); Mir Abd-ul Karim (assistant)

Country of origin: India

Dimensions: 6.7 x 29 x 29 m (22 x 313 x 313 ft); Mausoleum 33 x 57 x 57 m (108 x 187 x 187 ft); Dome height 35 m (115 ft); Minarets height 41.75 m (137 ft)

Material(s): Brick, marble, sandstone, plus 28 types of precious and semi-precious stones, including jasper, jade, lapis lazuli, turquoise, sapphire, carnelian

Declared a UNESCO World Heritage site in 1983, this monument to love is the mausoleum built for Mumtaz Mahal by her husband Shah Jahan (1592–1666), who is also buried there. A shimmering structure of predominantly white marble, it sits in a garden complex of approximately 17 hectares (42 acres) on the banks of the River Yamuna in Agra, in Uttar Pradesh.

In its design, the Taj Mahal combines Indian and Islamic traditions, which is appropriate since Mumtaz Mahal was Persian by origin. Islamic tradition favoured modestly decorated tombs surrounded by a *charbagh*, or paradise garden, an interpretation of paradise on Earth. And the four-section grid layout of the Taj Mahal complex reflects the simple style of the *charbagh* in which rivers would flow out from a central source towards north, south, east and west. Although the mausoleum is at the edge of the main garden, if the Midnight (north) garden on the other side of the Yamuna is included in the whole design, then it is more centrally positioned.

The cube-shaped mausoleum stands on a square plinth with minarets (over 40 m [130 ft] high) at each corner. Inside the tomb are the sarcophagi of Mumtaz Mahal and Shah Jahan, but their actual resting place is beneath and not visible. Crowning the tomb is the onion dome, also made of marble and itself 35 m (115 ft) high and decorated with a lotus-flower design, a sign of spiritual enlightenment.

The exterior walls are ornamented with bas-relief sculptures of flowers and vines in white marble and nature-inspired borders of *pietra dura* using polished jade, jasper and yellow marble. Inside, the walls are decorated with inlaid patterns – also in the form of plants and flowers – in precious and semi-precious stones, such as lapis lazuli, garnet and sapphire, cut and polished in the lapidiary technique. The tomb and gateways are embellished with calligraphic quotes from the Qu'ran; that on the *darwaza* (principal gateway) says, 'O Soul, thou art at rest. Return to the Lord at peace with Him, and He at peace with you.'

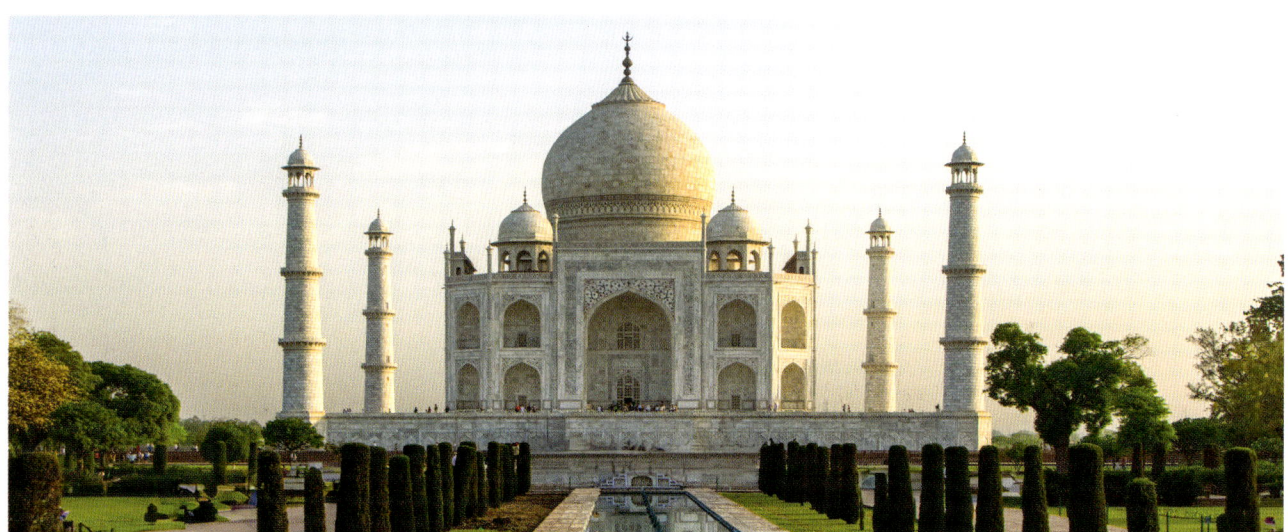

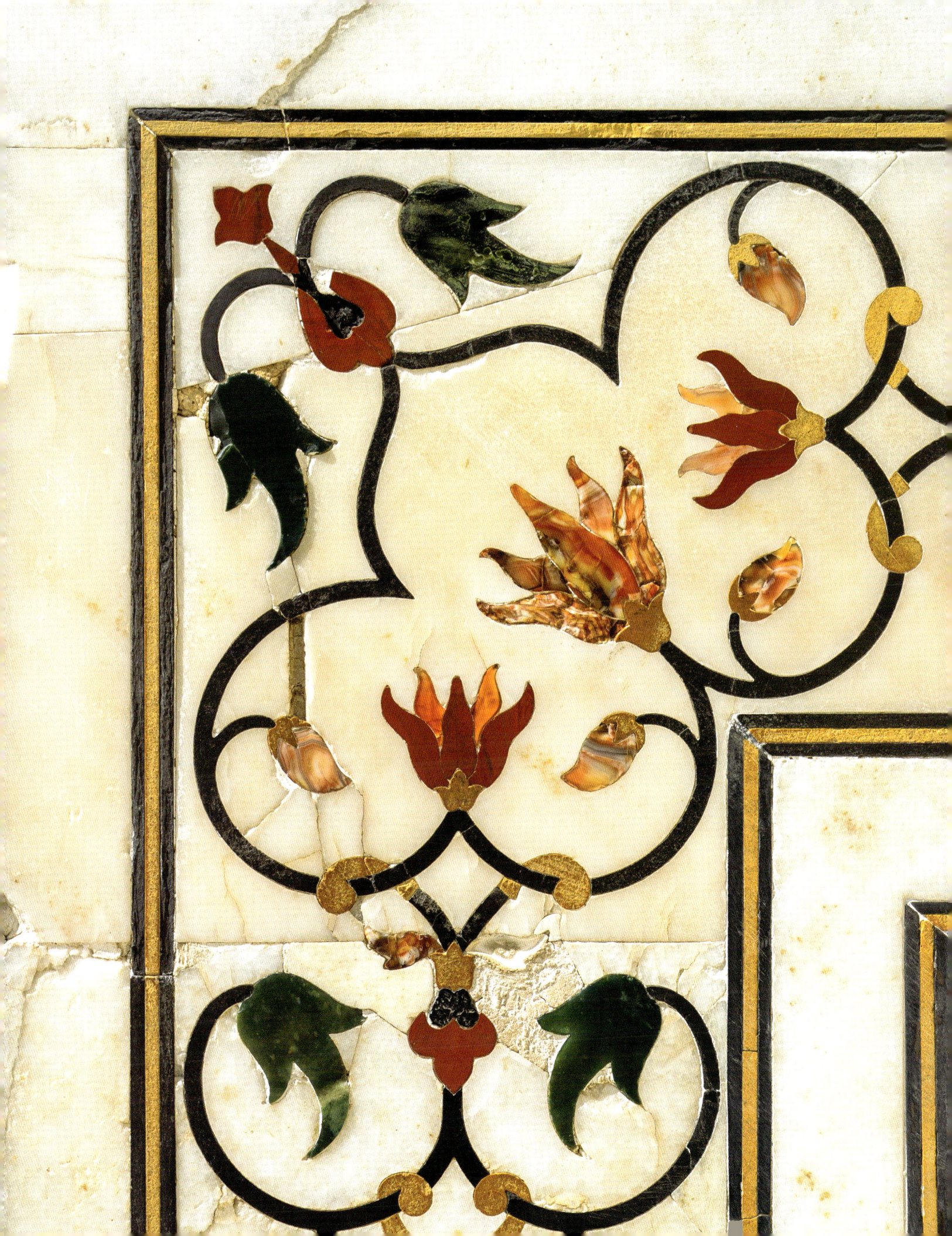

Lacquerware Screen
(*c.* 1685–1700)

Artist(s): Unknown

Country of origin: China

Dimensions: 321 x 624 x 2 cm

Material(s): Lacquer, coromandel lacquer and bronze inlaid in wood

Lacquerware objects were a popular form of art in East Asian countries, particularly in Japan and China where the techniques were refined by craftsmen over many millennia. Indeed, the oldest items of lacquerware (dating to the 7th millennium BCE) were burial ornaments found at the Kakinoshima archaeological site in Hakodate on the island of Hokkaido in Japan.

The most common form of lacquer was made from the sap of the unsurprisingly named Chinese lacquer tree (*Toxicodendron vernicifluum*). The sap was combined with wax and then painted over the surface of an object and left to dry. During the Tang and Song dynasties (618–907 and 960–1279 respectively), the art of lacquerware became more and more sophisticated, with the addition of carving, gold and silver motifs cut from thin sheets and inlays of mother of pearl. Layers of lacquer might be applied between various stages of decoration or built up so that in the case of the carving, a three-dimensional pattern could be created.

The 12-sectioned folding screen shown here is a beautiful example of coromandel lacquer, the type most commonly produced for export, though it was also popular with wealthy Chinese. Coromandel lacquer involved a variety of lacquering techniques, with the employment of mother-of-pearl or tortoiseshell inlays being a common feature. Screens were highly popular, and this one contains a rather whimsical composite image of Dutch ships arriving in China on the left-hand side, while in

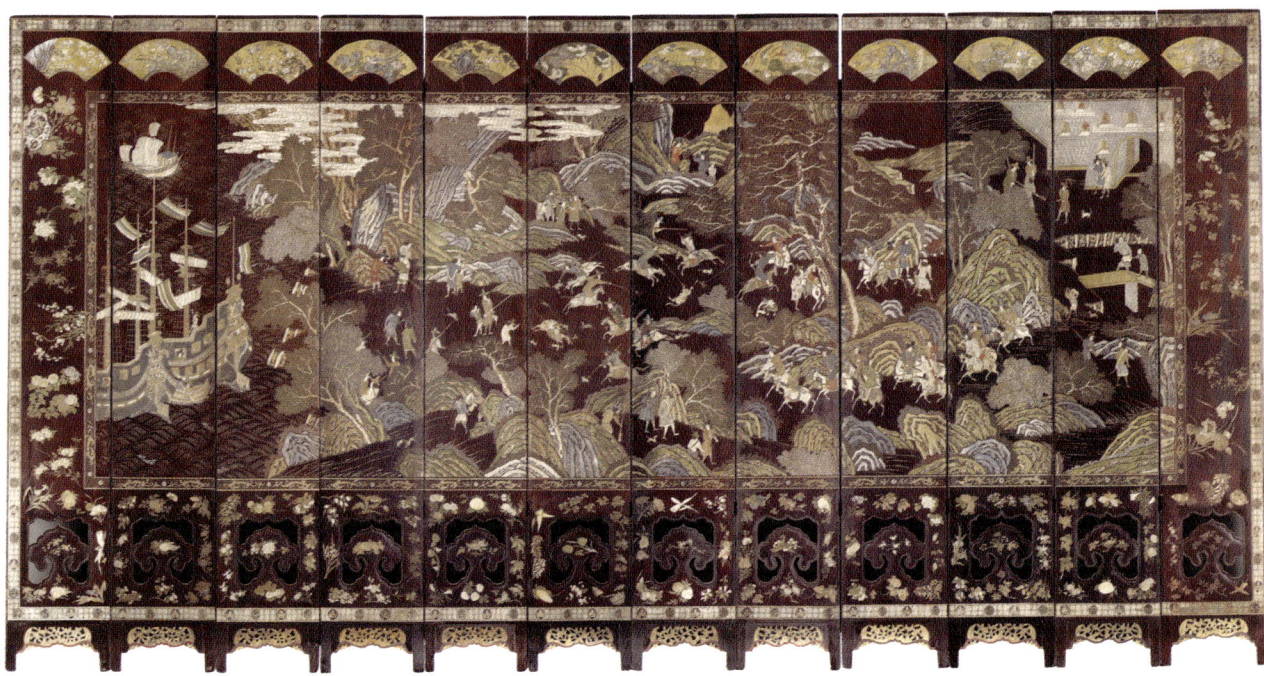

the middle Dutchmen can be seen hunting using a variety of weapons and, on the right, musicians on horseback playing their instruments with one or two slightly bemused-looking Chinese watching them. In contrast, the fan-shaped images along the top, the use of fretwork at the bottom of each panel and the decorations around the edges that include flowers such as chrysanthemums, cherry blossom, roses and peonies, as well as the border with its dragon motifs (dragons being an emblem of good fortune) around the central image, are all traditional decorative Chinese motifs designed to appeal to wealthy customers abroad.

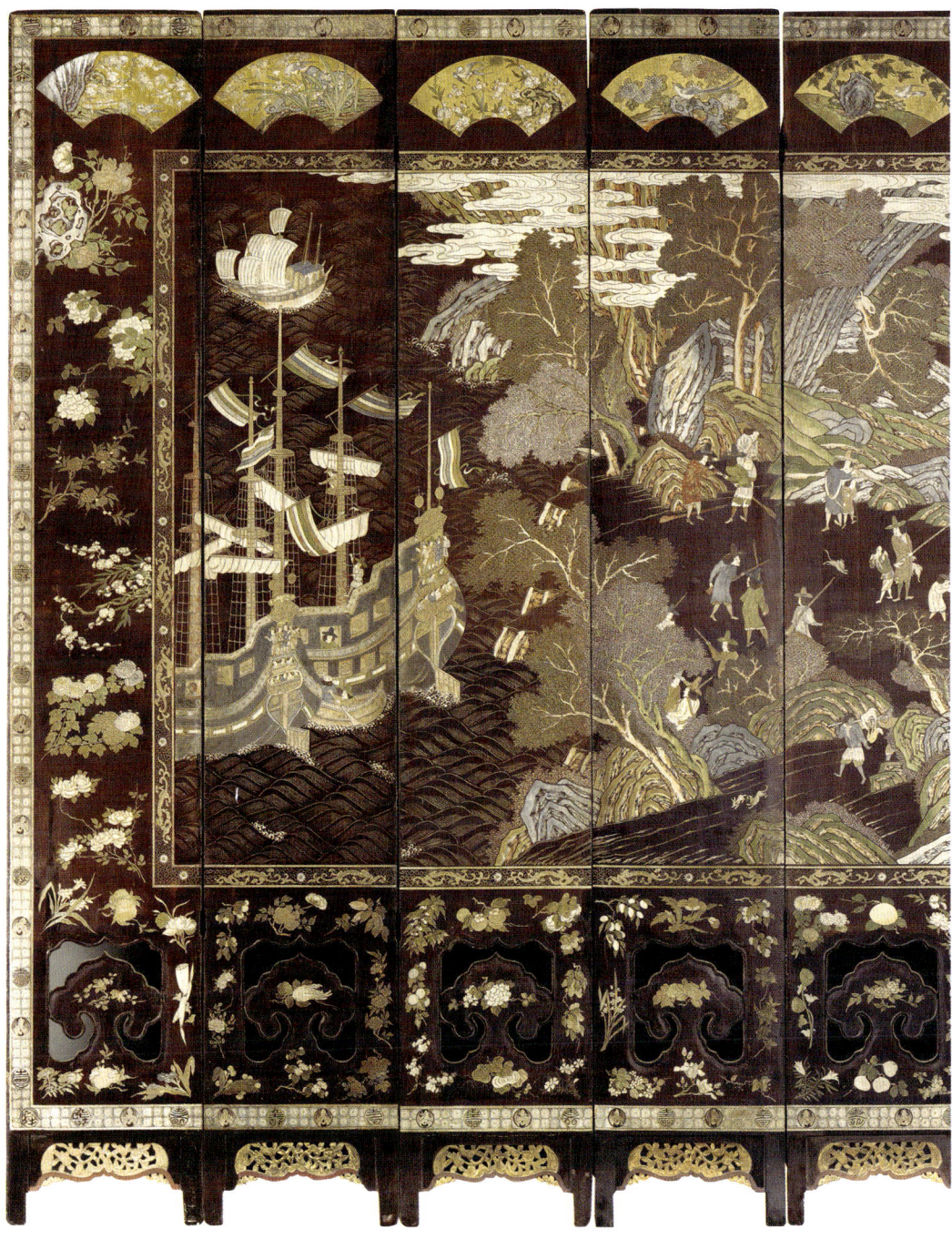

41 Netsuke
(1700–1900)

Artist(s): Unknown

Country of origin: Japan

Dimensions: 4 x 3.5 x 3.1 cm (1½ x 1¼ x 1 inches)

Material(s): Ivory

During the Edo period (1603–1868) in Japan, when both men and women wore kimonos, it was difficult to carry small objects around. Women would put items in the long sleeves of their kimonos, but for men it was more difficult because the things they needed were usually heavier and larger, such as bags of money or writing implements. So they suspended these belongings in a container known as a *sagemono* on a cord from the sash (*obi*) worn around their waists. Netsuke had been developed as basic fasteners (like a toggle) for *inro*, sets of small boxes that linked together and which were used to hold medicine or small seals. As *sagemono*s became more popular, netsuke were adapted to prevent the cord from slipping off the sash and, together with a small bead called an *ojime*, through which the cord ran, they allowed the cord to be loosened or tightened as needed.

The word 'netsuke' derives from two words: *ne* = root and *tsuke* = attached. At first, netsuke were quite plain in design, but as they became more popular, craftsmen took greater trouble over their creation and decoration, and netsuke were divided into different types, such as *karakuri-netsuke* that contained surprise elements like moving parts or *men-netsuke* that imitated Noh mask designs. *Inro* had most often been made from paper or wood and were decorated with lacquerwork, but *inro*, netsuke and the small *ojime* evolved into highly crafted objects. The material used still included wood and lacquer decorations, but some netsuke were carved from ivory or whale bone, while others included precious metals and semi-precious stones as well as coral and shell, or were created from nuts or bamboo and even teeth.

The makers of netsuke drew on a variety of areas for inspiration, including folklore, mythology and legends as well as the natural world, and they displayed an extraordinary attention to detail, as this example depicting a little family group shows, as well as a sense of humour (the figures here are themselves dressed in kimonos, each tied with an *obi*).

Over the years, after a more Western style of dress became more common in Japan, netsuke were less in use, but Westerners were fascinated by them and they have become collectors' items.

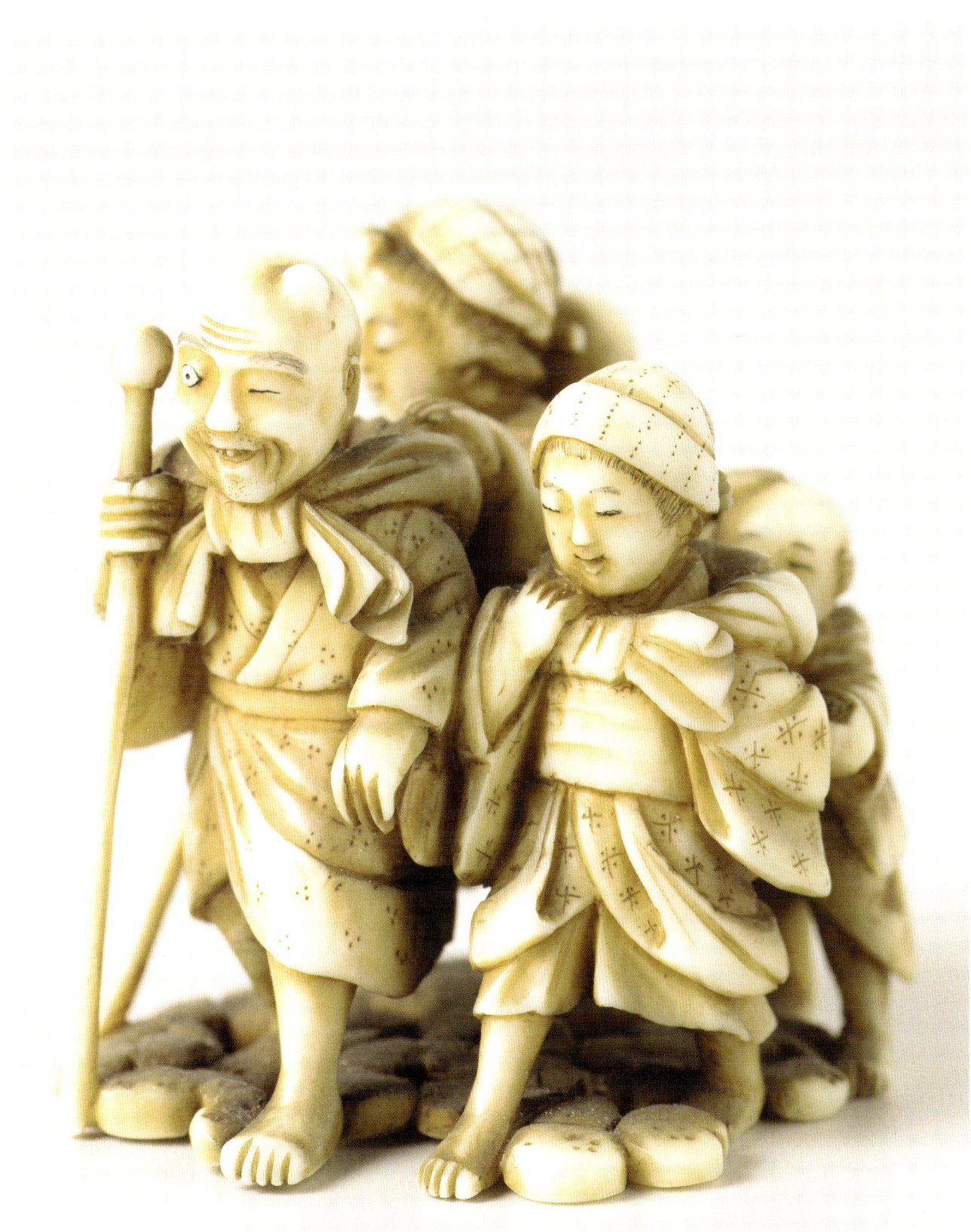

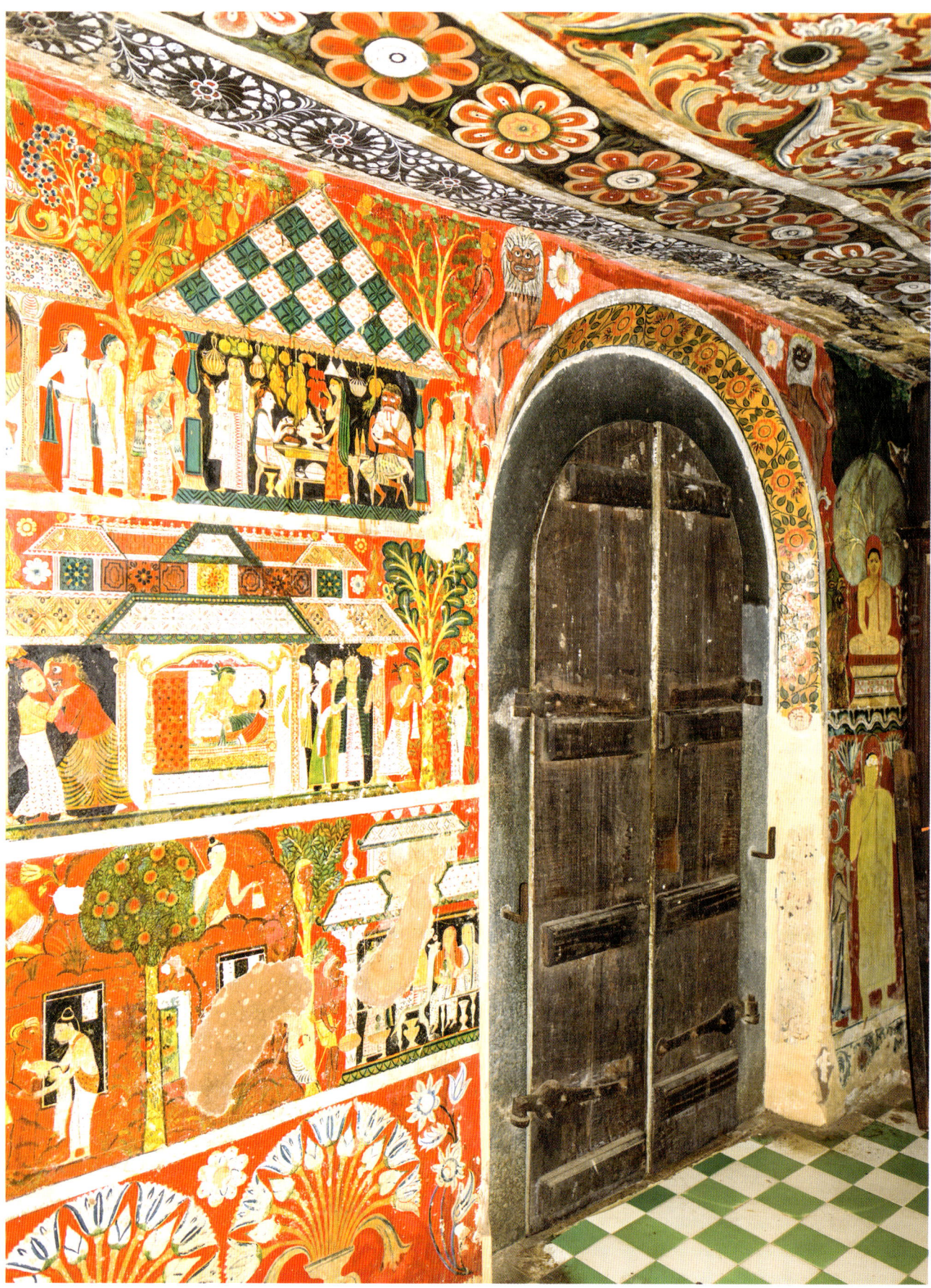

Mulkirigala Frescoes
(c. 1747–82)

Artist(s): Unknown

Country of origin: Sri Lanka

Dimensions: 7 temples on a rock (height 205 m/673 ft)

Material(s): Stone and paints made from clay, limestone and sand and vegetable dyes

Located in the far south of Sri Lanka, the ancient Buddhist temple of Mulkirigala Raja Maha Vihara was built in the 3rd century by the order of the king. Consisting of seven *vihara*s (monastic dwellings), it sits on a large, 205-m (673-ft) rock. One of the *vihara*s is also renowned as the site where a sapling was grown from a cutting taken from the Jaya Sri Maha Bodhi, a tree that in turn originated from the one under which Siddhartha Gautama attained enlightenment.

It was during the reign of the Kandyan king Kirti Sri Rajasinghe (1747–82) that the temple was refurbished and filled with Buddha statues and the magnificent frescoes that adorn the walls. While the Kandyan kings were keen to promote the arts and literature, the general level of education among the populace was low, and that included the monks, most of whom had not even attained *Upasampada* (ordination). This changed at the beginning of the Kandyan dynasty and monks began to preach Buddhism to the people. However, because literacy levels were almost non-existent, the monks advised their rulers that accounts of the Buddha's lives (the Jataka Stories) and Buddhist traditions should be painted on the walls of the temples in such a way that anyone could follow the narratives as in medieval European frescoes.

Working on a wet, white lime clay, the artists divided the walls into several rows and the stories were depicted from right to left. Each scene was then painted against a red background, using a restricted palette of some 40 shades. The paints were made by mixing various natural materials, such as clay, limestone and sand, with plant extracts and oils to create different colours. Variations exist between the frescoes painted in the up-country and low-country temples, including the height of each row of paintings and the complexity of the stories shown, with the low-country examples often being harder to understand. Artistically, the frescoes feature figures positioned in a style known as *Parshawa Darshi Kramaya* that shows the heads and legs facing to one side or another. As with the Kandyan fresco style, scenes are separated by trees, rivers or buildings, while other areas, including ceilings, are decorated with flower patterns, another common trait of the Kandyan era. Now a recognized archaeological site, it is a popular destination for visitors to the country.

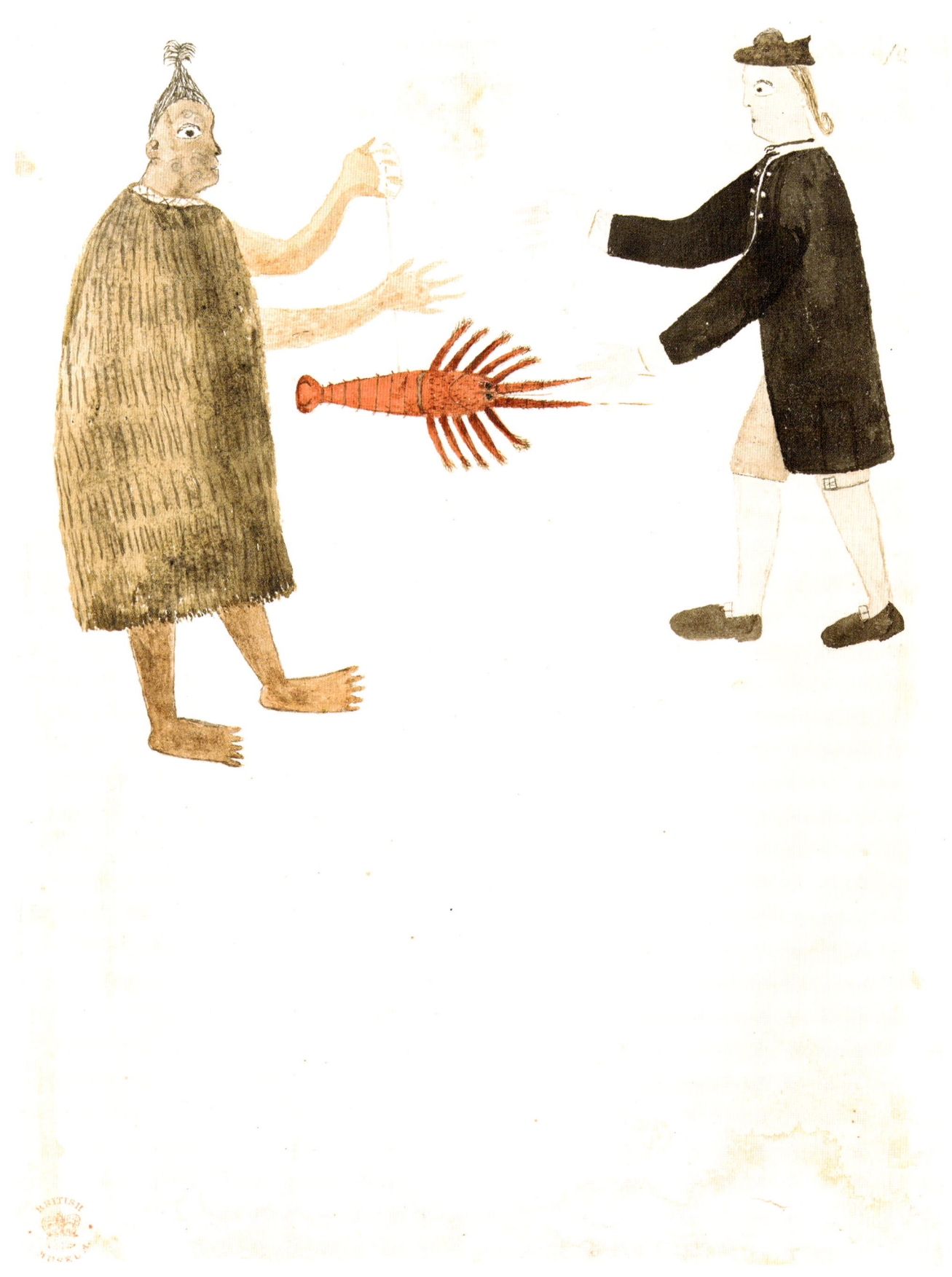

BRITISH

An English Naval Officer Bartering with a Māori
(*c.* 1769)

Artist(s): Tupaia

Country of origin: Aotearoa New Zealand

Dimensions: 26.7 x 21.0 cm (10½ x 8¼ inches)

Material(s): Watercolour on paper

The much-deliberated encounters, interactions and incursions by Europeans in Oceania were, as Nicholas Thomas writes, 'at times tense, but also rich and intimate, and the ramifications for both parties far-reaching'.[35]

From the viewpoint of Māori and European contact, one of the most fascinating encounters is captured by the Ra'iātean priest Tupaia, whose 'naïve' watercolour of a naval officer offering a handkerchief or a piece of barkcloth to a Māori man dressed in a feather cape in exchange for a red lobster is now an emblem of cross-cultural early meetings between these 'two worlds'.[36]

It is well recognized that Tupaia was an artist, scholar, warrior, linguist and navigator, who travelled from Tahiti to New Zealand with the scientifically inclined Joseph Banks and his retinue on HMS *Endeavour* in 1769–70. *An English Naval Officer Bartering with a Māori* captures the sorts of exchanges taking places during this early European voyage. A number of watercolour drawings exist from the expedition – images that were at first attributed to Joseph Banks. In 1998, however, the scholar Harold Carter discovered a letter from the English botanist which made plain that this painting – and other idiosyncratic sketches in the same collection – were by Tupaia. As Banks outlines in a letter to Dawson Turner, in 1812: 'Tupaia the Indian who came with me from Otaheite Learned to draw in a way not Quite unintelligible. The genius for Caricature which all wild people possess Led him to Caricature me & he drew me with a nail in my hand delivering to an Indian who sold me a Lobster....'

What is eye-catching about Tupaia's watercolour is its remarkable sense of acumen as well as a desire for knowledge about the lives of islander peoples. So it is not a complete exaggeration to say that Tupaia's sketches exhibit the ethnographic curiosity shown by European visitors to the Pacific islands. Moreover, another of his watercolour sketches, *Dancing Girl and Chief Mourner, Otaheite* (1769), from Tahiti, of an elaborate constructed funeral costume, is abstracted to the point that it would not go amiss among, say, the studies for costumes and décor by Picasso for the modernist ballet *Parade* in 1917. Tupaia's sketch has been referenced by a number of contemporary artists, including the Niuean-born New Zealand artist John Pule in his 1997 lithograph *Entanglements*.

Vasudhara Mandala
(1777)

Artist(s): Unknown

Country of origin: Nepal

Dimensions: 85.7 × 72.4 cm (33¾ × 28½ inches)

Material(s): Distemper on cloth

Originating from the Kathmandu Valley, this intricate mandala with its vibrant colours is the earliest dated example of a *paubha*, or traditional devotional painting, produced by the Newar in Nepal. The Newar have lived in the Kathmandu Valley in Nepal ('Nepal' is the Sanskrit, or literary, equivalent of 'Newar') for hundreds of years, and it was they who established the culture of the area. The descendants of various Indo-Aryan and Tibeto-Burman tribes, they have strong links with Buddhism and Hinduism.

Vasudhara is a Buddhist goddess (her name means 'stream of gems') who represents prosperity and wealth. She is often compared to the Hindu goddess Bhumidevi (who represents similar elements) and both Buddhists and Hindus would pray to these goddesses for abundant harvests. One tenet of Buddhism is to reject wealth, but it is accepted that appealing to Vasudhara is usually done to request good fortune for all.

Vasudhara also embodies the desire to learn and in this *paubha* she holds a sutra in her left hand representing the perfection of wisdom. Also on her left is a green image of the Bodhisattva Vajrapani; while on her right is a red image of the Bodhisattva Avalokiteshvara. To emphasize Vasudhara's role as a bringer of prosperity, there are depictions of Vajrapani's *yakshas* opening sacks of jewels and chests of treasure. The *yakshas* are male deities who are also associated with wealth and protection. Below Vasudhara is her attendant, Ila Devi. Four more *yakshas*, with yellow mandorlas (auras), protect the portals of the central mandalas. These are Manibhadra, Purnabhadra, Dhana and Veshavarna. Their consorts, the Gupta Devi, Sagputa Devi, Sarasvati Devi and Chandrakanta Devi, sit in the four corners. The mandala is also decorated with bands of lotuses and a ring of multicoloured flames, and in the corners of the outer square are four of the Pancha Raksha (protector goddesses). Vasudhara herself represents the fifth protector goddess. A lengthy description of the iconography in this mandala can be found in the text known as the *Vasndharoddhesa*.

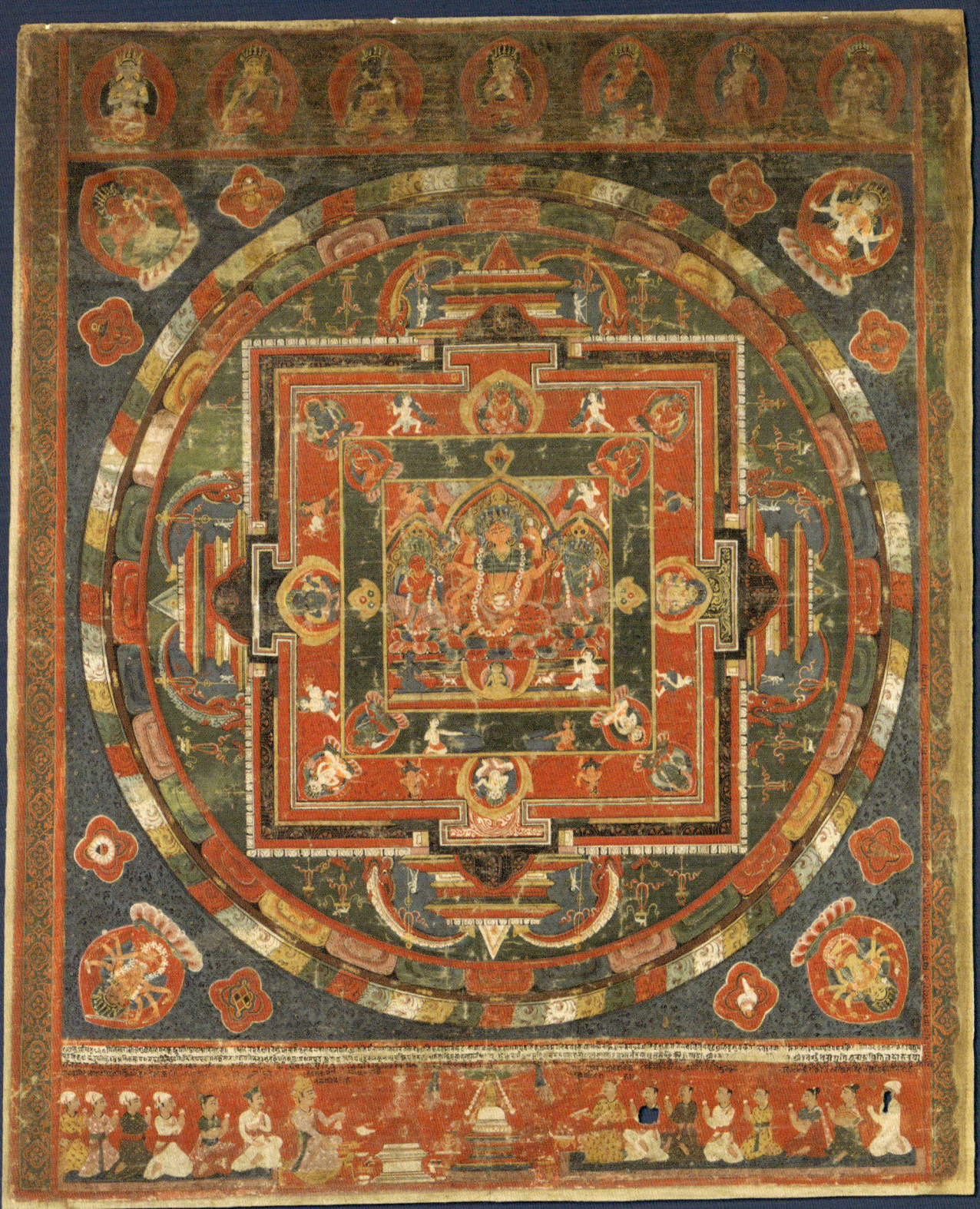

45 Feather Cloak (*'Ahu'ula*)
(Presented in 1778)

Artist(s): Unknown

Country of origin: Hawai'i, USA

Dimensions: 71 x 140 cm (28 x 55 inches)

Material(s): Fibre and feathers

Feathered objects were key to political and religious change in the Hawai'ian islands. Early voyagers (possibly from the Society Islands some 3,220 km/2,000 miles away) settled around 700–800 CE on the largely fertile islands, situated at the northernmost point of Polynesia. Relative isolation helped shape a highly idiosyncratic society in the form of chieftainship, religious custom and material culture. In 18th-century Hawai'i, political transformation was sparked by the veneration of one god figure in particular: the principal deity Kū – the god of war.

Feathered god images, woodcarvings, temples, staffs, sashes, helmets, capes and cloaks were all used to signify Kū's dominance. Heavy feathered cloaks (*ahu'ula*) denoted prestige and authority (*mana*) in connection with divine beings. Feathers were gathered and knotted into a fibre netting for the most influential of chiefs (*ali'i*). It is reported that King Kamehameha owned a cloak made from roughly 500,000 yellow mamo feathers plucked from some 80,000 birds. Chiefs tracked their genealogical lines back to creation gods, many related to birds that could fly between the living and deific realms. Akin to Tahitian *'maro'ura* (feathered girdles), these garments were indicative of Tahitian 'society's highest ranking kin-titles',[37] which were 'jealously fought over'.[38] Cloaks and other feathered garments were handed down through the generations, used to strengthen political connections and worn during warfare and religious ceremonies.

On arrival at Kealakekua Bay in Hawai'i on 26 January 1779, which coincided with the *makahiki* ritual and New Year festival, the local chief Kalani'ōpu'u greeted Captain Cook with his own ceremonial feather cloak and placed a feathered helmet (*mahiole*) on his head. Dressed in a chief's feathered cloak and helmet, Cook had been sanctified as the provisional incarnation of the god Lono. This *'ahu'ula* was 'worn by less powerful leaders' and is one of roughly 30 or so garments presented to Cook and his crew between 1778 and 1779. In an incident that was directly associated with 'the priests' reified... conception of Cook as the divine Lono' – 'the dying god', the captain was killed on 14 February at Kealakekua. Cook, now intrinsically linked with the deity Lono, had returned unexpectedly to the island after damage to the *Resolution*, and was subsequently caught up in a local power struggle. As leader, Cook was an unexpected returning force, which likely had to be restrained by Hawai'ian leaders. As Sahlins brilliantly identifies: 'Associated with *Kū* in their capacity as warriors, the King and his chiefs entertained ambivalent relations with Cook/Lono and his priests that seem altogether consistent with the cosmological antitheses of the Makahiki season ... and the more dangerous his relationship to the chiefs.'[39] Such was the intensely potent power and art of a Hawai'ian cloak.

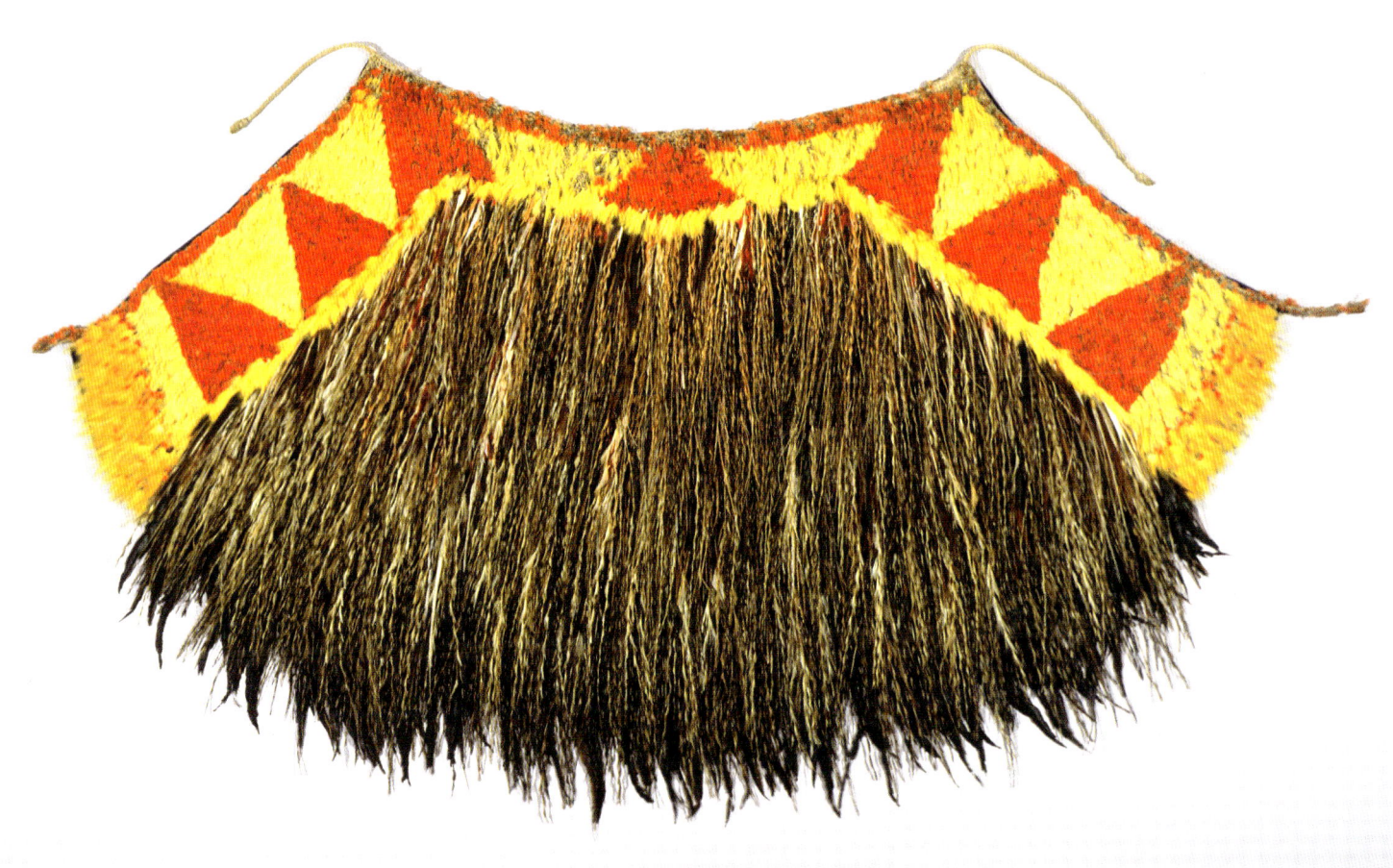

46 *Nelumbium speciosum* (now *Nelumbo nucifera*) (*c.* 1789–1814)

Artist(s): Unknown

Country of origin: India

Dimensions: 30 x 21 cm (12 x 8 inches)

Material(s): Watercolour on paper

Commonly known as the Sacred or Indian lotus, this delicate aquatic plant is a member of the family Nelumbonaceae, and is often confused with a waterlily. Lotus flowers are a common design motif in India and across other areas of Asia, thanks to their representation of enlightenment or purity of the soul. More often, though, it is the blue lotus flower that is depicted rather than this pink-tinged, ivory-white species.

This illustration is typical of the style of botanical artworks made for the collection of Dr William Roxburgh (1751–1815), who worked first for the British East India Company and then as Naturalist for the Madras government and Superintendent of the Calcutta Botanical Garden. Roxburgh created a collection of approximately 900 artworks that depicted plants he studied during his time in India, which was first published as part of his three-volume work *Plants of the Coast of Coromandel* (1795–1819).

Although the names of the majority of the artists who produced the artworks for the collection were not recorded, it is believed that they were trained in the techniques of intricate Mughal miniature painting. In all likelihood, the artists came from a long line of family painters because the tradition usually passed down from father to son. Brushes were hand-made and exceptionally fine, using hair shed by kittens or squirrels. They would have made their own watercolours, grinding mineral pigments such as lapis lazuli (for blue), malachite (for green), grading them by shade, or possibly using earth or insects, and then adding a form of gum arabic or glue to turn them into a paste. Using a drier-than-usual brush, the colour was generally applied more opaquely than is normal for watercolour, building up layers of wash on the paper.

Beautiful in its simplicity, the artwork represents the development of a centuries-old painting technique harnessed to a Western requirement for scientific accuracy in botanical artwork.

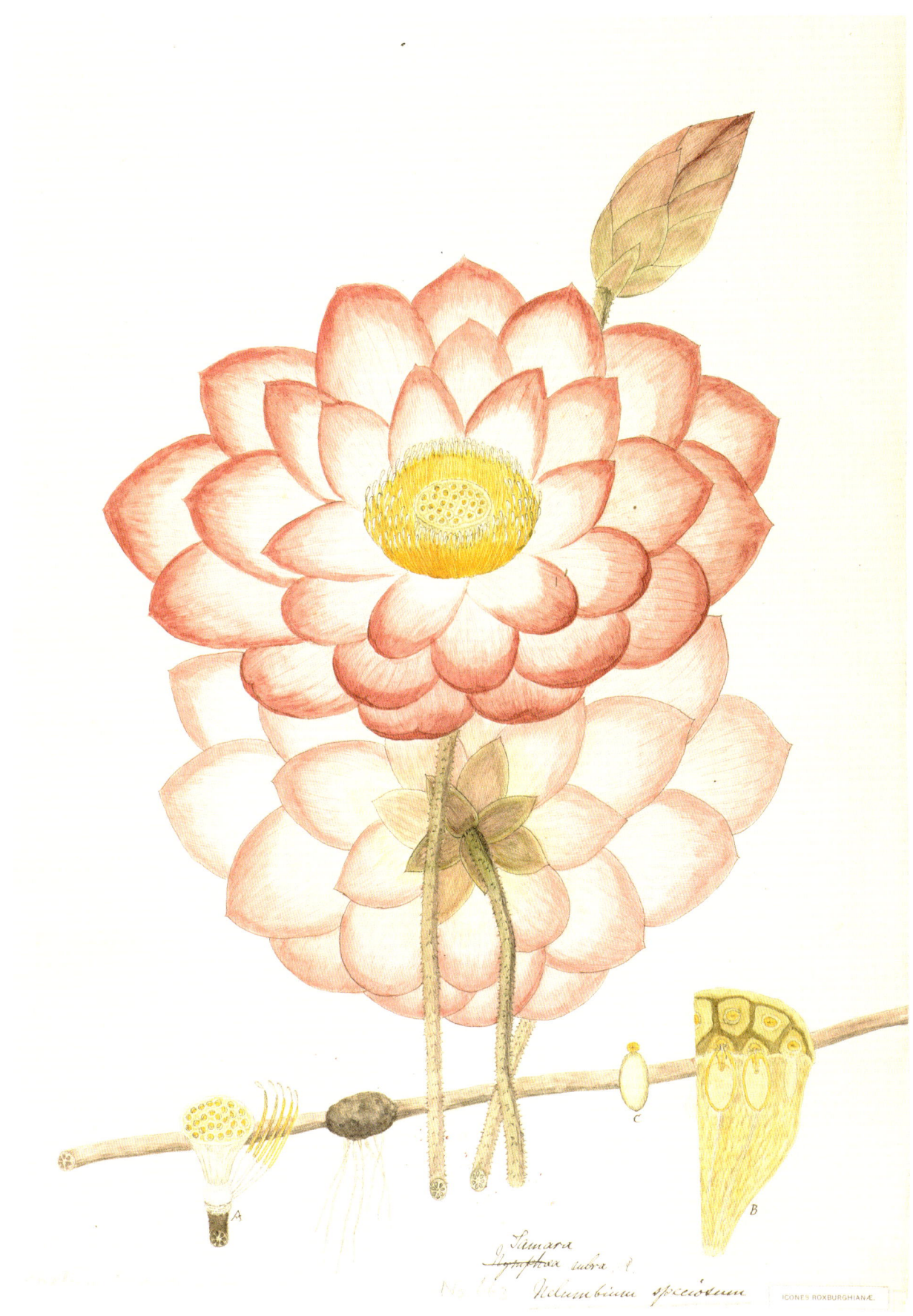

Samara

Nymphaea rubra ?

Nelumbium speciosum

ICONES ROXBURGHIANÆ

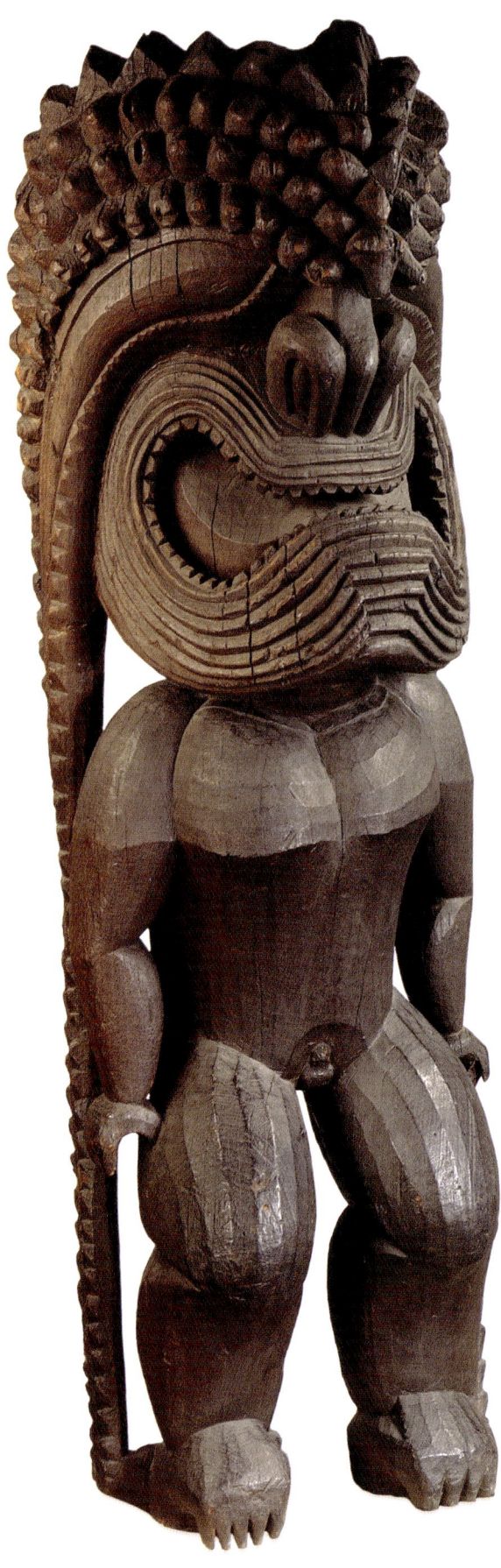

Kūkaʻilimoku (or Kū) Figure
(1790–1819)

Artist(s): Unknown

Country of origin: Hawaiʻi, USA

Dimensions: 267 x 69 cm (105 x 27 inches)

Material(s): Breadfruit tree wood

This temple *kiʻi* (statue, image or likeness) was donated to the British Museum in 1839 and is now a masterpiece of its Pacific collection. It's a powerful-looking statue with an enormous crest of hair and aggressive-looking mouth, cut from breadfruit timber (*Artocarpus altilis* sp.) and carved in the distinctive manner of Hawaiʻi's Kona region. An illustrated account by Jacques Argo, produced during an early French colonial expedition in 1817–20, shows an array of these colossal carvings at Kailua, in Hawaiʻi, in 1819. They were created during the reign of chief Kamehameha (*c.* 1758–1819) and erected to protect the temple ground (*heiau*). It is one of three existing Kū figures, the other two carvings being currently in the Bishop Museum, Honolulu, and the Peabody Museum of Natural History in Massachusetts, USA.

The great chief, who was the first to conquer and amalgamate the islands of the Hawaiʻian archipelago and become its first king, embraced 'Kū – the snatcher of land' – as his chosen god. Argo's image shows the Hawaiʻian *heiau* empty, with its statues in partial disarray, so the British Museum's large standing male figure may have been acquired from the temple grounds after its desertion. In general, Argo's image reflects state-sponsored 'discovery' at a time when the French and British naval powers were vying for colonial territory in the early part of the 19th century.

Adrienne Kaeppler has labelled Kū's countenance and its extensions 'the mouth of disrespect', where 'the chin juts forward and the mouth… is open wide (*oleʻole*), distends backward, shows teeth, and sometimes displays a protruding tongue'. Kaeppler has further suggested that such an expression is 'permissible in Hawaiʻian culture only by those at the very top [of society], or by enemies in war'.[40] Priests also called on the god Kū during rituals on the *heiau*, his rigid stance and belligerent expression demonstrating his power and readiness for war. The figure's hair is illustrated by four rows of animal heads, possibly dogs, one of the forms Kū could take on. The Hawaiʻian god Kūkā ʻilimoku took many forms, the god of war being just one manifestation.

With respect to this Hawaiʻian wood carving, Adrienne Kaeppler has proposed a connection between Kū and the Hawaiʻian god Lono. As such, Kū is counterbalanced by Lono, who, in his numerous indicators, is associated with peaceful agricultural activities. His hair likely amalgamates schematic pigs' heads that imply an added affinity with the deity Lono, the pig probably emblematic of wealth, with dogs and pigs also sacrificial animals. Collectively, the two competing forces illustrate the complementary characteristics of Hawaiʻian religion. As is well known, the colossal temple statues still hold profound importance for many Hawaiʻians. In 2010, the Bishop Museum in Honolulu gathered all three Kū figures on the islands; they had not been together for more than 170 years.

48 War Club (‘U‘u)
(Late 18th–Early 19th Century)

Artist(s): Unknown

Country of origin: Marquesas Islands, French Polynesia

Dimensions: 138 cm (54⅓ inches)

Material(s): Ironwood, sennet (coconut fibre) and human hair

‘**In all probability** Marquesan settlement pre-dates the beginning of the first millennium CE by at least a few hundred years, most likely to CE 700-900.’[41] Europeans first visited this key group of Polynesian islands in 1595, a violent encounter that ended in the death of more than 200 Marquesans. The islands were not visited again until Captain Cook's time in 1774, while the northwest islands were only spotted once more in 1791 by American and French sailors. An attempt by the London Missionary Society to establish a religious colony also failed in 1797. In the 19th century, whalers saw the Marquesas Islands as a vital refuelling stop where they traded cloth, metal, muskets and whales' teeth for timber and food stuffs.

In addition, Europeans were especially taken by widespread tattooing, with men adopting absolute body coverage. The custom was carried out by *tuhuna*, experts who fulfilled an ecclesiastic-like function. An engraving after Captain David Porter, who visited Nuka Hiva on the US navy ship *Essex* in 1813–14, illustrates *Mouina, Chief Warrior of the Tayehs* (1815, Wellcome Library, London) enveloped in tattoos. The Marquesan term for tattooing is *patu tiki*, ‘to tattoo’ or ‘to make *tiki*’, which the anthropologist Alfred Gell befittingly translates as ‘wrapping in images’. The warrior chief sports a triton shell trumpet with a toggle of human hair, a sperm-whale-tooth necklace, a wood and seed choker, and ivory or wood ear decorations, as well as a cloak and feather headdress. Most notably, he carries a war club (‘u‘u) in his left hand, which he points to with his right forefinger to indicate the weapon and staff of a warrior.

His club is strikingly similar to our own ‘u‘u. These bifacial clubs with a sequence of different yet similar *tiki* heads and faces watchfully staring in all directions, are ‘psychologically potent objects... [made] powerful by their metaphysical nature and their multiplicity’. And if we follow Gell's supposition that ‘art’ objects are persons in artefact form, then these objects are associated with the anthropomorphic chief/god image. As the French artist Paul Gauguin noted, ‘The basis of this art is the human body or face. The face, especially. You're astonished to find a face where you thought there was a strange geometrical figure. Always the same thing and yet never the same thing.’ Gauguin was denoting the recurrence of stylized *tiki* and schematic designs across the entirety of Marquesan material culture, especially the cleverness of its artistic play. This it to say, its formal variations, droll visual puns and ironic references ‘that kept the endless iteration of the same alive with the constant slip and surprise of minor differences’.[42]

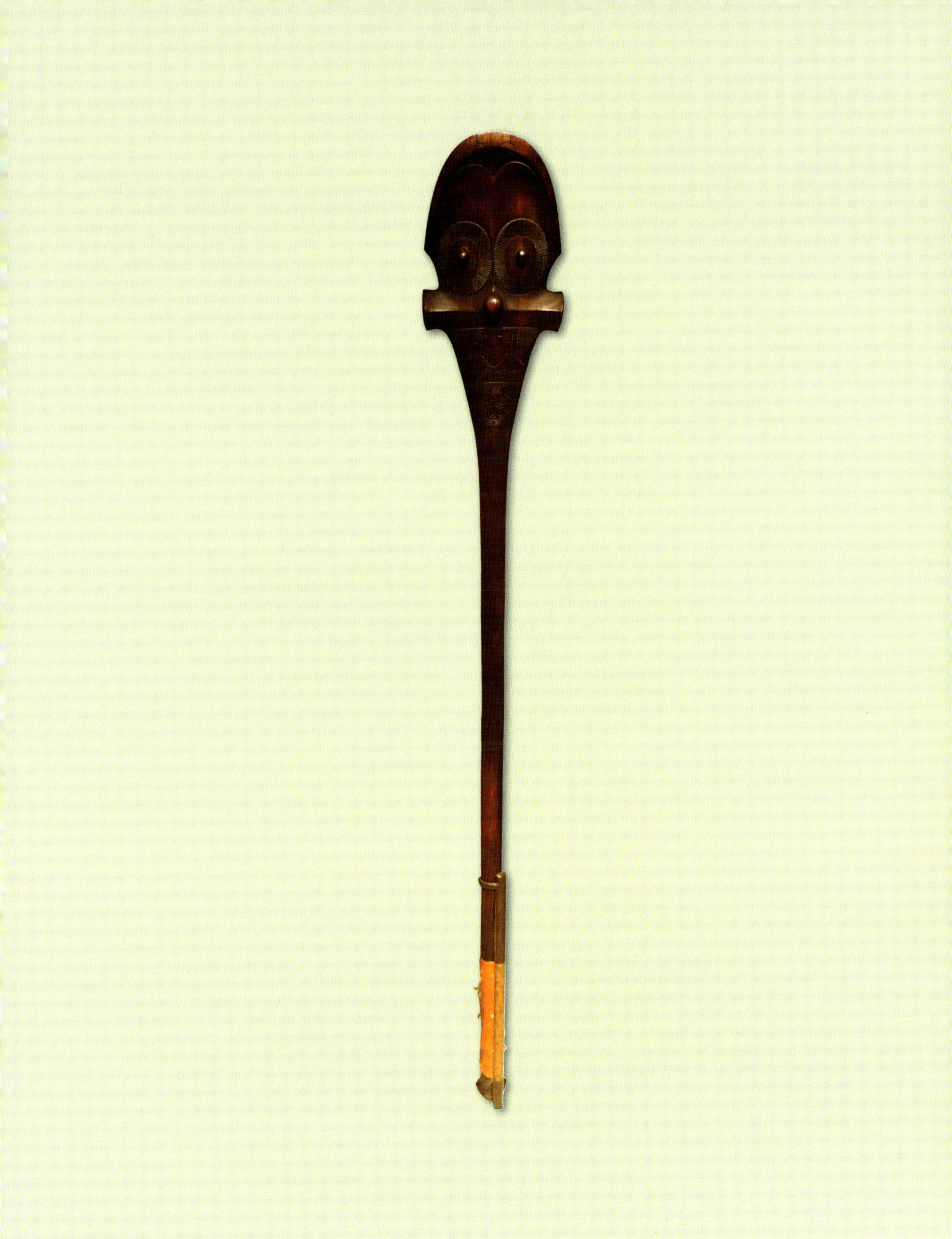

49 *Nō* Kimono
(Early 19th Century)

Artist(s): Unknown

Country of origin: Japan

Dimensions: 166 x 144 cm
(65 x 57 inches)

Material(s): Satin damask,
silk and metallic embroidery

Little evidence remains of the first Japanese fabrics. However, an 8th-century piece of silk garment in the Shōsō-in treasure house of Tōdai-ji Temple in Nara, as well as picture scrolls from the Heian period (794 and 1185) and especially the illustrious text *The Tale of Genji* (11th century), show aristocrats wearing luxurious silk robes and exquisite costumes. Prior to the introduction of European clothing, the customary attire was the Japanese kimono, which had no tailor-making or lining per se, but served as a basis for very stylish clothing patterns. Thus, traditional *Nō* costumes are kimonos of one sort or another. Surviving examples date mostly from the late Muromachi era of the Ashikaga Shogunate (1338–1573). A kimono consists of a rectangular body piece with wide sleeves and the collar and neck made from a single piece of material. The kimono is held together by an *obi*, a sash fastened around the hips or waist.

Japanese *Nō* theatre is an elaborate blend of music, dance, language, costume and high moral ideals. *Nō* is the tragic form of theatrical play in line with Zen ideas of self-control, humility, austerity of effort and economy of expression. The word means 'accomplishment' or 'perfected art' and is meant to articulate practical as well as artistic ambitions. Traditionally, major characters, the *shi'te*, wear costumes and masks, with both male and female roles played by men or young boys. *Nō* dramas can be divided into five major categories: plays about a specific deity (*kami*); 'battle plays' dealing with ghosts from the 12th-century Genji–Heike wars or heroic figures from Japanese history; *Kazura Nō*, or

'wig' plays, which largely focus on obsessive love; *Zatsu* or disparate *Nō* plays dealing with madness or obsession on the part the living or tales of spirits unable to vacate the human realm; and *Kiri*, stories of demons (*kichiku*) or supernatural beings illustrating the struggle between good and evil.

A typical *Nō* kimono requires highly sophisticated embroidery to depict, for instance, seashells, clouds, cherry blossom or the red and pink berries of the nandina plant that was thought to augur good fortune. Costumes of this kind also evidence a technique termed *nuihaku*, where gold leaf is pounded into the silk to create a glittering backdrop. The *Nō* costume shown here includes dandelions, cherry blossom and carriages that would have been used by the aristocracy.

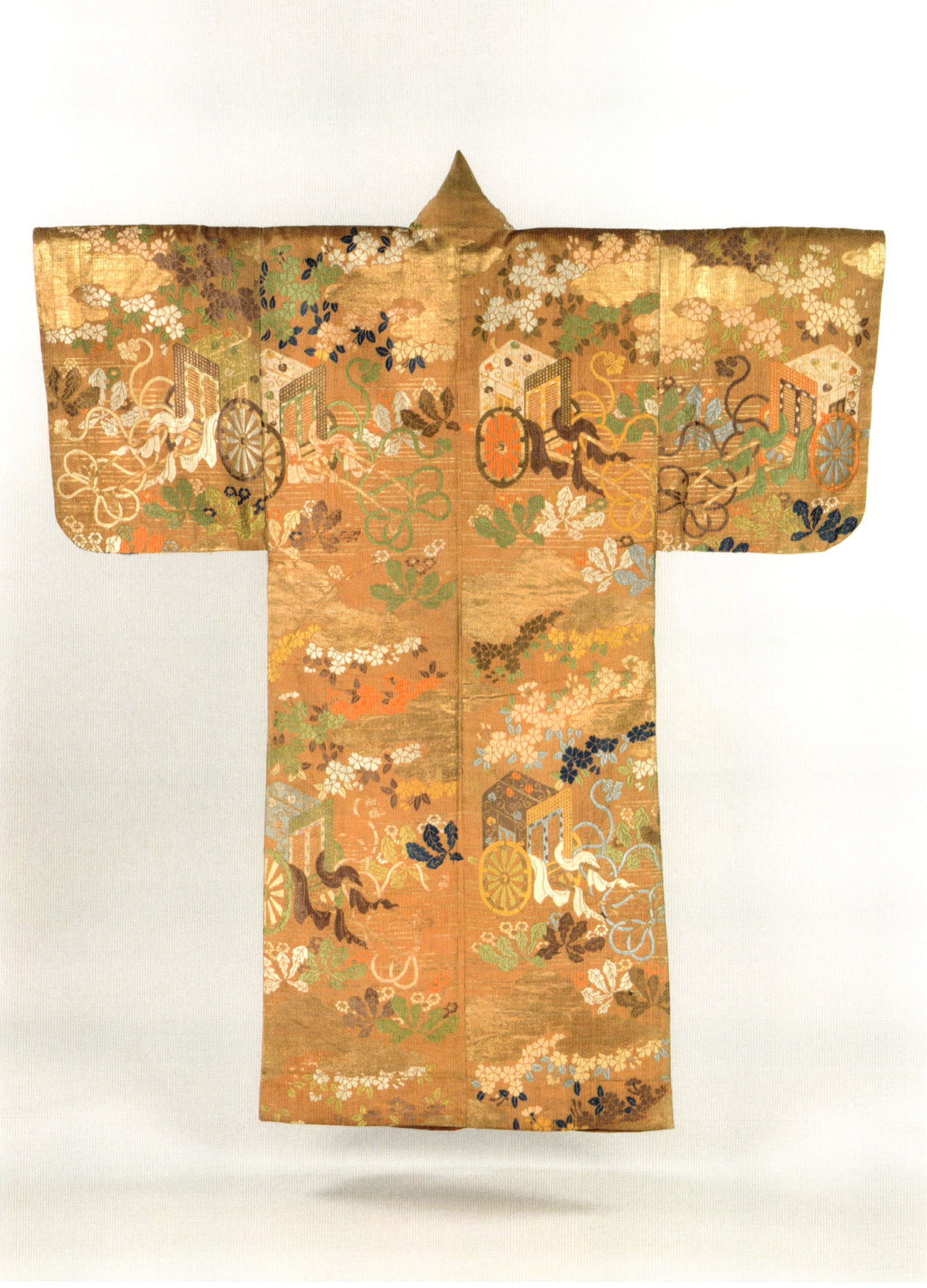

50 Broad Shield
(Early 19th Century)

Artist(s): Unknown

Country of origin: Australia

Dimensions: Height 92 cm
(36 inches)

Materials: Natural pigments
on wood

European colonial interests in Australia meant that countless Aboriginal peoples were dispossessed of land, devastated by viruses, killed, forced to inhabit government resettlement camps, separated from kin and their children taken away. Equally, Aborigines effectively lost touch with the Dreaming (their accounts and belief system underpinning creation), making it hard to resume their traditional life and rituals. By the end of the 19th century, it was assumed by the broader public that in the Southeast territories, Aboriginal art had completely died out. Through the colonial lens, this broad shield and other indigenous weapons are often obscured from real events and historically hard to unravel.

Nonetheless, as specialists in the artefacts of Southeast Australia have observed, the earliest interactions with European outsiders reveal a keen interest in the trade of Aboriginal artefacts. David Collins, who arrived with the First Fleet officials in February 1788, recorded that 'most of us have made collections of their spears, throwing sticks etc., as opportunities occurred.'[43] It is very likely that many shields, boomerangs, spears and spear-throwers were explicitly manufactured with trade in mind. Overall, the objects mirror a 19th-century European fascination with weapons and their aesthetic forms, many of which are elaborately decorated, their surfaces covered with intricately incised designs and coloured with earth pigments. Occasionally, the patterns have 'naturalistic' motifs like emu, possum or humanoid figures carved into the shield's surface. This aesthetic is highly representative of weaponry from New South Wales and Victoria. The richly burnished wood and sharply ribbed surface engraving add colour, feel and diversity to the shield. Regardless, most weapons have lost their elaborate vibrancy due to wear and tear. Originally, the incised surfaces and primary motifs were filled in and painted in similar or contrasting colours.

In all but a handful of cases, the most basic information about the weapon's origins – who made or used it, why it was made and for what reason – is lost. Southeastern shields were frequently employed in dance ceremonies or bartered as important artistic items. However, shields were chiefly used as defence against flying objects, or in close-range fighting, especially in battles for precious resources, land and women. Collins's early observations suggest that Aboriginal shields were also symbols of identity: 'It must be observed that the principal tribes have their peculiar weapons... [and] they extended this peculiarity even to songs and their dialects,'[44] he wrote. However, the shields are visual conundrums whose early history and 'signs' are largely enigmatic.

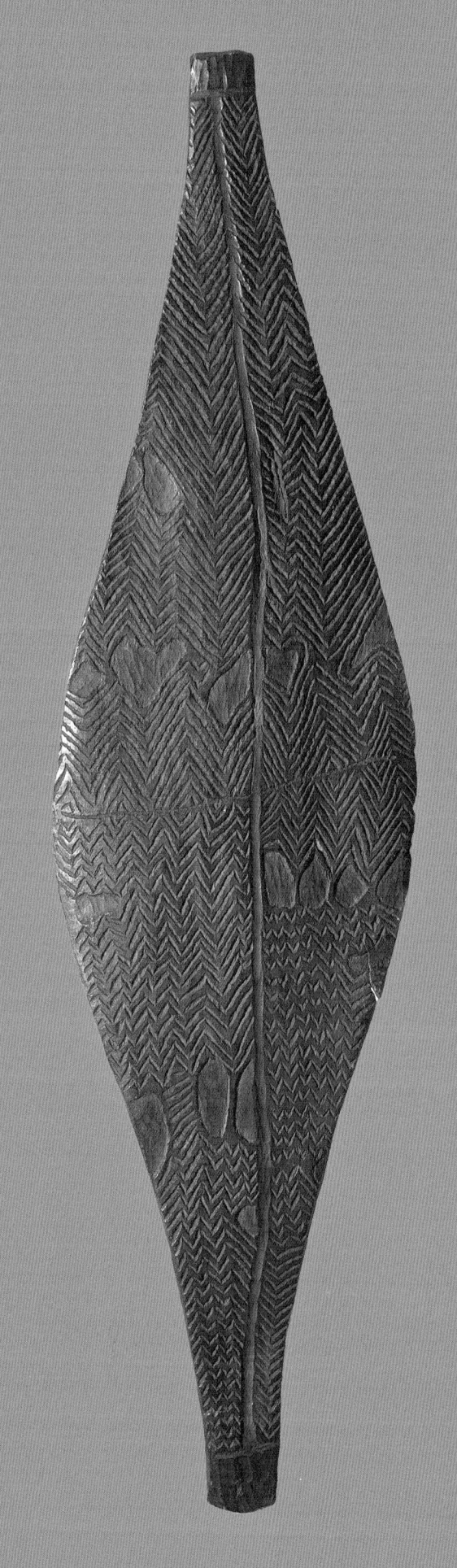

51 Hornbill Sculpture (*Kenyalang*)
(Early to Mid 19th Century)

Artist(s): Unknown

Country of origin: Sarawak, Malaysia

Dimensions: 57 x 86 x 14 cm (22^1/$_2$ x 34 x 5^1/$_2$ inches)

Materials: Wood, paint, cotton thread, plant material, wool

In any society, art has inestimable purposes. However, its principal application is to establish contact with the hidden realm. In traditional island societies, moreover, art helps groups maintain contact with the world of 'spirit' ancestors, gods and other preternatural entities. It also helps create coalitions between families and societal groups, promotes social status and reinforces political power, while enriching the visual appearance and force of the environment that people inhabit.

In Southeast Asian cultures, a universal belief system founded on a three-way concept of the cosmos frequently involves the representation of a large serpent, turtle, bird and so forth, upon which the whole universal fabric rests. In the cosmology of the Iban people of northwest Borneo, rhinoceros hornbills were formerly associated with headhunting, where an avian creature is believed to be an emissary to the god of war. Produced among the Iban, these large sculptures involve stylized representations of the Brahminy kite (*Haliastur indus*) and the Rhinoceros hornbill (*Buceros rhinoceros*). These are large species of forest bird whose beak is surmounted by a prominent horn-like protuberance, termed a casque and depicted in *kenyalang* sculpture as a spiralling form.

In Sarawak (one of the Malaysian parts of Borneo), *kenyalang* sculptures play a crucial role in ritual. The hornbill effigy is a powerful intermediary, possibly representative of the creator god, or a substitute for a human ancestor. In all instances, the kite and hornbill are associated with the upper world and maleness, while the netherworld concerns serpents, womanhood and cultivation. Hornbill statues are the showpiece of the *gawai kenyalang* ceremony held, in earlier times, by a prominent male leader, warrior or his descendants. Subsequently, *kenyalang* are a stand-in for the heads captured during fruitful expeditions, with hornbill effigies a marker of family status, personal triumph and achievement. In Iban society, the *kenyalang* were sanctified and raised on tall poles, and the lifeforce of the hornbill was believed to fly and diminish any enemy. Similarly, in *gawai burong* rites among Barito peoples of Borneo, hornbill sculptures are extravagantly bedecked on long wooden poles that symbolize the 'tree of life', joining together the upper and lower realms – the sky with the earth, male and female fertility, and the derivation of life and prosperity itself. Fabricating *kenyalang* was thought to be a perilous task that necessitated rituals, sacrifices and ceremonies to receive and honour the felled tree. In Iban culture, traditional styles of *kenyalang* have since been adapted to accommodate Christian and Muslim faiths.

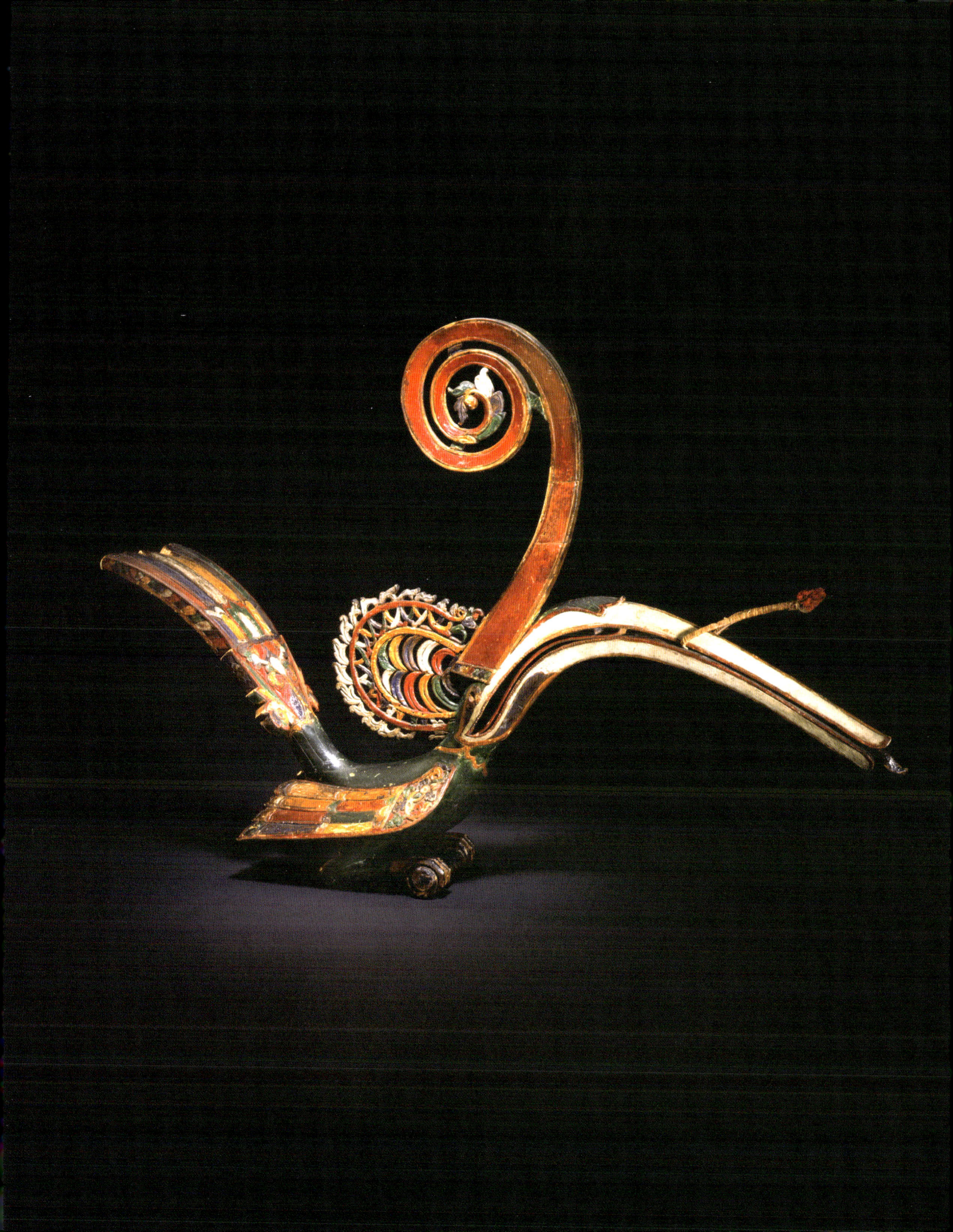

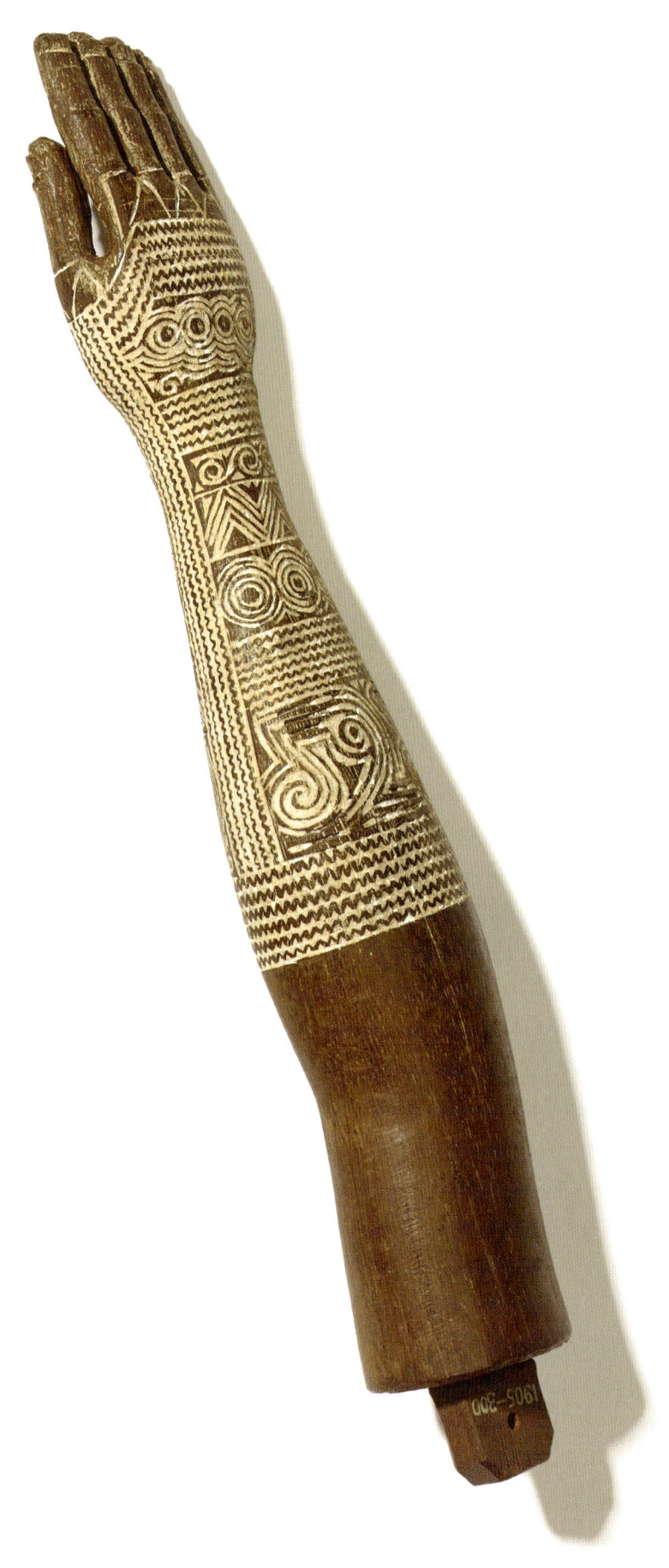

52 Model of a Tattooed Arm
(19th Century)

Artist(s): Unknown Kayan

Country of origin: Sarawak, Malaysia

Dimensions: 35 x 5.2 cm (13³/₄ x 2 inches)

Material(s): Wood

Like many non-Western cultures, Southeast Asians have differing views about the world and the accommodation of art within it. Of course, Western and Eastern cultures recognize the capability of 'art' to indicate authority and significance. However, in Western societies, art is generally appreciated in seclusion, such as in an exhibition setting. So it remains separate from the collective body and has no everyday practical purpose in the sense of a wider societal world view. Creative standards and otherworldly beliefs in Southeast Asia might correspondingly be connected with transitory approaches to art, including the tattoos on the body or face, 'conceived in part as a kind of screen behind and beyond which a deeper reality operates'.[45]

Tattoos (*tedek*) were at one time prolific throughout Southeast Asian society. In Borneo, tattooing was practised on both men and women, and differed according to a particular community. It was carried out with a piercing needle and a type of mallet, female tattoo artists driving the ink – extracted with 'soot', grease and sugarcane – beneath the skin.

For the Kayan people of Borneo, *tedek* recorded the accomplishments or triumphs of an individual, to affirm eligibility regarding marriage, to function as defensive symbols and indicate rank in a distinctly hierarchical Kayan society. Traditionally, designs such as the mythical *aso* (dog-dragon) or images of its eyes were sported by a chief to mark his highborn standing, while a 'plain' four-line design identified a lowlier person. Among the Kayan, boys were tattooed at important festivals, which involved the use of inked wooden blocks cut by men. A popular hook design, for instance, was first outlined manually or stamped onto the skin, customarily the thighs. Boys were also tattooed with uninterrupted lines on the thighs, hands, arms and shoulders, which could take many years depending on cost and ceremonial prerequisites.

This model of an arm illustrates designs that were deemed apt for a Kayan woman. Here they cover the forearm and back of the hands, but women's tattoos were similarly applied to the fingers, toes and thighs, entailing non-representational designs linked to the natural environment and fecundity. Tattooing was taboo during illness, bereavement or throughout the rice-planting season. And before tattooing, there were important rituals to be observed for the appeasement of spirits, with constraints put upon both the tattooist and the person being tattooed, including the consumption of special foods. More crucially, Kayan tattooing practice has importance beyond the worldly domain. As Hendrik Tillema explains of Apo Kayan *tedek*, the soul is first scrutinized by an otherworldly custodian, before traversing a bridge into the land of the dead. Granted that the underworld is a reflection of the living world, for this to occur, the darkly coloured tattoos must be whole in order to radiate and light up the way after death. Only then could the soul join up with its ancestors in the afterlife.

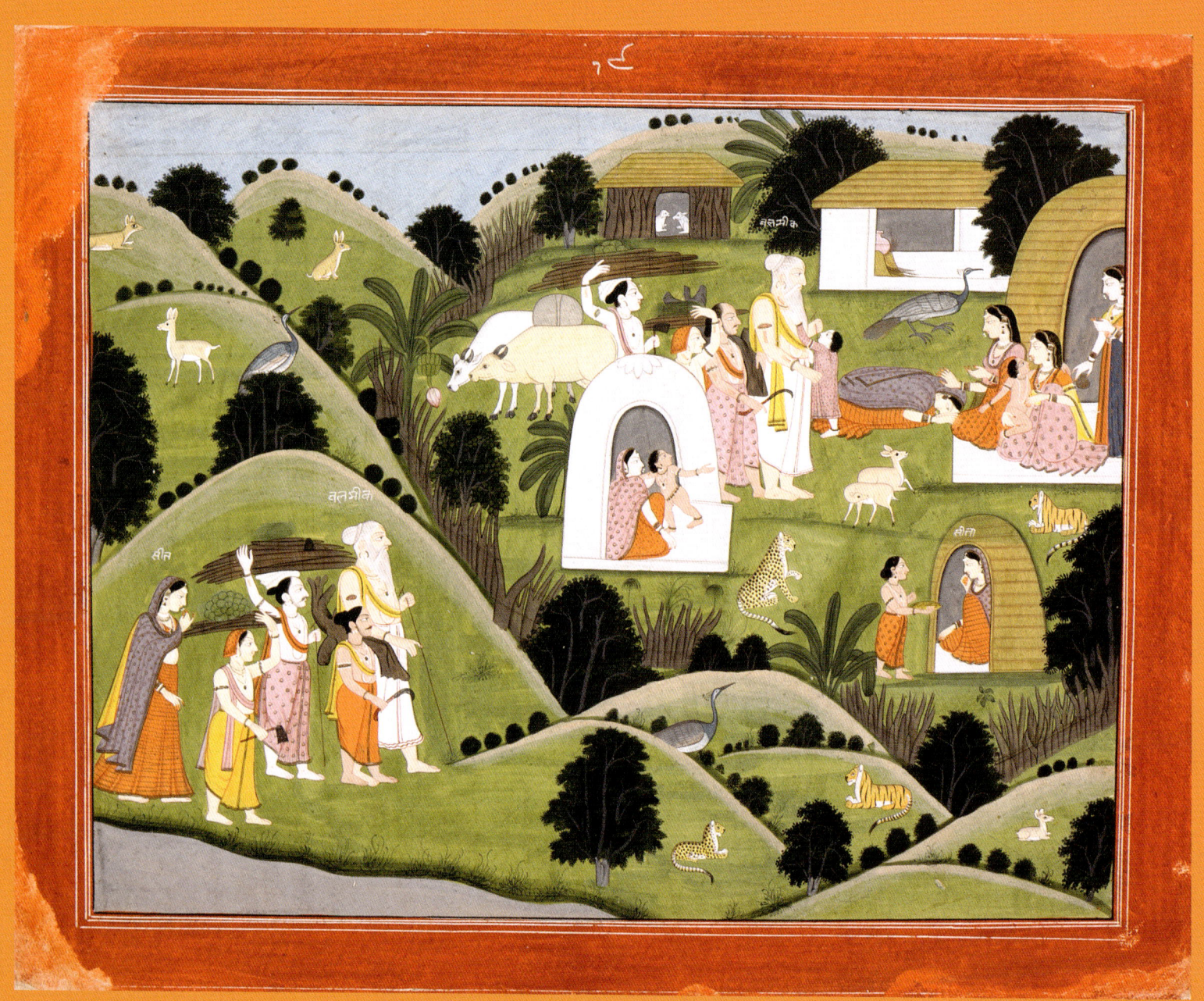

Hermitage of Valmiki, Folio from 'Nadaun' *Ramayana* (*c.* 1820)

53

Artist(s): Unknown

Country of origin: India

Dimensions: 27.9 x 36.8 cm (11 x 14½ inches)

Material(s): Opaque watercolour, gold and ink on paper

Kangra painting takes its name from the former princely state of Kangra-Lambagraon, which is situated in what is now Himachal Pradesh (of which Nadaun is a district), the northernmost state of India below the Himalayas. It became popular in the mid-18th century, having originated some decades earlier, and remained so until the mid-19th century.

Centred around the Pahari School of Painting, the Kangra style was developed by a family of Kashmiri artists who found a home at the court of Raja Dalip Singh, the ruler of Guler. These artists had been trained in the Mughal art style, which in turn had sprung from the art of Persian miniatures that focused on depicting the stories associated with Islamic figures and rulers. But living in Guler, the Kashmiri artists found themselves socialiing with local artists whose work was softer in style, using lighter colours and more influenced by nature and their surroundings. The result was that, as Kangra painting developed, its exponents moved away from the depiction of rulers, notable figures and events, such as battles and conquests, towards a celebration of life, nature and harmony and, in particular, a focus on the stories of the love between Krishna and Radha, the Hindu god of love and his consort, who is also considered by some to be an avatar of the goddess Lakshmi.

A central theme of Kangra painting is the evocation of *Shringara* (or *Sringara*) *rasa* (*rasa* meaning 'flavour'), which encompasses romantic love or the allure of beauty. In this image, the key figure is Valmiki, the poet-sage responsible for the *Ramayana*, the epic tale of the adventures of Rama. He is the large, white-haired and bearded figure shown in the group on the left that also includes Princess Sita, the wife of Rama, who has come to seek refuge in the hermitage where she gives birth to twin boys called Lava and Kusha. The same group then appears in the centre of the scene, where the princess pays homage to the wives of the sages by prostrating herself. Then she is shown once more in the bottom right-hand corner, being offered food while sitting in a hut. Throughout the scene, there are animals that in reality would normally be either hunting or hunted by one another, but the intention of the image is to promote a sense that within the hermitage everything could coexist harmoniously.

54

The Great Wave/Under the Wave off Kanagawa (1829–33)

Artist(s): Katsushika Hokusai

Country of origin: Japan

Dimensions: 28.5 x 38 cm (11¼ x 15 inches)

Material(s): Polychrome woodblock print, using ink and colour on mulberry paper

Hokusai's (1760–1849) *Under the Wave off Kanagawa* is part of a series of *Thirty-six Views of Mount Fuji*, begun circa 1829 and published in the early 1830s. Generally known as *The Great Wave*, it is one of the most renowned Japanese woodblock prints ever created, now duplicated on everything from Christmas cards to teacups.

The picture suggests humanity at the mercy of nature, a great wave breaking into foam-like-talons over helpless, tiny fishermen, with the similarly overshadowed Mount Fuji in the far distance. The wave's spume falls like snowflakes over the outline of its snow-covered peak – something that brings the diminutive-looking mountain momentarily closer into view. As with the pitching of a boat in high seas, one's vision heaves in and out, the oscillation created by watching Mount Fuji through a giant swell intensifying the painting's spatial and visual incongruities. The picture also relays a sense of things happening all at once, as if a single boat may well enter, pass through and exit the precarious channel: temporal events presented as a simultaneous occurrence and making for a highly avant-garde artwork.

Despite the influence of Western artistic conventions, the scene – where three little boats wallow in furious seas – is likely a summation of Hokusai's spiritual beliefs regarding Buddhism, centred on the fleetingness of life, and Shinto, to do with the absolute power of nature. Notably, the ambivalences in *The Great Wave* not only inform us of the natural disasters continuously wracking the Japanese islands, but also a social pattern of 'interaction and exclusion... across the centuries', not to mention the uncertainty inhabiting the nation's psychology in the early to mid 1800s, as Japan stood on the brink of the modern world, its chosen seclusion ended when American naval forces entered Tokyo Bay unsolicited in 1853 and forcibly imposed trade with the United States.[46]

In the modern European imagination, *The Great Wave* represents a timeless and geographically faraway nation. But it influenced European artists, with Hokusai's impact absorbed into Western prints and Modernist Japonisme. The image is printed on customary mulberry paper yet adopts a deep shade of Prussian or Berlin blue, an artificial dye invented in Germany and produced in China in the 1820s. So it is a cultural hybridism, 'a fusion of European materials and conventions with a Japanese sensibility' – largely the reason for its tremendous popularity.[47]

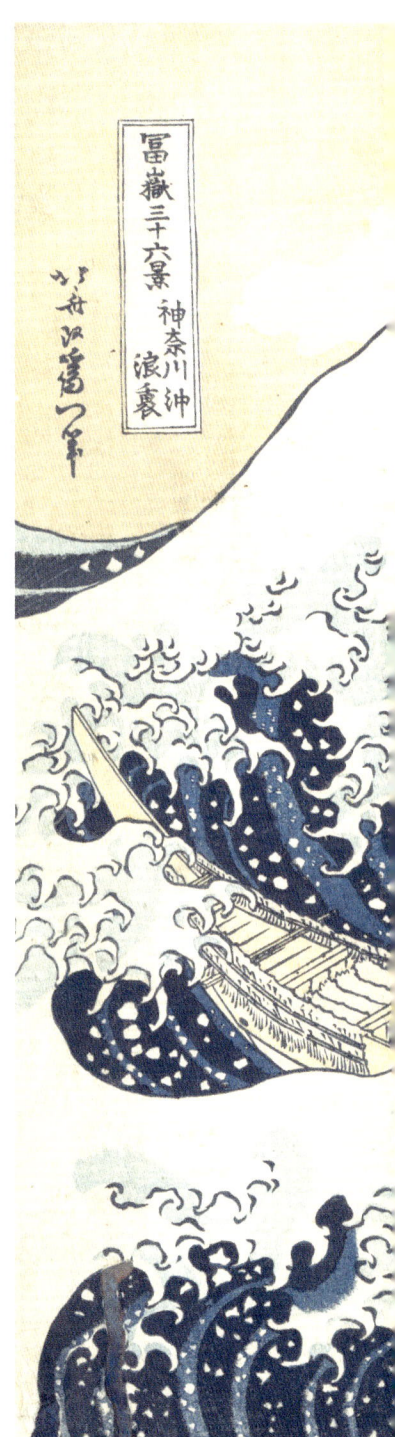

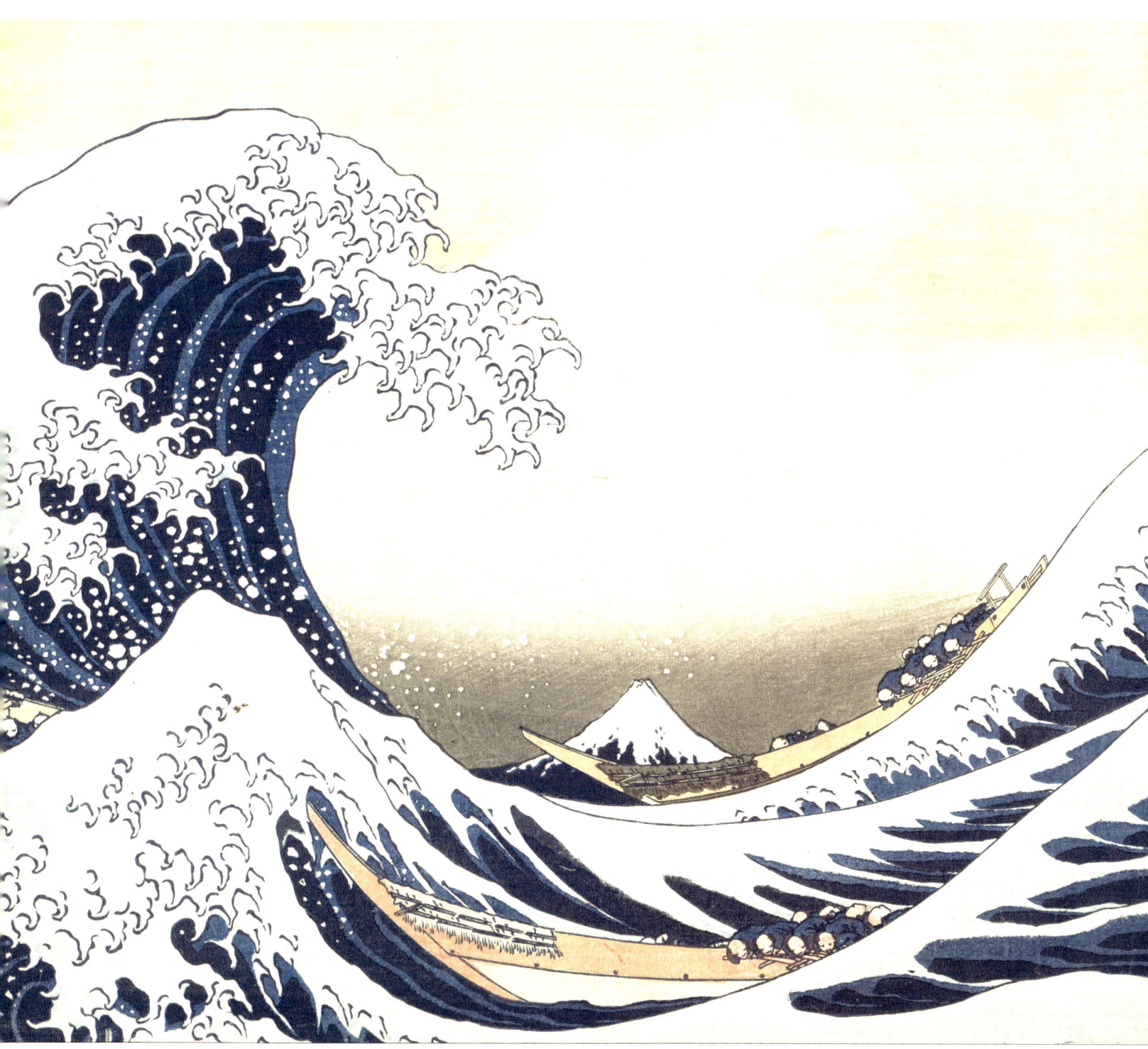

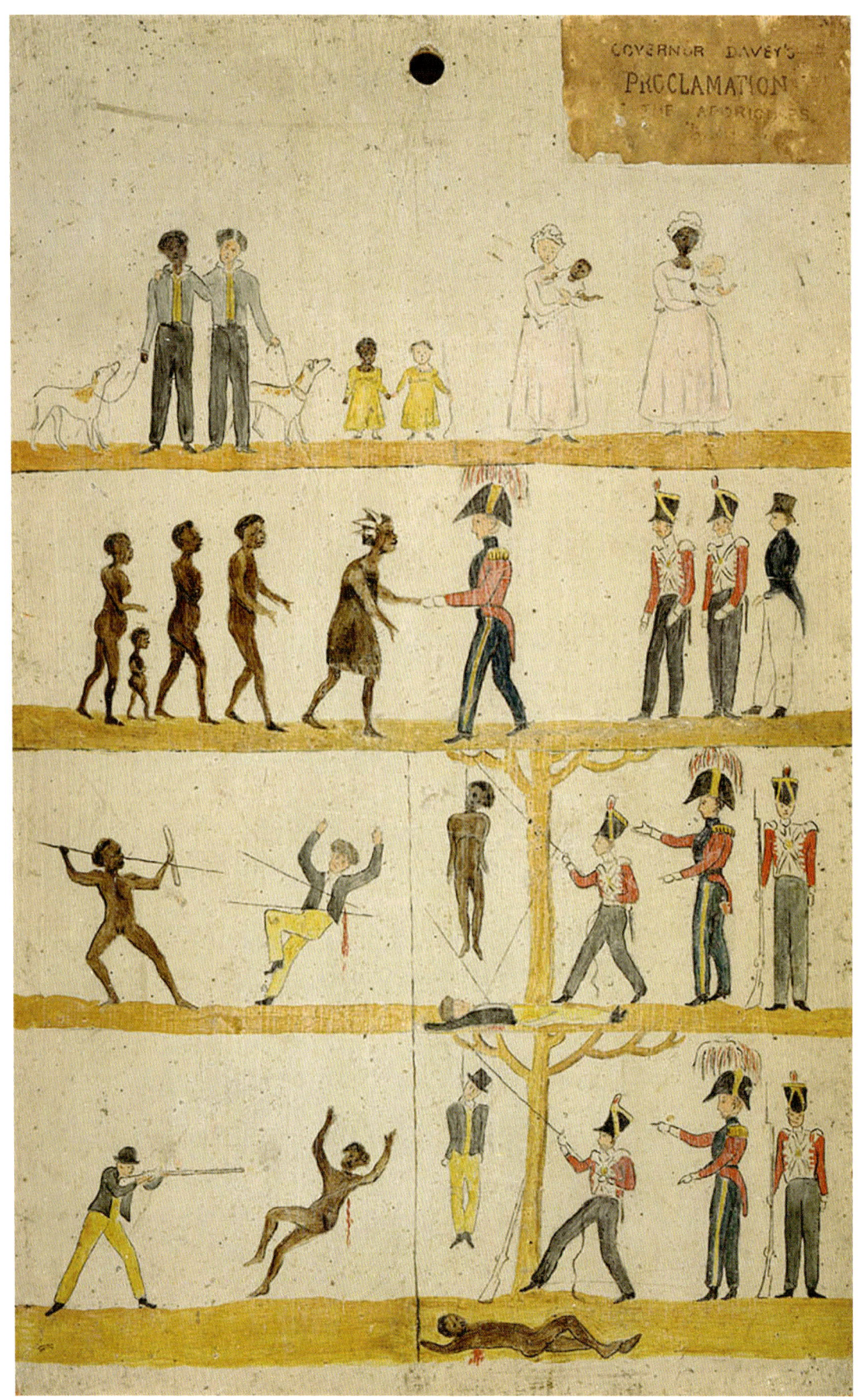

55 Proclamation Board
(1829–30)

Artist(s): Unknown

Country of origin: Australia

Dimensions: 38 cm (15 inches)

Material(s): Oil on pine

The terrible history of British rule in Tasmania began with settlement in 1803, followed by decades of armed fighting. Wanting to impart the British government's demands to the Aboriginal population, roughly 100 proclamation boards inspired by indigenous bark art were produced between 1829 and 1830.

The bark shelter art of Tasmania was first recorded by the French botanist Jean-Baptiste Leschenault de la Tour during an expedition to Maria Island in February 1802. As recounted, the botanist stumbled upon a small number of 'unusually well-made huts… covered with lines deliberately made, which resembled the tattooing of these people'.[48] In 1827, the chartered surveyor Henry Hellyer made known his sighting of huts in northern Tasmania, covered in charcoal drawings of animals and other symbols. Later, George Augustus Robinson, who travelled inland apprehending Aborigines for imprisonment in the Flinders Island settlement, relayed comparable accounts, as did surveyor George Frankland in a letter of 4 February 1829 to Governor George Arthur.

The outcome of these reports was the infamous 'Proclamation of Governor Arthur to the Aborigines'. In a faux-naïve European style, this form of visual communication was used to convey the requirements of the colonial government, the boards illustrating the impartiality of British law and the costs of violence, resulting in the exact same punishment for Europeans and Aborigines. More specifically, proclamation boards of the type reproduced here sought to relay that the killing of an Aborigine by a European and the killing of a European by an Aborigine would result in an equal fatal penalty – hanging. Somewhat bizarrely, at the top, the colonial idea of a 'local' form of visual expression depicts happy families and utopian friendship between indigenous and settler communities, while below, an Aboriginal chief and his group shake hands with the military Governor, accompanied by fellow European enforcers of British colonial law.

What colonists saw as a method to communicate with, and befriend, the indigenous population actually hid an unrelenting campaign to round up, capture and disinherit the Aboriginal Tasmanians still inhabiting their lands. In a way, the crude imitation of bark art highlights the lack of consideration given to Aboriginal people by Europeans, including seizure of their people and lands. In another, the proclamation boards raise 'issues of sovereignty, history and justice [that] remain unsolved in Australia today'.[49]

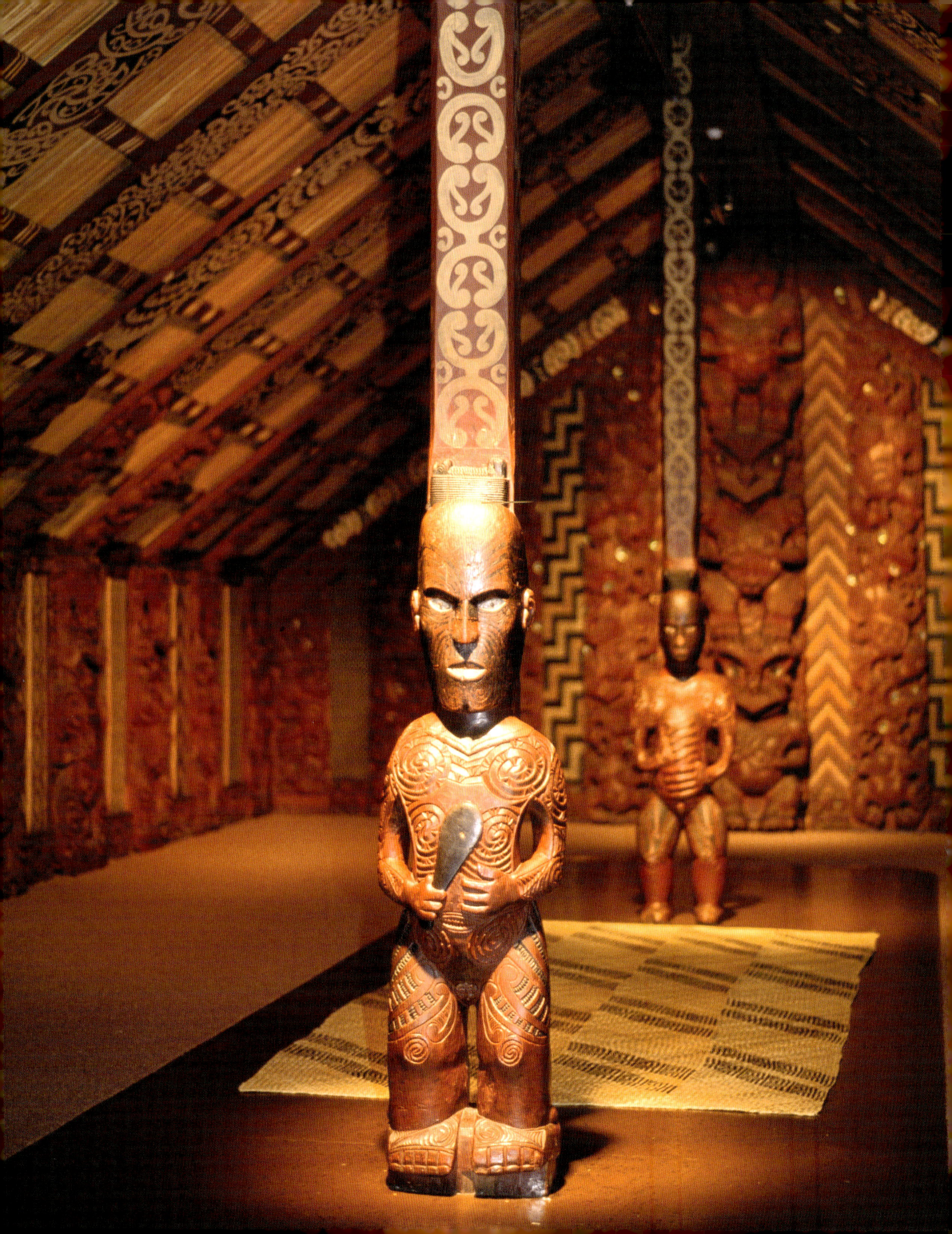

Te Hau-ki Tūranga Meeting House
(1840s)

Artist(s): Head carver: Raharuhi Rukupō

Country of origin: Aotearoa New Zealand

Dimensions: Original length x width 13.2 x 5.5 m (43⅓ x 18 ft); Height 3.7 m (12 ft)

Material(s): Wood

Te Hau-ki-Tūranga *whare whakairo* (carved house) – capable of being translated as 'spirit' or 'good-tidings from Tūranga' – is the oldest surviving Māori meeting house. Constructed during the 1840s at Ōrākaiapu pā, near Tūranga (known currently as Gisborne) in the North Island of New Zealand, it is likely to have been in use by 1845. It was built for the Rongowhakaata tribe or *iwi* under the auspices of the legendary carver and Māori leader Raharuhi Rukupō (c. 1800s–1873), also known by his anglicized name 'Lazarus' Rukupō.

In 1867, agents of the Crown took the much-prized building without permission of the Rongowhakaata owners, who immediately began lobbying for its return, but without success. Subsequently, the structure was transported to the Colonial Museum (now the Museum of New Zealand Te Papa Tongarewa, Wellington), where it remained until 2011, when Crown and tribal representatives arrived at an agreement as to its return.

Prior to the arrival of Europeans, the *pātaka* (storehouse) and war canoes (*waka*) were the most significant collectively owned objects and structures. Māori, living in coastal areas, quickly acquired metal tools from European travellers in the 18th century, the durability and razor-sharpness of these implements enlarging the production of carving. This eventually resulted in 'the external panels of raised *pātaka*... [being] embellished with detailed depictions of *tiki* and *manaia* ancestors, the prized resource of beached whales, and deities'.[50]

In the early 19th century, Pākehā (the Maori word for European) colonization, Christianity and land transference to European settlers had become urgent concerns for Māori. The carvings of *pātaka* also became far less important due to musket wars, land wars and other pressing issues. As a result, a new construction embodying *mana* (spiritual power and authority) – the *whare whakairo* – was developed specifically for the purposes of meeting and discussion. The meeting house resulted in a formal mix of a chief's house and the embellishments of *pātaka*, incorporating its exterior designs internally.

The interior and exterior of Te Hau-ki Tūranga was covered with carved *tiki* wall panels depicting ancestors of Raharuhi Rukupō and the adjacent Ngāti Kahungunu *iwi*, with whom Rukupō may have sought a political alliance. The building's rafters are also embellished with intricate repeating scroll paintings, which signify ancestral lineage. Complex ornamental lattice-work (*tukutuku*) between the upright wall panels likewise covers the interior of the meeting house. With the coming of Christianity to Aotearoa, and with an Anglican missionary established in Tūranga in 1840, European religious influence was evident. More crucially, the house was erected at a time of great political, economic, religious and technological change for Māori, influencing 'the form and function of an emerging meeting house architecture'.[51]

57 *Whakapakoko*
(*c*. 1840s)

Artist(s): Possibly Patoromu Tamatea of Ngāti Pikiao of Te Arawa

Country of origin: Aotearoa New Zealand

Dimensions: 83 x 15 cm (32¾ x 6 inches)

Material(s): Wood and paua shell inlay

This standing wooden sculpture (*whakapakoko*) is decorated with *rauponga* (carving of bold spirals), with the two figures possessing full facial *moko*, paua shells for eyes and evoking a Māori ancestor figure. The carving's provenance is contested, but the depiction of a large figure holding a smaller one in its arms is one of two Māori *tekoteko* (carved figures) that represent the Madonna and Child. This example, held in the Auckland War Memorial Museum, is believed to have been carved in 1840, while the other piece, at Te Papa Tongarewa, Wellington, was probably carved some decades later.

Christianity in Aotearoa New Zealand began to proliferate by the 1830s. As David Gaimster points out, 'The strength of missionary influence is illustrated by the chiefs Hōne Heke and Tāmati Wāka Nene citing their Christian faith as their reason for signing the Treaty [of Waitangi in 1840].'[52]

Anecdotal history suggests that both *tekoteko* were offered to local Catholic priests for use in the chapel at Matektu and at the Ōhinemutu altar. However, both were eschewed, being deemed pagan objects and inappropriate for Catholic worship. It was the scholar James Cowan who testified that Patoromu Tamatea, the Te Arawa carver, from Ngati Pikiao, fashioned this carving. We know that a Captain Gilbert Mair passed the sculpture on to the museum *c*. 1890, stating that the piece was carved, possibly in 1845, by an anonymous Māori convert for a Catholic church in the Bay of Plenty in the North Island of New Zealand.

According to Cowan, however, Tamatea offered the *tekoteko* to the Catholic chapel at Ruapeka Bay, Ōhinemutu, but the artist became so dispirited by its rejection that he joined the Māori Hauhau sect, which sought to modify Christian religious scripture to Māori beliefs. But as Roger Neich maintains, 'We can only assume that Cowan has invented his story from a mixture of scattered facts and much fiction.'[53] Neich also views the facial markings as male *moko* and connected to conceptual rather than misidentified iconography.

Alternatively, Allen Davidson has suggested that the carver conveyed the Christian concept of a miraculous conception through *moko*: 'Unlike the typical European representation of the Madonna and child, Mary has a full facial tattoo [...] traditionally used on a man.'[54] As such, the facial *moko* would appear to signify that the woman is a virgin. Whatever the precise reason for the facial tattooing, the *moko* indicates the figure's spiritual sacredness and exclusive status. Yet the carvings were manufactured during a period of intense 'missionization', 'institutional assimilation' and 'power and rhetoric' by the Church, so they probably epitomize a bigger issue as regards Māori responses to Christianity, cultural exchange and faith in a Māori belief system. In 1986, the present *tekoteko* held pre-eminence at the Pukekawa/Auckland Domain, when Pope John Paul II was greeted by Māori people and given a cordial reception.

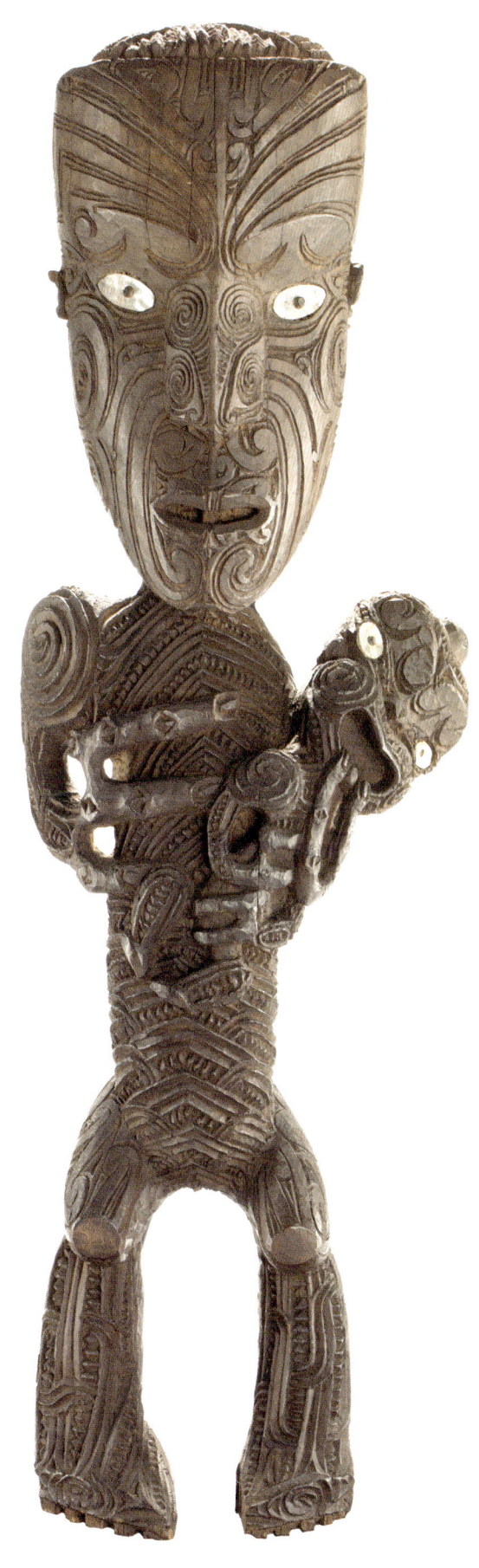

58 Trrou Körrou
(Mid 19th Century)

Artist(s): Unknown

Country of origin: Vanuatu

Dimensions: 3 m (9 ft 10 inches)

Material(s): Carved and engraved wood, blue and white pigment

This 'Blue Man' statue is from Malo Island in Vanuatu. It was purchased in Port Villa, Vanuatu's capital town on Efate Island, by members of the Korrigane Expedition in 1934–35. A precise date for its manufacture is unknown, but he is – alongside the *Lengnangulong* sacred stone – one of the most renowned Melanesian objects. What's so striking about the sculpture is its blue colouration, produced by a popular 19th-century European dye.

We know that in the initial decades of European arrival inbound goods and materials fascinated and impacted Melanesian islanders. By 1848, iron tools were being used in the southern Vanuatu island of Aneityum, which timber traders had been visiting for some two decades. European trading practices came at cost to Melanesian peoples. At Aneityum, visitors brought deadly diseases, and male labour at Anelcauhat was traded 'for rice and hard biscuit'. In the case of metal tools, traditional stone axes and axe heads were adapted to incorporate European blades, which cut down trees but also killed enemies. Guns were traded too in large numbers in the 1870s.

As traders and newcomers settled in the region, they brought with them manufactured cloth, beads and dyes. Manufactured in Hull, in 1852, Reckitt's Blue was a laundry whitener, the chemical amalgamation of imitation ultramarine and sodium bicarbonate. Reckitt's Blue quickly found its way into Pacific and African cultures, where the new whitener soon became a valuable item of exchange for its intense blue pigment. Made from hardwood or iron wood (*Intsia bijuga*), the present statue is painted in Reckitt's Blue.

The so-called 'Blue Man' is documented as having his own name, *Trrou Körrou*, said to denote 'he who stands before you and looks at you'. It's an apt title because he originally sat outside 'a men's cult house at Savkas village in south Malo'. 'Blue Man' is a 'grade' figure, in other words 'a figure which was raised to mark a man's achievement of one of the highest ranks in the graded or status-alteration society'.[55] Standing quietly in an exhibition hall in the Pavillon des Sessions, *Trrou Körrou*, together with other objects of cultural value from Vanuatu, displays an extraordinary 'gentleness and quiet power, an effect enhanced by its blue colour'.[56]

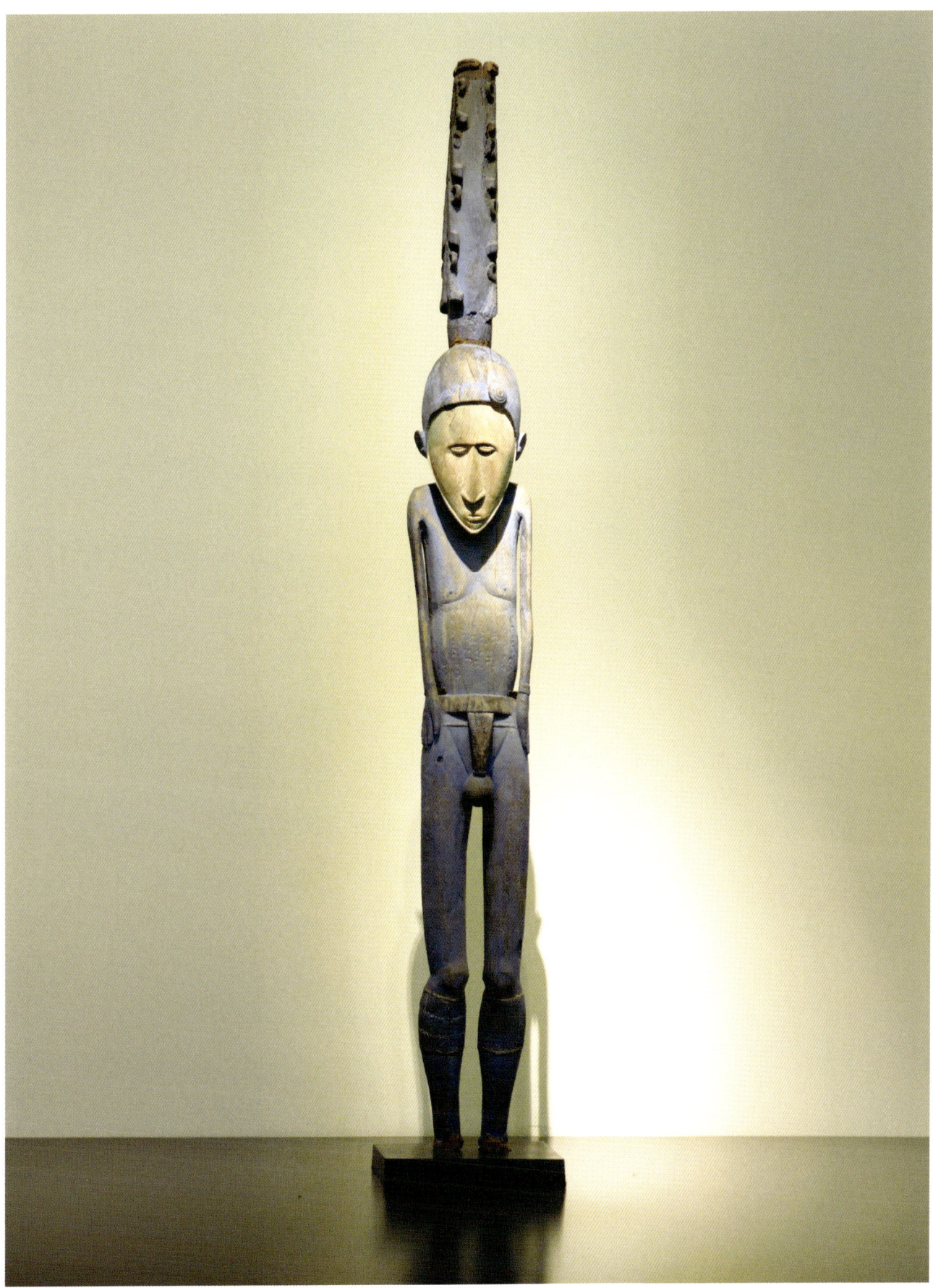

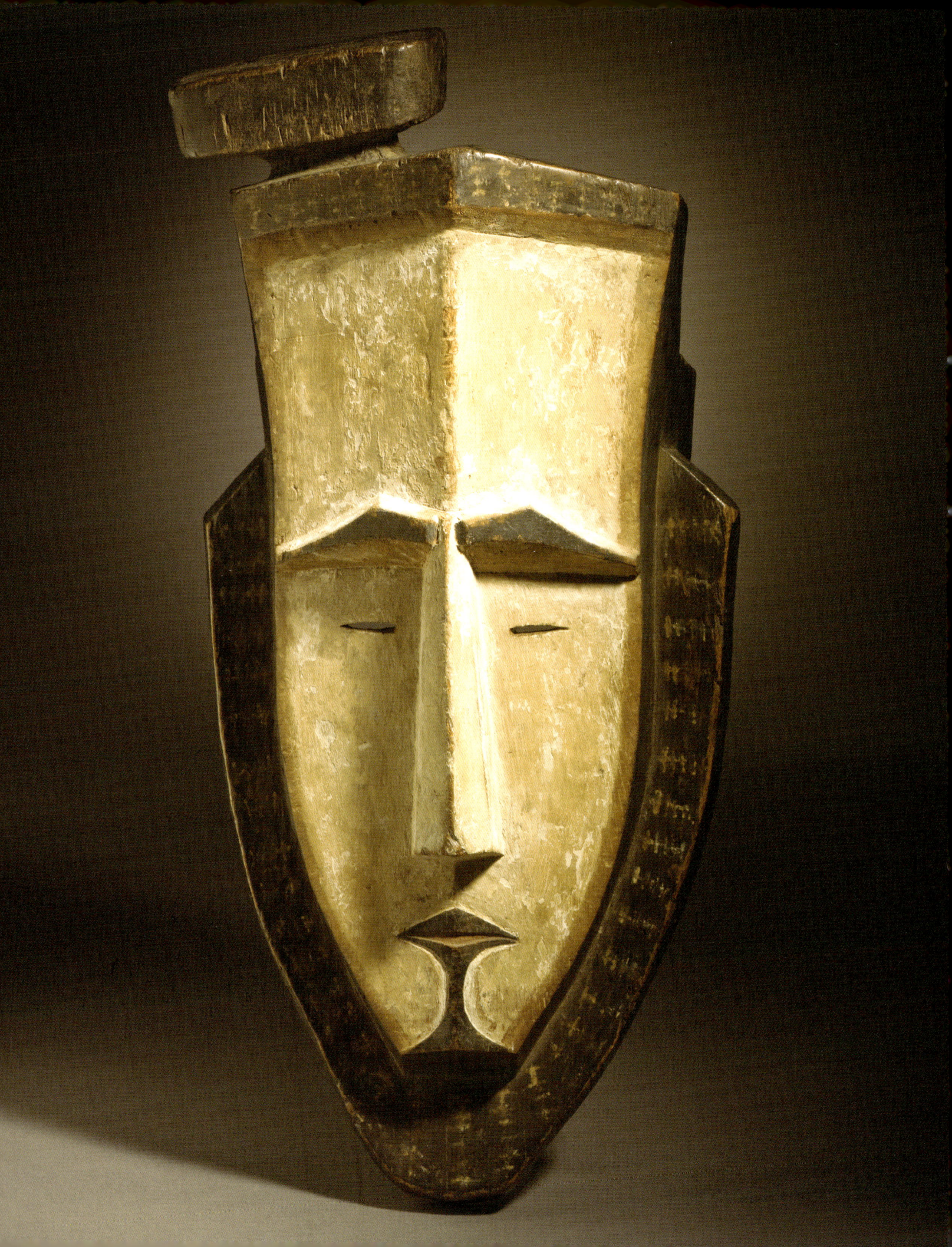

House Mask
(*c.* 1885)

Artist(s): Unknown

Country of origin: Mortlock (Nomoi) Islands, Caroline Islands, Micronesia

Dimensions: 53 x 24.1 x 20.3 cm (20⅞ x 9½ x 8 inches)

Material(s): Wood and pigment

Colloquially known as Nomoi, the Micronesian atolls of the Mortlock Islands include Etal, Lukunor and Satawan (Satoan). They are situated respectively south, southeast and southwest of Kuk, Chuuk and Pohnpei in the central Caroline Islands. Satawan atoll is believed to be the hub of masking traditions, but several *tapuanu* (masks) in early collections are accredited to Lukunor. One particular mask was acquired by the Hamburg Südsee Expedition in Truk, leading some researchers to consider that the custom stems from Melanesian interaction.

The Mortlock Islands are known for carved Nukuoro figures of gods and goddesses (Nukuoro is another atoll in Micronesia) as well as striking works carved from hefty breadfruit wood painted black and white and with an austerity of form found throughout the Caroline Islands. This mask was most likely produced for decorative purposes. As the anthropologist Mac Marshall observes, these objects now are called '*tapwpwaanu* … [a] mask-like spirit head carved of wood and set up on the gable of a Mortlockese canoe house or meeting house'.[57] But smaller versions were used in performance involving singing and dancing. As with the present work, they are flat, nominal carvings, the countenance characterized by sparing details cut out in very shallow relief, with a few touches in red to suggest the lips. The wing-like design of the eyebrows overlapping a T-shaped nose recall a bird in flight, while two small slits and a diamond-shaped ridge form the eyes and mouth.

Today, Mortlockese believe that the masks endured as both male and female couples. According to Adrienne Kaeppler, while distinctive to Micronesia, the masks can be associated with forms in Micronesia, Polynesia and Melanesia.[58] It is also speculated that they might have been used by executioners to do their duty faithfully and remain anonymous, but this has never been corroborated, and the notion seems entirely misplaced. A 1910 description by A. F. Krämer records that masks created by secret clutches called *soutapuanu*, sported in connection with songs and dances to battle destructive storms caused by the wind god Fangileng, helped protect the breadfruit crop.[59] By the mid-1930s masks could be bought and are still manufactured today for visitors to the islands.

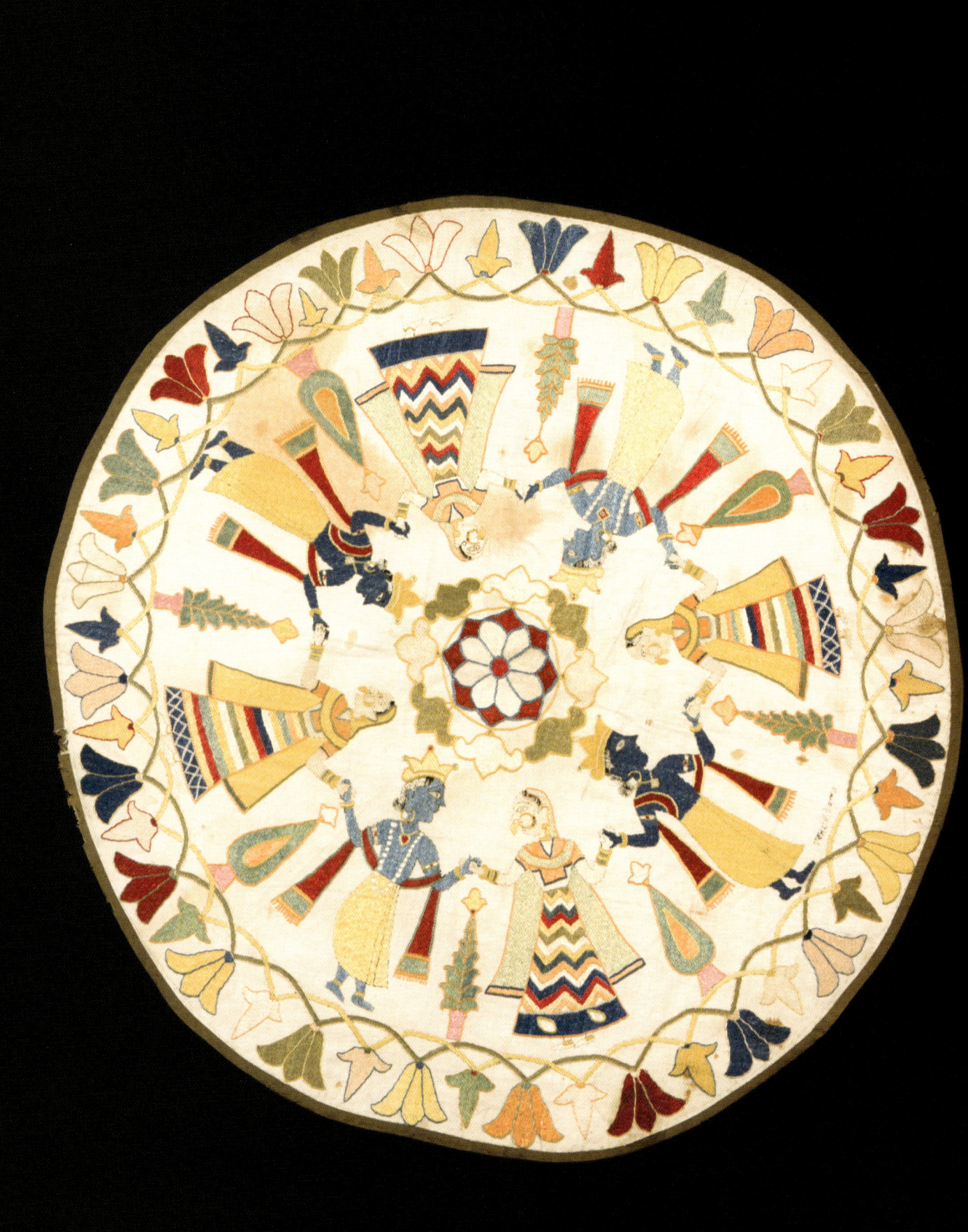

Rumal

(*c*. Late 19th Century)

Artist(s): Unknown

Country of origin: India

Dimensions: Diameter 69 cm (27 inches)

Material(s): Cotton with silk embroidery

The manufacture of textiles in the South Asian subcontinent goes back many thousands of years, the oldest remains of woven cloth having been found at the Bronze Age site of Mohenjo-daro. These remnants, together with the discovery of vats for dyeing cloth and bronze needles, are all evidence of the fact that this area of the world was much in advance of Western countries by some millennia in the weaving and colouring of cloth as well as its adornment with embroidery. Over the years textile production in the region was impacted by trade with the East and the West, as China supplied silk while demand from the West influenced what was produced – from the ancient Romans and Greeks to the Portuguese, Dutch and British from the 16th century onwards.

As weaving and dyeing techniques in the South Asian subcontinent developed, so too did embroidery styles, and many areas became renowned for their unique creations using a variety of different stitches as well as other forms of embellishment such as appliqué and mirrored glass. In Gujarat, particularly in the district of Kachchh (Kutch) and the Saurashtra peninsula, much of the embroidery work was generated by craftsmen known as Mochi, who turned embroidery into a professional occupation. The region built an important reputation for folk embroidery that involved designs handed down from generation to generation and which were used on a multitude of items, such as costumes for special occasions, babies' blankets, wall hangings and quilts. Brides were expected to bring numerous embroidered items with them as part of their dowries that were put on display at their wedding ceremonies.

Other embroidery motifs and decorative styles were influenced by Persian and Mughal art, incorporating flowers and animals of all kinds. In the 18th century, in the Himalayan region of Himachal Pradesh, the town of Chamba and surrounding hill states became the centre of the production of rumal. A *rumal* (also *rumal[l]a*) is a kerchief or cloth covering that refers either to a cloth worn by some Sikh men as an alternative to a turban or by other short-haired male visitors to the gurdwara (Sikh place of worship), or to the covering used to protect gifts or offerings to temple gods. Some Sikh households use a *rumal* to cover a small shrine or as a backdrop to it.

As with the example shown here, *rumal* were made from plain cotton or muslin cloth and embroidered with scenes from poetry or the life of Krishna. In this instance, the *rumal* is unusual because it is circular (the vast majority were – and are – either square or rectangular), but it highlights the *rasamandala* (circular dance) that is depicted, which is taken from a love poem called the 'Gita Govinda' describing the story of Krishna, his wife Radha and the *gopi* (female cowherders) who are devotees of Krishna. The *rumal* shows Krishna, Radha and the four *gopi* dressed in brightly coloured costumes and adorned with jewellery.

61 Fine Old Ancestor Figure (*Kandimboang*)
(Late 19th century)

Artist(s): Unknown

Country of origin: Papua New Guinea

Dimensions: Height: 42cm (161/2 inches)

Material(s): Wood, dog's teeth

Originating from the Murik Lakes in the East Sepik Province of Papa New Guinea, this wooden Ancestor Figure depicts a rather squat, young woman, her arms and hands by her sides resting forcibly on her hips. Although *Kandimboang* is a ubiquitous term for male and female carved figures, this type of sculpture was likely kept in the home of a high-ranking woman and used at special times to summon the manifestation and authority of beings whom they symbolize.

As anthropologists have observed, Murik figures embody female spirits that impart authority to young novices in a women's cult. 'They represented spirits that gave power, prophesies and love magic and taught that sexuality should be used for status, access to reserves and religious power.'[60] From the cult, inductees 'learned the power of seduction and beautification magic passed on from these female spirit figures.'[61] These carvings were also part of rituals for launching a canoe, and if men largely carried out trading voyages, they nonetheless acknowledged that 'the canoe travels on the strength of women'.[62]

Murik figures were carved by men but they were nonetheless clothed and decorated by women using skirts, bangles, necklaces and shell rings – ornamentation appropriate to the status of these spirits. The present figure is correspondingly adorned with a necklace made from dogs' teeth, a long-established type of exchange or wedding gift in New Guinea. Wooden representations of Murik woman sometimes have spirals carved into the shoulder blades, a symbol of the moon, indicative of the initiatory scarification process. It is reported that the spirits within are capricious, flirtatious, vain and easily offended. They were individually named and have the power of possession over the owner, who is said to elicit the voice of the spirit. In the lower Sepik area these objects were representative of individuals, kept in a basket and passed onto the first-born, or inherited from their mothers.

Murik initiation figures are known to include an image of maternal nurture, a small child perhaps, protectively shrouded between the figure's legs, something central to Murik society. All in all, the *Kandimboang* 'represents an ideal and physically strong image of Murik womanhood.'

We should not, of course, generalize about Melanesian material culture. Long ago, Kathleen Barlow recognized that gathering documentation in these cultures is 'a cumulative and on-going process.'[63] Nor should we generalize about the responsibilities and relations in Murik society or Melanesian cultures, because gender roles were fundamentally balanced and involved the esteem of women. As Bolton additionally observes, 'Outsiders often interpret Melanesian gender relations... as involving the oppression of women by men. In fact, it is impossible to generalize about anything, let alone about gender, in a region as complex as Melanesia... [where] hierarchy and oppression by no means always occurred along gender lines.'[64]

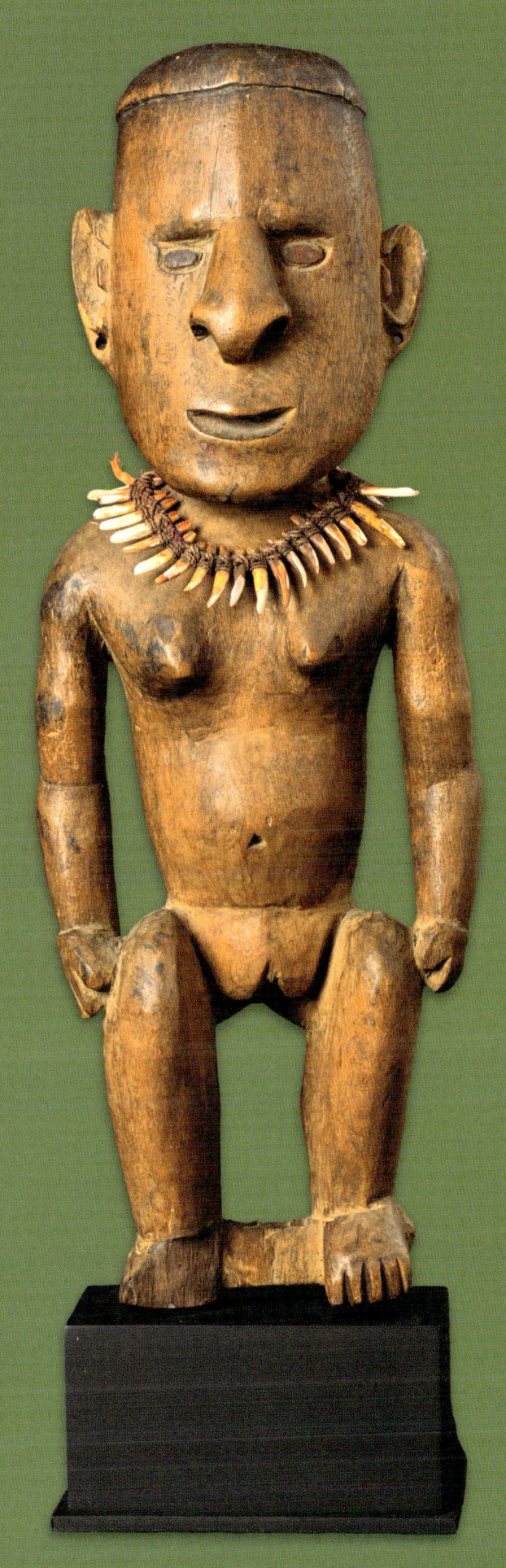

62 Malangan Figure
(Acquired 1884)

Artist(s): Unknown

Country of origin: Papua New Guinea

Dimensions: Height: 123 cm (48½ inches)

Material(s): Wood, shell, lime, red ochre, pigments, human hair, adhesive putty.

In a number of different island societies in New Ireland elaborate and complex funerary ceremonies are the reason for existing art. Large numbers of carvings and masks include wooden uli figures from the north-east coast and the idiosyncratic all-purpose *malangan* masks from the north. Here, it's worth reviewing the English term 'mask' because its stress on disguise does not easily translate into other cultures, where the concept of human articulation behind the mask is not appropriate and maybe entirely repudiated. The mask is not necessarily a separate entity, but should be considered alongside other attire and paraphernalia. As such, *malangan* funerary masks are part of the whole spectacle.[65]

Malangan ceremonies vary greatly among various cultures and often happen long after death. Although *Malangan* ritual display is meant to 'finalize' things by directing the deceased towards the spiritual realm, it also has an equivalence in life. Just as the deceased are transported to the spiritual realm, so younger members of society are relocated to the adult world.[66] The actual point is not just to say goodbye, but also to highlight the vivacity of those in the world who organize and stage these rituals. Hundreds of individuals may join the resulting feasting ceremonies, the climax of which is a dramatic show of *malangan* artefacts that relays a sense of an individual's identity.

Together with the ritual's vibrant music, singing, and resonating sounds from 'friction drums', it all suggests the preternatural. References to transformation include hybrid creatures, especially the images of a bird-snake or a bird ingesting a reptile. Images of alteration may include motifs such as a flying fish that is believed to be symptomatic of a chief's words journeying far and wide. As with Sulka masks (see page 150), *malangan* are highly varied yet retain the unambiguous stamp of a 'style', the consistent adoption of snail shells for eyes being just one example.

Some masks are made to be worn, others are for display, some retained and utilized periodically, while many are simply left to rot away.[67] Hence, the purpose of *malangan* theatrical displays is to allow the deceased to live on in the memory. Many *malangan* are now collectors' items, while the introduction of modern metal tools and commercial products actually altered the aesthetic involvedness of *malangan*.

The acceptance of Christianity has meant that carvings and masks are now largely commandeered by smel, concrete grave markers, that are far more abstract and unevenly manufactured.[68]

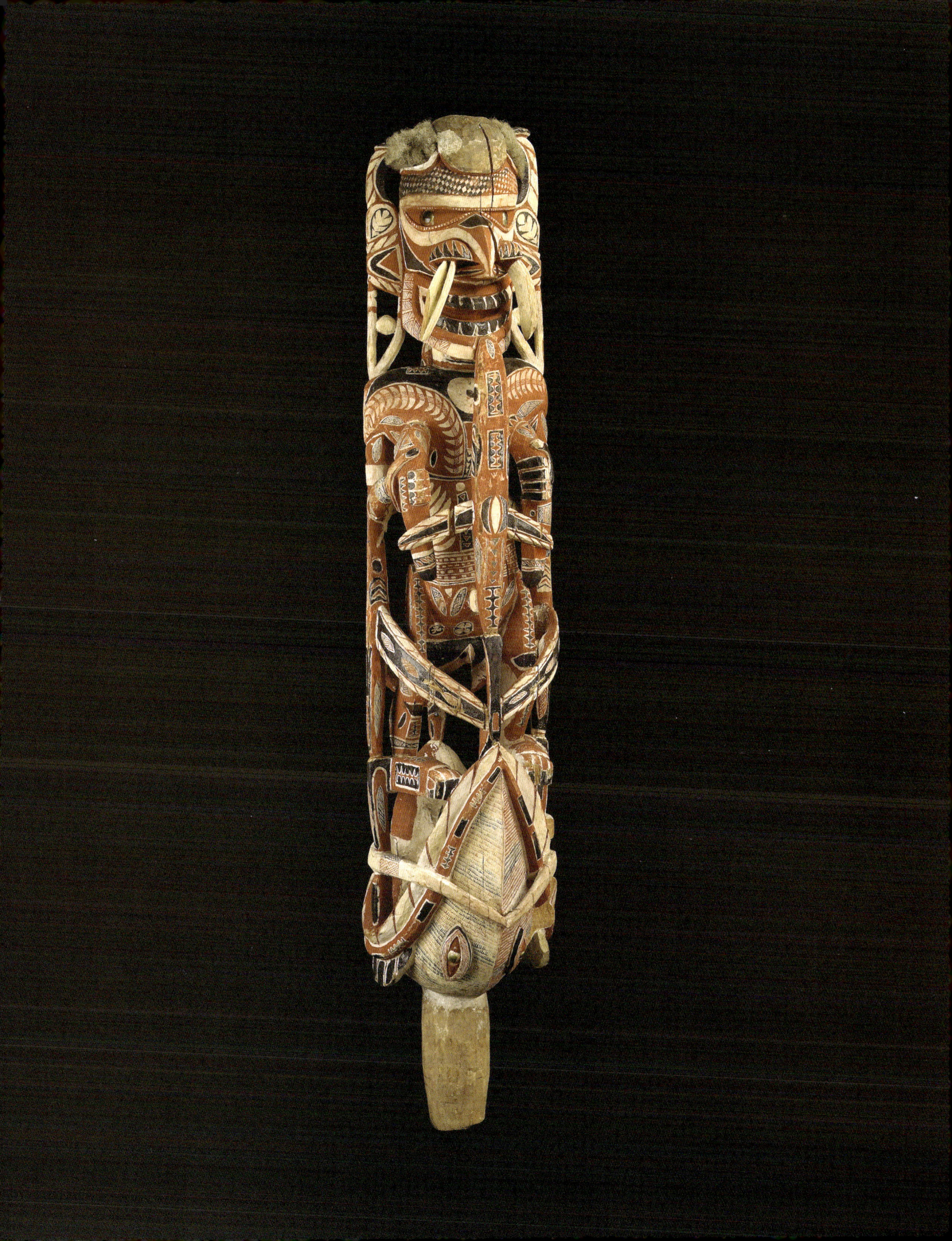

63 Tortoise-shell Mask, 'Crocodile Man'
(Acquired *c.* 1890)

Artist(s): Gizu of Nagir

Country of origin: Australia

Dimensions: 50 x 82 x 80 cm (19½ x 32 x 31½ inches)

Material(s): Tortoise shell, cassowary feathers, goa nuts, cowrie shell, pigeon feathers, pigments

This tortoise-shell mask (*krar*) is from the Torres Strait Islands, which lie between Australia's Cape York Peninsula and New Guinea, the region renowned for these highly elaborate and compound headdresses. *Krar* masks are among the most recognized works of art in Oceania. Typically, they appear in the shape of a fish or crocodile's mouth, topped with a human face that is imaginatively fashioned to startle and enthral onlookers.[69]

The masks are fabricated from the delicately-shaped exoskeleton of a hawksbill turtle – its plates steamed with hot stones to make them elastic. The plates are subsequently pierced, shaped, carved, dyed and profusely ornamented, often with cowrie shells, goa nuts, imported ochre and feathers from a New Guinea cassowary bird. Carved details are emphasized with lime and treasured European metals and fabrics are also adopted. In the featured 'crocodile man', 'the iron used for the outstretched hands and strands of calico were also incorporated.'[70] As such, it's a hybrid art form that parades composite imagery and materials, indicative of Western Torres masks.

So extraordinary are the masks that they were recorded by the maritime explorer Luis Váez de Torres in 1606, the first verified European study of any type of Melanesian art. This example is thought to have been made by someone called Gizu and obtained by the British anthropologist Alfred Cort Haddon (1855–1940) on Nagir island in 1888. Turtle-shell masks were purportedly traded and used by communities outside those that manufactured them, in induction and war rituals, as well as funerary ceremonies and increase rites, calculated to guarantee good harvests and plenty of fish and game. The ritual often involved senior individuals who wore the masks alongside ceremonial skirts made of swishing grass, acting out events derived from oral tradition. Worn over the head like a helmet, the mask allowed the wearer to dip down to disclose a human countenance, possibly epitomizing an ancestor-hero. We do not know the precise meaning of the 'crocodile man', but it is likely that the significance of the theanthropism varied from region to region. Torres Strait Masks typically feature sea creatures such as trigger fish and blackfish, perhaps expressive of a private totem.

In the early 20th century, the turtle-shell masks were rarely constructed, but we should not assume that this indigenous art form vanished with Western colonization. Mask-making continued at home and with those who migrated to the mainland. Ken Thaiday Snr is well known for his 'dance machines', begun in the 1980s, which include 'articulated' sharks, aircraft and other important characteristic aspects of island life.

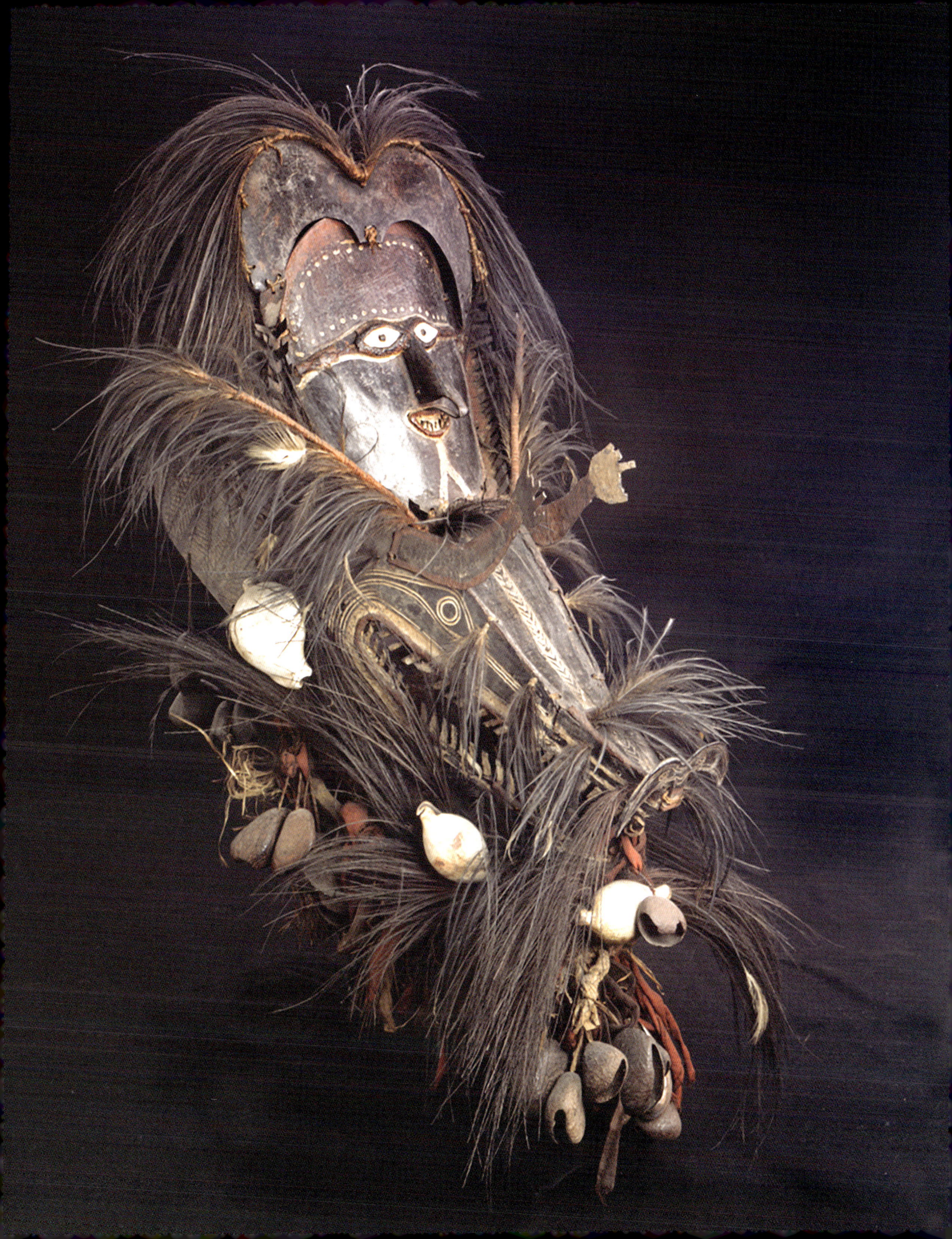

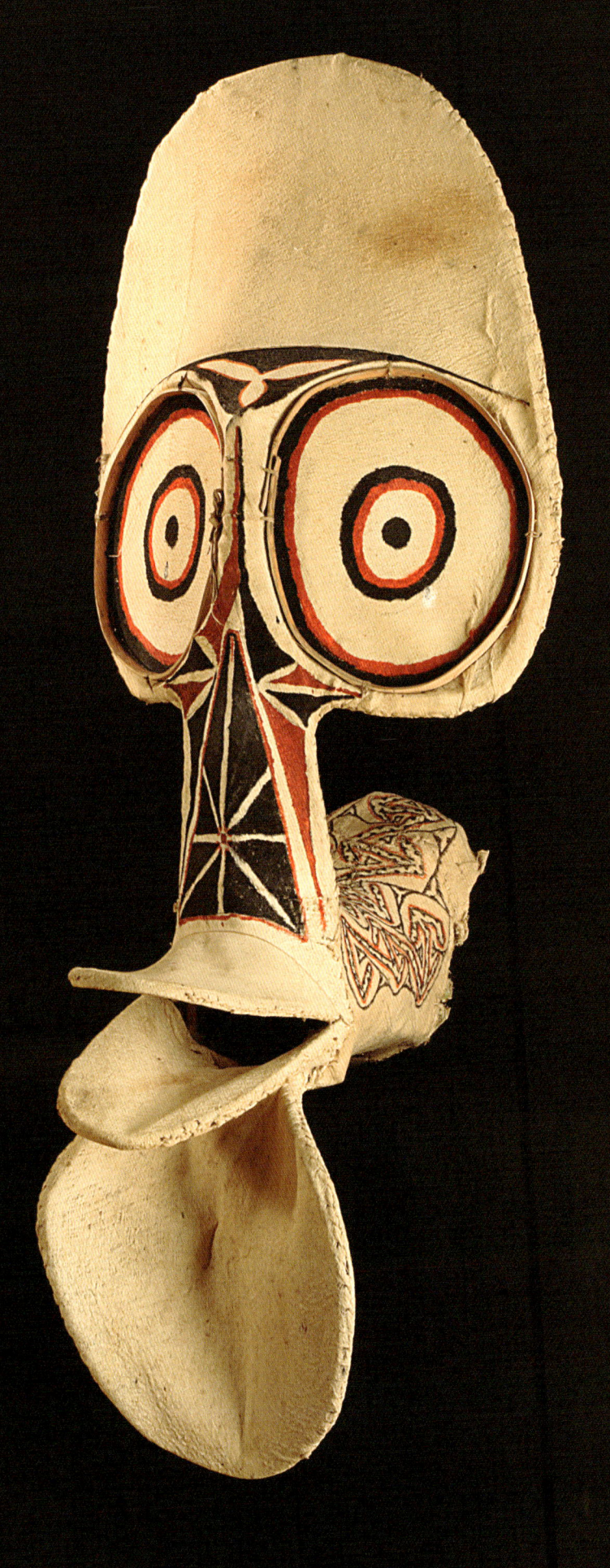

Painted Bark-cloth Mask
(Collected between 1890 and 1913)

Artist(s): Baining people

Country of origin: New Britain, Papua New Guinea

Dimensions: Approx. 120 x 68 cm (47¼ x 27¾ inches)

Material(s): Bark cloth

The Baining people are the original inhabitants of the mountainous Gazelle Peninsula of East New Britain Province in Papua New Guinea. Their artistic traditions include the production of bark-cloth masks. The most extraordinary variant includes large three-pronged constructions up to 4 m (13 ft) high. As a 1900 photograph of *hareiga* (headdress effigy) masks in performance reveals, the elephantine figures with tubular-shaped bodies, elementary limbs and giant heads border on performance art. Bark-cloth traditions combine sculpture, painting, music, dance, ritual and stories.

This fire-dance (*atut*) mask is constructed out of light and ephemeral materials and would be worn for a solitary ceremony, then dispensed with. In most cases, bamboo cane is overlaid with bark cloth and complemented by energetic patterns painted on the 'paper skin', typically in red and black hues. While some patterns are derived from wild vines, insects and pig intestines, contemporary designs embrace the tread of car tyres, church missionary crosses or mass-produced cloth, and may include flags and the 'thumbs-up' sign. Patterns are, however, partly adduced from the imagination and highlight individual creativity, elucidation and modification.

Baining masks vary considerably in shape, size and complexity, each with a distinctive type of headdress and flamboyant designs. The most characteristic type of bark-cloth mask entails a flat upper plate, which is circular or divided into two hemispheres, with a gawking, duck-like mouth from which extends a chin or tongue-like protrusion. Two large circles form large, accentuated eyes. Jane Fajans outlines three basic kinds of mask, '*avriski*, *anguangi* (*atutki*) and *alaspraka*', all of which are allied to a fire ceremony.[71] With rare privilege, masks are sported by men, the dancer concealed by fringes and supplementary filament skirts. The masks are created for daytime or nighttime ceremonies and denote departed spirits who have taken on the forms of animals or hybrid creatures. Accounts by Karl Hesse and Theo Aerts include the idea that Baining fire dances also involve the spirits, who reveal themselves during the performance.[72]

65 Khon Mask of Prince Rāma
(1890s–1920s)

Artist(s): Unknown

Country of origin: Thailand (formerly Siam)

Dimensions: 35 x 24 cm (13¾ x 9½ inches)

Material(s): Papier mâché, gold, wood, glass, silk, resin, metal lacquer

The Khon dance-drama in Thailand is a performing art that coalesces musical, oral, literary, ceremonial and handiwork elements. Khon involves graceful yet highly formalized dance movements, instrumental and vocal renditions, masks and opulent regalia. It portrays the story of Rama, the hero from the epic *Ramayana* (*Ramakien* in Thai), and the embodiment of Vishnu, who brings lawfulness and structure to life. The tales of Rama's life recount his journey in the forest, his legion of monkeys and his battles with the Thosakan, king of the giants, and his armed militia. *Ramayana*, the ancient Sanskrit legend, was once performed regularly across many parts of Southeast Asia, with the epic tale also represented in sculpture and painting in Myanmar, Thailand, Cambodia and Laos.

The Khon dance-drama was traditionally conveyed in the Siamese/Thai (Ayutthayan) royal court in the 16th and 17th centuries, but has since petered out. Masks, like the mask of Prince Rāma – fabricated from metal, wood and lacquered papier mâché and decorated with paint, gold leaf and small pieces of glass – are crucial to Khon performances. Combats in Khon require a very large number of players, so numerous masks are needed for gods, demons, monkeys, ogresses and royal men, for example. Unmasked players are traditionally women – celestials maidens, the wives and daughters of demons, and queens. The Prince Rama mask is distinguished by his green skin, graceful smiling features and highly elaborate crown – all indicative of royal characters.

Khon is currently staged for resident and visiting tourist audiences, and subsidized throughout national occasions. In one way, Khon epitomizes 'high art' forms fostered by early Siamese/Thai courts, while as a theatrical presentation, it can be understood and relished by audiences from very diverse societal circumstances. Khon has a dedicated principled purpose to reinforce respect, shared ideas and relationships, traditions and social values, not to mention upholding the universal concept of good over evil. Happily, then, UNESCO has accredited the significance of narrative and performance in the region's arts and culture by inscribing some of these forms – including the Khon masked dance-drama in 2018 – on the 'Representative List of Intangible Cultural Heritage'.

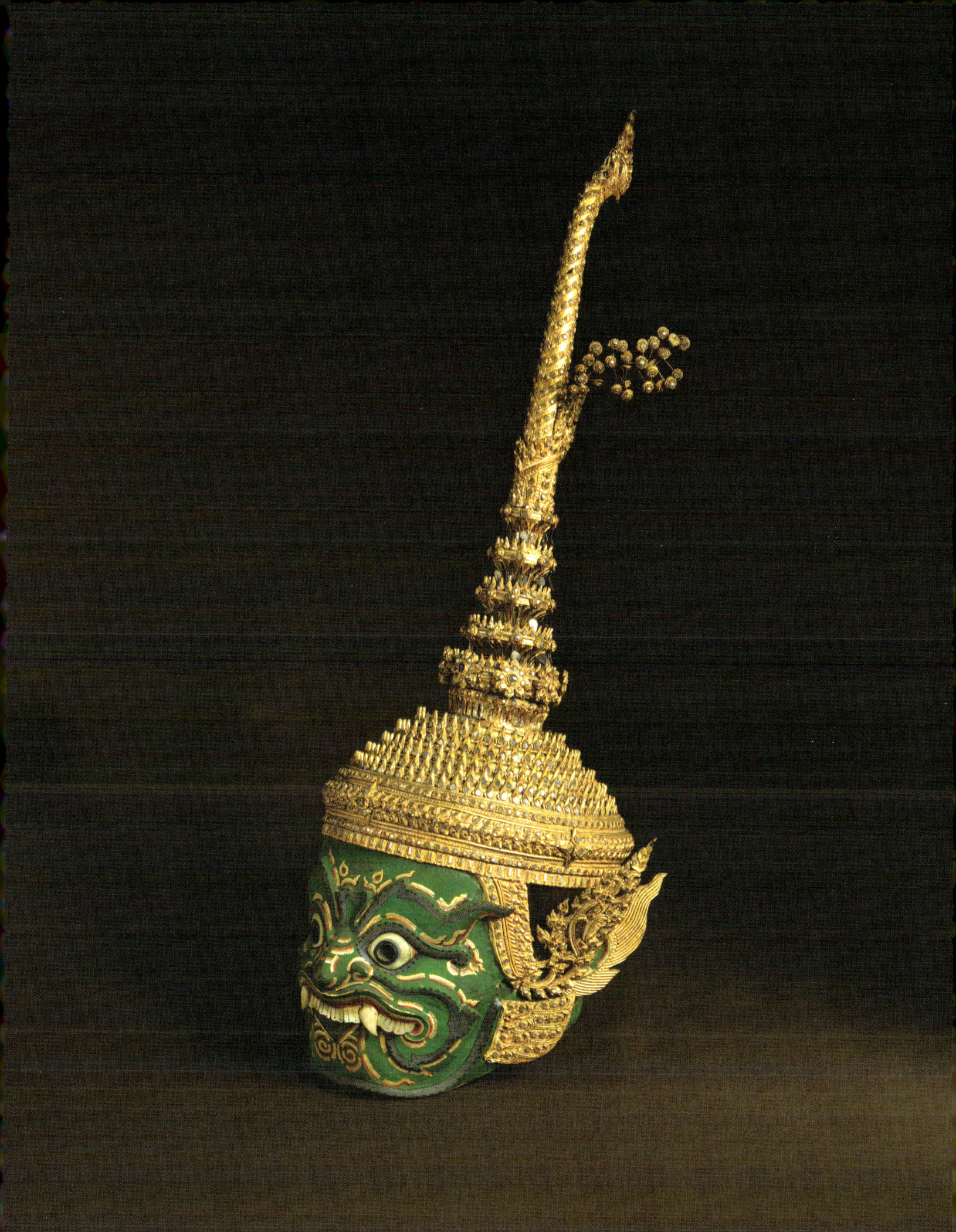

Kalikongu Feast Trough
(Acquired 1891)

Artist(s): Unknown

Country of origin: Solomon Islands

Dimensions: 8m (26ft)

Material(s): Carved wood, shell inlay and pigment

The Melanesian diet traditionally depended on root crops, leaf greens, fruits and nuts. Those in coastal regions naturally had a diet based on fish and seafood, while inlanders ate game like opossum and birds and fish from rivers. Pigs were a common feasting delicacy on islands other than New Caledonia. Coconuts were essential to the islander regimen and provided drinking 'water', oil and coconut cream. As a preservative and condiment, salt could be harvested, either extracted from trapped pools of salty brine, or from coconut husks and other plant matter or driftwood, by carefully preserving the salty ashes.

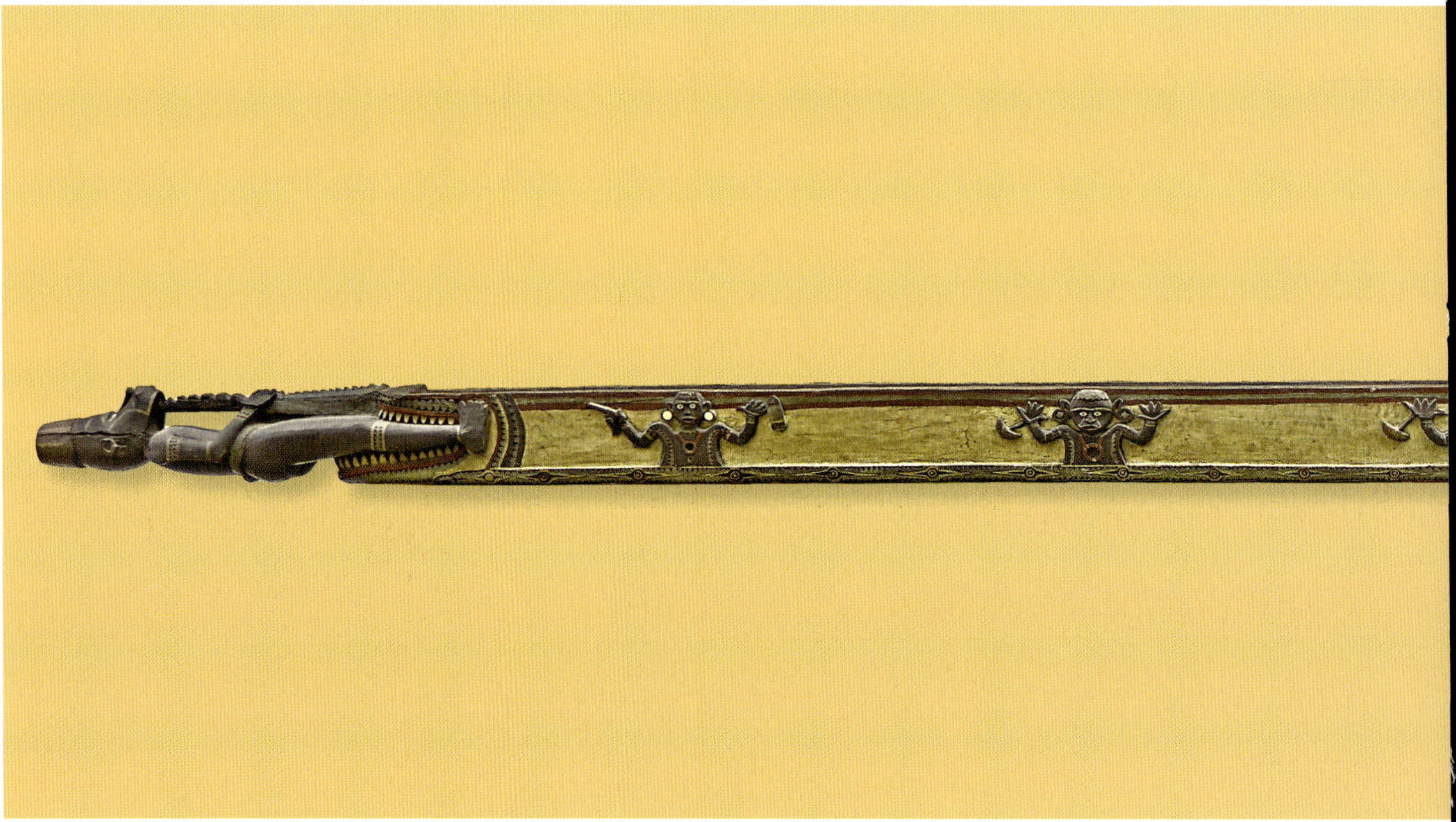

Food was traditionally roasted, steamed or boiled, with lots of stirring and pulverizing required. Hence the use of the term 'pudding' in the context of 18th-century Polynesian cooking is both fitting and highly enlightening. Melanesian feasting was a vitally important event and often the focal point of a specific rite. This 'trough' from the village of Kalikongu in the Solomon Islands would have contained a mixture of yams, taro and mixed nuts that were prepared for related headhunting sorties. It's a rare and striking artefact but hardly a 'bowl' in the traditional sense. Rather, it's a long trough in the shape of a crocodile that almost doubles as a canoe. While a human head is caught in a crocodile's huge jaws

at one end, its tail is grabbed by an anthropomorphic figure whose legs are devoured by a shark at the other. The trough also has carved images of warriors holding shields, clubs, hatchets and, in one instance, a revolver, a direct indication of its colonial history and influence.

Nicholas Thomas has made a convincing case for European traders emboldening the already highly competitive and expansionist culture of the Roviana people, whose traditional weapons were replaced by iron-bladed hatchets and muskets. Here, the violence was multiplied by Europeans seeking a labour force for Queensland, Fiji and other places. Hence a pattern of incursions and retaliations concerning inhabitants and European recruiters was recurrently lethal. On one particular 'voyage' to investigate supposed 'outrages' by HMS *Royalist* in 1890–2, Admiral Davis carried out retributive actions resulting in the shelling and looting of Roviana Lagoon villages, and the killing of villagers. In a correspondence of 1904, Davis condones the feasting trough's confiscation because of the consumption of cooked human flesh from this particular feast trough. According to Thomas Edge-Partington, Deputy Commissioner of the Western Solomons, however, the '[Roviana chief] Ingova assured me time after time that they never eat men from the trough; the heads are always there during the ceremony, but no human meat was eaten from it.'[75] The Kalikongu feast trough thus carries the histories of both indigenous and European violence, nonetheless expressed via a highly innovative and extraordinary form of Oceanic art, which has 'been seldom or never displayed, and seldom if ever published'.[74]

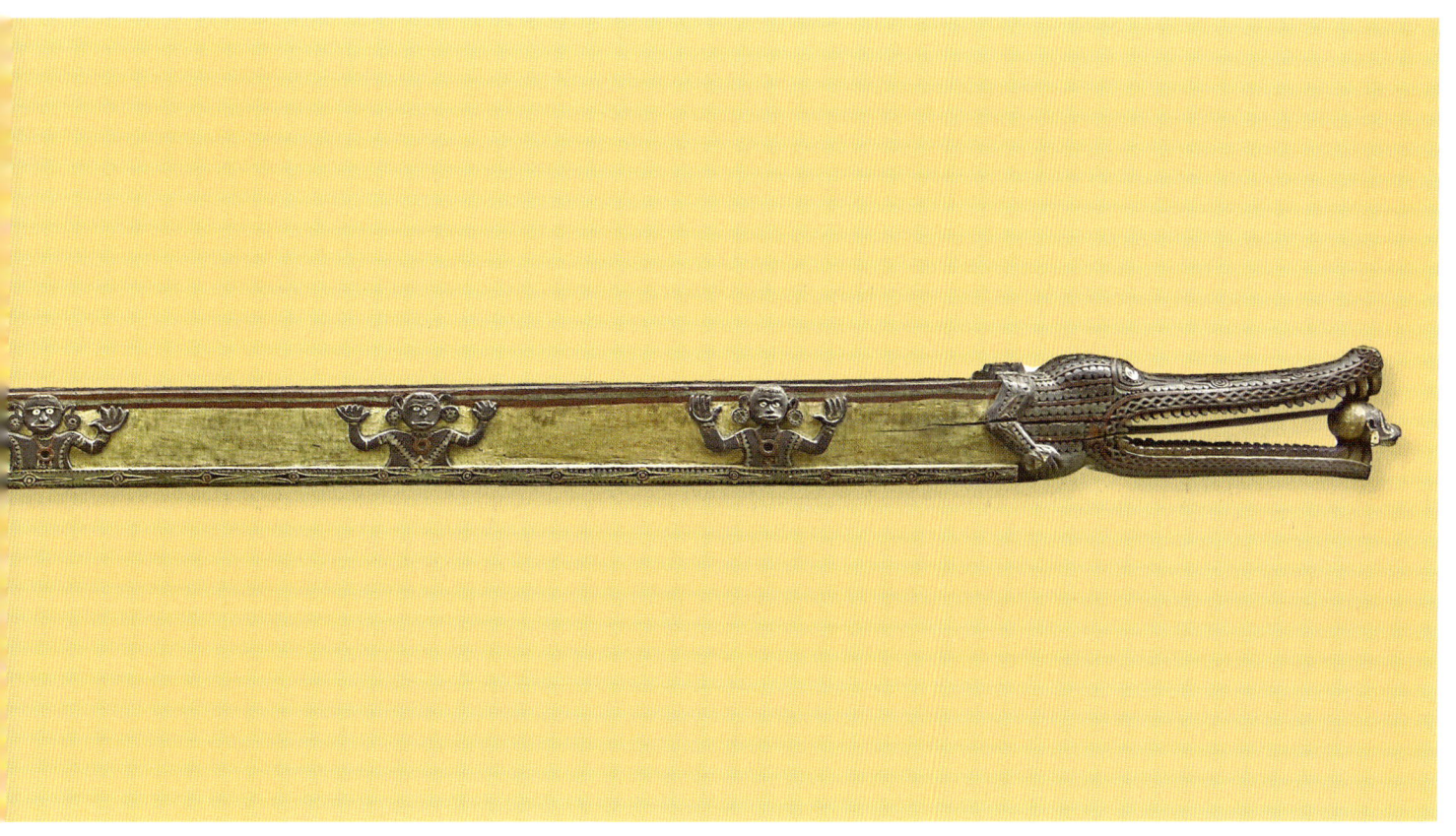

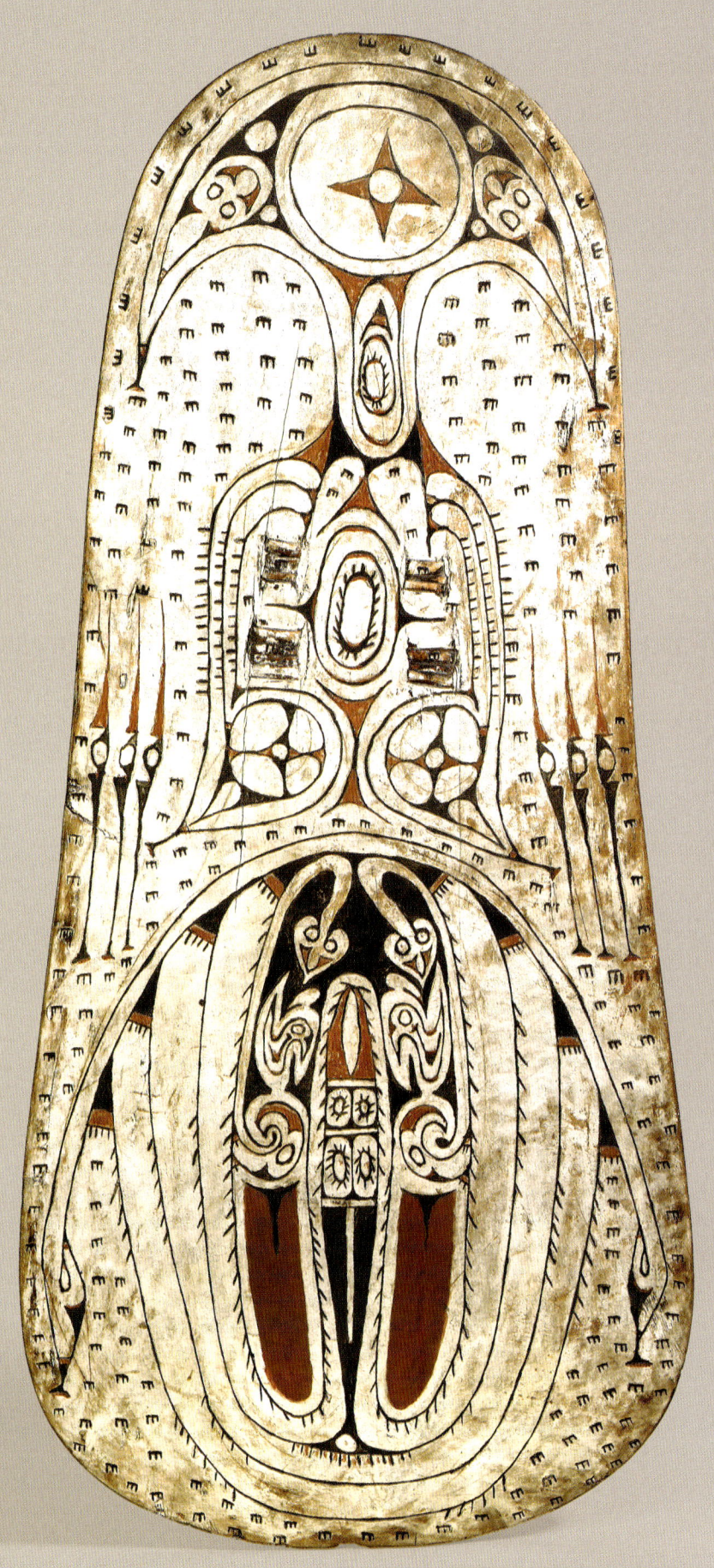

67 Painted Shield
(Acquired 1893)

Architect(s): Unknown

Country of origin: Papua New Guinea

Dimensions: 70.5 x 31.5 cm (28 x 12½ inches)

Material: Acacia wood, ochre, cane

In New Guinea societies, as in Europe and other places, weaponry was diverse, frequently embellished and greatly prized. Some of the most eye-catching were decorated shields, including this shield from the Trobriand Islands. This type of weapon was made throughout New Guinea and was typically carved out of individual cuts of acacia wood, scored and painted, but occasionally interlaced with cane and decorated with barkcloth, braids, twine or feathers.

The Trobriand shield is not simply a tool for defence against projectiles, but also a weapon. In the Trobriand Islands, the shields were smaller and made to deflect spears and arrows in close combat. A good number were unpainted, with only the boldest of fighters showcasing the shield illustrated, which has elaborate black and red motifs painted on a white background.

The shields are part of an age-old argument regarding the anthropology of art. The British anthropologist Edmund Leach interpreted the lower central portion of this shield as illustrative of female genitalia and a directly Freudian assessment that connected these objects with a dread of flying witches. From the point of view of the wounded, therefore, these anthropomorphic motifs could be deemed as malign and hostile apparitions.

In 2005 and 2006, Harry Beran – with the help of the Trobriand's Paramount Chief Pulayasi, Chief of Omarakana Village – actually distinguished the motifs on this particular shield. They consist of a red snake, who carried 'war magic to Kiriwina Island', and a red feather, a mark of the most courageous warriors. Insects, including the cricket, were highly venerated by combatants because of their speed of movement.[75]

The shield's lustre, dazzle or 'brilliance' is an intrinsic part of its design. Like many other objects in Oceania and Australia that are not weapons – wooden canoe prows, lengths of painted barkcloth, colourful-looking fabrics and bags included – they might appear to Western eyes as akin to modernist 'optical art', in which ocular illusions intimate feelings of movement, cryptic images, flickering and oscillating patterns as well as other highly destabilizing sensations. The artistic qualities of the New Guinea shields have correspondences that stretch across different genres and cultures, as well as across Oceania. More crucially, perhaps, Trobriand shields become highly 'aggressive instruments': 'Their designs were meant to dazzle, disorientate, intimidate and frighten…. The object at once powerful and unsettling – in the hands of a killer… simply terrifying.'[76]

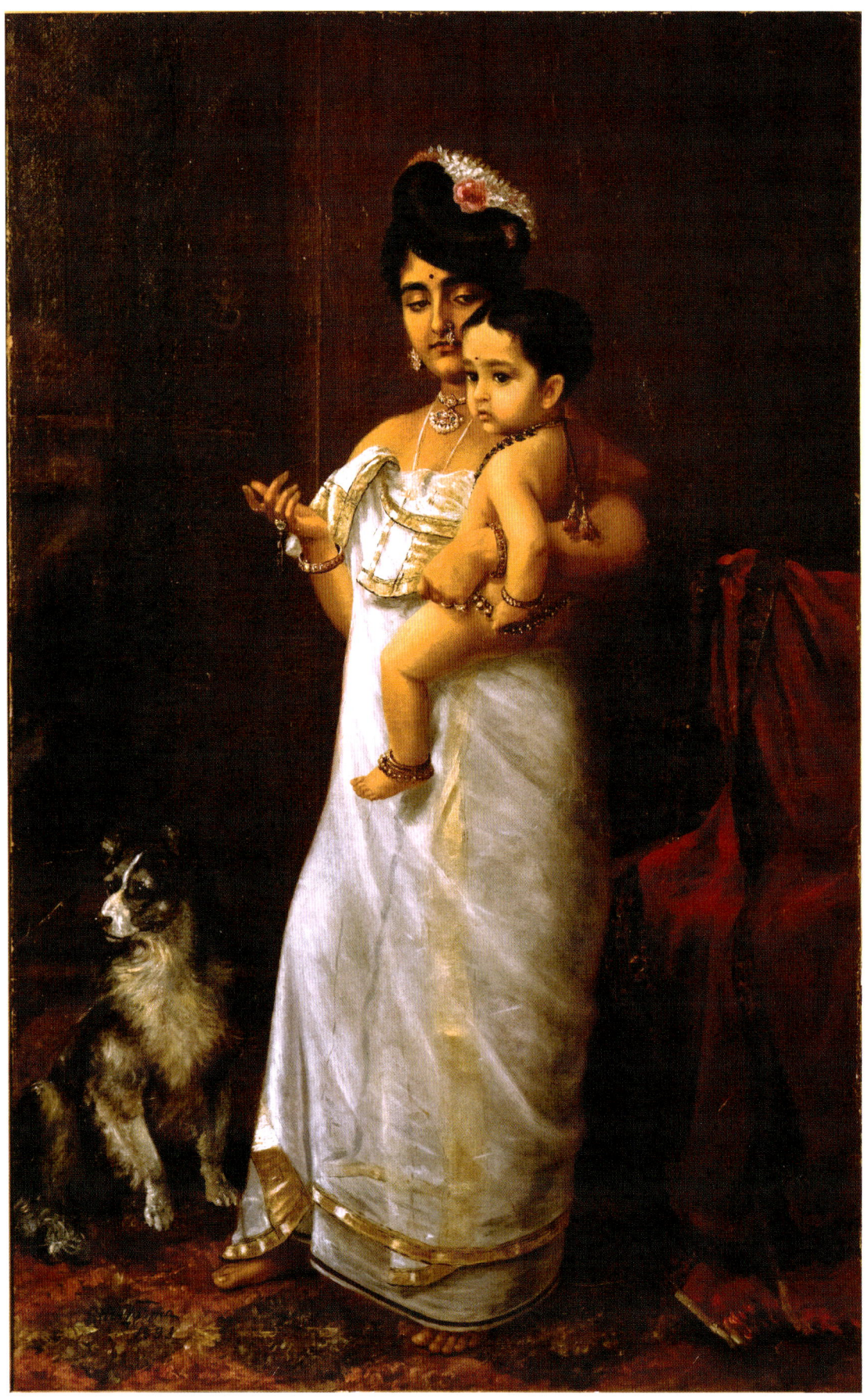

68 *There Comes Papa*
(1893)

Architects: Ravi Varma

Country of origin: India

Dimensions: 125 x 81 cm (49 x 32 inches)

Material(s): Oil on canvas

The art world has always been somewhat divided over the influence of Raja Ravi Varma (1848–1906), who has variously been described as 'the father of modern Indian painting' (Geeta Kapur in *When was Modernism: Essays on Contemporary Cultural Practice in India*, 2000) and 'kitsch' by the art historian Ratan Parimoo. What is undeniable is the role that Raja Ravi Varma played in fusing Indian iconographic art styles with the classical realism of European art that stemmed from the late 17th, 18th and 19th centuries, and this is evidenced by the work shown here.

Rich in tone and colour, this portrait shows Ravi Varma's eldest daughter, Mahaprabha Thampuratti, holding one of her sons, Marthanda Varma, in her arms. It is a scene that displays both the trappings of a well-to-do Indian family and some of the traditional European artistic influences in terms of the pose, lighting and symbols of domestic trappings, such as the dog sitting at Mahaprabha's feet (dogs are considered unclean in India). The work was well received in Western art circles and was shown as one of ten paintings of women in India by Ravi Varma at the Chicago World's Fair in 1893. Ravi Varma was forbidden from travelling to the exhibition, but he received a certificate of merit for his work.

Raja Rami Varma had been born into an aristocratic family in the kingdom of Travancore, which was in the state that is now Kerala, on the Malabar coast of India. Thanks to the familial connections of Rami Varma's wife to the Travancore royal family (which adhered to a matrilineal form of succession), Mahaprabha Thampuratti's daughter Lakshmi Bayi and her cousin Parvati Bayi (the daughter of Mahaprabha's younger sister) were adopted by the Travancore royals in 1900 and created Senior and Junior Ranis of Attingal respectively.

In addition to his Western-influenced paintings, such as this one, Raja Rami Varma drew on his training by both Rama Swami Naidu (in watercolour) and Theodore Jenson (oils) to produce numerous bright, colourful works that depicted scenes of Hindu literary figures and of the *Mahabharata, Ramayana* and *Puranas*. Many were then turned into lithographs and printed by the press that Rami Varma set up in Ghatkopar, Mumbai. The result was that for almost the first time, many families throughout India were able to purchase artworks for their homes. His legacy remains controversial, but 21st-century artists such as Pushpamala N. have drawn on his work for inspiration.

Tā Moko Panel
(1896−9)

Artist(s): Tene Waitere

Country of origin: Aotearoa New Zealand

Dimensions: 77 cm (30³⁄₁₀ inches)

Material(s): Wood

Aestheticizing non-Western art often draws criticism because Westernized terminology can appear inappropriate to, and perhaps an appropriation of, cultural artefacts created by indigenous societies. It is undeniably correct that there is hardly an accurate counterpart for this term in non-European languages, but even by Western standards the definition of 'art' – especially in the 20th century modernism – is often put in parentheses. Indeed, as Nicholas Thomas points out, 'almost every culture had some category of "valuables", and "valuables" were typically carefully and elaborately produced artefacts.'[77]

In the case of this wonderfully instructive relief carving by Tene Waitere (*c.* 1854−1931) of a *tā moko* (tattoo) panel, the latter approach is highly deceptive because it was intended to illustrate tattoo patterns for the ethnologist and curator Augustus Hamilton's *The Art Workmanship of the Māori* (1896−1900). In fact, the artist exploited European sponsorship to try out a highly non-conventional approach to sculpting the face, which is depicted in three-quarter profile. It is probably the earliest such departure from a traditional frontal image in the Rotorua region, the panel demonstrating the master carver's fascination with experimental composition and technique.

Born among his Ngāti Tarāwhai *whānau* (family) in Ruato, on Lake Rotoiti, Waitere was trained by celebrated carvers such as Wero Tāroi and Anaha Te Rāhui, whom he extolled in a well-known letter of 22 September 1926: 'Among the experts, Wero was a very great expert with great name among Te-Arawa for his carving. Te Arno also was a very great expert before Anaha Te Rāhui, a great expert well known to the Government... [T]hese elders taught me the ways of the Māori for teaching the knowledge of carving.' His major projects included the Rauru, the famous meeting house carved for a Rotorua hotel, held at the Museum fur Völkerkunde in Hamburg. The Rauru was not a tribal house per se but rather an individual commission from a Pākehā [European-descent] hotel keeper, Charles Nelson.

A list of Waitere's carvings takes in a wide spectrum and larger multiplicity than those by other contemporary carvers. His carvings often helped fill an intense demand for 'authentic' replicas of traditional objects for sale to Europeans like Hamilton in the 1890s. Besides the *Tā Moko Panel*, Waitere worked on smaller commissions, including tobacco pipes, walking sticks, canoe paddles (*hoe*), golf clubs, mirror frames and replicas of customary artefacts, that were all created primarily for the European market. As with many other indigenous artists, he made objects specifically for sale in a burgeoning 'art' market. So, this type of object was 'not extracted from the flow of ordinary life, from the community or ceremonial use; [but] arguably "out of context – works of 'art'", dare we say it – in the first place.'[78]

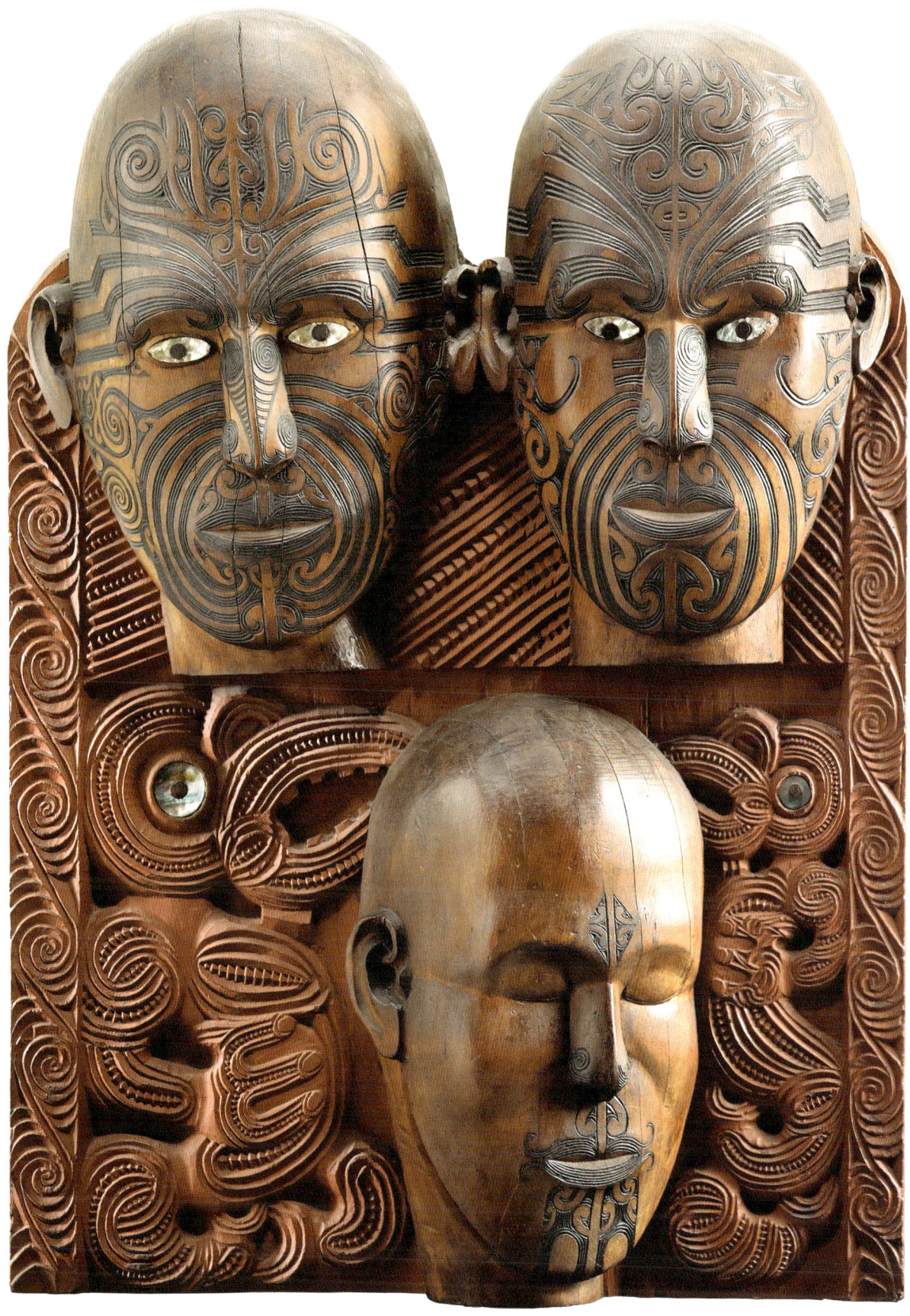

70 *Melons*
(1899)

Artist(s): Daoud Corm

Country of origin: Lebanon

Dimensions: 60 x 73 cm
(23½ x 29 inches)

Material(s): Oil on canvas

Daoud Corm (also known as Dawoud al Qorm) (1852–1930) was a pioneer of modern art in Lebanon. His talent as a draughtsman was spotted by two Jesuit priests who offered him a position teaching art at the local missionary school in exchange for giving him Italian lessons. The lessons proved useful when Corm left Lebanon in 1870 to go and study art in Rome at the Accademia San Luca under Roberto Bompiani. He then moved to Belgium for a few years, working as an official painter to the royal household under King Leopold II.

On his return to Beirut, Corm set up his studio and produced portraits of the great and the good of Beirut society, using as his calling card an image of his work on a portrait that he had made of Pope Pius IX while in Rome. He then established Maison d'Art, which not only formed the backdrop to his painting career but also sold art materials to others and offered facilities for them to develop their photographs in the shop's darkroom and, in doing so, helped to develop the growing Lebanese modern art movement. His influence was such that he mentored a young Khalil Gibran (1883–1931), the author of *The Prophet*.

Corm's artistic style reflects various influences, including the Renaissance masters and later Italian artists whom he studied in his late teens, which is exhibited in both his portraits and his religious paintings. He was not a natural landscape artist, the results looking somewhat simplistic and stilted, but he also completed various still lifes, such as the work shown here depicting melons. The formality of the styling and perspective of the image owe much to the Dutch and Spanish still lifes that were popular in the 17th and 18th centuries. The brushwork is assured and clean in style, also suggesting a return to simplicity and a counterpoint to the Impressionist style that was growing in popularity across Europe at the time he was there studying.

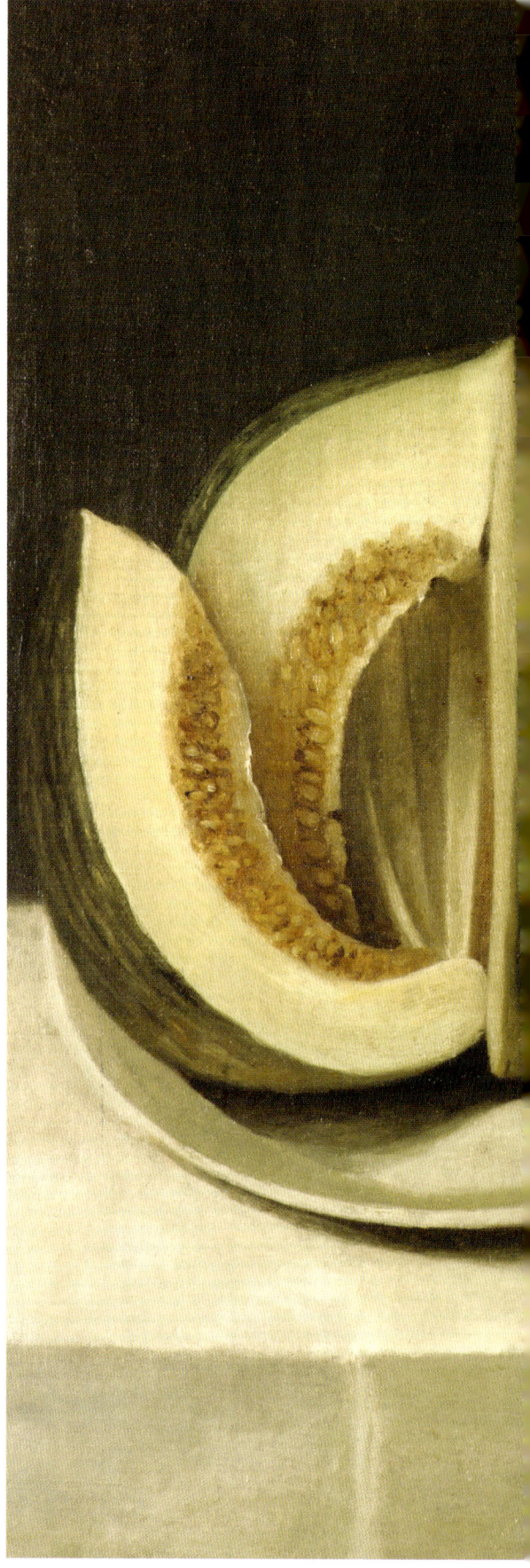

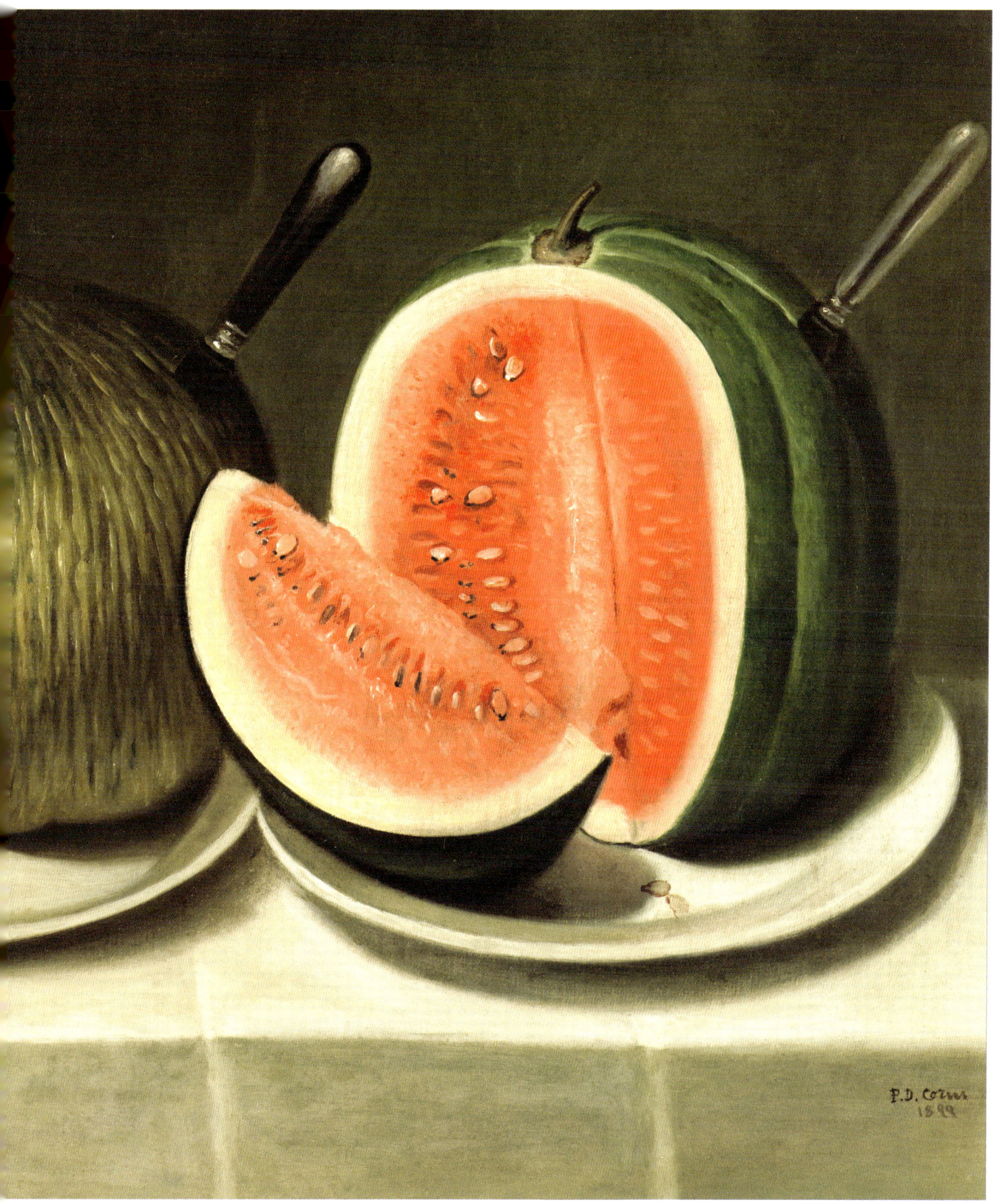

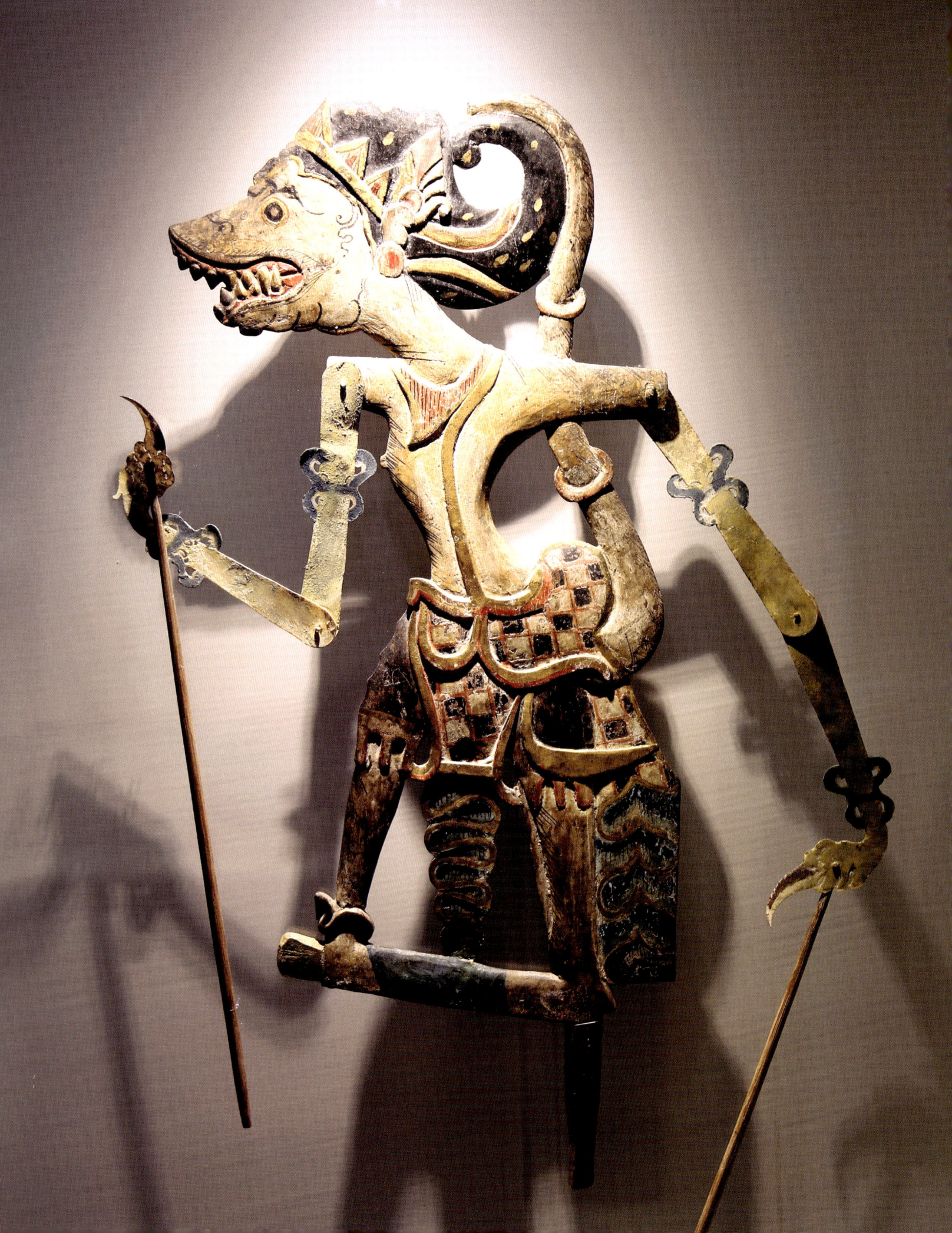

Wayang Klitik Puppet
(*c.* 1900)

Artist(s): Unknown

Country of origin: Java, Indonesia

Dimensions: Approx. 60 cm (23½ inches)

Material(s): Wood, metal and natural pigment paints

Narrative plays an important part in Southeast Asian art, with tales performed in numerous ways, and epic literature recounted via wall paintings, sculptures and relief carvings. Traditional storytelling – often handed down orally – was a vital means of communicating philosophical and religious ideas as well as social customs. And it's still practised today.

There are various types of performing arts, including the 'Theatre of Shadows' or *wayang*, where the shadows of puppets are cast on to a blank screen, a genre widely thought to have originated in Java. The Javanese term *wayang* is said to stem from the Malay word *bayang* ('shadow'), which suggests that shadow plays are a homegrown performing art associated with familial veneration, since the 'Theatre of Shadows' is intended to represent ancestor figures. Experts on *wayang* have alternatively argued that this is not credible because the word for *wayang* in High Javanese and Balinese, *ringgit*, does not mean shadow but rather refers to 'dancers', 'theatre' or 'actor'.

The specific colours given to the puppets to typify the characters also demonstrate that it is not just shadow that is crucial to the play.[79] Through *wayang*, the Javanese recognize 'stories from long ago', which are mainly derived from two great Hindu Indian epics: the *Ramayana* and the *Mahabharata*. The puppet illustrated here represents Hanuman, the Hindu white monkey god, son of Batahara Bayu, the wind god, in the *Ramayana*. Hanuman can be identified here by his long fingernail (*kuku pancanaka*), a symbol of both his divine origin and the supernatural powers that help kill his enemies. In Javanese eyes, Hanuman is honourable, courageous and noble, and helps Rama – an embodiment of Vishnu and the rightful heir to the throne – win back his kidnapped wife, Sinta, from the evil demon Rawana. However, as Fiona Kerlogue points out, in all Southeast Asian stories 'the battle is not simply one of good against evil; characters… provide lessons about duty, self-discipline and honour, much discussed by audiences.'

Creating a puppet like Hanuman was no easy task because it involved highly skilled work by different artisans. It was manufactured mostly out of wood (as here; this is termed a *wayang klitik*) and sometimes metal or buffalo leather, then painted. Flexible arms and handles were manufactured from thinner strips, and appended to the body and arms so the *dalang* (puppeteer) could manoeuvre it. Traditionally, performances last through the night, the *dalang* controlling up to six puppets at any one time, with music (often gamelan), voices and songs performed by the puppet master to provide ambience. Today, the 'Theatre of Shadows' maintains a combination of pagan, Hindu and Muslim features, its tradition still very much alive.

Sulka *Susu* Mask

(*c.* 1900)

Artist(s): Sulka people

Country of origin: New Britain, Papua New Guinea

Dimensions: 90 cm (35 inches)

Material(s): Rattan, vegetable pith, fibre, feathers, natural pigments

New Britain is an island northwest of Australia. In the past, its archipelagos were occupied, apportioned and disputed intermittently by Britain, France, Germany and Australia. Regardless of the events and impact of colonialism, in some parts of the Bismarck Archipelago the abundant array of mask-making traditions have been remarkably impervious to change, some surviving unremittingly today. Some of the most spectacular are the masks of the Sulka, recognized for their multiplicity and size.

Manufactured out of highly transitory materials such as vegetable pith, plant fibres and natural pigments, *susu* masks were used in initiation rites and funeral ceremonies. Among the many languages, cultural arrangements and numerous art forms in New Britain, 'secret societies' openly interact with formidable ancestral spirits. The masks largely depict human spirits, but some have animal attributes such as the form of a python, an important ritual reptile that illustrates spiritual strength and is frequently shown curving along the back of the human head and out through the mouth. By becoming a member of these secretive and restricted groups, men learned to hone their mask-making skills and master ritualistic dances and songs. When initiated, a member could wear and perform in these ritually imbued objects without fear of injury.[80]

The mask shown was probably manufactured from strips of spongy white pith from the interior of a reed (a species of liana), which was stitched on to a basketry or wicker framework, a highly rare method of manufacture not seen elsewhere in the Pacific Islands. Ritual motifs and bodily particulars of the mask were painted on the outside in an assortment of brilliant colours, applied at the eleventh hour to prevent the natural pigments fading. Originally, the colour of this mask would probably have been a darker red or vermilion but has now faded.

The mask was at its most dazzling during a performance. Photographs of a Sulka mask in performance *c.* 1980s also show the wearers with a long, shaggy-looking shawl and skirt made of riven palm leaves.[81] The wavering fringe of the energetically moving costume would have augmented the theatrical character of this highly idiosyncratic mask – 'a performance aimed at creating the effect of a revelation', Monica Jeudy-Ballini explains.[82] The dancers are presaged by a trumpeting conch shell and shouts from tribesmen, who mix with now singing and dancing womenfolk. The dance is short – perhaps only 10 minutes or so – the masks eventually sent back to the forest to decay. The impact of the dance was intended to create 'emotional turmoil' in the onlookers, expressed as 'joy, love, nostalgia, affliction, depression or any other conflicting feeling'.[83] As Eric Kjellgren points out: 'In recent decades, some artists across the region have revived or revitalized other art forms once largely abandoned, and in some places… they have pioneered a growing contemporary art movement.'[84]

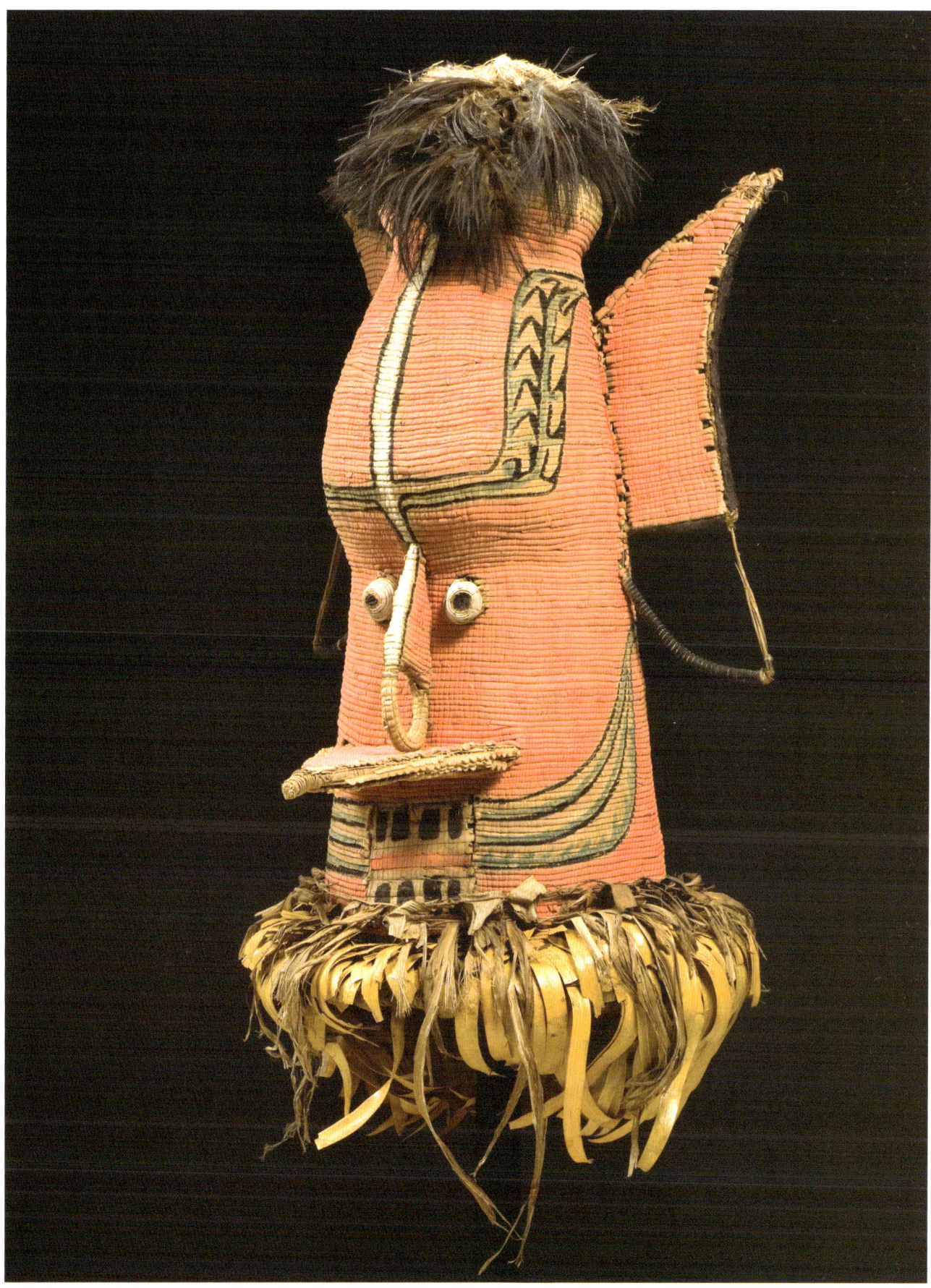

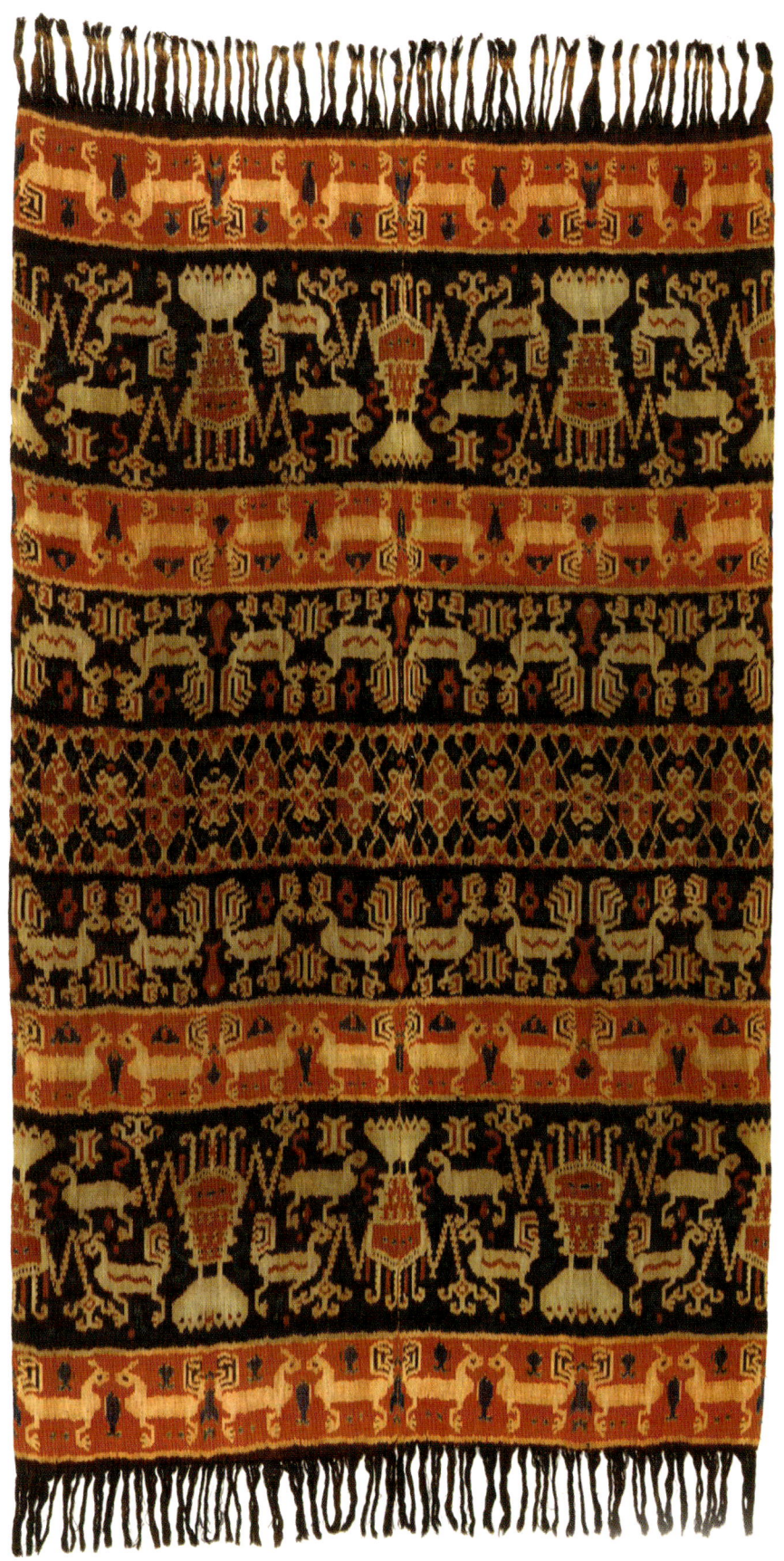

Hinggi Cloth (Man's Mantle)
(*c.* 1900–20)

Artist(s): Unknown

Country of origin: Indonesia

Dimensions: Approx. 2.54 x 1.27 m (100 x 50 inches)

Material(s): Cotton and natural vegetable dyes

In Indonesia and mainland Southeast Asia textiles are connected to the spiritual and ritual character of life and death. In the 20th century, studies by Dutch ethnologists, who were fascinated by the structural networks of these societies, focused on the 'symbolic dualism' of Indonesian beliefs.[85] As in all societies, social organization is highly multifaceted, but as Fiona Kerlogue explains, 'the balance between male and female worlds lies at the core of representation in Indonesian culture'.[86] Essentially, clan knowledge about aesthetic traditions takes place in secret, with vital information transferred through visual representation on, say, a materfamilias's sarong.

Another feature of what is, fundamentally, a patrilineal cultural system is the allocation of duties, with men basically accountable for wood carving and metalwork, and women for fabrics, floorcoverings and basket weaving.[87] Here, the exchange of gifts is also categorized in terms of male and female: 'textiles, ivory bangles, glass beads, pottery and pigs considered female, and given by the wife's family. The gifts from the husband's side include gold jewellery, horses, weapons and in earlier times slaves also.'[88]

Textiles also have a spiritual and ritual dimension, with unearthly forces frequently ascribed to such fabrics. For instance, the golden colouration of a nobleman's *hinggi kombu* (three-coloured wrap including red dye or *kombu*; simpler *hinggi* use only two colours of dye) from the east of the island of Sumba is said to convey preternatural powers.[89] Fabrics of this kind were only borne by noblemen and worn at special times to project authority and prosperity.

In east Sumba, dominant indigenous *ikat* (tie-dyed) fabrics are part of traditional dress worn at ceremonial exchanges or used as grave goods to indicate traditional wealth and standing. Importantly, Marie Jeanne Adams has analysed the patterns of decorated cloths in east Sumba and found that the designs on *hinggi* cloths parallel the organization within traditional village groups. As such, the structural principles of the *hinggi ikat* cloth shown here seem to echo related patterns regarding the social alteration of east Sumbanese society. As Kerlogue further observes: 'This visual trope of almost symmetry, of balance and mediation, is prevalent in visual arrangements in many media in Southeast Asia, but perhaps most striking in textiles.'[90]

Charles F. Goldie in His Studio with Patara Te Tuhi from *Maoriland Photographs*
(1901)

Photographer: R. Love Edwards

Country of origin: Aotearoa New Zealand

Dimensions: 170 × 250 mm (6¾ x 10 inches)

Material(s): Gelatin silver photograph

Charles F. Goldie (1870–1947) is perhaps New Zealand's preeminent painter. Born in Auckland in 1870, he became a highly promising art student with a 'continental education' that included the prestigious Académie Julian in Paris, France, where he enrolled in July 1893. Goldie returned to Auckland in mid-1898, his career beginning in earnest in 1900 with a number of Pākehā (people of European descent) and Māori portraits exhibited at the Auckland Society of Arts. As one critic remarked, Goldie received 'the *grand prix* in popular estimation' for paintings 'far-and-away superior to anything... ever seen in Auckland... [and] the result of his [Parisian] training...'.[91]

While Māori relatives of Goldie's 'sitters' (he worked from models in the studio and/or from photographs[92]) revered these depictions of their antecedents, 'many Māori were deeply suspicious of the making of "naturalistic" portraits of living individuals and their potential for inappropriate use'.[93] The latter attitude clashed with the European desire to record the physiognomies and *tā moko* (tattooing) of Māori. Goldie's renown has been augmented by endless sensationalizing newspaper accounts to do with unrivalled market prices, thieveries, defacements and fakes. As the New Zealand art historian Roger Blackley identifies: 'The intellectual and physical neglect suffered by Goldie's paintings throughout the modernist period must in part be regarded as a form of revenge for this public renown.'[94]

Although some Māori rightly fought the seizure of their likenesses, others celebrated portraiture, cognizant that their captured image would develop *taonga* (treasured possession) in and of itself. '[I]n Māori terms it is the *mana* [authority, prestige, influence] of the portrait subject that is paramount, and a poor quality photography can take precedence over a sumptuous oil painting.'[95]

Pātara Te Tuhi, as a warrior and editor of the earliest Māori-language broadsheet, was a consistent voice for Māori grievances regarding Pākehā and a powerful advocate for portraiture, not to mention something of a cosmopolitan, who toured England in 1844. The careful photographic set up showing Te Tuhi accompanied by his unfinished portrait, drinking a cup of tea and with his workaday clothing visible beneath a splendid Māori cloak, demonstrates his effective participation in manufacturing a likeness and culture for subsequent Māori peoples of Aotearoa. As Leonard Bell has argued, 'Goldie's depictions of Māori were carefully calculated constructs... [the painter's] models for *Darby and Joan* and *The Widow* [both 1903]... primarily raw materials to be manipulated; fashioned to fit the artist's and European audience's requirements.'[96] More crucially, the photograph demonstrates native intervention in usurping the cultural forms and contexts of the settlers, and establishing a distinctive Māori response to the account of British colonial art.

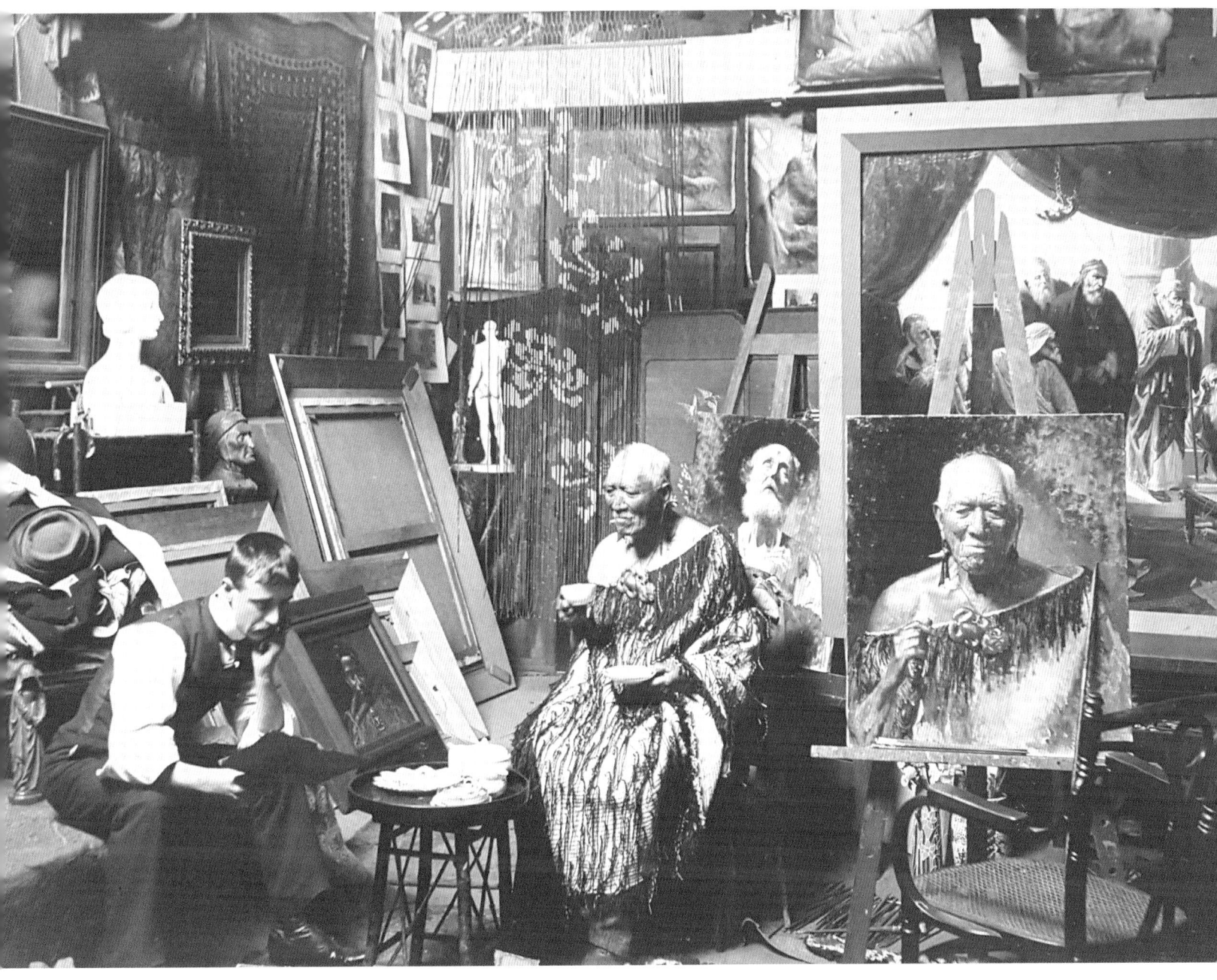

75

The Pioneer
(1904)

Artist: Frederick McCubbin

Country of origin: Australia

Dimensions: Left panel: 222.5 x 86 cm (871/2 x 34 inches); Centre panel: 224.7 x 122.5 cm (881/2 x 481/4 inches); Right panel: 223.5 x 85 cm (88 x 332/2 inches)

Material(s): Oil on canvas photograph

'The large canvas is divided into three panels to enable the painter to give pictorial insight to three episodes in the life history of those strong spirits who opened up this continent.'

The Age, 16 August 1905 (on Frederick McCubbin's *The Pioneer*)

Fredrick McCubbin's 1904 triptych was painted not long after the six British colonies – New South Wales, Victoria, Queensland, South Australia, Western Australia and Tasmania – federated, on 1 January 1901, to become the Commonwealth of Australia. McCubbin's triptych is identified with the Heidelberg School of painting, its name taken from a village near Melbourne where artists enjoyed painting *en plein air*. This new 'Australian style' was founded against the backdrop of nationalism and federalism in the late 19th century, picture-making reaffirming the socio-political attitudes of the time.

The practice of Heidelberg painters such as Tom Roberts (1856–1931) and McCubbin (1855–1917), essentially summarized the aesthetic ideology of the age. These older painters strived for a more thorough aesthetic relationship with the land, a type of story-telling that would give 'cultural meaning to a particular landscape'.[97] The bush-life bathos of *The Pioneer*, is revealing of such an approach. In the left panel, our two settlers have penetrated deep into the scrub, while in the next, 'exuberant Nature' falls under the pioneer's axe, tamed by the 'slow dogged struggle' of their free work. Undoubtedly, the ideology of the time saw these 'strong spirits who opened up this continent' helping to pioneer a new Australian nation. The final panel shows a youth tending the neglected grave, presumably of our pioneers. 'In the distance the spires and bridges of a glorious young city tell of the joys that another generation is reaping from the toil of the once lusty pioneers now gone to dust', wrote the Melbourne Age.

Despite the rather mawkish sentiments of the *Age*, McCubbin's triptych is full of ambiguity and questions. 'Why does the youth visit the seemingly unattended grave maker? Has the city forgotten?', asks Christopher Allen. How did the couple's personal sacrifices and heroic struggle become the apparent prosperity revealed by the 'glorious young city'? Are the pioneers an expulsed Adam and Eve restored by their labour, 'the child they have produced… of a new heroic race'?[98] As Allen surmises, McCubbin's painting tends to divulge far more than the *Age* would like to concede.

One outcome of the Heidelberg creed is that the Aboriginal people are rarely seen in the Movement's imagery, its ideology of declaring the lawfulness of the settler's enterprise tending to supersede Aborigines' intimacy with their lands. This might simply be viewed as a sign of colonial racial discrimination associated with the intensification of European Australia nationalism, but there is more to this issue. As Allen notes of the landscapes made by the settlers of Australia, the indigenous population is deeply, albeit very indecisively, caught up with Europeans' efforts to occupy their lands: 'It is generally true that the figure of the Aborigine appears in Australian art at moments of uncertainty or doubt, but is absent from the relatively few moments of unqualified confidence.'[99] Painted 15 years after the highpoint of the Heidelberg idiom, one other fact is omitted from McCubbin's picture: the reality of municipal and countryside wage-labour, and how 'from the safe vantage point of Melbourne or Sydney, the life of the settler was [now] something of a romantic dream.'[100]

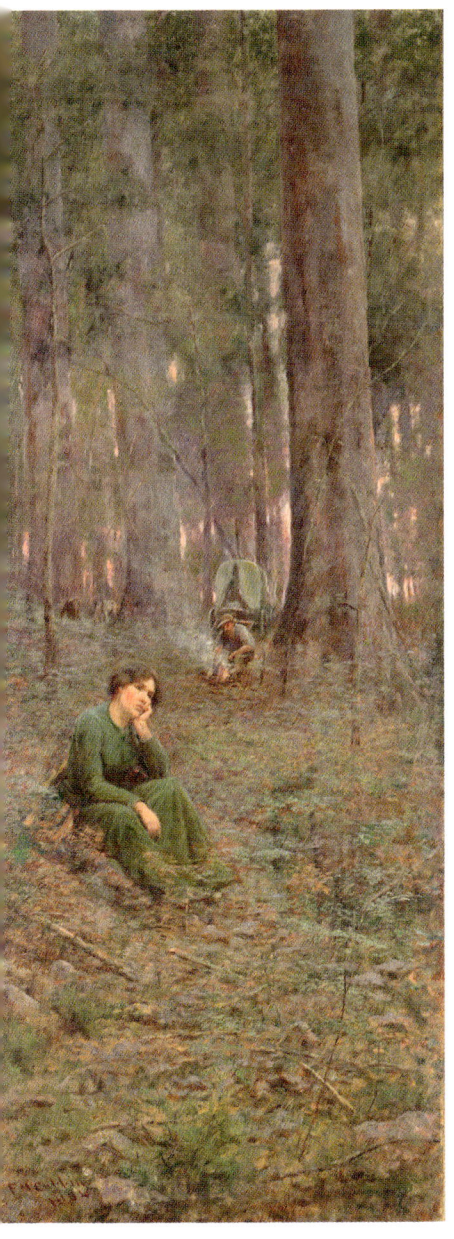
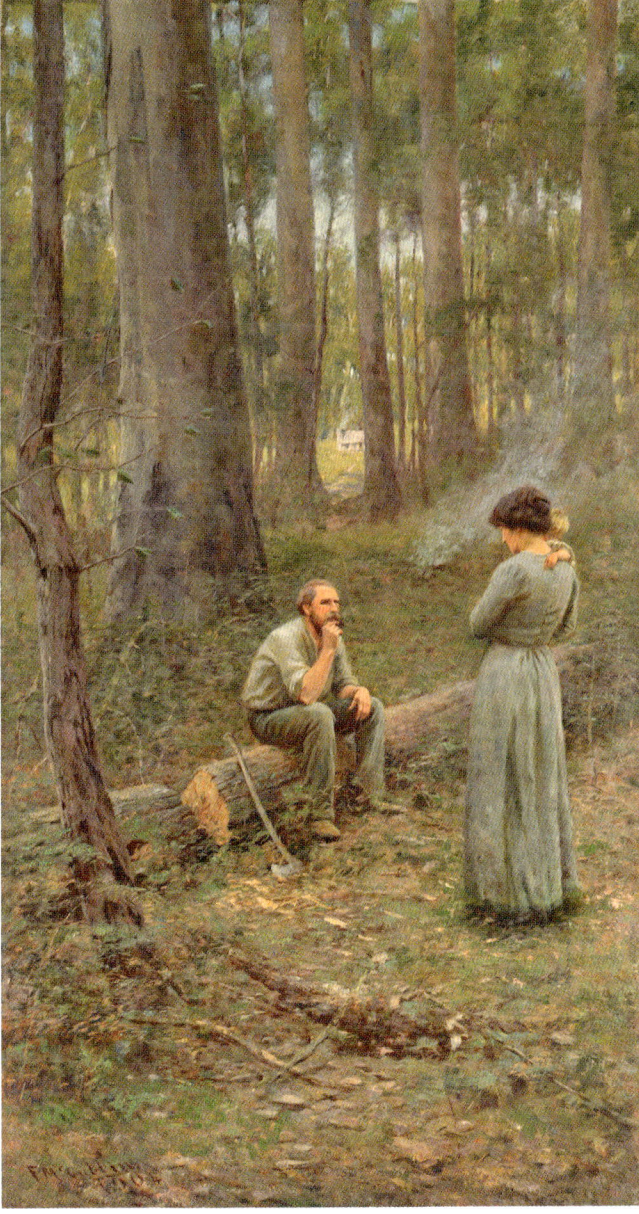
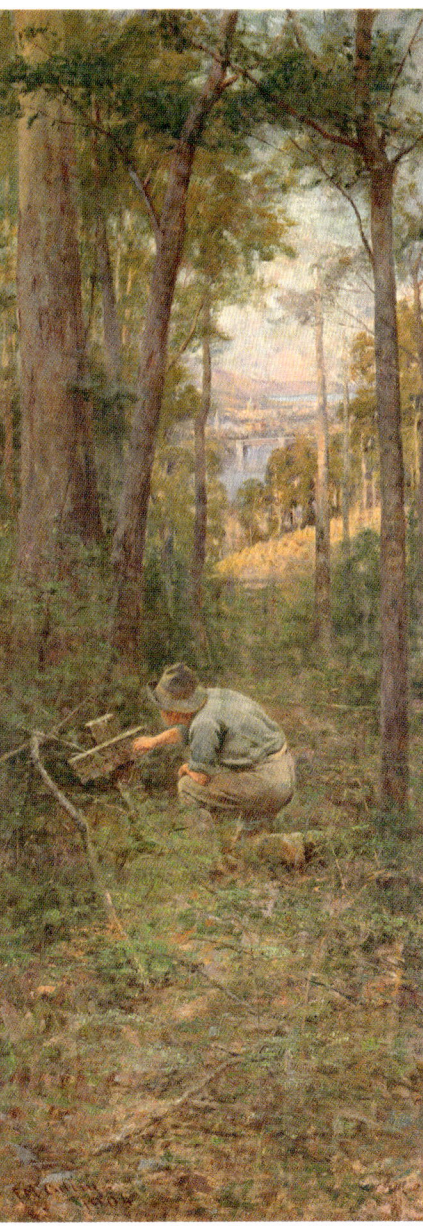

76

Portrait of Mrs Háromi
(*c*. 1907)

Artist(s): Gottfried Lindauer

Country of origin: Aotearoa New Zealand

Dimensions: 76.9 x 60.2 cm (30¼ x 23¾ inches)

Material(s): Oil on canvas

The paintings of Gottfried Lindauer (1839–1926), alongside the work of C. F. Goldie, remain the most renowned and popular images of Māori in New Zealand. It is not known why Lindauer left his native Bohemia for New Zealand in 1894. It was probably due to a desire to escape obligatory military service, the lure of newspaper articles about Aotearoa, and a visit, in 1873, to the Vienna World Exposition, where he likely encountered art by Māori.

Arriving in Wellington, Lindauer visited Nelson, where he made his first Māori portraits. In Auckland, in 1875, he met Henry Partridge, who commissioned him to paint portraits of prominent Māori figures, while an exhibition in Wellington in 1877 drew in well-known Māori chiefs, who commissioned their own portraits. At the New Zealand Industrial Exhibition in Wellington, the celebrated ornithologist Sir Walter Buller – also a barrister, native Land Court judge and major patron of Lindauer – exhibited nine of the artist's Māori portraits. In his *Galleries of Maoriland*, Roger Blackley forcefully contends that Buller's unscrupulous activities helped build a substantial fortune to boost his ethnological collection, including acquiring Lindauer's remarkable series of Māori portraits.[101]

Ironically, these portraits – in which chiefly claimants are shown wearing native *kākahu* (cloak, garments), displaying ancestral *moko* (tattooing) and festooned in *taonga* (treasured possessions) or sporting a traditional *wahaika* (hand weapon) – were part of a process that saw the handover of land across the board from traditional ancestral ownership to single settler title. In contrast, other Pākehā (people of European descent) sought to foster and secure Māori cultural *taonga tuku iho* (treasures of an earlier time). On a family trip to Europe in 1901–2, Lindauer met Josefa and Vojtěch Náprstek, who purchased two Māori portraits, including *Portrait of Mrs Háromi*, eventually sent to the Náprstek museum in Prague (in today's Czech Republic). Háromi wears a *korowai hukahuka*, a flax cloak with black braids, and *mako* (shark tooth) earrings, her long black hair embellished with *huia* (*Heteralocha acutirostris*) tail feathers to bestow further beauty and dignity. Though the identity of the subject is unclear, the facial tattoo comprising of *ngutu pūrua* (tattooed lips) and *moko kauae* (a tattooed chin) shows 'the shadow maker's' deep knowledge of Māori tattooing practices.[102] His portraits may include detailed attention to Māori *moko* and *kākahu*, but his 'journeyman' paintings are not, ethnologically speaking, exactly of the essence. They are, intentionally or not, a European construct concerning 'old-time' Māori – a sentimentalized picture of a society and culture mistakenly believed to be dying. Nonetheless, his paintings were beloved by many Māori as memorials to *whānau* (family) or *iwi* (tribe/people).

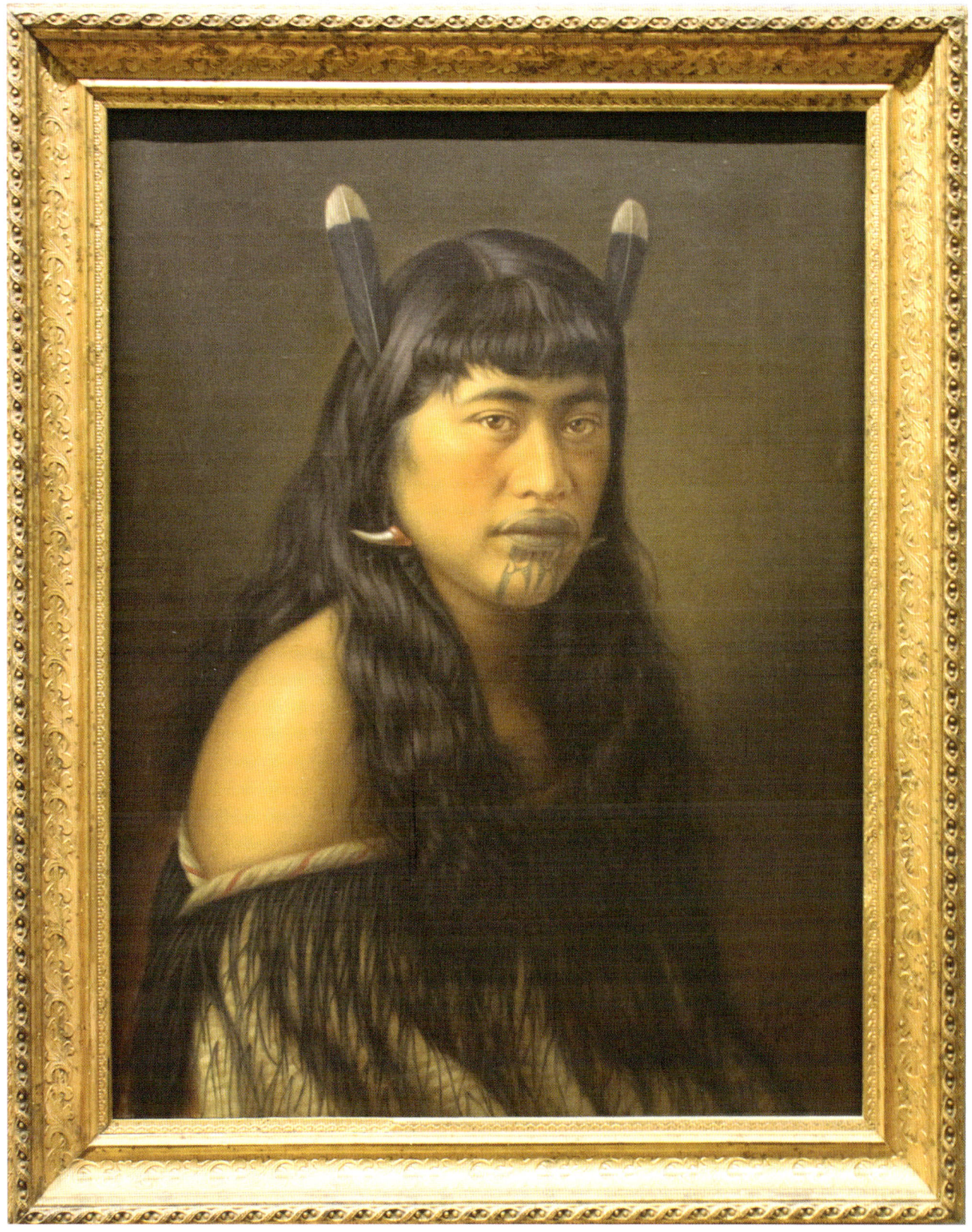

River Scene on the Banks of the Tigris
(1920)

Artist(s): Abdul Qadir Al-Rassam

Country of origin: Iraq

Dimensions: 61.5 x 91.5 cm (24¼ x 36 inches)

Materials: Oil on canvas

Abdul Qadir Al-Rassam was a pioneer of modern Iraqi painting and a leader of the realism movement in the country. Born in 1882 in the *vilayet* (administrative province) of Baghdad during the rule of the Ottoman Empire, he attended the military college in Istanbul, the capital of the empire at the time, where he also studied drawing and painting. He was attracted to the Realism movement that had begun in France in the late 1840s. This approach to art abandoned the romanticism which had dominated both art and literature and attempted to portray subjects in a more natural and truthful manner.

Al-Rassam developed his painting in this European style while he pursued his military career in Istanbul, learning to use an easel, which was uncommon in this part of the world. When he retired, Al-Rassam decided to return to Baghdad, which was now under monarchical rule, but his wife and children refused to go with him, so he lived alone, painting and teaching art both privately and in local schools. He died in 1952. Although he travelled to various European countries to study further, it is for his work in Baghdad that he is best known. Along with three other Iraqi artists – Mohammed Hajji Selim (1883–1941), Asim Hafidh (1886–1978) and Mohammed Saleh Zaki (1888–1974) – Al-Rassam promoted the Realism style and, together, these four were known as the Ottoman artists.

For the most part, he painted landscapes and scenes of everyday life in Baghdad. This charming view shows the River Tigris, one of his most popular subjects. While there is a clarity and sense of mannered precision about his style, Al-Rassam was not above manipulating the proportions of buildings and other features – and even adding motifs – to create atmosphere and accentuate the panoramic effect of his viewpoint.

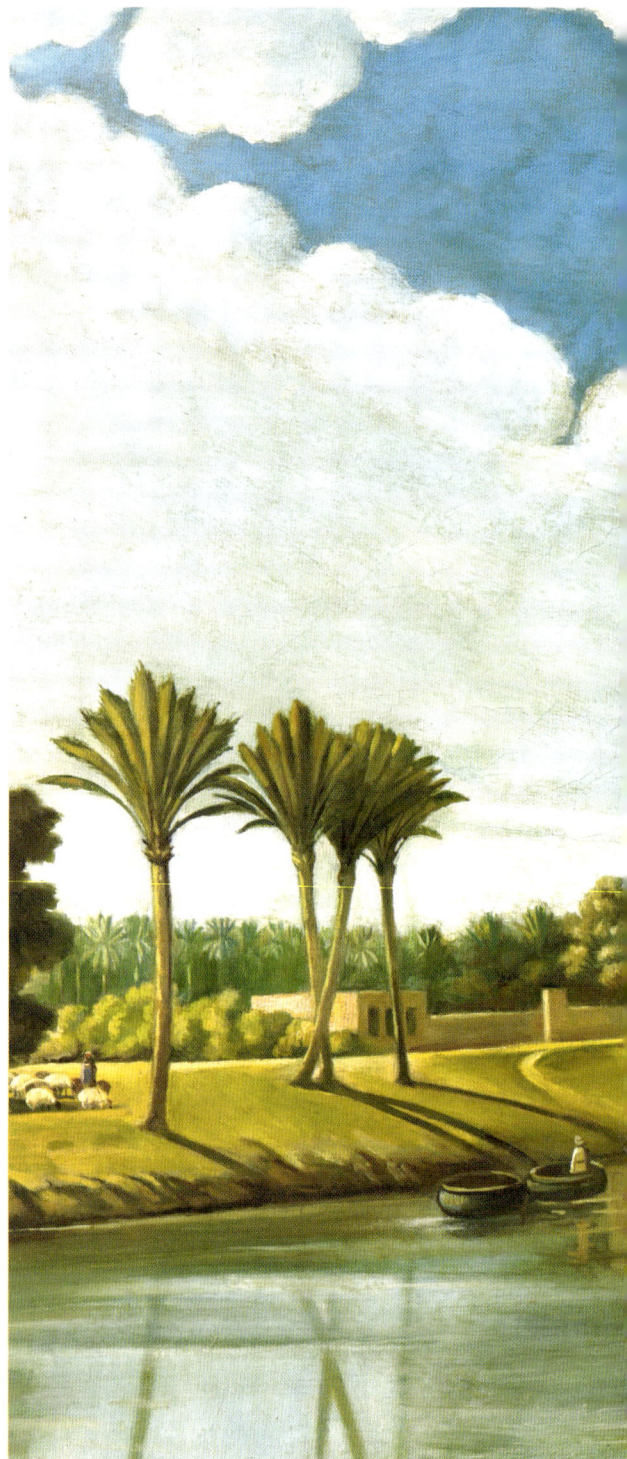

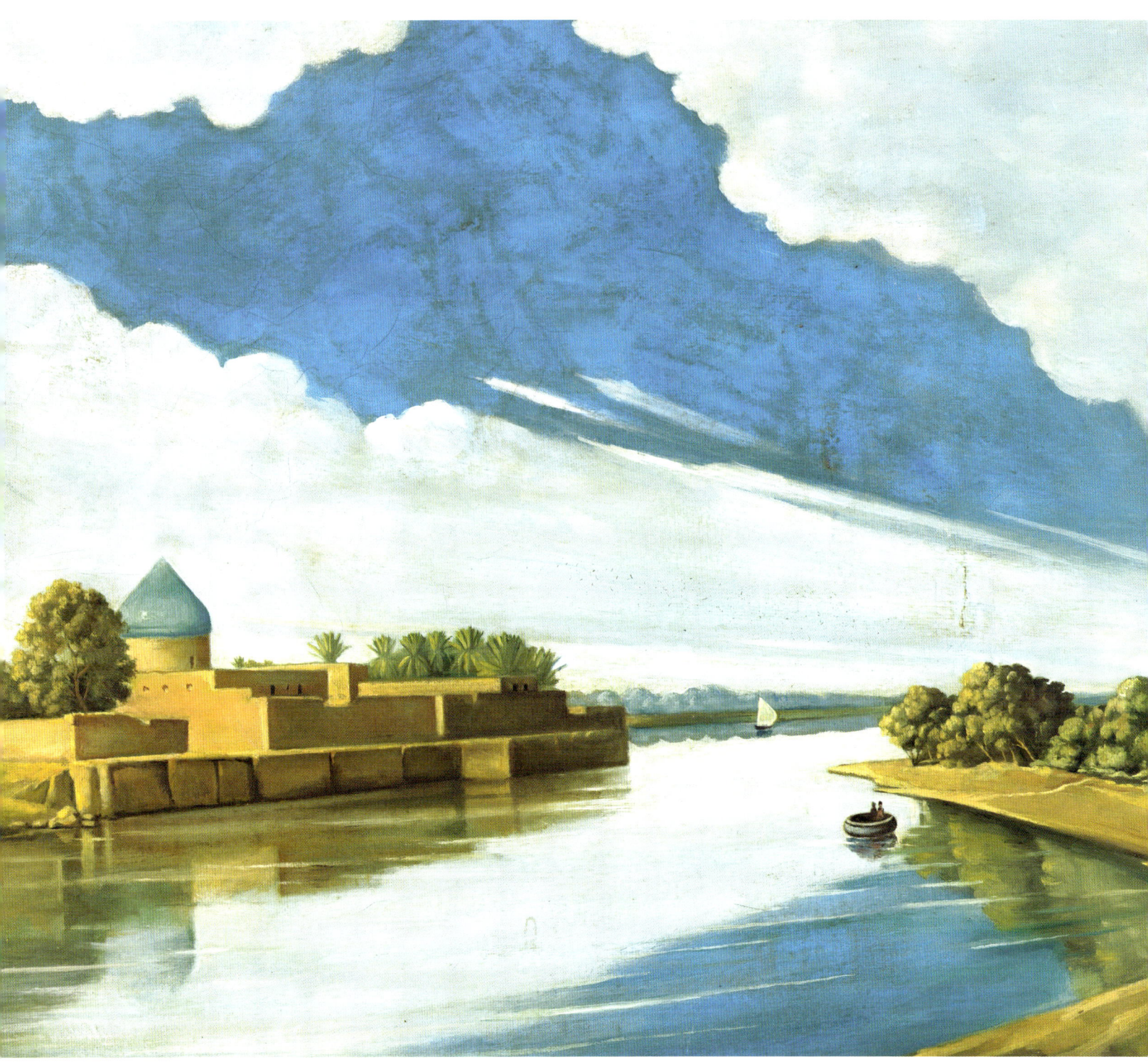

78 Stick Chart
(1920s)

Artist(s): Unknown

Country of origin: Marshall Islands

Dimensions: 74 x 91 cm (29 x 36 inches)

Materials: Wood, shells

Artistic, mythical and divine ideas form the cultural universes of Polynesian and Micronesian seafarers, the connection between widely scattered islands, skies and seas across colossal distances making up the physical and conceptual world of the Oceanic mariner. While most ancient art and architecture – from ancient Greek to Egyptian monuments – prioritizes the philosophical permeance of things, by comparison early islander voyaging was, and still is, a dynamic, active and time-based art to do with wind power, the skyline and the investigation of the unfamiliar. For millennia, Pacific peoples 'presupposed no fixed place except the guiding orientation of the stars'.[103]

Famed for their sophisticated navigational skills, canoes and other large ocean-going vessels, Pacific navigators made use of natural phenomena as a guide with 'reflection, refraction, the shadow phenomenon, and several other ancillary wave actions... well understood by the Marshallese'.[104] These patterns were visualized on Polynesian stick charts – 'mnemonic devices to teach and to refresh the memory before heading out to sea'.[105]

This *mattang* is one of three types, the others being *meddo* and *rebbilib*, and is basically used for instructional purposes – an intellectual map containing traditional seafaring knowledge. Information encoded in the chart is indicated by the arrangement of wooden strips comparative to one another and by the shapes of opposed curved sticks that intersect. For instance, arched sticks designate the altered course taken by ocean swells and chaotic seas redirected by the presence of an island. The *meddo*, from the Marshall Islands, is of the kind collected by Robert Louis Stevenson (University of Pennsylvania) in the mid 19th century, with cowrie shells or coral pieces representing islands and likely courses to plot between land masses and associated ocean swells. *Rebbilib* is different, with many more shells indicating the position of islands in the Marshallese group. As such, this *mattang* stick chart is a palpable representation of how Marshallese pilots intellectualize their environment and particularly the oceanic topography and waterways between isles. Unlike Western navigational charts, distances are only roughly implied and the framework largely symmetrical to convey an unpretentious set of conditions. The *mattang* is akin to a map, but it is not taken onboard the sailing vessel because the information is stored primarily in the navigator's memory. The chart is made from wood with unassuming ties that bind the framework together and form an ocean that mariners can safely comprehend on dry land and recollect at sea. Hence, as Sean Mallon astutely observes, for cohorts of Oceanic seafarers, discovering, roving and settling among the various atolls and islands in the Pacific was no accident: 'it was a necessity of life, an act of imagining, knowing and remembering the ocean.'[106] In short, Oceanic voyaging for Polynesians and Micronesians was an accomplished and highly considered enterprise.

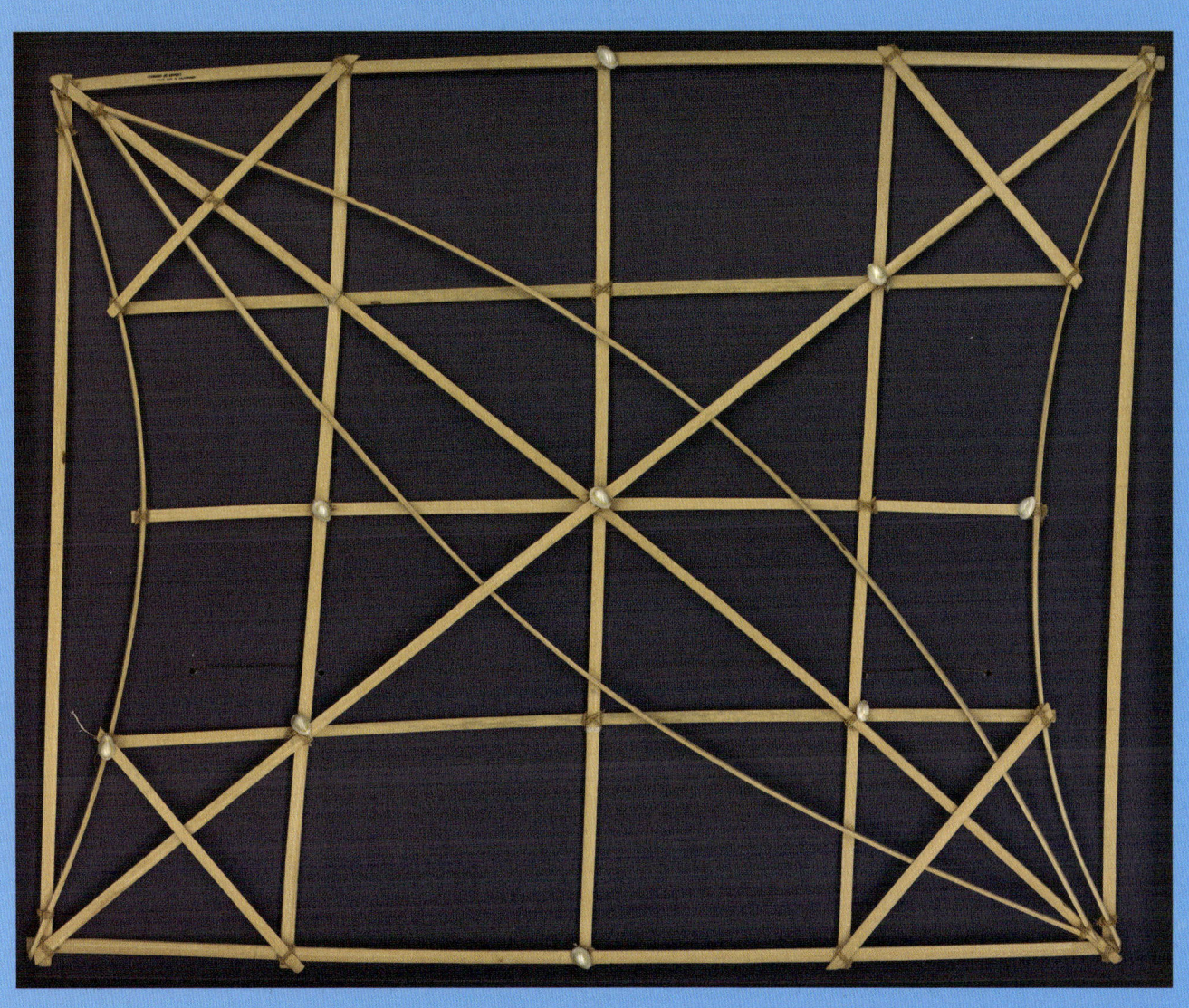

79 A'a Deity Figure
(Before 1921)

Artist(s): Unknown

Country of origin: Rurutu, Astral Islands, French Polynesia

Dimensions: Height 117 cm (46 inches)

Material(s): Sandalwood

The story of this A'a deity figure, 'an icon of Pacific art *par excellence*',[107] is both vivid and momentous. In August 1921, A'a was one of a number of Polynesian god images sent by newly converted Rurutuan chiefs to the London Missionary Society on Ra'iatea in the Society Islands. In 1837, missionary John A. Williams celebrated it as one of 'the [Christian] trophies of Victory', later recalling that 'Aa [sic], the national god of Rurutu, excited considerable interest; ... He is said to be the ancestor by whom their island was peopled, and who after death was deified.'

It is a striking work, with a top-heavy frog-like head, large rounded stomach and various secondary figures covering its surface that suggest its propagative powers, expressing the important theme of multiplicative procreation in pre-Christian Rurutuan society and religion. The figure cast a spell over modernist artists absorbing 'primitive' art, such as Roland Penrose, Pablo Picasso and Henry Moore. Its interior cavity can be opened from the back, so it is likely a reliquary for the ancestral bones of an important chief. However, given that Polynesian artefacts were crafted primarily for powerful élite *ari'i* (chiefs), the precious commodities found inside may well embody genealogical power, imbuing hereditary chiefs with the spiritual lifeblood of ancestors and reaffirming their connection to forebears.

Other stories suggest that A'a was made following the introduction of Christianity, via narratives concerning the hero-traveller Amaiterai (possibly the same character, or a combination thereof) who visited London in advance of European missionaries. The Amaiterai hypothesis has an undeniable reciprocity – 'A'a is from Rurutu and resides in London's British Museum, while... Christianity, brought from London, now inhabits the island nation.'[108] Collaborative research revealed a red feather from a Kuhl's lorikeet (*Vini Kuhlii*) – indigenous to the neighbouring Rimatara island – inside A'a's cavity, alongside barkcloth and human hair. Sandalwood 'is not thought to be endemic to Rurutu' (albeit a few trees were previously known to exist), but the tree is found on neighbouring islands. Rather than tying the work to an individual locality or intention, these discoveries throw new light on A'a's travels and points of interchange.

This was an extremely difficult time for Polynesian societies, with Europeans visitors bringing new technologies, ideas and disease that radically altered and challenged traditional ways of life. As with the Hoa Hakananai'a statue (see page 48), the forfeiture of A'a by islanders was not an isolated incident in pre-Christian Polynesia cultures. In times of environmental and societal stress Polynesian gods could easily be relinquished, so it is not a surprise that A'a's surrender happened alongside devastating disease and Rurutuan conversion to Christianity. Ironically, A'a is now something of a global celebrity and an 'idol' in the 21st century, thanks to William Epsom's 1932 poem 'Homage to the British Museum'.

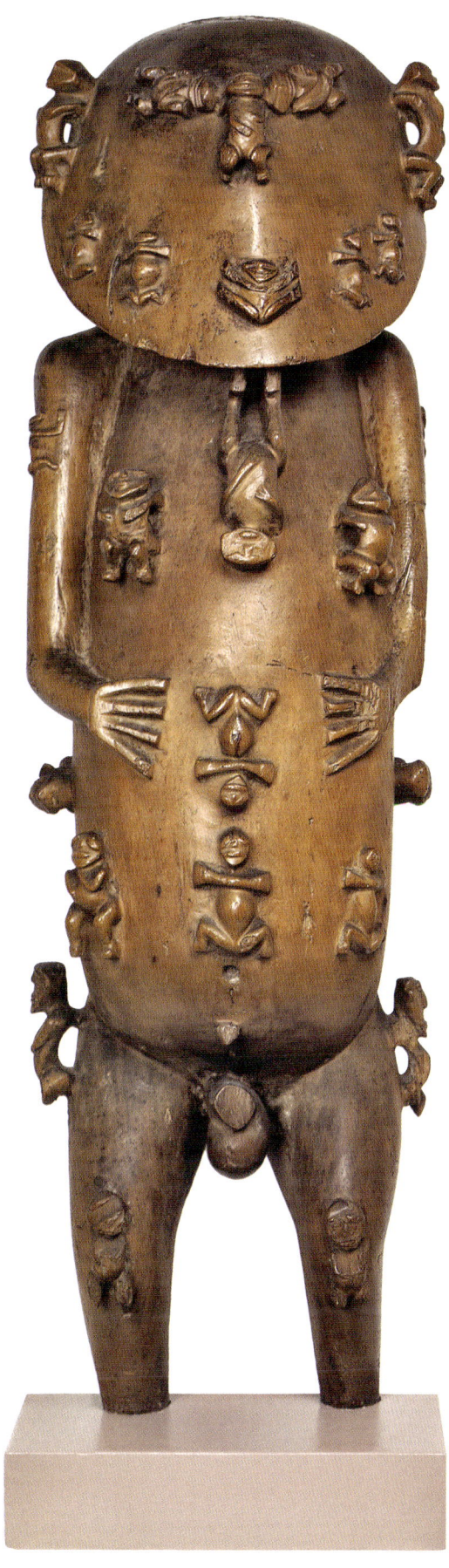

80 Betel-gear Bag
(Before 1925)

Artist(s): Unknown

Country of origin: Solomon Islands

Dimensions: Length 63 cm (25 inches)

Material(s): Banana fibre, plant fibre, shells

Fabrics, baskets, bags and other household items are produced throughout Melanesian and Polynesian society. 'Ngwa'i, or bags, in which men and women store individual items, were part of ordinary attire with some designed to be highly decorative, in the same way people adorned their own bodies.'[109] In the Solomon Islands, there are effectively four basic types of ngwa'i. Photographic evidence shows that loom weaving was still in use in the Santa Cruz Islands (part of the Solomon Islands) c. 1900 but halted after the ushering in of European cloth. Bags can be distinguished by the sort of fibre used, as well as their size, shape and decorative design; this bag is made from the fibres of a variety of banana palm. Banana spathe (a modified leaf, not the fruit) is beaten and the vegetable matter extracted, dried and knotted into long lengths for plaiting.

It is relatively easy to identify the origin of a bag from Santa Cruz, because it is embellished with large shells (and sometimes, although not in this case, made out of flying fox fur), so very likely a personal item for a chief. As some specialist writers recount, in Malaita, in the Solomon Islands, 'Some men used their bags to proclaim daring secret offences committed successfully by themselves and their clan, displaying prowess and the power of their ancestral ghosts.'[110]

The bag from Santa Cruz seen here is used for betel-chewing gear, which is very similar to a pestle and mortar. Betel nut is the seed of the Areca palm (*Areca catechu*) and chewing habits are widely prevalent in parts of Africa, Asia and the Pacific. In the Solomon Islands its use is extensive, with areca nut slaked with lime or tobacco to produce pleasant intoxicating effects. According to the *Encyclopaedia of Papua and New Guinea*, Betel nut is a factor in gift-giving ceremonies, including marriage, and as conciliatory gifts to spirits.

Besides being practical objects, in Pacific cultures bags, baskets and other textiles are containers of metaphor as well as allegories for life. In Māori tradition, *kete tāniko* – a kind of satchel – is one of the three baskets of knowledge reclaimed by the god Tāne, which held sacred information. On the island of East Ambae, in Vanuatu, a proper blanket conveys a moral lesson. Indigenous peoples relay a folktale about a young man caught in the cold without a suitable garment to keep him warm. Despite his best efforts, he fails to acquire a much-needed mantle, so covers himself with dry bananas leaves, but nonetheless dies. As Lissant Bolton identifies, it's a moral tale reinforcing the meaning of kinship and close interpersonal ties: 'he has no close relationships of gift exchange by which he could command one.'[111]

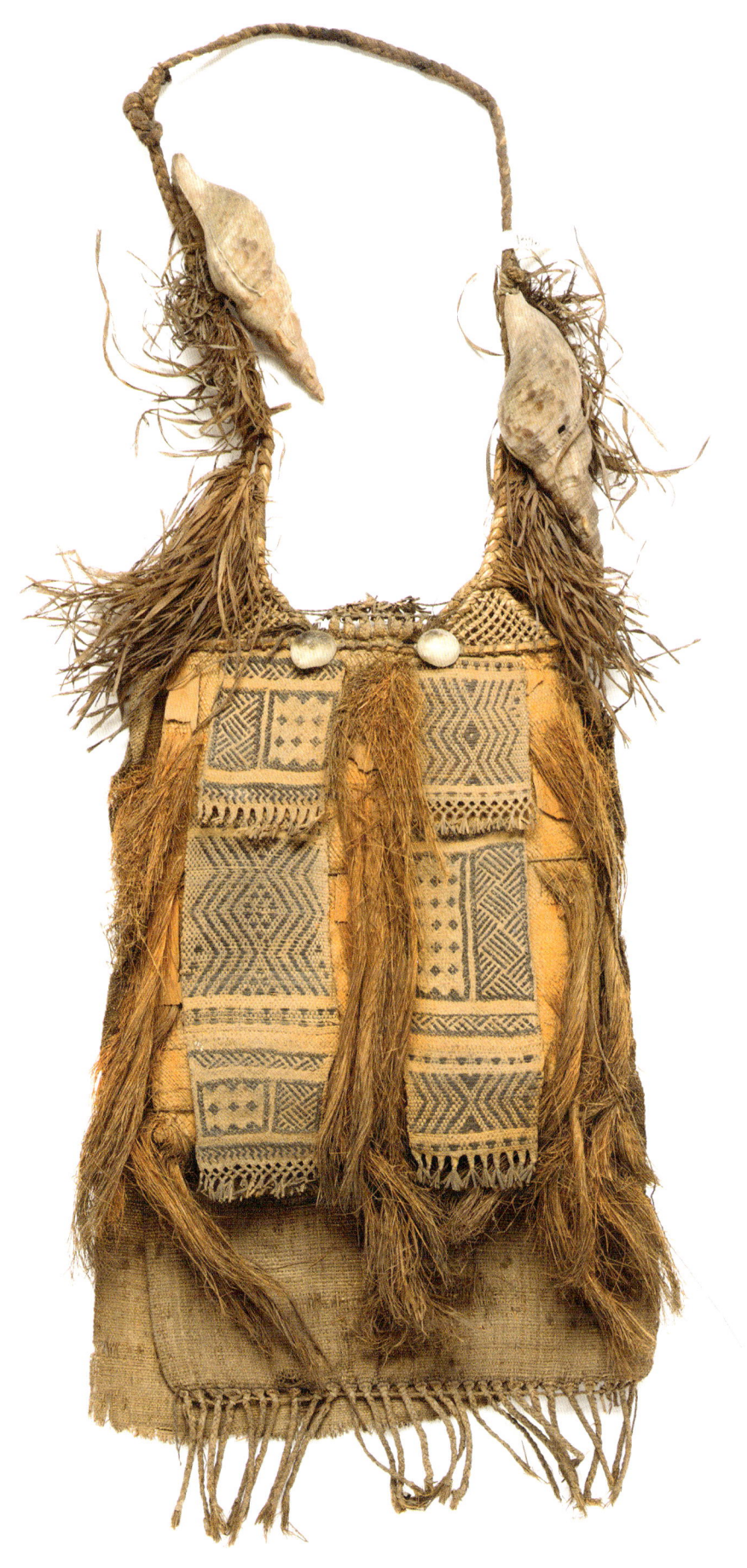

81 *Nguzunguzu*
(Collected 1929)

Artist(s): Unknown

Country of origin: Solomon Islands

Dimensions: Height 17 cm (6¾ inches)

Material(s): Wood, shell inlay

This Solomon Islands canoe-prow figure (*nguzunguzu*) has been reproduced in no less than half a dozen books of Oceanic art and has become a symbol of the Western Province. Subsequently, it now appears on everything from money to t-shirts to postages stamps and is thus a local symbol of the Solomons. It's an impressively striking artefact with overstated but finely balanced features. Its bold shapes, striking beautification and tonal contrasts immediately draw the eye. In addition to extended facial features, intense staring eyes and large circular ear formations, a 'figure style characteristic of imagery from the New Georgia (Roviana) Islands', the carving has near-kinetic lines of intricate shell inlay.[112] But the figure 'is arresting, above all', writes Nicholas Thomas, 'because of its determination of expression'.[113] With its head, beak and wings pointing down, moreover, might it intimate resignation or the proffering of something?

Beyond this aestheticizing, *nguzunguzu* – variously known as a *musu musu* or *toto isu* – have a history prior to the arrival of European colonialism. *Nguzunguzu* was of a genus produced by a certain era, a culture and an economic system of a specific kind, not a society and culture lost in time. For illustrative purposes, this canoe prow has characteristics that are divergent from, say, the figurehead carving currently in the Museum of New Zealand Te Papa Tongarewa and collected prior to 1805, so *nguzunguzu* very likely have a shifting aesthetic history beyond early European appreciation.

Documented reports of war canoes and canoe-prow figureheads largely occur in the narratives of travellers, government spokespersons and other visitors to the Solomon Islands between the 1880s and 1930s. As anticipated, these accounts describe a connection between the figureheads and defensive spirits, their function elaborated by the anthropologist Edvard Hviding: 'They are depicted as holding either a human head (for success in headhunting) or a bird (for navigational aid) in the hands. A *toto isu* was lashed to the bow of every departing New Georgian war canoe to ensure safe passage and success in warfare; its wide-open staring eyes were supposed to ward off any troublesome maritime spirits.'[114]

Archaeological research has considerably improved our understanding of *nguzunguzu*, especially its connection with headhunting and role as 'part of a singular and prestige economy in the New Georgia region'.[115] In Hviding's opinion, this *nguzunguzu* was likely made before European pacification, so it may not necessarily have been a sign of peace. Given evangelical pacification in the Pacific region, it is reasonable to assume the bird motif may have become one on so-called 'mission war canoes'. Perhaps prow figureheads were polyvalent objects whose possible meaning changed with the individual geographical and historical situation?

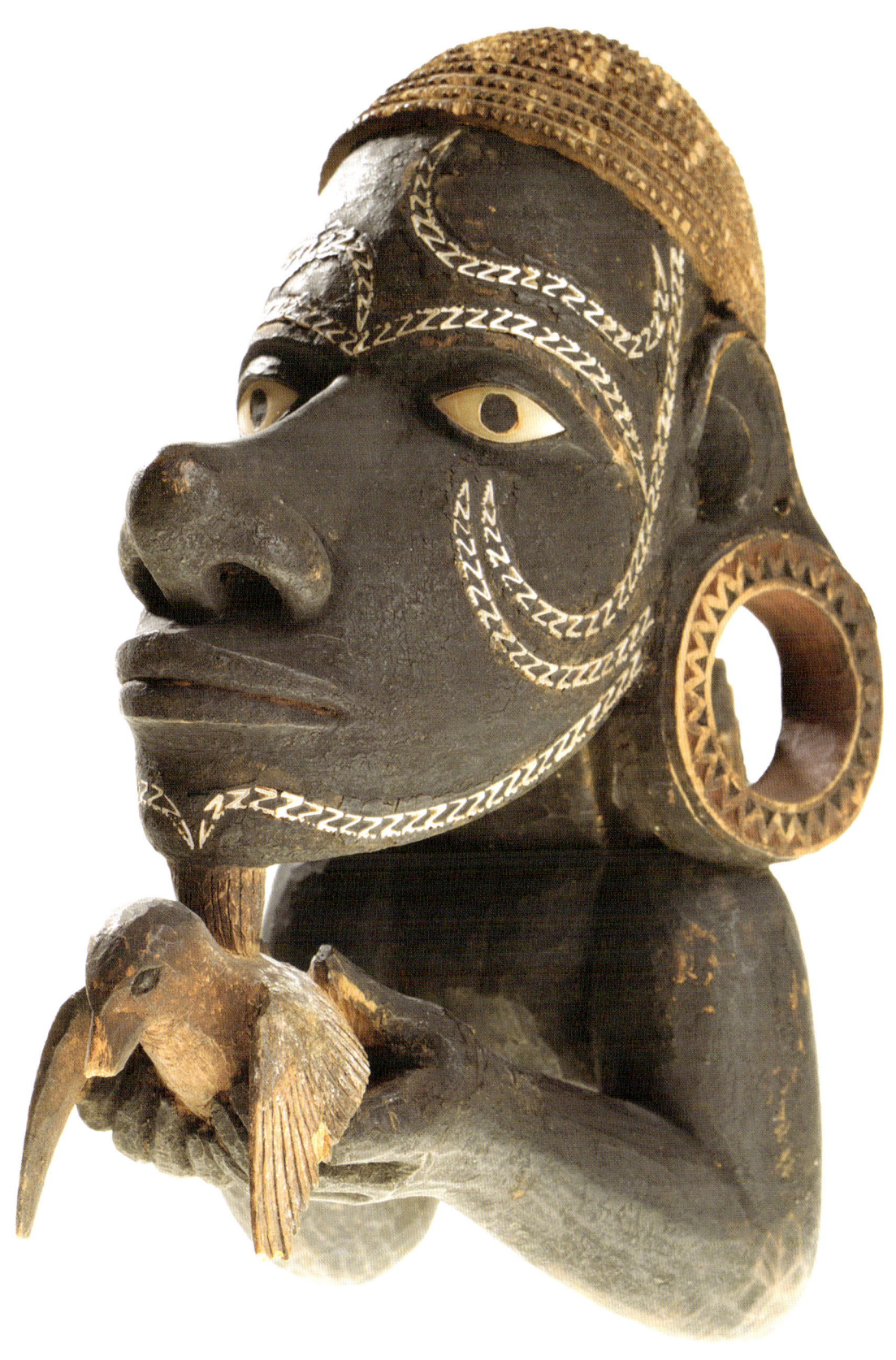

82 *Village Group* (1938)

Artist(s): Amrita Sher-Gil

Country of origin: India

Dimensions: 62 x 84 cm (24 x 33 inches)

Material(s): Oil on canvas

Influenced by both her Indian heritage (her father was a Sikh Indian aristocrat) and her access to a European education at the Santa Annunziata art school in Florence, Italy, and later at the Académie de la Grande Chaumière and the Ecole des Beaux-Arts in Paris, Amrita Sher-Gil (1913–41) produced work that fused the traditional Mughal Miniature and Pahari School styles of painting with the more contemporary European styles of the post-Impressionists in the early 20th century. The inspiration of the Renaissance as well as painters such as Amedeo Modigliani and Paul Gauguin are evident in the paintings that she created of everyday Indian life as is that of the art of Rabindranath Tagore and his nephew Abindranath.

Village Group is indicative of the pared-back style that she developed, with a somewhat languorous, Modernist figurative style that contrasts with the animation of the gestures of the women and children depicted here as they chat and go about their work, such as spreading chillies out to dry as the woman on the right is doing. It also represents Sher-Gil's interest in highlighting the role of women in Indian society at the time. Her Hungarian opera-singer mother, who came from an affluent family too, encouraged Amrita's artistic talent, and her passionate nature was obviously inherited by her daughter – who enjoyed a bohemian lifestyle, indulging in a number of affairs before and during her marriage to a Hungarian cousin, Dr Viktor Egan. Sher-Gil's belief in the rights of the underprivileged and her support of Mahatma Gandhi's ideals underlined her wish that her work should portray everyday Indian life rather than the privilege of her own upbringing.

Sher-Gil's somewhat precocious talent (she started painting seriously at the age of eight) and her quick study of artists in Italy and France led to her first success, when her painting entitled *Young Girls* (1932) won both a gold medal from and election as an Associate of the Grand Salon in Paris in 1933. Much of her work, her lifestyle and her early death at the age of 28 have led to comparisons with Frida Kahlo, and she is now viewed as a pioneer of modern Indian art.

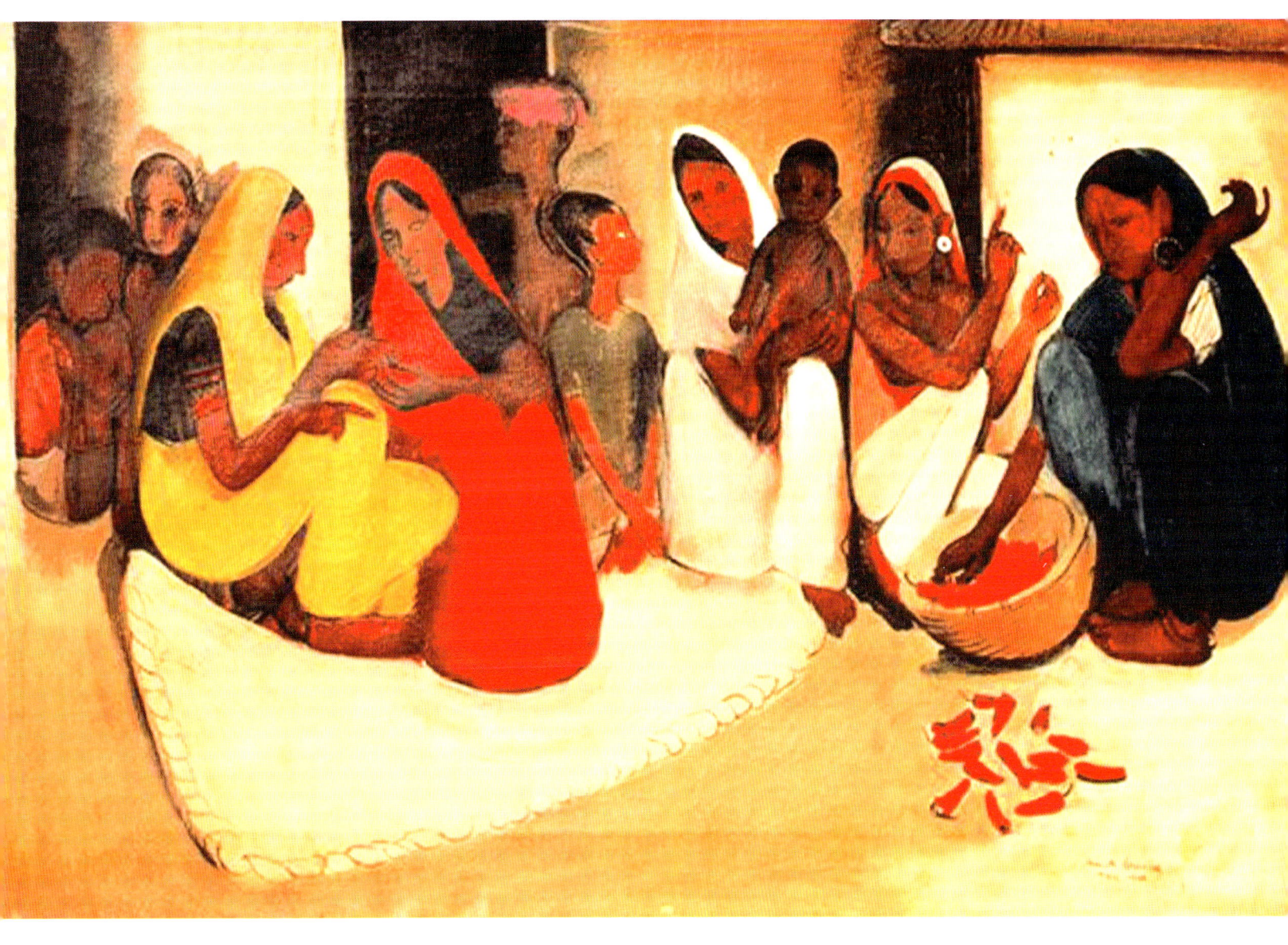

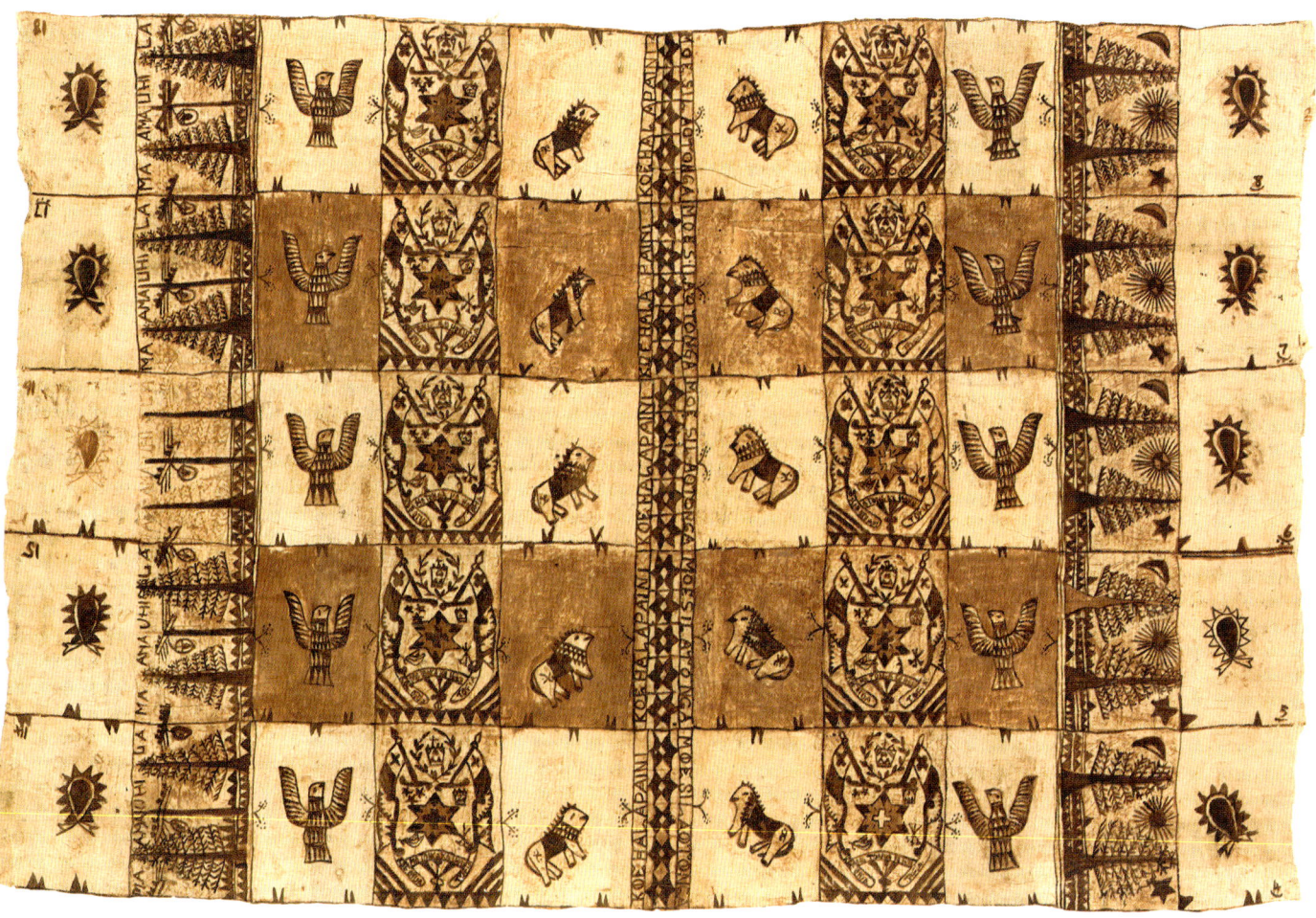

Ngatu
(1943–5)

Artist(s): Unknown

Country of origin: Tonga

Dimensions: 196 x 160 cm (77 x 63 inches)

Material(s): Barkcloth

This type of *ngatu* (barkcloth) from the Pacific was first taken to England after Cook's voyages in the 1770s, when Tongan *ngatu*, Hawaiʻian *kapa* and other barkcloths (known as *tapa* in most parts of the Pacific) were cut up and distributed as tasters among connoisseurs. They even became modish among London ladies who sought to adapt their clothing by 'incorporating *tapa*, which has thus been a cross-cultural fabric for nearly 250 years'.[116] Captain Cook's wife Elizabeth used it to make a waistcoat for his anticipated return in 1780.

Traditionally given as ceremonial gift in Tongan society, barkcloth was intended 'to constitute sanctity, to define a ceremony, to wrap around a body, to bear knowledge or to effect a gift',[117] and was also wrapped around the body of a chief, a ceremonial dancer, a betrothed couple, newborns and the deceased. Elizabeth Cook's gift was prophetic: Cook's bones were wrapped in Hawaiʻian barkcloth after his death in 1779.

Ngatu production is a very special type of art making, which is simultaneously but not exclusively a work of 'art' in the standardized sense. Bias toward works of tribal sculpture by men and a general perception of barkcloth as merely decorative in intent have tended to relegate this type of work to a 'secondary category' of artistic and cultural creativity, but it should be noted that decorated *ngatu* were not created for aesthetic purposes. As Queen Sālote Tupou III of Tonga (1900–65) observed: 'the history of our people is written in our mats' – by which she meant *kie hingoa* – 'mats named and filled with genealogical histories, myths, legends, historical events, people, and places.'[118] Fay Ginsburg acknowledges too that, *tapa*, like other cultural products, is used to help 'heal disruptions in cultural knowledge, historical memory, and identity between generations, people and places'.[119]

Manufacturing of barkcloth involves a highly labour-intensive process of preparing raw materials, beating the bark (usually from a paper mulberry tree) and its fibres, gumming several sections together with plant substances such as arrowroot, and concocting the pigments and dyes. Adrienne Kaeppler, who has studied Tongan *ngatu* from World War II, has identified airplanes such as the British Spitfire and Lockheed P-38 warplane used by the American Air Force in World War II, and notes that traditional designs have been transformed by the introduction of representational motifs. *Ngatu* traditionally reference place, genealogy and specific historical moments, but also include images such as European figures, the passing of Halley's comet, sporting events, bicycles and even the establishment of electricity on Polynesian islands. In contemporary art, John Pule (b. 1962), a Niuean artist who lives in New Zealand, has imaginatively taken *tapa* (called *hiapo* in Niuea) and re-used it for his own artistic purposes (see page 196). Often venerated for its beautification, therefore, 'the art of barkcloth, the art of *tapa*', as Sean Mallon astutely puts it, 'is neither paper thin nor skin deep'.[120]

84 *Ned Kelly*
(1965)

Artist(s): Sidney Nolan

Country of origin: Australia

Dimensions: 122 x152 cm (48 x 60 inches)

Material(s): Oil on panel

Sidney Nolan (1917–92) was one of the most significant Australian artists of the post-World War II period. He is celebrated for his representations of the bushranger Ned Kelly, an historical figure who was hanged in Melbourne Gaol on 11 November 1880. Painted between 1945 and 1947, the Ned Kelly paintings focus on the ambivalent bush-life of the Kelly Gang, a painterly meditation on folly, violence, daring, anti-authoritarianism and the question of individual responsibility.[121] In Kelly, Nolan conjured a powerful mix of the early settler mentality (see *The Pioneer*, page 156) with the antithesis of the pioneer, the criminal bushranger/folk hero, Kelly.

Kelly was eternally deemed a scoundrel, martyr and (rather improbably) a champion for social justice – 'the image of the anti-hero in home-made armour […] irresistibly romantic.'[122] Nolan claimed that these paintings were about 'Kelly as a poetic rebel reformer who did something to our world.'[123] The painter also wrote that the Kelly saga was 'a story arising out of the bush and ending in the bush', the Australian landscape fundamental to his enthusiasm for the events.

Landscape itself was a crucial component of the Kelly series – a story that gives significance to place. Regarding the Australian scenery, Nolan explained in a letter in 1942 that '[there] was the thought we [artists] would learn to tell our own story.'[124] Nolan's paintings frequently mix highly colourful and arresting images with an erudite faux-naïve style. In *Ned Kelly* (1946), the bushranger rides out into an expansive and luminous landscape dotted with trees on the far horizon and coupled with an ominous-looking sky. These paintings convey a deep sense of alienation where the outlaw scours the seemingly empty and capacious plains. Kelly is always depicted wearing his home-made suit of shadowy armour, the story, in fact, flourishing precisely because of 'the strange darkness of the helmet.'[125] In the present work, the outfit morphs – centaur-like – with his horse, the sky visible in the rectangular slot of his helmet. Nolan explained that this framing device was intended to create the 'maximum sense of space'. The play of 'flat' surface planes is typical of the series, the 1946 *Ned Kelly* cleverly fashioning the subtle suggestion of both faraway clouds and gun-smoke from the outlaw's rifle. In the present (1965) version, the strangely disembodied figure lying on the ground reflects Nolan's statement that the Kelly paintings were a post-war reflection on violence.

The Ned Kelly series finally entered the National Gallery of Australia in 1977, and their display at the Metropolitan Museum of Art in New York not long after Nolan's death strengthened their standing as one of the most outstanding series of Australian paintings of the era.

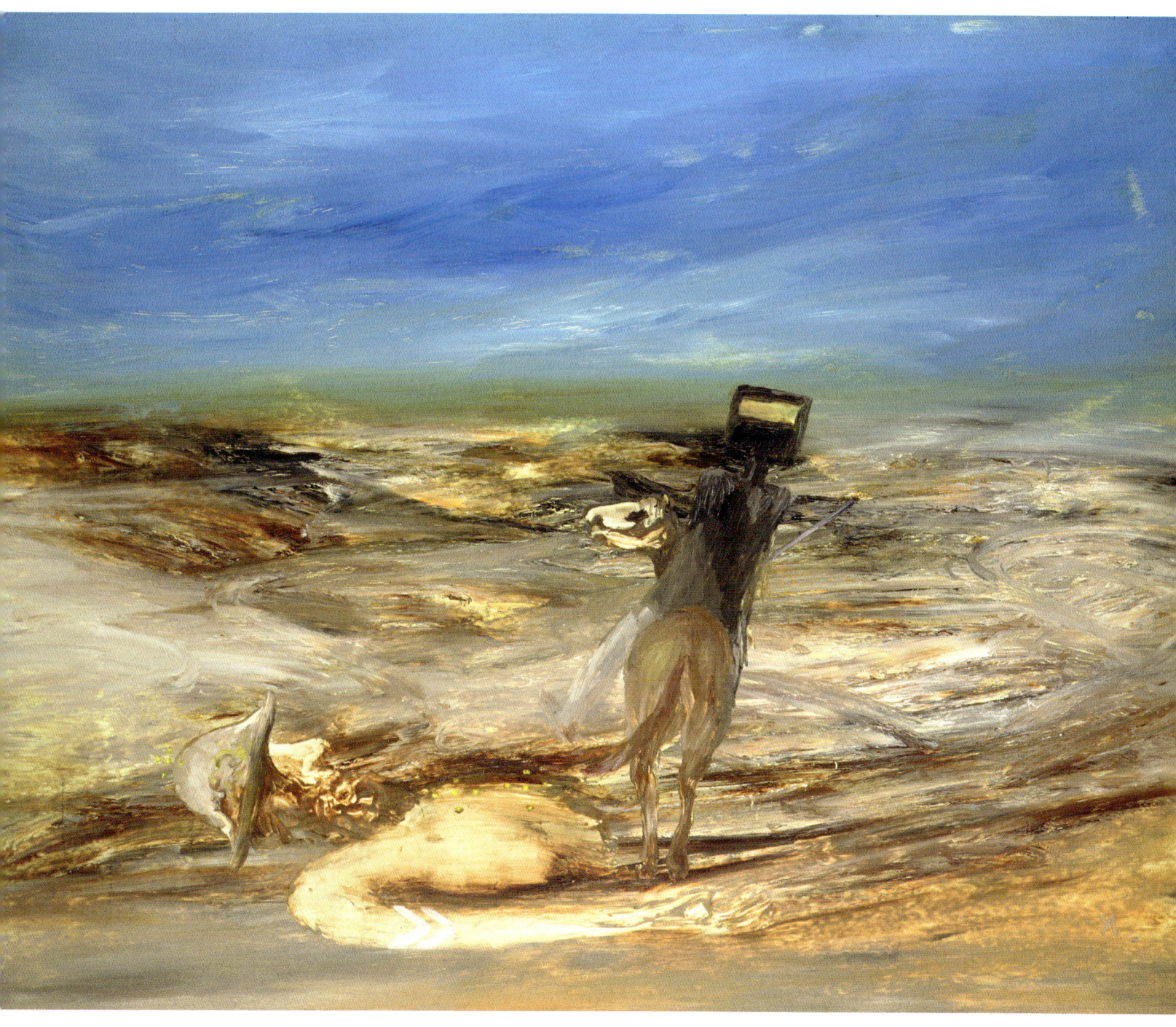

85

Washday at the Pā
(Front cover image from the photographic series)
(1964)

Artist(s): Ans Westra

Country of origin: Aotearoa New Zeland

Dimensions: 28.4 x 25.4 cm (11¹/₄ x 10 inches)

Material(s): Gelatin silver

Washday at the Pā, photographed and written by Ans Westra (1936–2023), was 'a bulletin for schools'[126] and meant as a reader for children – an old-style journal or picture book covering an ordinary day at home for one Māori *whānau* (extended family). It was published in 1964 by the School Publications Branch of the Department (now Ministry) of Education in a post-World War II era of nationalist growth and Māori urbanization. But Westra's book became the focus of Māori protest, led by the Māori Women's Welfare League (MWWL) and resulted in its withdrawal from New Zealand schools. In August 1964, the scandal become a national debate. As Westra, who spent many months living among rural Māori, well-meaningly argued, 'The booklet was never meant to portray a typical Māori family. It is just a story of a happy family living in the country. It shows the warmth of family relationships.' (*The Dominion*, 4 August 1964)

From a critical Māori perspective, particularly the MWWL, it undermined their work. One member, Wikitoria Bennet, wrote to *The Evening Post* to report that 'younger children are influenced by what they see and the photographs show sub-standard housing and living. The Māori school child is immediately placed at a disadvantage with his European schoolfellows and becomes the butt of their derision.'[127] Indeed, statistics for 1961 showed that a large percentage of Māori lived in sub-standard housing.

Washday also raised the larger issue of Māori rights, particularly the representation of Māori and the possibility of 'othering' while doing so. Ultimately, this fictionalizing manufactured an accustomed feeling of spiritual malaise for Māori. The *Washday* story about the family's move to a new house provided by the state was one of the major challenges faced by Māori women and children during urbanization in the 1950s and 1960s. It's a reality that brought the MWWL into being, something shared by thousands of people when the government introduced a policy of 'pepper-potting' (sprinkling) Māori in suburban areas dominated by Pākehā (those of European descent). This strategy 'ignored the trauma caused by the contrast from previous rural Māori homes, where families were surrounded by kin networks of social and material support'.[128] So the original 'ghost book' – two revised editions of *Washday* were later published in 1964 and 2011 – has become something of a conundrum. On the one hand, there is a recognition of the brilliance and power of Westra's photographic images, while on the other, knowledge and perspectives have revealed very different and 'continuing meanings for Maori and the history of education in Aotearoa New Zealand'.[129] As Georgina Stewart and Hêmi Dale further point out, *Washday* should perhaps be considered a type of national *taonga* (treasure or, 'commodity or value item') as well as 'a parable or learning story on which we can draw for thinking about biculturalism as it plays out in Aotearoa New Zealand'.[130]

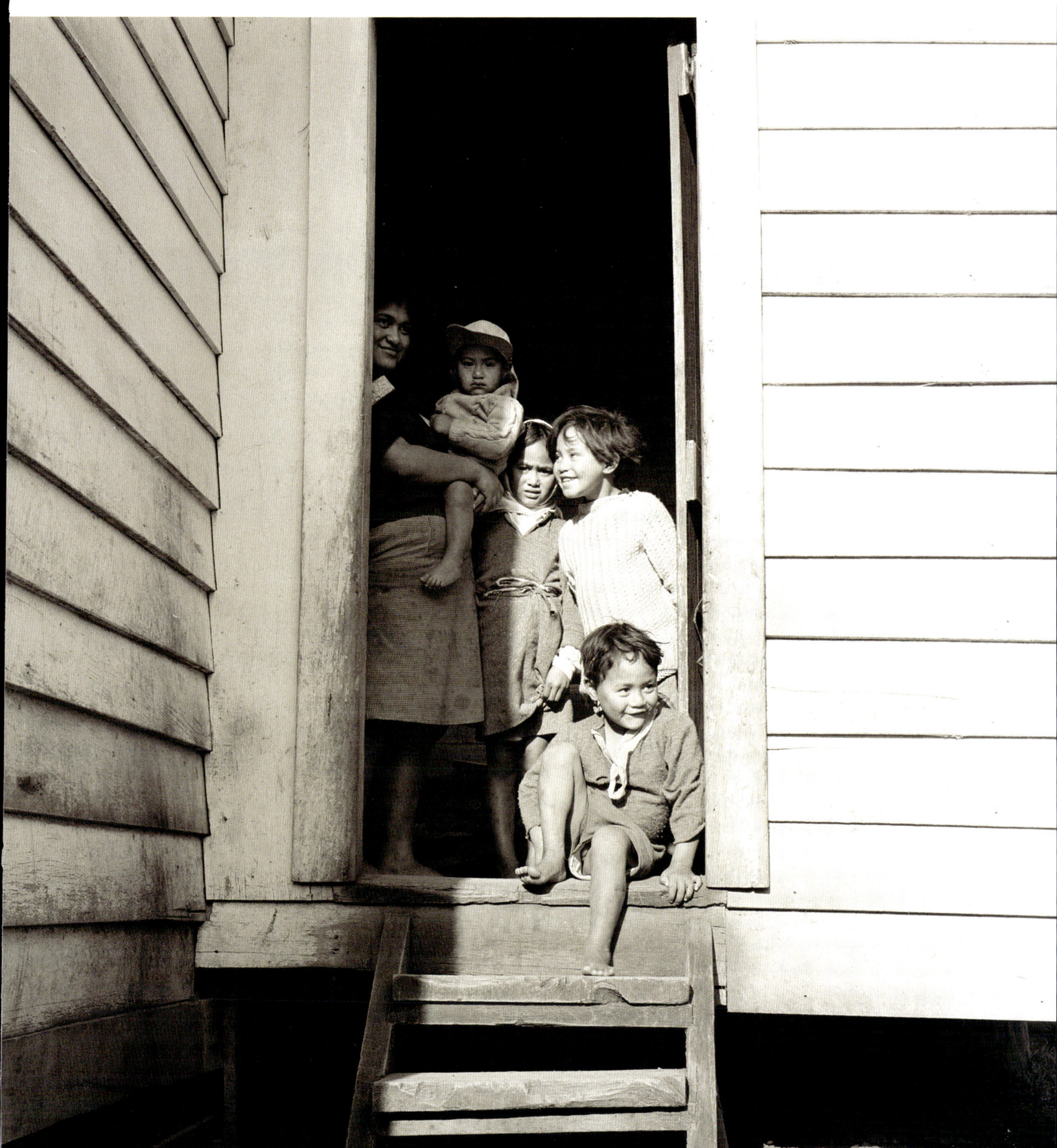

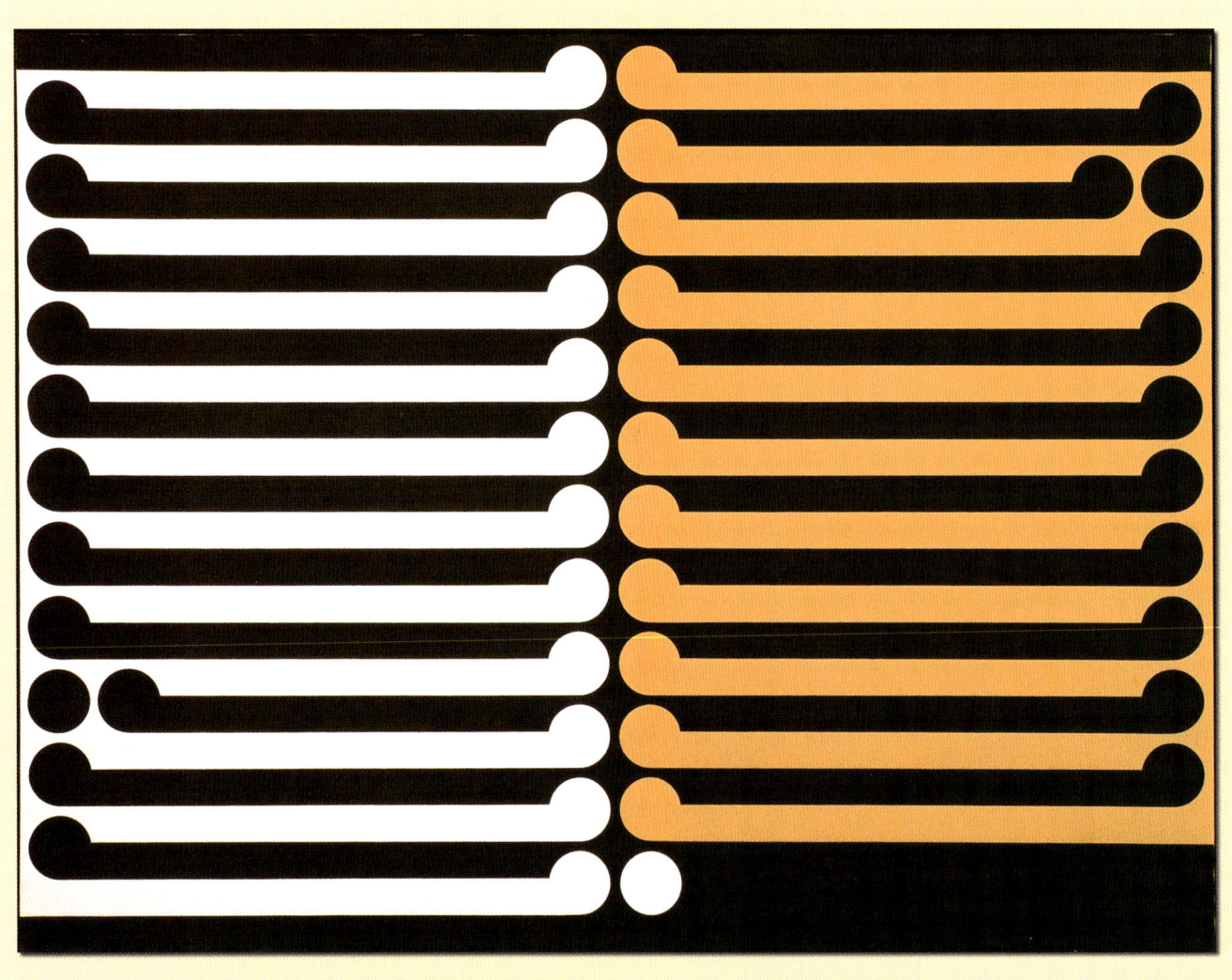

86

Kahukura
(1967–68)

Artist(s): Gordon Walters

Country of origin: Aotearoa New Zealand

Dimensions: 138 x 152.3 cm (54 ⅓ x 60 inches)

Material(s): Acrylic and PVA on canvas

Between 1935 and 1939, Gordon Frederick Walters (1919–95) worked as a commercial artist while studying art part-time in Wellington, New Zealand. Familiar with European artists' use of tribal art from Africa and the South Pacific, and assessing Western art and culture, Walters advanced a homegrown form of modernist primitivism.

In his work, certain *koru* (loop or coil) motifs from Māori art appear alongside forms of American and European geometric abstraction. *Kahukura* is part of a sequence of works that incorporate his distinctive bar-and-circle design and are evocative of Frank Stella's abstract *Black Paintings*, which Walters greatly admired. As Walters later recalled, 'black and white' resonated throughout the world of international art.[131]

In *Kahukura*, Walters manufactures an 'optical shimmer' that renders the picture surface visually volatile,[132] its optical 'hum' transforming 'the activity of seeing into a bodily experience'. As Damien Skinner has further observed of *Kahukura*: 'Two cultures, Māori and Pākehā [white settler], are locked into a relationship that never settles into a hierarchy but remains dynamic.'[133] Conversely, when Walter's exhibited his 'mature' style (*c.* 1966), he saw almost no formal or stylistic ties with Māori art, his starting point being modernist abstraction. As he told Michael Dunn, 'The forms I use have no descriptive value in themselves and are used solely to demonstrate relations. I believe that dynamic relations are most clearly expressed by the repetition of a few simple elements.'[134] It's a striking statement, given that *Kahukura* uses Māori headings: *Kahukura* being a 'personal name', or 'the name of several *atua* [gods or spirits] and ancestors', according to the *Māori Dictionary*.

Critically, for Māori, the *koru* denotes renewal and has a privileged position in art. Hence its adaption by Pākehā artists like Walters in the 1980s and 1990s was seen as questionable in some quarters. In response to this, in 1993, Walters told Michael Smythe, 'in my case all I have done with the *koru* motif is make reference to it and naturally, since I'm a contemporary Pākehā artist, the result is not Māori art.'[135] These polarizing attitudes to art and culture fundamentally boil down to either unauthorized borrowing/theft or commandeering as a kind of tribute. Walters's '*koru* series', as it was known, was effectively rooted in international art overseas and a number of Māori modernists in the 1970s drew attention to what Walters was producing by engaging with *koru* on their own terms. As Francis Pound intelligently observes of *Kahukura*: 'The first painting on canvas to have a full stop preceding a blank is *Kahukura*, [which] stands out in white and black… a potentially fertile entity… [that is] safe… from the likely accusations of a faux ethnic folksiness.'[136]

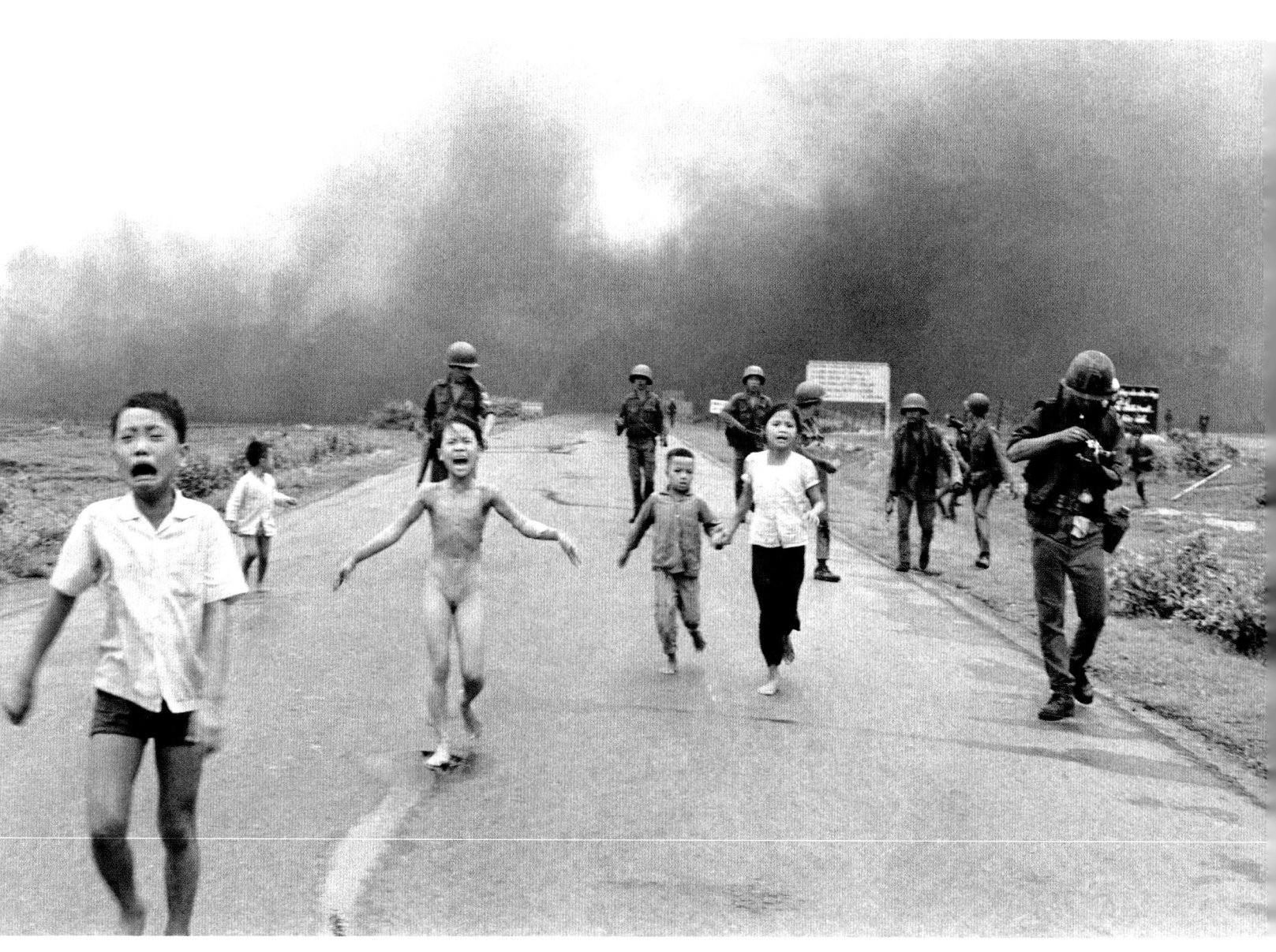

87

***Vietnam, Napalm* Photograph of (from left) Phan Thanh Tam, brother of Kim Phúc, Phan Thanh Phouc, youngest brother of Kim Phúc, Kim Phúc, and Kim's cousins, Ho Van Bon and Ho Thi Ting (1972)**

Photographer: Nick Ut
Country of origin: Vietnam
Dimensions: Not applicable
Material(s): Photograph

This news image by the Vietnamese-American photographer Huýnh Công Út (professionally known as Nick Ut [1951–]), originally titled 'The Terror of War', was a transformative instant in a conflict that seemed to limp on endlessly. The United States entered the fray in 1964, when North Vietnamese torpedo boats struck an American destroyer in the Gulf of Tonking. By 1968, almost half a million American servicemen were involved in hostilities with South Vietnam against the communist Viet Cong insurgents and soldiers from North Vietnam. Ut's Pulitzer Prize-winning photograph, taken on 8 June 1972, was labelled 'Napalm Girl' and captures the image of a seriously injured nine-year-old named Phan Thi Kim Phúc. It is an 'iconic' image because it makes a wider emotional plea as to the horrors of war, but it is also a document of the 'conflict' and the wider historical events. In the photograph, South Vietnam children flee Trang Bang village after being torched by a misdirected napalm strike. Disastrously, a South Vietnamese Air Force Skyraider '... dropped the napalm around 12:30pm,' Ut later told Mark Edward Harris of *Vanity Fair* (on 3 April 2015). A joint British and American film crew also captured in real time and in full colour Kim Phúc and other badly burnt children. However, it was Ut who netted what Henri Cartier-Bresson termed 'The Decisive Moment.'

Highway 1 to Trang Bang was, as now, an essential route joining Saigon with Cambodia. Equally horrifying, however, is that recordings released in 2002 divulged a conversation in which President Richard Nixon asks Henry Kissinger 'to think big' vis-à-vis dropping 'the nuclear bomb' on Vietnam. The idea was swiftly rejected by Kissinger, but the following month Nixon instructed the largest intensification of the war since 1968. In the taped discussions, Nixon reproaches Kissinger for his concerns regarding civilian fatalities. 'I don't give a damn,' the President says. More specifically, on 12 June 1972, Nixon, with his chief of staff, H. R. Haldeman, mulls over Nick Ut's photograph. 'I'm wondering if that was fixed,' Nixon pondered. 'Could have been', Haldeman replies.[137] But as Ut stated after hearing the release tapes: '[My] photo was as authentic as the Vietnam War itself ... That terrified little girl is still alive today and has become an eloquent testimony to the authenticity of that photo. That moment thirty years ago will be one Kim Phúc and I will never forget.'

Nixon eventually withdrew US combatants and a peace treaty was signed in Paris on 27 January 1973.

88 *Yuelamu (Honey Ant Dreaming)*
(1980)

Artist(s): Clifford Possum Tjapaltjarri

Country of origin: Australia

Dimensions: 229.5 x 366.5 cm (90¼ x 144¼ inches)

Material(s): Synthetic polymer paint on canvas

Associated with the modern-day Papunya Tula school of painting, the art of Clifford Possum Tjapaltjarri (*c.* 1932–2002) is full of geographical and spiritual significance that typically re-affirms associations between Aboriginal land and ceremony, adopting an extensive range of symbolic representations.

The subtitle refers to the term universally used in Aboriginal Australia – the 'Dreaming', or 'Dreamtime', which evolved out of attempts by Aborigines to explain their religious values to 19th-century Europeans. The Dreamtime registers with various Aboriginal languages: the Yolngu term *wangarr*, the Walpiri *djukurrpa* and the Arrernte (Aranda) *altyerrenge* are agreed as standards. A verbatim interpretation might be 'belonging to dreams' or 'of dreams', but the inference of 'Dream' is inapt because, as some Yolngu rightly believe, *wangarr* is not dreaming per se but reality.[138] As Howard Morphy puts it, 'the Dreaming is as much a dimension of reality as a period of time... [where] the Dreamtime has never ceased to exist, and from that point of view of the present it is as much a feature of the future as it is of the past.'[139] It has nothing to do with the subconscious nature of dreams and is far from commonplace reality. Aborigines use the Dreaming to characterize the spiritual, moral and natural order of the cosmos and the balance between it and humanity. It typically involves the doings and heroic acts of mythological beings and creator ancestors, who adopt different forms, create everything in the world and decree the directives of societal and spiritual conduct.[140]

Tjapaltjarri's painting portrays the ceremonial camps associated with the Honey Ant Ancestor at Yinyalingi, a site north of Papunya, *c.* 240 km (150 miles) northwest of Alice Springs (Mparntwe). Ceremonies are held during abundant rain when the soil can sustain large foraging groups. So '[*Yuelamu*] reflects seasonality, the cyclical nature of good seasons, and concentrations of people and ceremony.'[141] The life of the Australian honeypot ant (*Camponotus inflatus*) is intricate yet short-lived. Worker ants gather nectar from mulga trees and take it underground, where the bellies of storehouse ants are stuffed with honey. Honey ants are an esteemed food source with extraordinary medicinal and antimicrobial properties.[142]

In the painting, the fruitfulness of Yinyalingi is signified by juicy-looking grubs at the edges and around the camps demarcated by U-shaped forms. This work also maps mythological events on the landscape and lives of the ancestral beings, while the happenings of the Dreamtime are demarcated by adroitly applied dots, lines and geometric shapes. Viewed from above, seemingly through morning mists represented by the two pale parallel bands, the eye zones in and out on an extraordinary array of pattern and colour. Tjapaltjarri's painting is a magnificent testament to the imagination, power and resilience of the Aboriginal peoples and their culture.

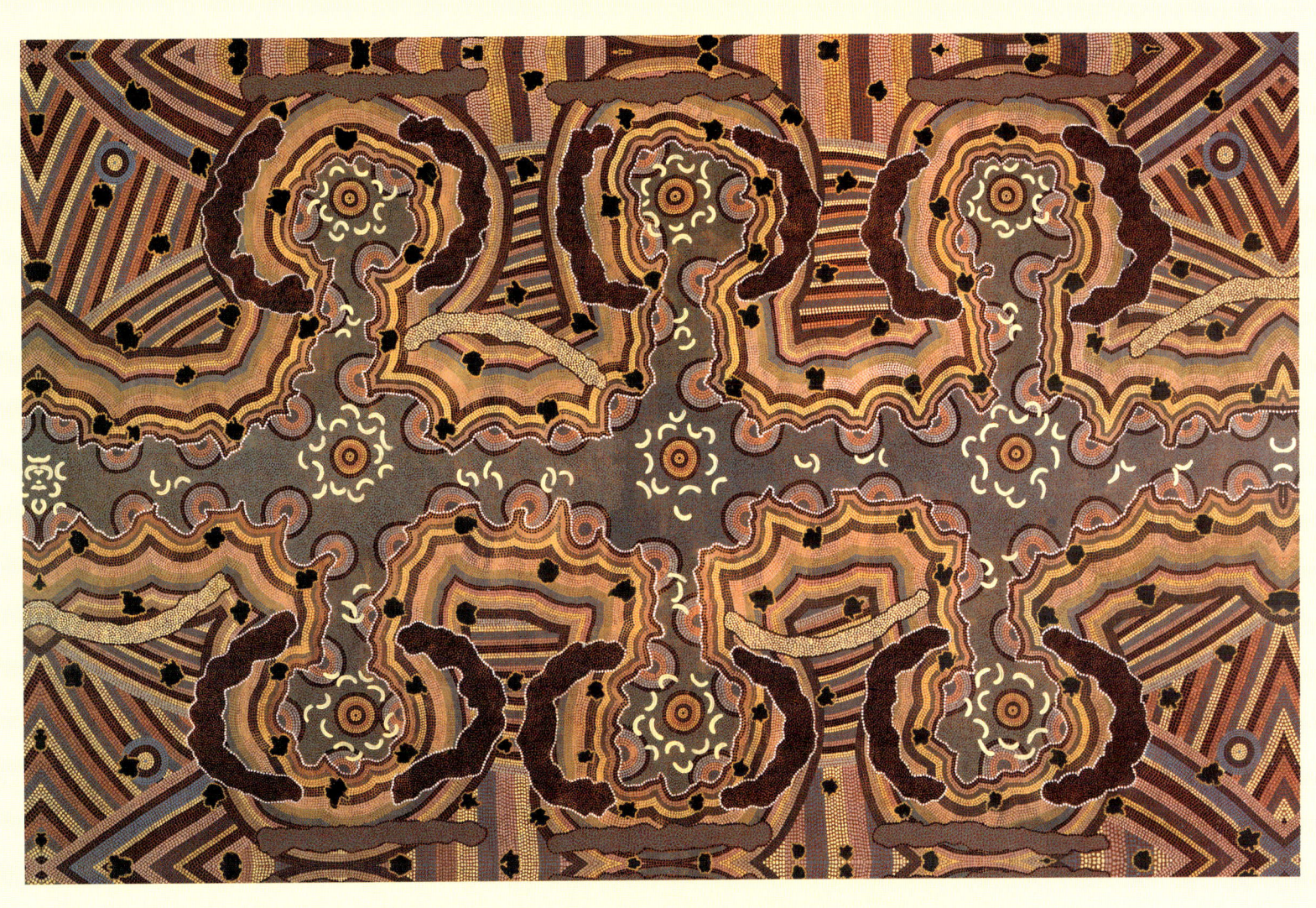

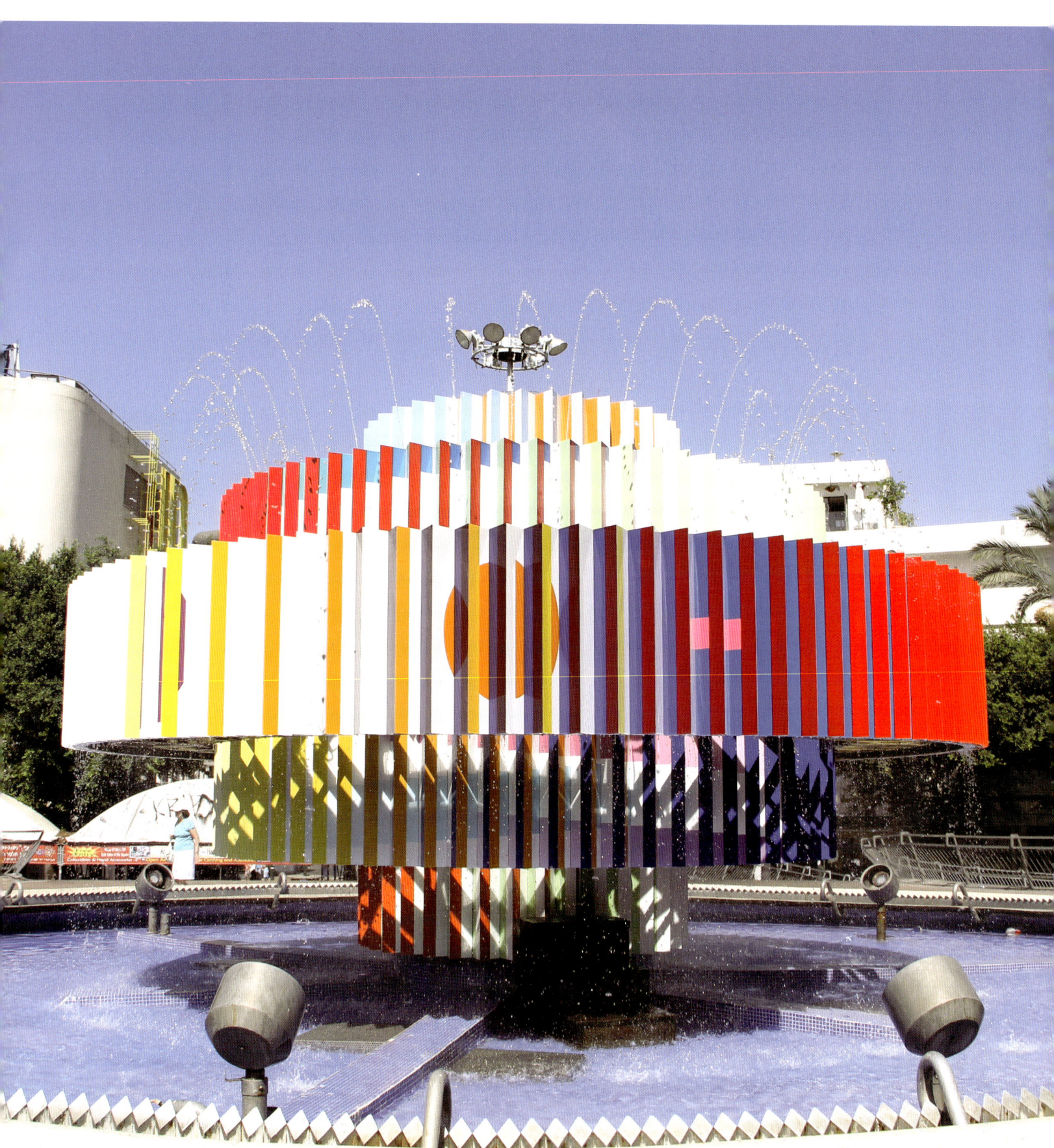

Fire and Water Fountain
(1986)

Artist(s): Yaacov Agam

Country of origin: Israel

Dimensions: Height 9 m (29½ ft); Diameter 6 m (19¾ ft)

Material(s): Sheet metal, water, music and fire

Renowned as one of the pioneers of kinetic art, Yaacov Agam (né Yaakov Gipstein) (1928–) was born in Israel, but has lived in Paris, France, since the early 1950s. His experimental work in the areas of both optical and kinetic art, along with his sculptural achievements, have led to the creation of such diverse pieces as the world's largest Hanukkah menorah, in New York (2005), the fountain in La Défense in Paris (1975) and the winner's trophy for the 1999 Eurovision Song Contest. He has held exhibitions around the world and, in 1996, he received the Jan Amos Comelius Medal from UNESCO for his development of the 'Agam Method' which has contributed to the visual education of children.

An entrancing example of how he has combined the movement of kineticism with his dynamic use of colour, Agam spent ten years developing the *Fire and Water Fountain* that formed the centrepiece of the Dizengoff Square in Tel Aviv in Israel. It was, as Agam described it, a five-dimensional work, involving 'many time operations related', by which he meant that a variety of elements were combined within the work and interlinked to perform in a coordinated manner. The fountain consisted of several rotating 'wheels', affixed to which were slim rectangles of aluminium in a multitude of colours. In addition, a flame of fire would appear periodically from the top of the fountain, while water sprayed out at other times and in different directions. And all of this was accompanied by music, giving the viewer an ever-changing experience.

Although the fountain was originally installed in 1986, it was completely refurbished in 2012. At the time, Agam was filmed in Dizengoff Square explaining his work, whose inspiration he said was Heaven (*esh ve máyim*), with the rainbow effect of the colours on the revolving tiers of the fountain representing a rainbow that he saw as 'our covenant with God'. He went on to say: 'Time cannot be repeated, time cannot be expected... I introduced the unexpected in a work of art. So, my work[s] of art change; they are beyond the visible; appear[ing], disappear[ing]. And there's always an element of the invisible.'[143]

Sadly, due much to maintenance issues but mainly to local council plans to redevelop Dizengoff Square, the fountain was dismantled in 2016 and only partially replaced two years later, without the unique decorations and effects that made the fountain so unique. While no plans appear to be in place for its full reinstallation, Yaacov Agam's work, which can now be seen in a museum dedicated to his creations in Rishon LeZion, Israel, stands as a testimony to the way in which art in the Middle East/western Asia continues to inspire in the 21st century.

Mural, Ceiling of Frere Hall
(1986–7)

Artist(s): Syed Sadequain Ahmed Naqvi

Country of origin: Pakistan

Dimensions: 42.5 x 21.3 m (140 x 70 ft)

Material(s): Wooden panels

Syed Sadequain was a pioneer of the Hurufiyya movement that began in the 1950s and aimed to blend traditional Islamic art styles, such as calligraphy, with a modern aesthetic in art, avoiding Western art forms. This soon became popular in various parts of Asia and North Africa. Sadequain, a master calligrapher, was considered to have sparked a renaissance in Islamic calligraphy not least because he was also a prolific poet.

Born in 1930, Sadequain's career was driven by his belief in humanity, his desire to portray the reality of life, particularly the lives of working people. He often created works for public buildings for free and gave away many of his creations to fans. While much of his work has been destroyed, he produced some 15,000 artworks in many media, ranging from drawings, paintings and illustrations, such as that for Albert Camus's novel *L'Etranger*, to works of calligraphy and murals. A largely figurative painter, he created more than 45 murals in various public buildings across Pakistan, India and the Middle East but, sadly, some of the earlier ones are missing. The mural that he produced for the ceiling of Frere Hall in Karachi, Pakistan, was his last and one of his largest.

Sadequain commonly painted subjects in quite sombre, often monochromatic, tones but the incomplete mural in Frere Hall is much more colourful. Incomplete at the time of his death in 1987, it is known by the name of 'Al-ardh-o-was-samawaat' (sometimes just 'Arz-o-Samawat') meaning 'Earth and the Heavens', because those words encapsulate the subject of the mural and are incorporated in it. Around the ceiling, there is a deep border that depicts the earth – from fields of crops to mountains and rivers – as well as figures working the land and looking up to the heavens. Elsewhere, there are angels shown fighting devils and a variety of curious, otherworldly shapes that indicate the celestial bodies. The mural consists of many panels, but it is now at risk due to a lack of maintenance. It remains, though, as a testament to the power of this multi-award-winning artist's imagination and exemplifies the uniqueness of his style.

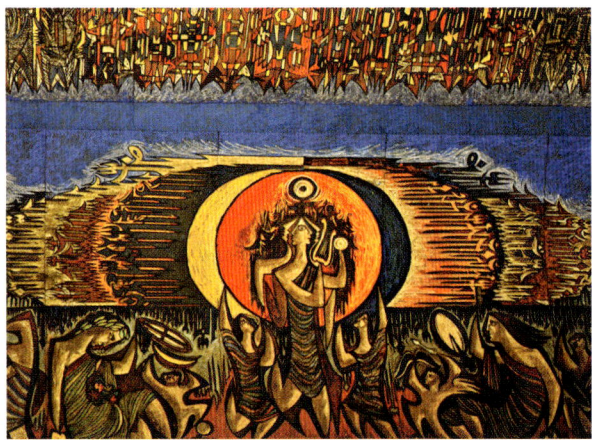 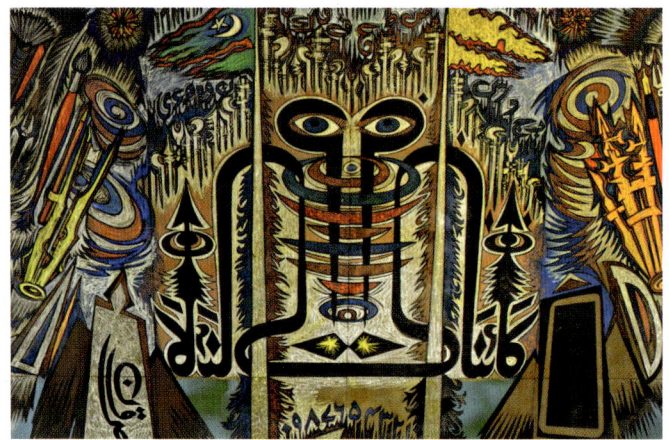

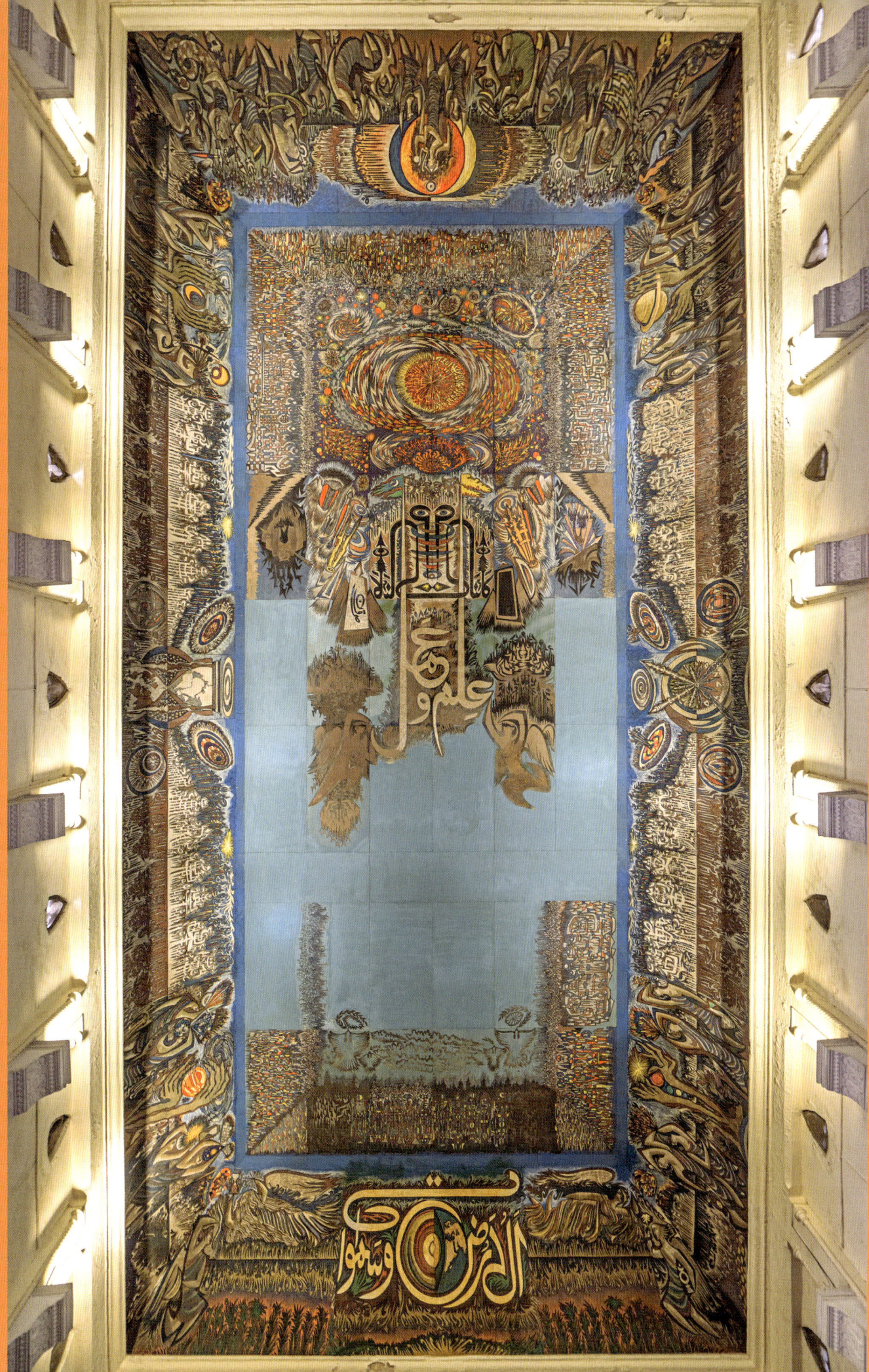

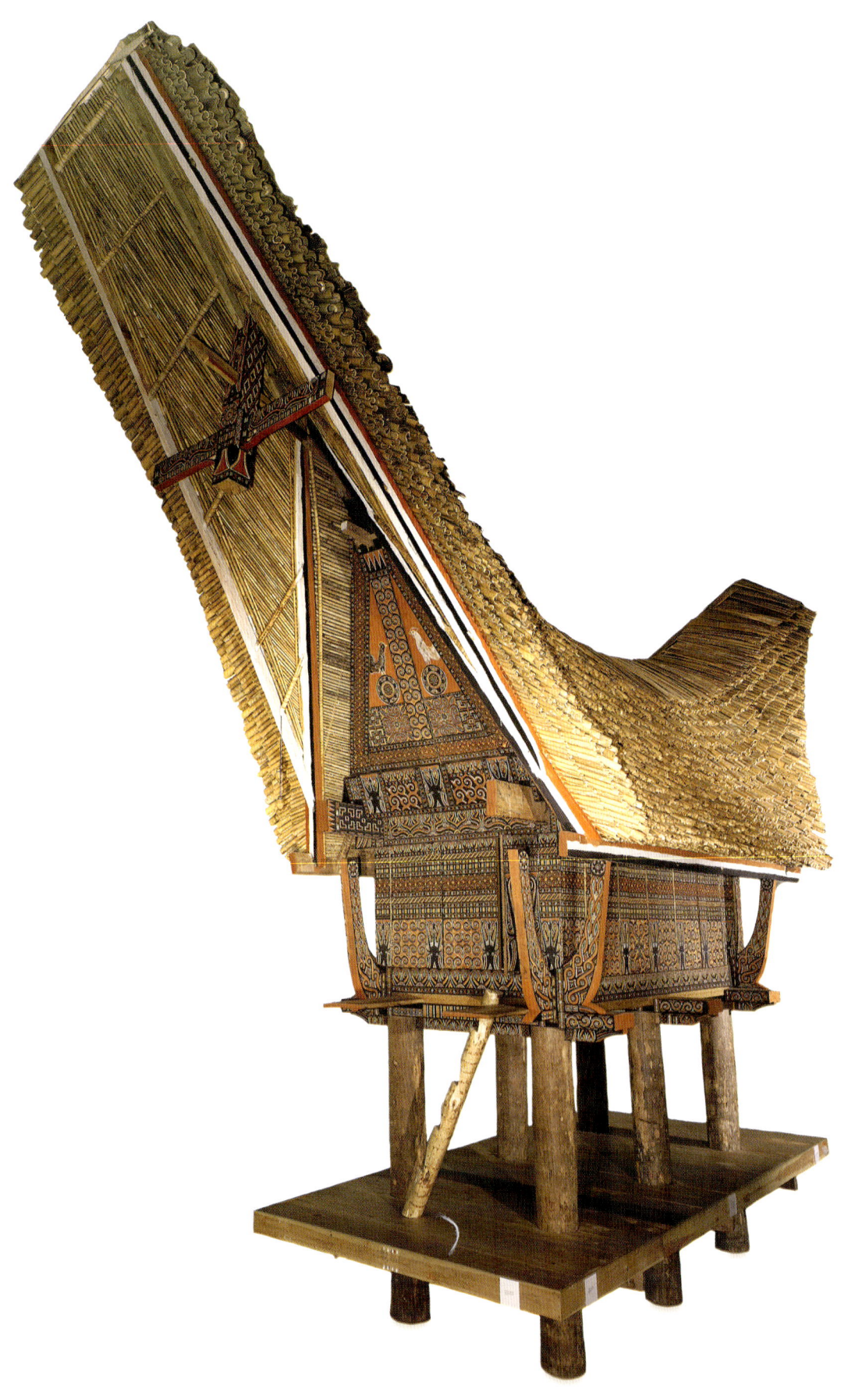

Rice Barn (*Alang*)
(1987)

Architect(s): Unknown

Country of origin: Indonesia

Dimensions: Approx. 8 x 3 x 11 m (26¼ x 10 x 36 ft)

Material(s): Wood, bamboo and rattan

Traditional houses of the Torajan people (who live in a mountainous part of Sulawesi) are designed to fulfil environmental and spiritual requirements. Sometimes an additional structure along with the house is the granary (*alang*), also providing sacred and practical functions. 'Rice, the staple of so many South-East Asian societies, is treated with the greatest reverence,' writes Roxana Waterson.[144] This granary was built and decorated by a group of Torajan craftspeople at the behest of the British Museum for the exhibition 'Toraja: Creating an Indonesian Rice Barn' at the Museum of Mankind in London, in 1987.

Architecturally, the granary and the noble 'origin-house' (*tongkonan*) are similar: an amalgamation of uprights or posts holding up a sizeable saddle-like roof with a three-tiered dissection of the structure. This type of building is ubiquitous throughout the region and probably dates back to the Bronze Age. The design is highly practical, and its architectural form endures because it also satisfies symbolic and aesthetic concerns. The space below the main floor is for animals, the middle section for human dwelling and the loft used to store items associated with the spirit world.

The architecture of Southeast Asia is generally constructed with social, ritual and cosmological interests in mind. The *tongkonan*, theoretically at least, echoes an ideal shared heritage, though in reality, the house belongs to the immediate family and a 'group of people who claim descent from it'.[145] An individual ménage typically preserves connections with roughly four *tongkonan*. A person's identity is bound up with the physical nature of the house, the home also being a material symbol of the social body and its remembrances.

Among the Toraja, who are notably conscious of social ranking, an *alang* that, like this one, is covered with elaborately carved designs and buffalo motifs, is understood to be intended for a high-ranking family. The granary was not only used for the storage but associated with gift-giving to ancestor spirits and gods, so intrinsically linked to kinship and the family's ancestral home. For example, bundles of rice were frequently laid out at the precise cardinal points on behalf of the intended. Sacred house dividers (*ampang bilik*) separated the space into important or sacred zones – 'designated functions in accord with *aluk to dolo*, the way of the ancestors'.[146] In the clan house, these dividers signify areas of life and death. Although it is essentially a private dwelling, it nonetheless has a public function where visitors meet, resolve conflicts and organize marriage ceremonies, funerals and other rituals.

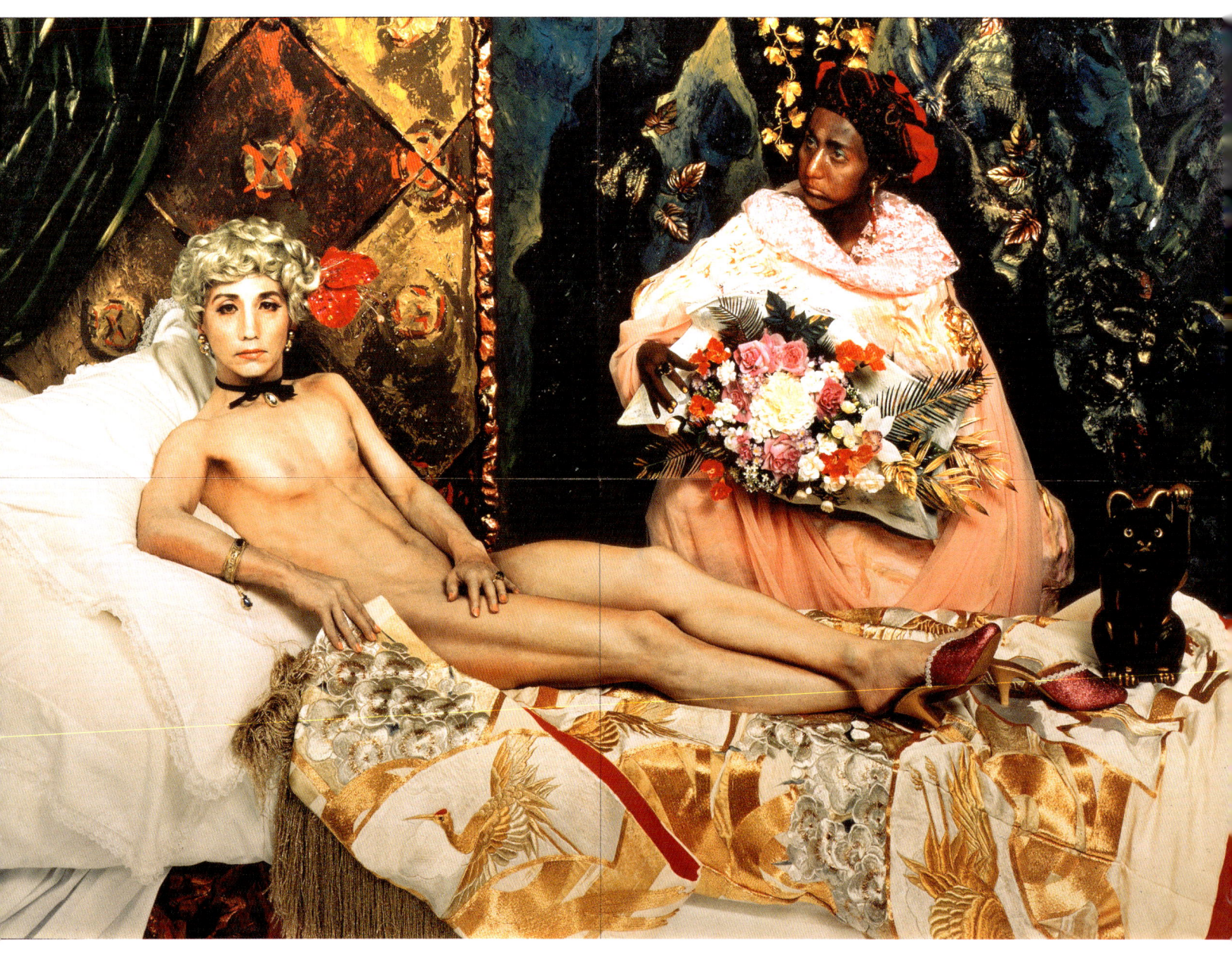

92 *Portrait (Futago)*
(1988)

Architects: Yasumasa Morimura

Country of origin: Japan

Dimensions: 3.43 x 2.40 m (11¼ x 7¾ ft)

Material(s): Colour photograph, transparent medium

In an age of 'selfies', the photographic work of Yasumasa Morimura (b. 1951) appears highly prophetic. The present trend of self-portraiture has equivalences with his art, but as the artist has stated, 'there is also something decidedly different about it.'[147] An element of 'disguise' likewise runs through Morimura's work, and in *Portrait (Futago)* the artist becomes a stand-in for both Manet's modern Olympia and her 'African' servant.

In *Olympia*, Manet satirizes the politely titillating and exploitative salon nude. In choosing paintings by Manet and other artists, Morimura recreated the original settings in plaster and photographed himself masquerading and clad (or unclad) in the celebrated poses of the figures. And by opting for a symbol of French modern art, Morimura draws together a complex web of art historical references and creates a handmade history of art. In *Portrait*, sex work – the real subject of Manet's painting – is drolly allied with the commodification of Western art in Japan, particularly modern photographic reproductions that appear to flatten and negate Manet's painterly style. Morimura's pastiche likewise draws our attention to the fluidity and insecurity of gender, ethnic boundaries and stereotypes as well as societal taboos, particularly transvestism and the attitude to the nude in Japanese art and society. Additionally, *Portrait* might allude to the popular Japanese habit of tampering with photographs and the use of plastic surgery to Westernize Japanese eyes: '[Morimura] challeng[ing] both Western and Japanese notions of good taste and, indeed, of art itself.'[148]

In one sense, Morimura's image points to the commodification of art by misappropriating, 'sabotaging' and making pastiches of famous images. In another, *Portrait* (its subtitle *Futago* means 'twin') taps into the contemporary idiom and term under which 'appropriation' navigated 'postmodernism'. Postmodernism contested the lowly status of the picture, the notion of the author and the ritualistic value or 'aura' of the original artwork. The artist could not have ignored the teachings of Walter Benjamin and his highly influential 1936 essay 'The Work of Art in the Age of Mechanical Reproduction', given 'an upsurge of interest in Benjamin [that] took place in Japan during the 1960s [onwards]'.[149] Essentially, Benjamin postulated that the 'aura' of the singular, exclusive artwork suffers a loss to duplicability; albeit this may not be anything to lament, unlocking highly democratizing options in photography and cinema.[150] Morimura would likely have been aware of Benjamin's radical idea that the photograph was a 'multiple without an original'. The theory seems to echo the Japanese artist's view that 'by resisting the push to view history as accepted fact, I set out to destroy its authority,' and that his 'artistic expressions are an extension of [...] acts of destruction and recreation'.[151]

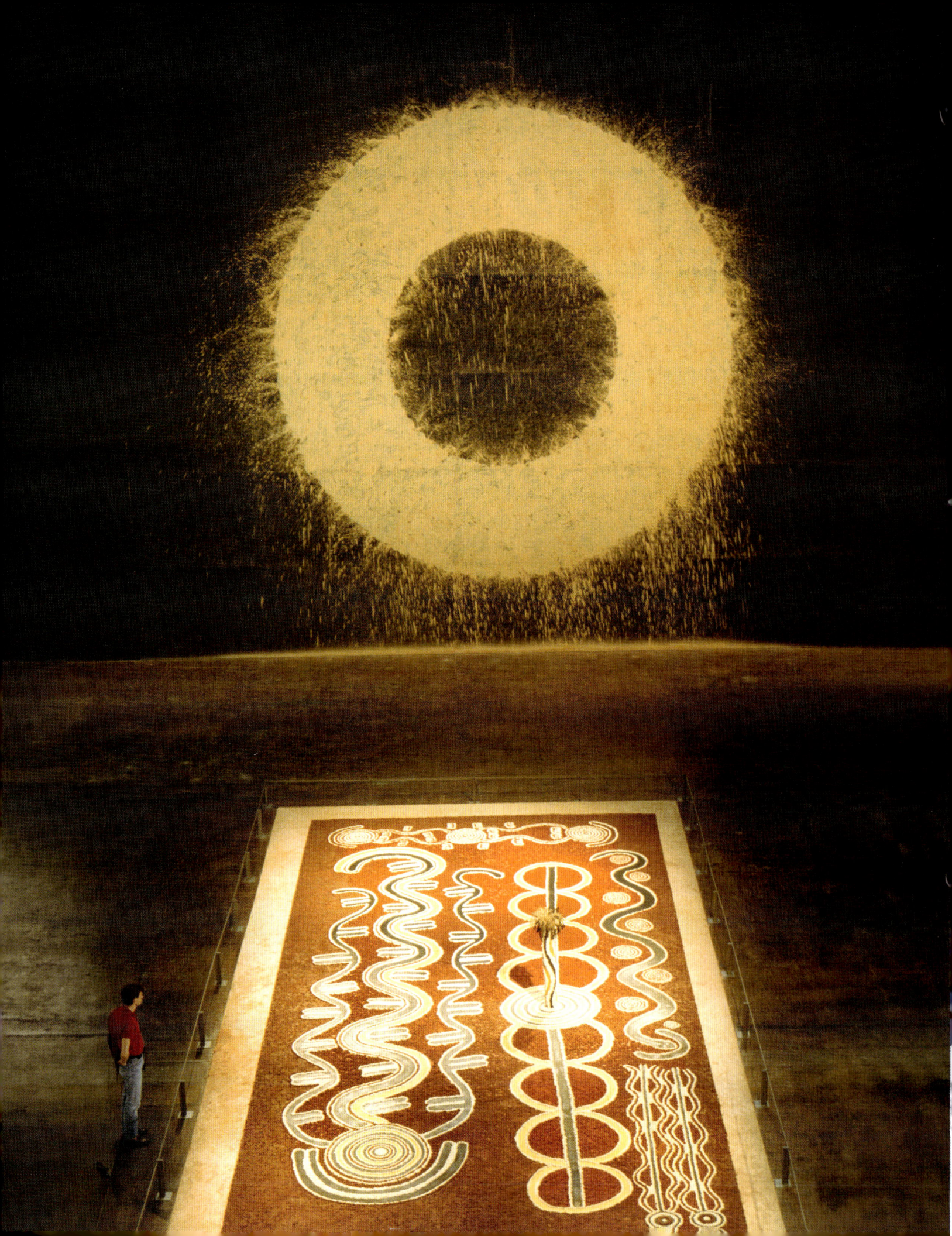

93

Yarla (Yam Dreaming)
(1989)

Artist(s): Paddy Jupurrurla Nelson, Paddy Tjapaltjarri Sims, Paddy Cookie Tjapaltjarri Stewart, Neville Japangardi Poulson, Francis Jupurrurla Kelly and Frank Bronson Jakamarra Nelson

Country of origin: Australia

Dimensions: 10 x 5 m (32¾ x 16½ ft)

Material(s): Earth pigments and other natural materials

The exhibition '*Magiciens de la terre*' ('Magicians of the Earth') took place at the Musée National d'Art Moderne, Centre Georges Pompidou and the Grand Halle, La Villette, both in Paris, from May to August 1989. Its organizer, Jean-Hubert Martin, set out to curate nothing less than 'the first truly international exhibition of worldwide contemporary art'. Martin presented works by more than 100 artists from 50 countries, and to this day the exhibition is seen as a vitally important challenge to the Western 'primitivizing' canon. In part, it was mounted as a corrective to the famous 'Primitivism in 20th-century Art' exhibition at MoMA (Museum of Modern Art) in New York in 1984. '*Magiciens*' was the beginning of the professed 'global turn' – a serious call for investigation into post-colonial attitudes to curating and the need for a global art discourse regarding the colonial rewriting of history;[152] essentially, '*Magiciens*' mounted a challenge to Western art-historical attitudes to the so-called 'primitive' and the yardstick of 'authenticity' levied by the art market. It is still one of the most debated, provocative and maverick exhibitions of its time.

While 'Primitivism' at MoMA displayed objects that were in virtually every instance manufactured chronologically prior to the 20th century, in '*Magiciens*' the art and artists presented were contemporary. For the exhibition, a group of artists from Yuendumu in northern Australia installed this ceremonial Yam Dreaming (an Aboriginal origin story, see page 182, relating to yams) painting, *Yarla*. It's an impressive type of desert art and manner of ceremonial painting usually prepared on a soil or a ceramic surface. Yarla was placed directly in front the English sculptor Richard Long's large red mud circle, the entire installation inviting comparisons with magical circles and materials born of the earth. The pairing was seen as a pioneering interchange that signalled the growing scope and complexity of global artistic practice and curation. As the curator Jean-Hubert Martin claimed, 'Those objects which have a spiritual function for the human mentality, objects which exist in all societies... possess[] an aura.'[153] This assumption that art in non-Western cultures was intrinsically 'magico-religious', as opposed to the general forfeiture of the spiritual in Western societies, was particularly irksome. This was 'primitivism' reconfigured, without mentioning the fact that Aboriginal peoples were habitually subject to involuntary resettlement and far worse. Moreover, as Jean Fisher astutely observed in 1989, '... though the Yuendumu earth paintings made the show, it was not mentioned that, as the late aboriginal anthropologist Eric Michaels has described, they operate a creative video-production-and-broadcast unit reinvented in relation to aboriginal law.'[154]

94 Hands of Fatima
(1989)

Photographer: Laila Shawa

Country of origin: Palestine

Dimensions: 89 x 70 cm (35 x 27½ inches)

Material(s): Oil and acrylic on canvas

Laila Shawa (1940–2022) was a Palestinian artist who was a prominent exponent of Islamo-Pop art, using it to comment on political topics that affected the country of her birth, Gaza, and the impact of the conflict between Palestinians and Israelis on Palestinians in general. She employed various forms of media, such as graffiti, photography, painting, silk-screen printing and sculpture, to explore the subjects that interested her in series of works such as *The Walls of Gaza* and *Gaza III*. Commenting on her work, Shawa said, 'From the privileged vantage point of the artist, I try to consider all sides of any question. Through my multi-layered approach, I express the dichotomies, ironies, and hypocrisies to which others seem less attuned.'

With an education in Egypt at the Leonardo da Vinci Institute and in Italy at the Academy of Fine Arts in Rome, Shawa embraced the Italian Pop art scene before returning first to Gaza and then spending time variously in Beirut in Lebanon, London in the UK, and the US, all the while examining themes that interested her, such as politics, violence against women and children, injustice and persecution.

The 'hands of Fatima' is an alternative name for the *hamsa/khamsa* symbol that can be traced back to the days of ancient Mesopotamia (part of modern-day Iraq). Associated with traditions in the Middle East/western Asia and the northern parts of Africa, the motif of an open right hand featuring the 'evil' eye denotes divine protection and mystical feminine power. In various cultures, it is related to symbols – such as the Hand of Mary and the Hand of Venus – that represent fertility, successful pregnancies and the auspicious rearing of babies, and Shawa spent time studying its history in ancient cultures such as those of Assyria and Egypt.

Hands of Fatima (part of the artist's *Women and Magic* series) is rooted in Pop art with its vibrant colours and patterns, but its subject and motifs are indicative of Shawa's aim to highlight the plight of women in the Middle East and the violence wrought against them, along with the enforcement of wearing a veil (to which she objected, as a sign both of men's fear of Western influence on Eastern traditions and of female acquiescence to patriarchal rule). It also showcases her use of folklore and mystical imagery. Shawa's art continues to resonate and her works can be seen in collections around the world.

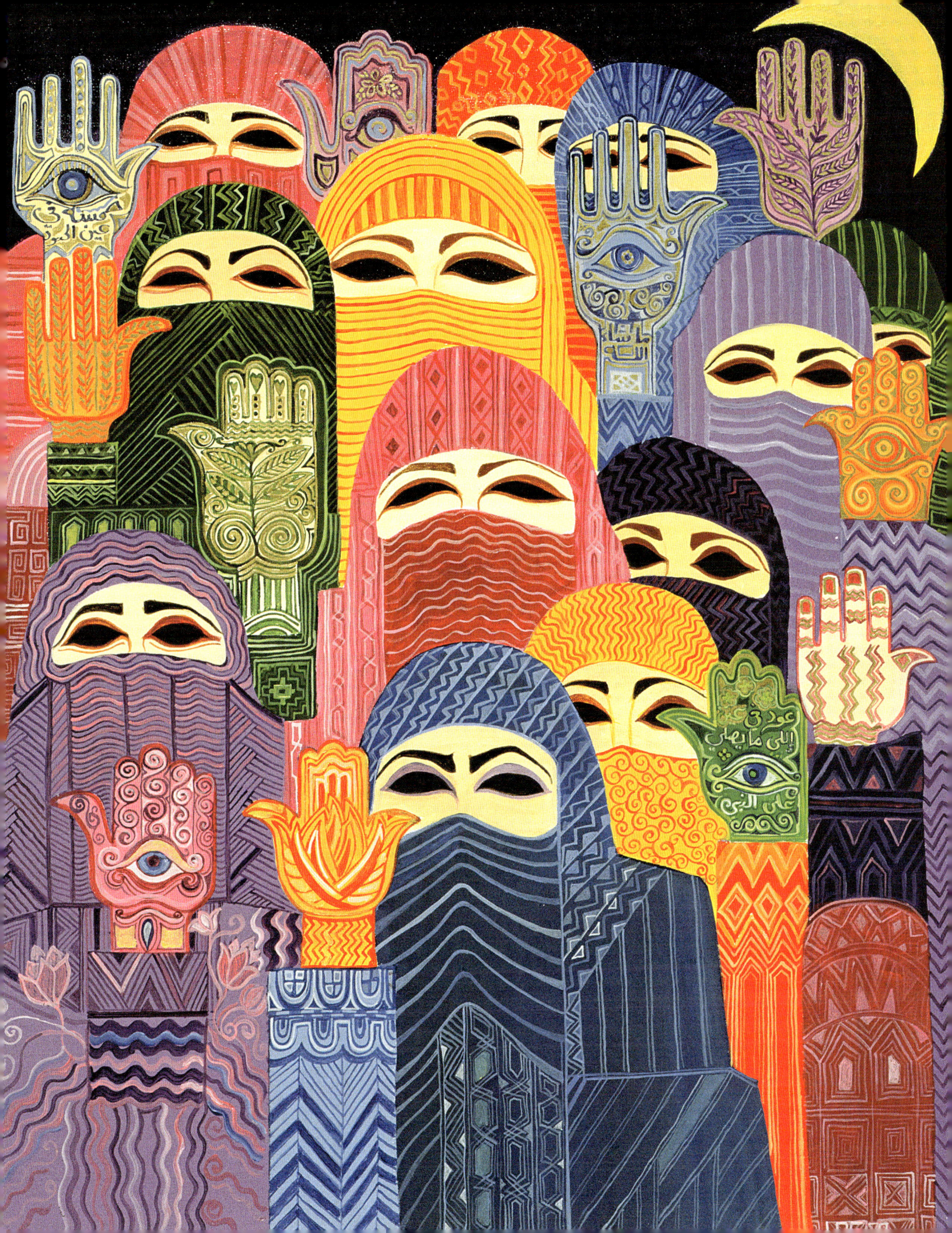

Take these with you when you leave
(1998)

Artist(s): John Pule

Country of origin: Aotearoa New Zealand

Dimensions: 188 x 185 cm (74 x 72 ¾ inches)

Material(s): Oil on canvas

The history of Pacific people's strange and frequently ill-fated encounters with the Europeans has always been full of contradiction. In truth, the taxonomies of Western science, literature and art have repeatedly been used or promoted at the expense of indigenous societies. The cultures of the Pacific and Aotearoa unquestionably had their own mythologies, art and histories regarding the European 'other', but Niuean (a Polynesian island associated with New Zealand) images include highly cultivated depictions of their own peoples, flora, fauna and wider environment.

These inextricably intertwined yet oddly undetermined histories are similarly part of John Puhiatau Pule's (b. 1962) art. His etchings, lithographs and paintings adapted a Niuean *hiapo* (barkcloth) aesthetic system to suit his own art – a system that greatly influenced barkcloth design in the islands of Tonga and Sāmoa in the mid 19th century. But as Nicholas Thomas has recognized, 'Pule's... paintings of the early to the mid-1990s "look like" *hiapo* but do not really resemble them at all.'[155] It's probably more accurate to say that works such as *Take these with you when you leave* 'echo... the tonalities, structure and graphic invention of Niuean *hiapo*'.[156]

Born in Liku, Niue, Pule immigrated to New Zealand in 1964. He is not only a prominent figure in the New Zealand art scene, but also a contemporary artist with a significant bearing in Pacific art. His re-imaginings of historic *hiapo* have consistently reinterpreted the moot relationships between Pacific histories and contemporaneous global concerns, which has resulted in a richly textured, intelligent and wide spectrum of images. Pule deftly intermingles European Modernist idioms (Munch, Matisse and Picasso) with Christian fresco cycles from the Italian Renaissance, and the circular formations of *kapkap* ornamentation from New Ireland and the Solomon Islands. Furthermore, his artwork habitually references past Pacific histories, including Cook's voyages, Māori stories and art.

Pule's 'signature' is a fretful mix of recognizable and unrecognizable creatures, with 'strange bird or lizard-like predators with gaping jaws... in a landscape of myth [that speaks] of transformation and transgression, of theft and loss, but also consumption and growth'.[157] In the early 2000s, his work changed radically to include strange atmospheric spaces and 'surreal cloudscapes' connected by vines or the sinews of climbing plants. Images of veins, stems and arterial routes imply a correlation between our organic selves and the origins, journeys and paths we take in life. Fundamentally, Pule's paintings take us 'wherever it is that we want to go' and reveal an open-minded – real and imagined – world.

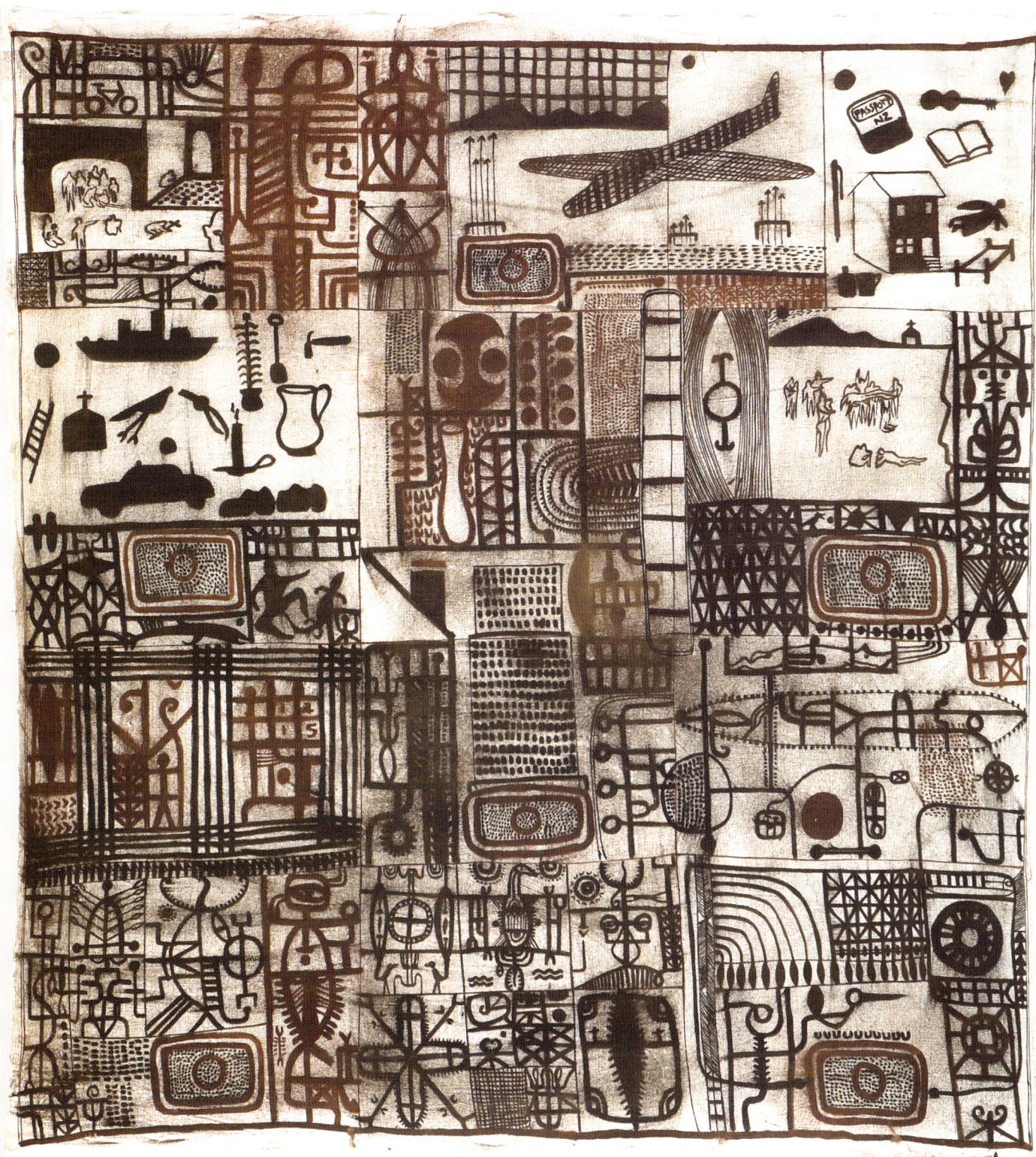

96 *Rent Collection Courtyard*
(1999)

Artist(s): Cai Guo-Qiang, assisted by Long Xu Li and nine guest artisan sculptors

Country of origin: China

Dimensions: 108 life-sized sculptures of varying heights

Material(s): Clay, wire and wood armature

The Chinese artist Cai Guo-Qiang (b. 1957) is perhaps best known for his suggestive pyrotechnical art practice, works that make use of coloured explosives to 'paint' the sky. Cai's art runs the gamut of exploratory oils, black gunpowder illustrations, sculptural installations and coloured explosive art: art which often relays the forces of destruction, violence, happenstance and ephemerality. Other works allude to ancient mythology, cultural history and Eastern belief systems, as well as present-day political, social and cultural concerns. One pyrotechnic artwork involved trying to lengthen the Great Wall of China using two explosive fuse lines. In Cai's work, destruction is on a par with creation, the only coefficient being transformation itself. Although these pyrotechnic displays are a marker of Chinese inventions, according to the artist they are also attempts to manufacture a larger, world-wide reciprocity between different cultures and audiences.

In September 1999, as a recipient of the Venice Biennale Golden Lion and the Praemium Imperiale awards, a very different conflagration engulfed Cai's work. His *Rent Collection Courtyard* re-imagines a well-known Socialist-Realist sculpture made in the late 1960s by members of the Sichuan Academy of Art, commissioned during the Cultural Revolution. The original piece is sculpted in the tradition of the famous Terracotta Warriors of Qin Shi Huang (see page 22) and comprises more than 100 life-sized figures that illustrate the 'brutal exploitation of the peasants' and their 'simmering anger' towards pre-Revolutionary landlords.[158]

In Beijing, reproductions of the original in fibreglass were adjusted to create a far more commanding image of propaganda under Communist – as opposed to Feudal – rule. Cai's installation became the subject of a lawsuit, with the artist and the Biennale sued for patent contravention, which appeared a long way from the Chinese belief in a 'people's art'.[159] Detractors maintained that Cai was bowing down to Western arrogance vis-à-vis the Cultural Revolution, his Biennale installation also seen as disparaging a sculptural work still lauded in China today. Cai has always argued that his installation was fundamentally a figurative and aesthetic response to both Venice's history and Renaissance sculpture. In the artist's re-working, the unfired clay was left to dry out and fall to pieces, the entire installation destroyed at the end of the exhibition. Other versions, including the New York *Rent Collection Courtyard* (2008), also remained incomplete. It seems that Cai's interpretation of the original concept intimates how things have altered over time and how 'its deliberate state of non-completion'[160] proffers the possibility, the optimism and the belief that circumstances will also change for future generations.

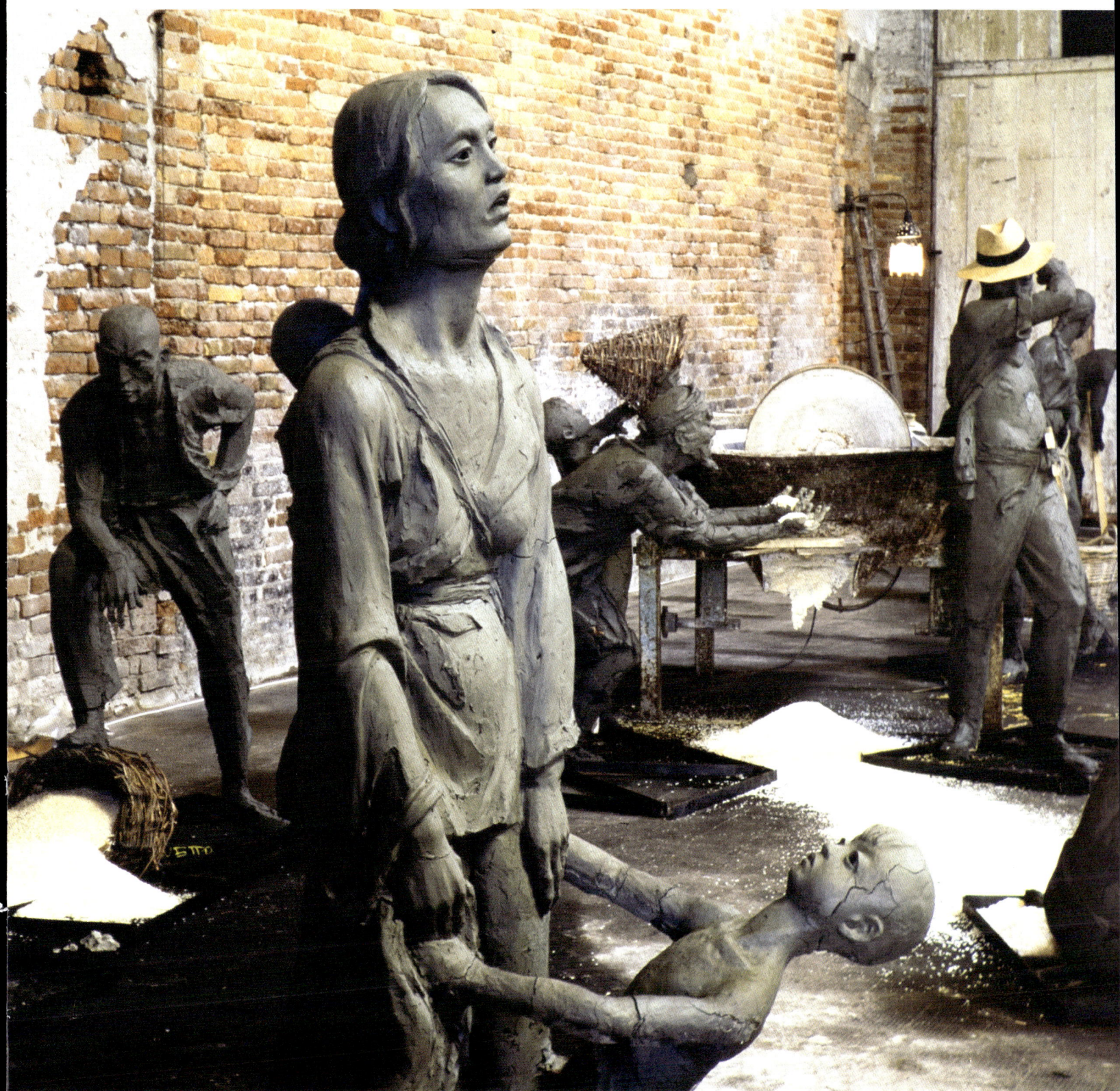

Vertical Form, Counter Rotating
(2006)

Artist(s): Andrew Drummond

Country of origin: Aotearoa New Zealand

Dimensions: 9 x 0.5 m (29½ x 1½ ft)

Material(s): Stainless steel and various materials

Andrew Drummond's practice traverses the boundaries of art, science and engineering, his work unlike any other New Zealand sculptor. Impressed by Marcel Duchamp's works, Drummond (b. 1951) produced a number of innovative pieces for his graduation show in Ontario that established the foundation of his later performance-based practice. *Spiral of Light*, *Suitcase* (both 1975) and *7 x 7 x 7 x 7 Circles* (1976) saw him don a white lab coat and boiler suit with cloth helmet to generate an aura appropriate to his ritualistic performances. To a degree, Drummond aligned himself with modernist 'worker artists' like Pablo Picasso, Georges Braque, Alexander Rodchenko and Joseph Beuys, who had dressed as scientists, mechanics, aviators and technicians.

Themes of transformation, ritual, spectacle, abjection, alchemy, allegory and the body as political agency are all central to Drummond's art. *Filter Action* (1980) similarly relied on repetitive, ritualistic echoes of arterial and circulatory systems. Reflecting on the aesthetic relationships in his work, the artist made a striking connection between *Filter Action* and his motorized *Vertical Form, Counter Rotating*. As he explained:

> It took me back to 1980 when I was planning *Filter Action* and what was going on in my thinking. Then an image emerged from that day, and it was [the idea of] counter-rotating. As I scribed the circle, I drew in both directions and [made] the same actions I did during the performance, and they were always counter-rotational.... [161]
>
> The idea of rotation has gone on from time immemorial – since the invention of the wheel – so it is pretty central to my practice.... My more recent sculptures respond to cyclical principles by using the fickleness of the wind to demonstrate how quirky machines are in comparison to the human sensory system.... My machines do not just do what they do: they also inform us about the environment and play on an age-old idea of the transformative moment. [162]

From this perspective, there is continuity between Drummond's early performance art and his later machine sculpture, and a reaction to a progressively perplexing, uncanny modern world. *Vertical Form, Counter Rotating* refers to seeds and seed pods from the native *kōwhai* tree, but also straddles boundaries between purportedly archaic forms – its structure suggestive of Ottoman minarets – and futurist technologies, modern art-world sculptured forms, materials and ecological interests. As such, *Vertical Form*, 'provides an indication of where society has to move into the sustainable future while at the same time remaining located in the realms of beauty and dream.' [163]

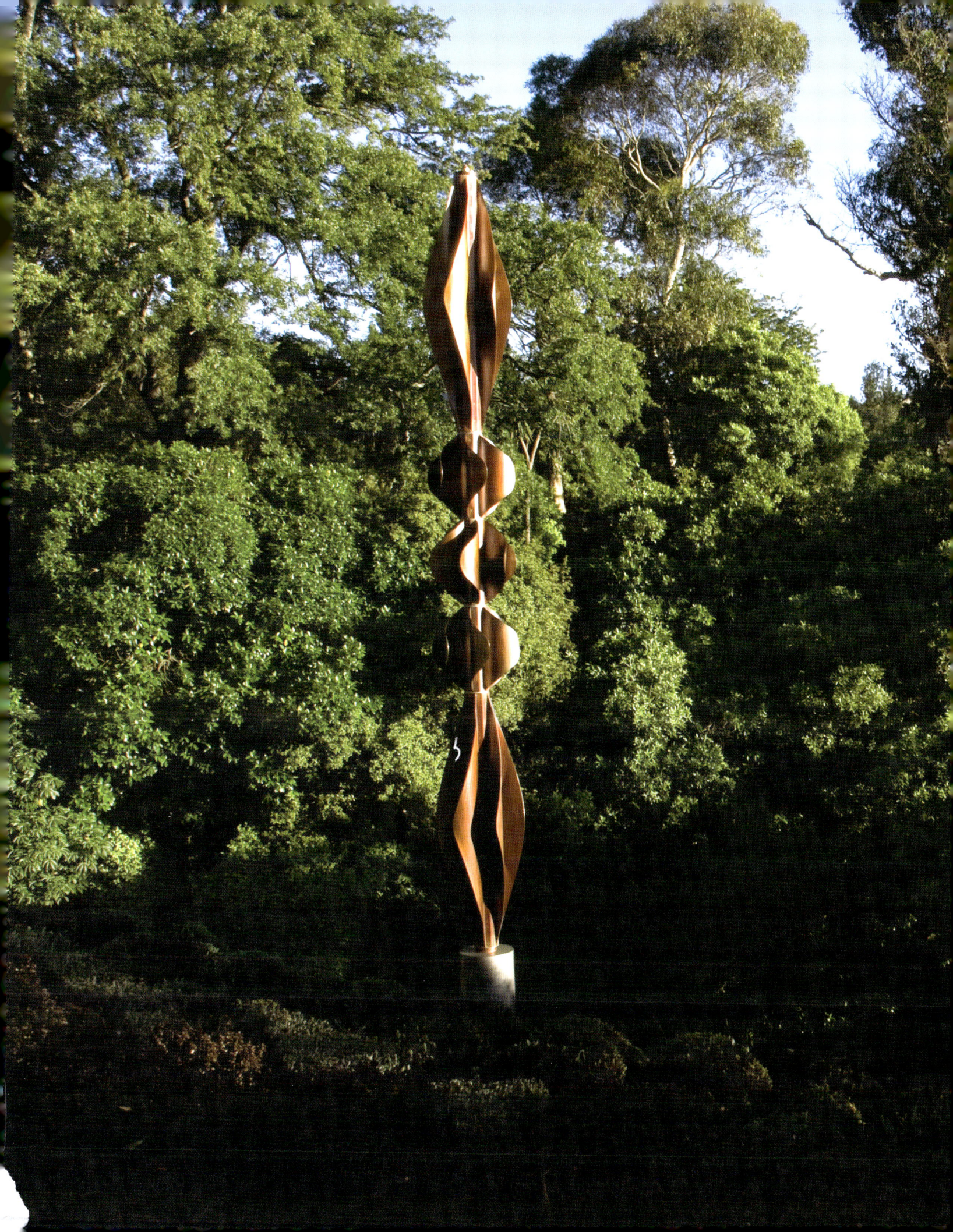

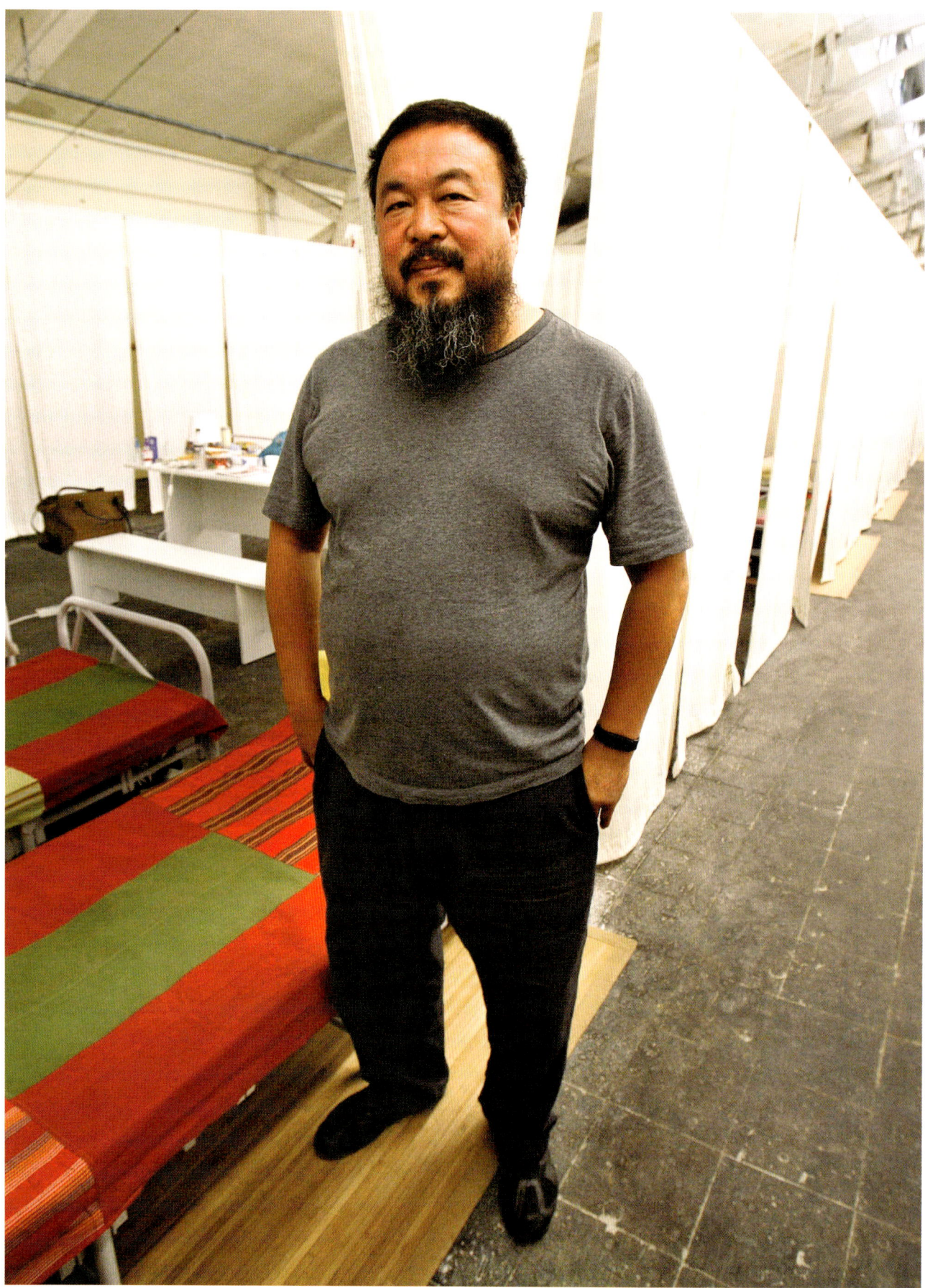

98 *Fairytale*
(2007)

Artist(s): Ai Weiwei

Country of origin: China

Dimensions: Not applicable

Material(s): 1,001 Qing-dynasty wooden chairs (1644–1911), luggage, dormitories

Ai Weiwei is an internationally recognized artist, curator, writer and architect. He was born in Beijing, China (in 1957), but lives and works in Berlin, Germany. His work includes assemblages, 'readymades' and frank and moving activities that offer humane pleas for social justice, operating in a place between art and social activism, frequently muddying the waters between the two.

In 2007, the artist devised *Fairytale*, a work that he called 'a sociopolitical readymade',[164] which brought together 1,001 Chinese – including farmers, manual workers, street sellers and students, many of whom had never had the chance to travel within China, let alone abroad. Ai arranged for them to visit Kassel, Germany, for one of his, and at the time *Documenta* 12's, largest and most ambitious projects. The 'tourists', as Ai labelled them, were separated into five 'waves' of 200, each group visiting for one week. They stayed in a hostel specially devised by the artist in an old textile factory. Here Ai housed them in small, partitioned dormitories divided by white sheets and with decorative bedspreads made to his specifications. He spread 1,001 chairs from the Qing dynasty through the exhibition venue as well as constructing *Template* (2007), a large *plein air* assemblage made from destroyed Ming- and Qing-dynasty houses, with wooden windows and doors salvaged from properties in northern China's Shanxi Province, bringing attention to China's speedy development at the expense of traditional material culture.

For *Fairytale*, 'tourist' uniforms, which the group were not compelled to adopt, were concocted and accompanied by corresponding luggage to suggest visual branding. Cameras and sound recorders allowed the 'tourists' to detail their thoughts about the town, in which they were free to wander. The concept was simple, but the organization highly complex and bureaucratic (some participants were denied passports and visas), drawing attention to the realities of the 'freedom' to move or migrate internationally. As one art historian observed, travelling in this way requires procuring a national identity, and must be politically sanctioned, if not comprehensively acknowledged.[165] Moreover, the way Ai handled his 1,001 visitors highlighted the globalized spectacle of mass migration. The artist's strategy also introduced ideas of mass verses individual experience. The movement of individuals and groups implied the type of travel embarked on not for tourism but for economic or political necessity.

Of course, *Fairytale* can be seen as a comment on the way a globalized format for very large exhibitions, including *Documenta*, expanded in the 1990s and 2000s. We can trace this globalism back to the *Magiciens de la terre* show in 1989 (see page 192), which first pondered contemporary art from a global perspective. From Ai's standpoint, however, travel to a literal art world and veritable fairytale setting, which was also home to the Brothers Grimm and their dark folktales, for *Fairytale* hinted at the shady side of 'globalization's glib surface of easy mobility'.[166]

99 Infinity Mirrored Room –
Filled with the Brilliance of Life
(2011/2017)

Artist(s): Yayoi Kusama

Country of origin: Japan

Dimensions: 295 × 622.4 × 622.4 cm (9¾ x 20½ x 20½ ft)

Material(s): Mirrored glass, wood, aluminium, plastic, ceramic and LEDs

As part of the Pop art, Minimalist and feminist idioms, Yayoi Kusama (1929–) – alongside Takashi Murakami (1962–), the 'Warhol of Japan' – was an important artist to emerge from Japan in the early 1960s. In 1957, she moved to the United States, settling in New York where she took part in a number of significant exhibitions during 1960–4. Kusama showed alongside a coterie of Minimalist, Conceptual and Pop artists, gathering acclaim from critics.

Swapping sculpture for installation, Kusama quickly became a fixture of the 1960s New York art scene. Her initial 'Pop' exhibitions included 'Aggregation: One Thousand Boats Show' at the Gertrude Stein Gallery in 1963, and she first exhibited her *Infinity Mirror Room – Phalli's Field* (or *Floor Show*) at the Castellane Gallery in 1965, featuring soft polka-dot sculptural forms and mirrored walls that created a feeling of unending space.

Kusama also began to put on her 'Happenings' and embraced late 1960s 'hippie' and psychedelic counterculture by organizing events that included painting the naked bodies of participants in brightly coloured polka dots. *Soul Under the Moon* (2002), using mirrors, ultra-violet lights and other detritus such as plastic, nylon thread, timber and synthetic paints, continued her series of 'Infinity Mirror' rooms from the early 1960s. The artist has repeatedly stressed the crucial role the spectator occupies in her infinity rooms and how they experience the works under ever-changing circumstances: 'For it is the viewer who changes the shape constantly by [their] change in position relative to the work.'[167]

Infinity Mirrored Room – Filled with the Brilliance of Life was created especially for the artist's travelling retrospective exhibition, 'Yayoi Kusama', held in 2011 and 2012. As the title intimates, it intends to envisage and conceptualize life as a form of 'brilliance'. Here, the spectator is directed along a reflected walkway (through mirrored tiles on the walls and ceiling) suspended over a shallow pool. Hundreds of minuscule dots of light, throbbing and varying in colour, at times progressively and on occasion suddenly, are hung from the ceiling and mirrored in every surface. Like pinpricks in the sky at night, the dots suggest a boundless universe. 'Our earth is only one polka dot among a million stars in the cosmos. When we obliterate nature and our bodies with polka dots, we become part of the unity of our environment,' Kusama once remarked.[168] To a degree, the immersive spaces of the infinity rooms not only demolish the watertight barriers between art and viewer, but also bring us into Kusama's extraordinary internal world. In amalgamating aspects of Minimalism, Conceptualism and Pop art, and in criss-crossing traditional and contemporary techniques, Kusama's mirrored realm echoes many major developments in art practice over the years.

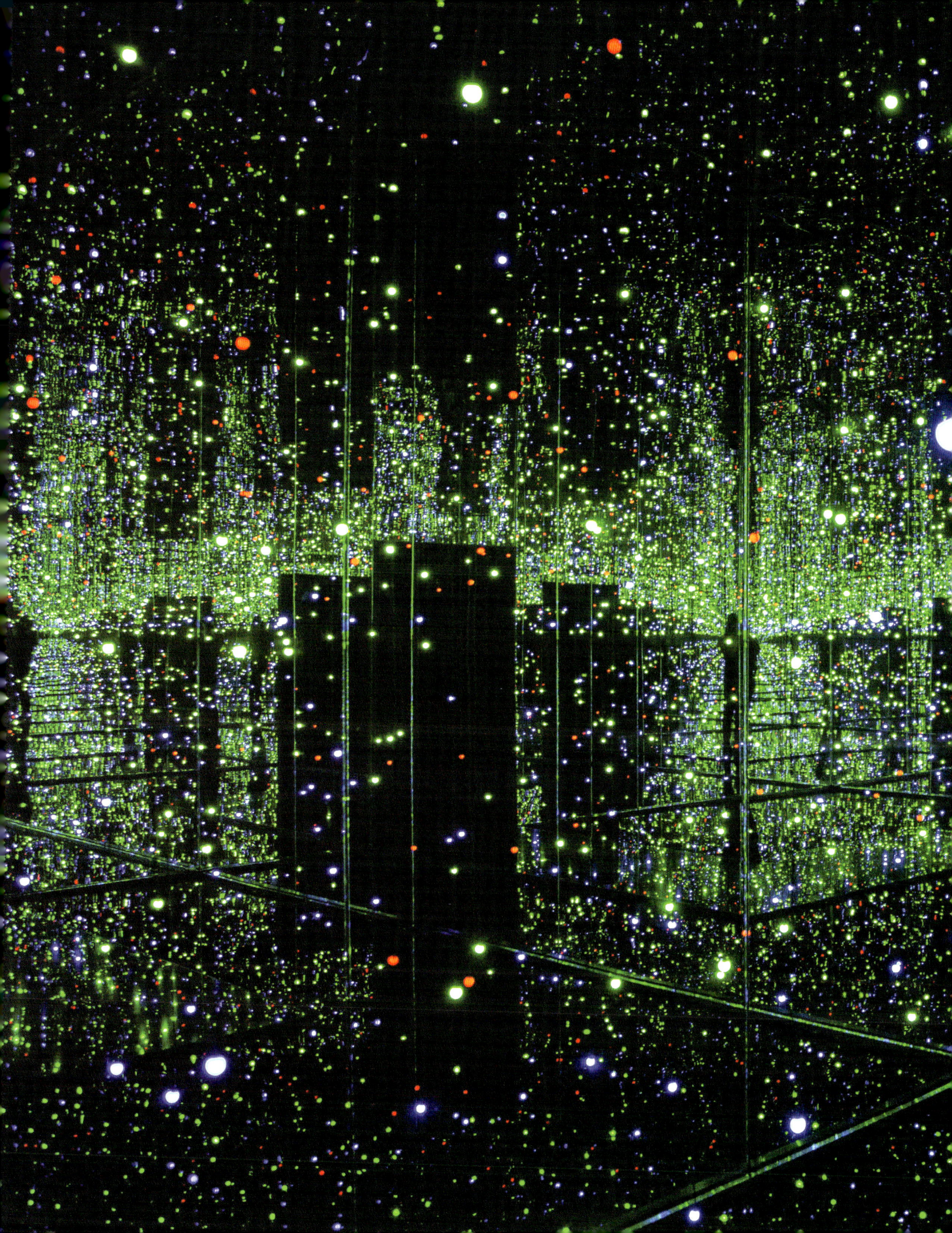

100 *Absentee (Self-Portrait)* (2023)

Artist(s): Christian Hidaka

Country of origin: United Kingdom

Dimensions: 1.95 x 1.3 m (6⅓ x 4¼ ft)

Material(s): Oil tempera on linen

Christian Hidaka (né Ward) was born in Noda, in Japan, in 1977 (to a British father and Japanese mother). In 1981, his family relocated to the UK, where Hidaka studied fine art. He currently lives and works in London, but his works are widely exhibited and held in various collections internationally.

Hidaka's artistic concerns include a myriad of visual and literary references, from Palaeolithic wall painting to Chinese Song dynasty landscapes, old Japanese photographs, Islamic and Buddhist art, French Modernist painting and poetry, and science fiction. Connective threads underpinning his work include theatre, architecture, 'the history of painting and the art of memory'.[169] In recent exhibitions, the gallery is construed as a theatrical space with paintings and murals effortlessly allied, the exhibition becoming an artwork or theatrical entity in itself. Recent works, including *Absentee (Self-Portrait)*, develop connections between performance and art. In these, Hidaka adopts what he terms a 'Eurasian' mode of picturing, a transitional space where East and West, old and new, happen simultaneously.

In *Absentee*, the figure is derived from a British newspaper story showing a North African migrant stumbling from a boat onto Dover beach in England. But the painter did not feel it quite right to use the migrant's face, so he used his own, and the picture morphed into something else entirely. For the absentee's outfit, Hidaka applied designs by Picasso for the 1917 Jean Cocteau ballet *Parade*, specifically the white whorls and stars that play loudly over the cobalt blue of a trapeze artist's leotard. As Hidaka has explained, 'I have referenced the arabesques on the costume of the acrobat in Picasso's *Parade* because this acrobat leaps from star to star, and for me these stars are akin to constellations of references.'[170] The emblematic crane and turtle depicted above and below in the painting are ciphers in Zen Buddhism, illustrative of a spiritual journey. Red coral at the edge of the stage perhaps intimates 'the mobility of commodities', but it is also one of the 'seven precious materials' of Buddhism and is possibly a reference to the alchemical process relating to creativity. The appearance of the wind god Zephyr high up in the rafters may also be a sign of the creative winds of change.

In Hidaka's painting, decorative touches appear on the floor and the proscenium, including intricate Islamic floor patterning and brightly coloured flowers taken from an ancient Italian fresco. Another esoteric and 'off-centring' note is the spectre thrown onto the wall – the 'absentee' perhaps? – haunting the picture. The way Hidaka's absentee is ushered in on Zephyr's west wind is possibly a reminder of the journeys that migrants and refugees embark upon in war or peace. If *Absentee* triggers images of globalized itinerary, diversity, throwing caution to the wind, it nonetheless combines these references with the magical expression of movement and the artistic agility of an acrobat, who is 'lightfootedly set' and bounds amid 'constellations of references'.

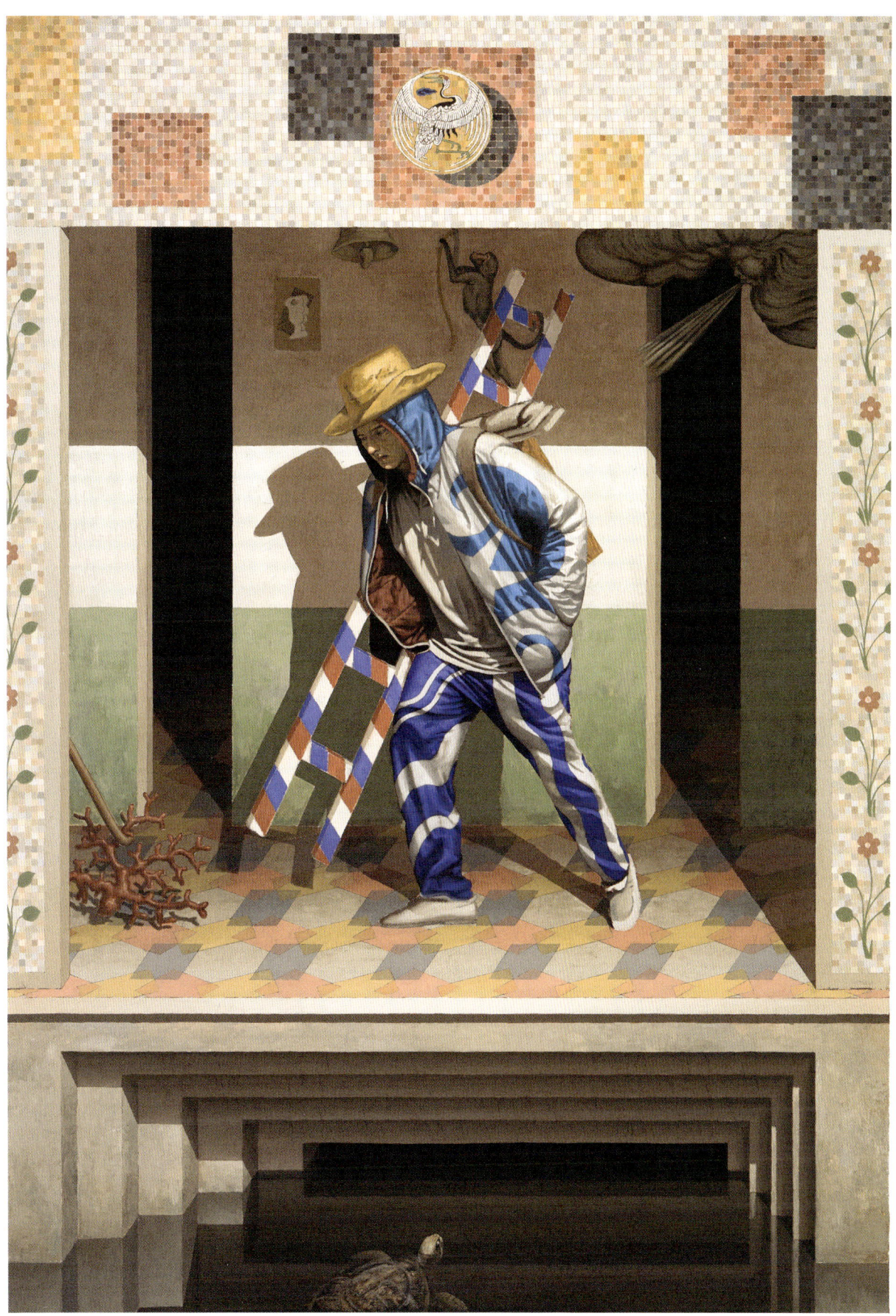

Bibliography and Notes

The numbers in brackets and accompanying page references refer to the annotations and the pages on which they appear throughout the text.

Publications:

Adams, J., Hooper, S. Nuku, M., *A'a: A Deity from Polynesia: British Museum Object in Focus*, The British Museum Press, London, 2016. (107 – p. 164)

Adams, M. J., 'Structural Aspects of a Village Art', *American Anthropologist*, New Series, vol. 75, no. 1, February 1973, pp. 265-279. (85 – p. 153)

Allen, C., *Art in Australia: From Colonization to Postmodernism*, Thames & Hudson, London, 1997. (98, 99 & 100 – p. 156), (122 – p. 174)

Allen, M. S., 'Revisiting and revising Marquesan culture history: new archaeological Investigations at Anaho Bay, Nuku Hiva Island, *Journal of the Polynesian Society*, vol. 113, No. 2, June 2004. (41 – p. 102)

Applin, J., 'Yayoi Kusama: Infinity Mirror Room – Phalli's Field', London, 2012. (167 – p. 204)

Bacus, E. A., et al, *Interpreting Southeast Asia's Past*, NUS Press, Singapore, 2008. (17 – p. 43)

Bail, M., 'Ned Kelly, Artist', in *Sidney Nolan's Ned Kelly: The Ned Kelly Paintings in the National Gallery of Australia*, N.G.A., Canberra, 2002. (125 – p. 174)

Barlow, K., 'Achieving womanhood and the achievements of Women in Murik Society: Cult Initiation, Gender Complementarity, and the Prestige of Women', in Lutkehaus, N. C. & Roscoe, P. B. (eds), *Gender Rituals: Female Initiation in Melanesia*, Routledge, London, 1995. Also see Bolton, L., 'A tale of two figures, Journal de la Société des Océanistes, 2018. (61, 62 & 64 – p. 128)

Barlow, K. *COMA* Bulletin. (63 – p. 128)

Bennet, W., *The Evening Post*, August 1964. (127 – p. 176)

Berger, J., *The Success and Failure of Picasso*, Penguin, London,1980. (28 – p. 65)

Blackley, R., *Galleries of Maoriland*, 2018, Auckland University Press, New Zealand. (97 – p. 158)

Blackley, R., *Goldie*, Auckland Art Gallery Toi o Tamaki, in assoc. with David Bateman Ltd, Auckland, 1997. (91, 92, 94, 95 & 96 – p. 154)x

Brunt, P., Thomas, N., Mallon, S., Bolton, et al, *Art in Oceania*, Thames & Hudson, London, 2021. (9 – p. 30, (22 – p. 49), (27 – p. 61), (35 – p. 93), (38 – p. 96), (42 – p. 102), (50 – p. 119), (55 & 56 – p. 122), (60 – p. 128), (74 – p. 139), (76 – p. 141), (77 & 78 – p. 144), (81 – p. 150), (103 – p. 162), (106 – p. 162), (111 – p. 166), (113 – p. 168), (132 & 133– p. 179), (134 – p. 181), (156 – p. 196)

Buchloh, B., Interview with Jean-Hubert Martin), 'The Whole Earth Show', *Art in America*, vol. 77, No. 5, May 1989. (153 – p. 193)

Burman, E., *Terracotta Warriors: History, Mystery and the Latest Discoveries*, Weidenfeld & Nicholson, London, 2018. (5 – p. 23)

Burt, B., Akin, D. & Kwa'ioloa, M. *Body Ornaments of Malaita, Solomon Islands*, University of Hawai'i Press, Honolulu, 2009. (109 & 110 – p. 166)

Caruana, W., *Aboriginal Art*, Thames & Hudson, London, 1993 (3rd ed. 2012). (138, 140 & 141 – p. 182)

Cohen, J. I. et al, 'Art History, Postcolonialism and the Global Turn', *Art Margins*, vol. 12, issue 2, June 2023. (151 – p. 193)

Curiger, B. in Birnbaum, D., Butler, C. H., Cotter, S., *Defining Contemporary Art*, Phaidon, London, 2011. (166 – p. 203)

Davidson, A. K., *Aotearoa New Zealand: Defining Moments in the Gospel-Culture Encounter*, WCC Publication, Geneva, 1996. (54 – p. 120)

Dillion, M. et al, *China: A Cultural and Historical Dictionary*, Curzon, Surrey, 1988 [1998]. (2 & 3 – p.23), (31 – p. 71)

Drummond, A. Email to Author. (161 – p. 200)

Dunn M. in *The Art of the East*, Könemann, Cologne, 1999. (19 – p. 45), (20 – p. 46), (34 – p. 81)

Dunn, M., *Gordon Walters*, Auckland City Art Gallery, Auckland,1983. (134 – p. 179)

Ebony, D., *Art in America*, October 2000. (159 – p. 198)

Elliott, M. & Thomas, N. (eds), *Gifts & Discoveries: The Museum of Archaeology and Anthropology Cambridge*, Scala Publishing, London, 2011. (49 – p. 117). (69 & 70 – p. 132)

Fajans, J., *They Make Themselves: Life Cycle, Domestic Cyle and Ritual among the Baining*, PhD diss., Stanford University, 1985. (71 – p. 135)

Fahr-Becker, G., Hesemann, S., Dunn, M. (eds), *The Art of East Asia*, Könemann, Cologne, 1999. (1 – p. 16), (7 – p. 25), (12 & 13 – p. 38), (29 & 30 – p. 65), (88 & 89 – p. 153)

Finlay, J., 'Imperfect Machines and Atmospheres', in Hay, J. et al, *Andrew Drummond: Observation/Action/Reflection*, Christchurch Art Gallery Te Puna o Waiwhetu, Christchurch, 2010. (162 – p. 200)

Finlay, J., (Email to the author), January 2024. (169 – p. 206)

Fischer, J., 'The Invisible Labyrinth', *Art Forum*, September 1989. (154 – p. 193)

Furuhata, Y., 'Animating Copies: Japanese Graphic Design, The Xerox Machine, and Walter Benjamin', in Beckman, K. (ed), *Animating Film Theory*, Duke University Press, Durham NC, 2018. (149 – p. 191)

Gaimster, D., *Director's Choice: Auckland Museum*, Scala Books and Heritage Publishers Ltd., London, 2018. (52 – p. 120)

Ginsburg, F., 'Indigenous media: Faustian contract or global village?', in *Cultural Anthropology: Journal for the Society of Cultural Anthropology*, vol. 6, no.1, 1991. (119 – p. 173)

Green, A., *Southeast Asia: A History in Objects*, British Museum/Thames & Hudson, London, 2023. (146 – p. 189)

Haase, C.-P., 'The Art of the Book', in Phillip, F. C. (ed), *Arts of the East*, Hirmer, Munich, 2017. (33 – p. 74)

Hansford, P., 'From Nowhere to Somewhere via Anywhere: Andrew Drummond's Art of Prototypes', in Hay, J. et al, *Andrew Drummond: Observation/Action/Reflection*, Christchurch Art Gallery Te Puna o Waiwhetu, Christchurch, 2010. (163 – p. 200)

Harper, J., 'BLACK, WHITE and OP: Links between Gordon Walters, Brigdet Riley and Victor Vasarely', in Ross, J. & Simmons, L. (eds), *Gordon Walters: Order and Intuition*, Walters Publication, Auckland, 1989, p. 27. (131 – p. 179)

Harris, P., Zhou Daguan, *A Record of Cambodia: the Land and its People*, Silkworm Books, Bangkok, 2007. (24 – p. 54)

Harrison, C. and Wood, P. (eds.), *Art in Theory: 1900–2000: An Anthology of Changing Ideas*, Backwell Publishing, Oxford, 2003. (150 – p. 191)

Harrison-Hall, J., *China: A History of Objects*, The British Museum, Thames & Hudson, London, 2017. (32 – p. 71)

Heermann, I., (ed.), *Form Colour Inspiration: Oceanic Art from New Britain*, Arnoldsche, Stuttgart, 2001. (80, 82 & 83 – p. 150)

Hesse, K. & Aerts, T., *Baining Life and Lore*, University of Papua New Guinea Press, NCD, 1996. (72 – p. 135)

Honour, H. & John Fleming, J., *A History of World Art*, Laurence King Publishing, revised 7th ed, 2016 [2009]. (148 – p. 191), (160 – p. 198)

Hooper, A. & Huntsman, J. (eds.), *Transformation of Polynesian Culture*, The Polynesian Society, Auckland, 1985. (108 – p. 164, Alain Babadazan)

Huffman, J. L., *Japan in World History*, OUP, New York, 2010. (46 – p. 114)

Hviding, E., *Guardians of the Marovo Lagoon: Practice, Place and Politics in Maritime Melanesia*, Pacific Islands Monograph Series 14, University of Hawaii Press, Honolulu, 1996. (114 & 115 – p. 168)

Jessup, H. I., *Art and Architecture of Cambodia*, Thames & Hudson, London, 2004. (25 – p. 55),

Jong, E. de, *Making a Living between Crises and Ceremonies: The Practice of Everyday Life of a South Sulawesi Highland Community in Indonesia*, Brill Open, Leiden and Boston, 2013. (145 – p. 189)

Joselit, D. in Foster, H. Krauss, R. et al, *Art Since 1900*, Thames & Hudson, London, 2016. (164 & 165 – p. 203)

Kaeppler, A. L., *The Pacific Arts of Polynesia and Micronesia, Oxford History of Art*, OUP, Oxford, 2008. (40 – p. 101), (51 – p. 119), (57 & 58 – p. 125, (118 – p. 173)

Kerlogue, F., *Arts of Southeast Asia: World of Arts Series*, Thames & Hudson, London, 2004. (16 – p. 43), (45 – p. 111), (86, 87 & 90 – p. 153)

Kjellgren, E., *Oceania: Art of the Pacific Island in the Metropolitan Museum of Art*, The Metropolitan Museum of Art, New York, Yale University Press, New Haven and London, 2007. (84 – p. 150)

Kleiner, F. S., Mamiya, C. J. & Tansey, R. G. (eds), *Gardner's Art Through the Ages*, 11th edition, vol. I, Harcourt College Publishers, 2001. (14 – p. 38), (20 – p. 46)

Krämer, A. F., *Inslen un Truck*, Hamburg, 1935. Cited in Feldman, J. & Rubinstein, D. H., *The Art of Micronesia*, exhib. cat., The University of Hawaii Art Gallery, Honolulu, 1988. (59 – p. 125)

Liang, E., *The Winking Owl*, University of California Press, Berkeley, 1988. (158 – p. 198)

Ledderose, L., *Ten Thousand Things: Module and Mass Production in Chinese Art* (The A. W. Mellon Lectures in Fine Arts, Bollingen Series, XXXV, 46), Princeton University Press, Princeton, 1998. (6 – p.23)

Lewis, P. H., 'Changing memorial ceremonial in northern New Ireland', *Journal of the Polynesian Society*, vol. 82, no. 2, 1973. (68 – p. 130)

Lindauer's letter to Náprstek, see Filip, A. & Musil, R., 'The View from Central Europe: A Bohemian artist in New Zealand', in Mason, N. & Stanhope, Z. (eds), *Gottfried Lindauer's New Zealand: The Māori Portraits*, Auckland Art Gallery Toi o Tāmaki, Auckland University Press, Auckland, 2016. (102 – p. 158)

Lipset, D., *Mangrove Man: Dialogues of Culture in the Sepik Estuary*, CUP, Cambridge, 1997. (58 – p. 128)

McAloon, W., *Gordon Waters: Prints and Design*, Adam Art Gallery Tā Pātaka Toi, Victoria University of Wellington, Victoria, 2004. (135 – p. 179)

MacGregor, N., *A History of the World in 100 Objects*, Allen Lane, London, 2011. (15 – p. 41), (21 – p. 49), (47 – p. 114)

Mack, J., Masks: *The Art of Expression*, The British Museum Press, London, 2013. (65, 66 & 67 – p. 130)

Maskill, D., 'Colonial Myth Busters', *Association for Art History*, vol. 44, no. 1, February 2021. (93 – p. 154)

Morphy, H., *Aboriginal Art*, Phaidon, London, 1998. (10 – p. 31), (43 & 44 – p. 106), (48 – p. 117), (139 – p. 182)

Neich, R., *Carved Histories: Rotorua Ngāti Tarawhai Woodcarving*, Auckland University Press, Auckland, 2001. (53 – p. 120)

Newell, J., *Pacific Art in Detail*, The British Museum Press, London, 2011. (105 – p. 162)

Oliver, D. L., *Ancient Tahitian Society*, University of Hawaii Press, Honolulu, 1974, and Filihia, M., 'Oro-Dedicated "Maro 'Ura" in Tahiti: Their Rise and Decline in the Early Post-European Contact Period', *The Journal of Pacific History*, vol. 31, no. 2, December 1996. (37 – p. 96)

Parmentier, H. '*L'Art Khmer classique, Monuments du quadrant nord-est*', 2 vols., L'Ecole française d'Extrême-Orient, Paris, 1939. Summarised in Jessup, 2004. (11 – p. 34)

Pound, F., *Gordon Waters*, Auckland University Press, Auckland, 2023. (136 – p. 179)

Rawson, J., *Mysteries of Ancient China: New Discoveries from the Early Dynasties*, G. Braziller, New York, 1996. (4 – p. 23)

Sahlins, M., *Islands of History*, University of Chicago Press, London, 1985. (39 – p. 96)

Salmond, A., *The Trail of the Cannibal Dog: Captain Cook in the South Seas*, Allen Lane, London, 2003. (36 – p. 93)

Sayers, A., *Australian Art*, OUP, Oxford, 2001. (97 – p. 156), (123 – p. 174)

Sayers, A., 'Kelly's Words, Rousseau and Sunlight', in *Sidney Nolan's Ned Kelly: The Ned Kelly Paintings in the National Gallery of Australia*, N.G.A., Canberra, 2002. (121 & 124 – p. 174)

Setsuda, R., 'Visitors': Interview with Christian Hidaka & Takeshi Murata, Le Forum, Tokyo, The Hermès Foundation, 2022, p. 30. (170 – p. 206)

Sri Kuhnt-Saptodewo et al, in *The Art of East Asia*, 1999. (79 – p. 149)

Stewart, G. & Dale, H., *Reading the 'ghost book': Māori talk about Washday at the Pā, by Ans Westra*. Video J. of Educ. and Pedagogy 3, 2 (2018). https://doi.org/10.1186/s40990-018-0014-2, 2018, p. 3. (128, 129 & 130 – p. 176)

Thomas, N., *Paper skin: Barkcloth Across the Pacific*, Queensland Art Gallery, Museum of New Zealand Te Papa Tongarewa and Queensland Museum, Brisbane, 2009. (116, 117 & 120 – p. 173), (155 & 157 – p. 196)

Waite, D. B., 'Art and Ethnographica from the Solomon Islands', in *Captain Cook and the South Pacific*, The British Museum Press, London, 1979. (112 – p. 168)

Waterson, R., *The Living House: An Anthropology of Architecture in South-East Asia*, Tuttle Publishing, Vermont, 2009. (144 – p. 189)

Westra, A., *Washday at the Pā*, 1964. (126 – p. 176)

Websites:

https://www.britannica.com/event/Tumulus-period. (18 – p. 45)

https://www.britishmuseum.org/collection/object/E_Oc1903-1007-1. (73 – p. 139)

https://www.britishmuseum.org/collection/object/E_Oc-6317. (75 – p. 141)

Collins, D., 'Nixon, The A-Bomb, And Napalm', CBS News, 28 February 2002. https://www.cbsnews.com/news/nixon-the-a-bomb-and-napalm-28-02-2002/. (137 – p. 181)

Davenport, William H., 'Marshall Islands Cartography', Web. 09 Jun 2023, http://www.penn.museum/sites/expedition/?p=747 (104 – p. 162)

Dong, A. Z., Cokcetin, N., Carter, D.A., Fernandes, K.E. 2023. Unique antimicrobial activity in honey from the Australian honeypot ant (Camponotus inflatus) PeerJ11:e15645 https://doi.org/10.7717/peerj.15645 (142 – p. 182)

https://emuseum.nich.go.jp/detail?langId=en&webView=&content_base_id=100201&content_part_id=0&content_pict_id=0. (8 – p. 26)

Gan, R. et al, 2020, p. 5 and p. 7. https://museumvolunteersjmm.com/2020/05/07/every-stone-tells-a-story-2/. (26 – p. 59)

https://www.ribaj.com/culture/yayoi-kusama-infinity-mirror-rooms-tate-modern (168 – p. 204)

https://www.youtube.com/watch?v=ZIjNqCjfmrA (Park West Gallery film featuring Yaacov Agam, 2012). (143 – p. 185)

Yasumasa, M., 2018. https://shugoarts.com/en/news-en/6707/. (147 & 151 – p 191)